Intellectuals and the Search for National Identity in Twentieth-Century Brazil

This book discusses twentieth-century Brazilian political thought, arguing that whereas Rio de Janeiro intellectuals envisaged the state and the national bourgeoisie as the means to overcome dependency on foreign ideas and culture, São Paulo intellectuals looked to civil society and the establishment of new academic institutions in the search for national identity. Ronald H. Chilcote begins his study by outlining Brazilian intellectuals' attempt to transcend a sense of inferiority emanating from Brazilian colonialism and backwardness. Next, he traces the struggle for national identity in Rio de Janeiro through an account of how intellectuals of varying political persuasions united in search of a political ideology of national development. He then presents an analysis by São Paulo intellectuals on racial discrimination, social inequality, and class differentiation under early capitalism and industrialization. Last, the book concludes with a discussion on how Brazilian intellectuals challenged foreign thinking about development through the state and representative democratic institutions, in contrast to popular and participatory democratic practices.

Ronald H. Chilcote is professor of economics and political science at the University of California, Riverside. He is a founder and managing editor of the bimonthly journal *Latin American Perspectives* and is the author or editor of more than two dozen major books.

Intellectuals and the Search for National Identity in Twentieth-Century Brazil

RONALD H. CHILCOTE
University of California, Riverside

CAMBRIDGE
UNIVERSITY PRESS

CAMBRIDGE
UNIVERSITY PRESS

32 Avenue of the Americas, New York, NY 10013-2473, USA

Cambridge University Press is part of the University of Cambridge.

It furthers the University's mission by disseminating knowledge in the pursuit of
education, learning, and research at the highest international levels of excellence.

www.cambridge.org
Information on this title: www.cambridge.org/9781107071629

© Ronald H. Chilcote 2014

First published 2014

Printed in the United States of America

A catalog record for this publication is available from the British Library.

Library of Congress Cataloging in Publication Data
Chilcote, Ronald H.
Intellectuals and the search for national identity in twentieth-century
Brazil / Ronald H. Chilcote.
pages   cm
ISBN 978-1-107-07162-9 (Hardback)
1. Intellectuals – Political activity – Brazil – History – 20th century.
2. Brazil – Intellectual life – 20th century.   3. Political culture – Brazil – History – 20th
century. 4. Nationalism – Brazil – History – 20th century.
5. National characteristics, Brazilian.   I. Title.
F2538.C47   2014
305.5'5209810904–dc23   2014009768

ISBN 978-1-107-07162-9 Hardback

For Brazilians of all persuasions who have enhanced my understanding of Brazil, its culture and politics, and from whom I learned a great deal.

Contents

Preface

My early work in Portugal brought me in contact with the opposition to the Salazar dictatorship, as well as with young African students in Lisbon. I wrote about the opposition and conditions in Portugal and about the revolutionary independence movements that challenged the Portuguese empire in Africa, culminating in my being forbidden to return there until the coup of April 25, 1974, deposed the dictatorship and formally acknowledged independence for the African colonies. During the summer of 1964, I visited Brazil, just after the military had seized power, and I met young intellectuals such as Leôncio Martins Rodrigues and Theôtonio dos Santos in clandestinity and wrote a piece about the coup (1964). During a sabbatical leave in 1967, I spent two months in Rio de Janeiro, where I was able to interview most of the intellectuals who had participated in the founding of the Higher Institute of Brazilian Studies (Instituto Superior de Estudos Brasileiros [ISEB]). I carried on with other interviews after reaching Recife and Olinda, Pernambuco, where I lived for a year and came into contact with many other intellectuals. At the time, I envisaged two serious studies: one on intellectuals in pursuit of a national culture and the other a study of contiguous communities in the backlands of the Northeast.

Until the death of Stalin in 1953, prominent intellectuals in Brazil had tended to cluster around the Brazilian Communist Party (Partido Comunista Brasileiro [PCB]), and during the early 1960s, the party split, with a pro-Chinese wing forming the Communist Party of Brazil (Partido Comunista do Brasil [PC do B]). My study of these intellectuals became a book (1974) and contributed to a bibliography on the Brazilian left (1980). I also organized a series of colloquia that brought together scholars of Brazil and Portuguese Africa (see 1972), as well as fieldwork in the

Northeast (1969–1971 and 1982–1983) that led to another book (1990), but my commitment to a study of intellectuals never wavered. Indeed, during the mid-1980s, I conducted additional interviews, drafted an introductory chapter, and published two journal articles (both in 1985) on the theme. When at the turn of the century I was able to dedicate more time to writing, I returned to the interviews and the books, newspaper clippings, ephemera, and pamphlets on which this book draws. Rather than simply identify the interviews, I have integrated some of their content into the stories they tell through the brief profiles I weave through my book, especially about Rio de Janeiro and São Paulo intellectuals. The intent here is also to show how intellectuals of different persuasions and outlooks can cluster together as they work toward ambitious goals aimed at shaping culture around an autonomous national identity. Some of them are prominent, others less well known, but I take seriously their institutional participation and devote some attention to their scholarly productivity and activism. I include a lengthy bibliography, including some of their work, drawn from the tens of thousands of sources I have gathered over the years. The sources cited in the book are occasionally referenced with some detail, whereas others are included to give the reader a sense of the scope of an intellectual's contribution. As succinctly as possible, I try to characterize their writings, not with a desire to provide a review essay, but to show the reader how their intellectual productivity has evolved over time. These materials are now in the Special Collections of the Tomás Rivera Library of the University of California, Riverside; a finder guide is available at http://library.ucr.edu/content/collections/spcol/universityarchives/uo12.pdf.

Over the years, Brazilians have been receptive and supportive of my fieldwork, and in a small way I have tried to repay them by devoting portions of four years as a Fulbright professor, teaching graduate courses and working with Brazilian doctoral students in political science and sociology at the Universidade Estadual de Campinas (UNICAMP) and the Universidade Federal de Ceará (UFC) in Fortaleza. This commitment has yielded new and interesting experiences and learning for me and brought me closer to an understanding of Brazilian culture, political economy, and academic life.

I must especially thank my wife, Frances, and our sons, Stephen and Edward, who spent years with me in the field. At last, I can formally thank Marie Zentai for her early work on the interviews and her exhaustive research in my collection of Brazilian materials. My work is largely of my own making, but I am indebted to the Brazilians who I interviewed and

FIGURE I The image of renowned sociologist Florestan Fernandes is drawn from the Fundo Florestan Fernandes and the special collections of the Universidade Federal de São Carlos, Brazil, where his library is now housed. Thanks to Ana Alibris and to João Roberto Martins for locating and allowing use of the image. The image also appeared on the cover of the now-defunct journal *Revista Praxis*.

to those who read and offered extensive suggestions on the manuscript, in particular Jawdat Abu-el-Haj of the UFC and James Green of Brown University, who read the manuscript in various drafts, and Luiz Carlos Bresser-Pereira, who read portions of an earlier draft. I have always appreciated the encouragement of Thomas Skidmore over the years, especially his insistence that I finish this project. I appreciate the extensive editing that Barbara Metzger, who has read all my recent work, gave to an early draft of the manuscript. Finally, I am grateful to Deborah Gershenowitz, senior editor for American and Latin American History at Cambridge University Press, who remained committed and encouraged revisions and publication of my book.

List of Acronyms

ABPN	Associação Brasileira de Pesquisadores Negros (Brazilian Association of Black Researchers)
ACM	Associação Cristão de Académicos (Christian Association of Academics)
ALN	Ação Libertadora Nacional (National Liberation Action)
ANL	Aliança Nacional Libertadora (National Liberation Alliance)
AP	Ação Popular (Popular Action)
ARENA	Aliança Renovadora Nacional (National Renovation Alliance)
ASN	Ação Social Nacionalista (Nationalist Social Action)
CAPES	Coordenação de Aperfeiçoamento de Pessoal de Nível Superior (Coordination for the Improvement of Higher Education Personnel)
CEBRAP	Centro Brasileiro de Análise e Planejamento (Brazilian Center for Analysis and Planning)
CEDEC	Centro de Cultura Contemporânea (Center for Studies of Contemporary Culture)
CESIT	Centro de Sociologia Industrial do Trabalho (Center for Research in the Sociology of Industry and Labor)
CESO	Centro de Estudios Socioeconómicos (Center for Socioeconomic Studies)
CGT	Comando Geral dos Trabalhadores (General Command of Workers)
CLACSO	Consejo Latinoamericano de Ciencias Sociales (Latin American Social Science Council)

COB	Confederação Operária Brasileira (Brazilian Workers' Confederation)
COLINA	Comando de Libertação Nacional (National Liberation Command)
CONCLAT	Coordenação Nacional da Classe Trabalhadora (National Confederation of the Working Class)
CPC	Centro Popular de Cultura (Popular Center of Culture)
CUT	Central Única dos Trabalhadores (Unified Workers' Central)
DASP	Departamento Administrativo do Serviço Público (Administrative Department of Public Service)
ECLA	Economic Commission for Latin America. Established by the United Nations in 1948 and became ECLAC in 1984 when it admitted Caribbean nations
ESG	Escola Superior de Guerra (Superior War College)
IBESP	Instituto Brasileiro de Economia, Sociologia e Política (Brazilian Institute of Economy, Sociology, and Politics)
IMF	International Monetary Fund
ISEB	Instituto Superior de Estudos Brasileiros (Higher Institute of Brazilian Studies)
IUPERJ	Instituto Universitário de Pesquisas de Rio de Janeiro (University Institute of Research of Rio de Janeiro)
MDB	Movimento Democrático Brasileiro (Brazilian Democratic Movement)
MNU	Movimento Negro Unificado (Unified Black Movement)
MPB	Música Popular Brasileira (Brazilian Popular Music)
MR-8	Movimento Revolucionário do 8 de Outubro (Eighth of October Revolutionary Movement)
MST	Movimento dos Trabalhadores Rurais Sem-Terra (Movement of Landless Rural Workers)
ORM	Organização Revolucionária Marxista (Marxist Revolutionary Organization)
PACS	Políticas Alternativas para o Cono Sul (Alternative Policies for the Southern Cone)
PC do B	Partido Comunista do Brasil (Communist Party of Brazil)
PCB	Partido Comunista Brasileiro (Brazilian Communist Party)
PCBR	Partido Comunista Brasileiro Revolucionário (Brazilian Revolutionary Communist Party)
PD	Partido Democrático (Democratic Party)

PDS	Partido Democrático Social (Social Democratic Party)
PDT	Partido Democrático Trabalhista (Democratic Labor Party)
PFL	Partido da Frente Liberal (Liberal Front Party)
PL	Partido Liberal (Liberal Party)
PMDB	Partido do Movimento Democrático Brasileiro (Brazilian Democratic Movement Party)
POLOP	Política Operária (Worker Politics)
POR	Partido Operário Revolucionário (Revolutionary Workers' Party)
PPS	Partido Popular Socialista (Popular Socialist Party)
PRP	Partido Republicano Paulista (São Paulo Republican Party)
PSB	Partido Socialista do Brasil (Socialist Party of Brazil)
PSDB	Partido da Social Democracia Brasileiro (Brazilian Social Democratic Party)
PSR	Partido Socialista Revolucionário (Revolutionary Socialist Party)
PSR(T)	Partido Socialista Revolucionário (Trotskista) (Trotskyist Revolutionary Socialist Party)
PT	Partido dos Trabalhadores (Workers' Party)
PTB	Partido Trabalhista Brasileiro (Brazilian Workers' Party)
PUC	Pontifícia Universidade Católica (Pontifical Catholic University)
SUDENE	Superintendência do Desenvolvimento do Nordeste (Superintendency of Northeast Development)
ULTAB	União dos Lavradores e Trabalhadores Agrícolas do Brasil (Brazilian Laborers' and Agricultural Workers' Union)
UME	União Metropolitano dos Estudantes (Metropolitan Union of Students)
UNAM	Universidad Nacional Autónoma de México (Autonomous National University of Mexico)
UNE	União Nacional dos Estudantes (National Union of Students)
UNESCO	United Nations Organization for Education, Science and Culture
UNICAMP	Universidade Estadual de Campinas

USP	Universidade de São Paulo (University of São Paulo)
VAR-Palmares	Vanguarda Armada Revolucionária-Palmares (Palmares Revolutionary Armed Vanguard)
VPR	Vanguarda Popular Revolucionária (Popular Revolutionary Vanguard)

INTRODUCTION

The Intellectual in Theory and Practice

We begin by clarifying what an intellectual is. The Italian thinker Antonio Gramsci (1971) identified two types of intellectuals: traditional intellectuals, such as teachers, priests, and administrators (who specialize in the production of ideas and knowledge and perform the same functions from generation to generation and who may have expressed their quest for knowledge in oral and written discourse, in poetic or plastic expression, in historical reminiscence or writing, or in ritual performance), and organic intellectuals (who are directly connected to classes in society and actively organize interests, seek power, and gain control). Many writers have focused on this activism and how intellectuals may engage with and shape public life. C. Wright Mills (1963: 299) looked at the public intellectual, suggesting that independent artists or writers were "among the few remaining personalities equipped to resist and to fight the stereotyping and consequent death of genuinely living things.... If the thinker does not relate himself to the value of truth in political struggle, he cannot responsibly cope with the whole of life experience." Paul Baran (1988) considered the intellectual the conscience of society and the representative of progressive forces – a social critic concerned with analyzing and working to overcome obstacles to the achievement of a more humane and rational social order. Edward W. Said (1996) saw the values of the intellectual as integrity, rigor of thought, conscience, and disdain for dogma, and he cautioned that intellectuals were nevertheless at risk of being lured by money, power, or specialization: "Insiders promote special interests, but intellectuals should be the ones to question patriotic nationalism, corporate thinking, and a sense of class, racial or gender privilege" (xiii). He considered intellectuals "endowed with a faculty for representing, embodying, articulating a message, a view, an attitude, philosophy or opinion to, as well as for, a public" (11) and believed that they could be nurtured within the university or the corporation while maintaining autonomy and creativity in their work (74–75).

Intellectuals sometimes are seen as a social class. Alvin Gouldner (1979) identified intellectuals and the technical intelligentsia as constituting a new class – secularized, cosmopolitan, and multinational, more public than private in its activities, more marginal and alienated in a technocratic and industrial society, and associated with an anonymous market for its products and services – that he saw emerging everywhere. He contrasted his conception with interpretations of intellectuals as benign technocrats (Daniel Bell and John Kenneth Galbraith), a master class or socialist intelligentsia that exploited society (Nicolai Bukharin), a group of dedicated professionals who merged with the old moneyed class to form a collectively oriented elite (Talcott Parsons), the servants of power and the old moneyed class (Noam Chomsky and Maurice Zeitlin), and a flawed universal class, elitist and self-seeking (his own earlier position). Regis Debray (1981: 21–23), examining the relationship between intellectuals and power, viewed the intelligentsia as including liberal professionals as well as senior administrative personnel and as too heterogeneous to constitute a collectivity. The Brazilian political economist Luiz Carlos Bresser-Pereira (1981) identified an intermediate stratum in the form of a techno-bureaucracy that had emerged through the apparatuses of the state to exercise influence in the contemporary world. He saw the new class as having taken hold in some socialist countries, whereas in capitalist nations a mixed type of production had evolved. Even in decline, in his view, capitalism more effectively resisted the techno-bureaucracy.

These descriptions of intellectuals and especially the notion that they constitute part of a new class call to mind Karl Marx's identification (in an unfinished chapter at the end of *Capital)* of intermediate classes, the significance of which has only recently received scholarly attention. Dale Johnson (1982: 24), although considering it inappropriate "to posit professionals or any category of knowledge ability or technical expertise as constituting a universal class," pointed to the decline, with the process of capitalist accumulation, of the old petty bourgeoisie of independent producers, small farmers, and merchants and the rise of a new salaried intermediate class composed of technical, administrative, and professional employees that mediated between capital and labor.

This idea is reminiscent of Nicos Poulantzas's (1975) concept of "new petty bourgeoisie" made up of white-collar employees, technicians, supervisors, and civil servants. Poulantzas was concerned with designating positions in the social division of labor and distinguishing between productive and unproductive labor. For example, at the economic level, supervisory personnel are exploited like other labor, but at the political level, they participate in the exploitation of the working class. Poulantzas suggested that their position reflected both their dominant role in the social division of labor and their political domination by capital. Erik Olin Wright (1978: chapter 2, esp. 95–96) took issue with the distinction between productive and unproductive labor and emphasized "contradictory locations within the class structure" as a means of characterizing the position of managers and supervisors and certain categories of employees who maintained some control over their labor process but were positioned between the petty bourgeoisie and the working class.

This backdrop leads to a set of assertions about the role of intellectuals in contemporary society:

1. *Intellectuals may engage with society*: "An effective collaboration between intellectuals and the authorities which govern society is a requirement for order and continuity in public life.... Yet there is always a degree of tension between the two levels and various forms of consensus and dissensus prevail in the relations between intellectuals and the ruling powers of society" (Shills, 1972: 21).

2. *Intellectuals tend to reject inherited and prevailing values*: Kuhn (1970), in contrast, argued that paradigms of intellectual activity and thinking tend to persist until major new scientific understandings of revolutionary proportions come along.

3. *Intellectuals value originality*: Shills pointed to the genius of the individual, whereas Gouldner (1979) emphasized the autonomy arising from specialized knowledge or "cultural capital."

4. *Intellectuals are ideological*: "The disposition toward ideological construction is one of the fundamental properties of the human race, once it reaches a certain stage of intellectual development" (Shills, 1972: 28). Gouldner related ideology to autonomy and held that professionalism became intellectuals' public ideology.

5. *Intellectuals control culture*: Gouldner (1979: 19) saw intellectuals as constituting "a cultural bourgeoisie who appropriates privately the advantages of an historically and collectively produced cultural capital."

6. *Intellectuals constitute a sort of class*: As we have seen, Gouldner viewed intellectuals as a new class, subordinate to the old moneyed class but in de facto control over the mode of production and the means of administration. He distinguished at least two elites in the new class: "intelligentsia whose intellectual interests are fundamentally 'technical' and ... intellectuals whose interests are primarily critical, emancipatory, hermeneutic, and hence often political" (48). He acknowledged a struggle between the old and new classes over the protection of individual rights, harassment of the old class to secure material interests, cultivation of alliances with the working class, and advocacy of a welfare state. The new class was "a cultural bourgeoisie" – "the relatively more educated counterpart ... of the old moneyed class. Thus the New Class contest sometimes has the character of a civil war within the upper classes. It is the differentiation of the old class into contentious factions" (18). Shills, in contrast, referred to a vague hierarchy in which the lower stratum learned from the higher. He argued that intellectuals did not yet form a community bound together by a sense of mutual affinity and attachment to a common set of rules and identifying symbols, although subcommunities with these features did exist. Debray (1981: 202) also distinguished between a lower and a higher intelligentsia, the latter seeing the former as "backward and dangerous": "Whereas the lower intelligentsia exhibits solidarity, the high intelligentsia displays complicity; the former makes collective demands, the latter devises individual strategies." He maintained, however, that the intelligentsia could not be defined by its position in the material process of production: "It is not a class" (21).

7. *Intellectuals make revolutions with their ideas*: For Gouldner, the "new class" was increasingly involved in political life and inclined to shape revolutionary society in theory and practice. He was less interested in bourgeois revolutions than in "the collectivization of private property that increases the means of production at the disposal of the state apparatus" (1979: 11). Although its activity in mobilizing the masses was often disguised, ignored, or distorted, the new class not only was sometimes politically revolutionary but also constantly revolutionized the mode of production in its subordinate position to the old moneyed class.

My search for an understanding of the intellectual draws from Gramsci and approximates that of Carl Boggs (1993), exploring the changes in intellectual life that accompanied capitalist modernization and especially "the political dimension of intellectual activity as it unfolds within the ongoing struggle for ideological hegemony" (ix). Boggs understood the crisis of modernity as linked to the conflict "between technocratic and critical modes of thought, between structures of domination and embryonic forms of opposition visible in the emergence of new social movements" (xiii). He saw intellectuals as involved in a counterhegemonic struggle that went beyond Gramsci's notion of the organic intellectual, envisioning "an engaged, critical, public intelligentsia whose activity is grounded in social projects, constituencies, and movements" (8). This new type of intellectual, he argued, was to be found in the mass media, education, trade unions, the university, popular and social movements, artistic communities, and even the state (9), and under organized state capitalism "a new dialectic between technocratic and critical intellectuals" was emerging (180) as the numbers of traditional and progressive intellectuals diminished.

Many years ago, I began my study with a deep interest and curiosity about Brazilian intellectuals, their ideas, their role and influence in academic life, and their participation in a society seeking to escape its colonial past. My study, however, intends to serve as a basis for comparative study relevant to shifting intellectual outlook and experience in particular situations. For instance, Debray (1981) suggests that an intellectual may move beyond an intellectual's vocation. He illustrates by identifying changing generations of French intellectuals, beginning with the Parisian intellectuals from 1880 to 1930, a professoriate linked generally to the Sorbonne; after 1930 until the 1960s, when new publishing houses fostered a "spiritual family" comprising the intelligentsia and their editors and included Sartre, Gide, Camus, Mauriac, and Malraux; and after 1968, when intellectuals shifted from their publishers to the mass media as journalists, advisers, and so on. Debray is concerned with the relationship of intellectuals and power. As he focuses on three generations of French intellectual life, he shows for each stage the replacement of a degenerative cycle with one of critical intelligence. He depicts the impact of capitalist development on the mind, the distortions of intellectual life, and the false consciousness that pervades contemporary media-oriented society.

Generational changes among intellectuals in the United States are also obvious and may help us in understanding the trajectory of the intellectual in Brazil. A major problem is the entrenchment of progressive intellectuals in academe and their marginalization or retreat altogether from public life during the twentieth century, as in the case of the United States (see Paul Gorman, 1996, and John Carey, 1993, for useful overviews). With the Great Depression of the 1930s, intellectual life flourished under the communist, socialist, and other leftist progressive political parties. Newspapers and journals prospered as intellectuals, comprised of public-spirited academics within the universities and public figures, many of them immigrants from Europe, focused on solutions to the many problems of their era. Many of them came to be known as the New York Intellectuals whose contributions to American culture were substantial in all walks of life but who began to withdraw as the Second World War wound down and the Cold War evolved during the 1940s. The journal *Partisan Review* was at the center of these intellectuals' lives. They including Philip Rahv and William Phillips, who were influential since its founding, and Dwight Macdonald, F. W. Dupuy, and Mary McCarthy, all of whom joined the editorial board in 1937. Other early participants included Sidney Hook and James Burnham, whereas in the early 1940s Diana Trilling, Paul Goodman, and Alfred Kazin were involved, and a bit later a young group of writers such as Irving Howe, Daniel Bell, and Saul Bellow joined their ranks. Their story is revealed through fascinating appraisals, including Alexander Bloom's comprehensive intellectual history (1986) and Terry Cooney's treatment (1986) of the formative period before 1945, Harvey Teres (1996) explores radicalism during the 1930s and the culture wars of the 1940s, Howard Brick (1986) delineates the tension between socialist and sociological theory during the 1940s, and David Laskin (2000) emphasizes the role of women in the movement. Alan Wald has explored this period through three major studies, with the first (1987) looking at the New York Intellectuals and the rise and decline of the anti-Stalinist left from the 1930s to the 1980s; the second (1994) delving into the literary left with essays on the revolutionary left and the relation between radical artistic practice and politics; and the third (2002) exhaustively portraying major intellectuals and writers in the United States and their leftist activities in the first half of the twentieth century, in particular their affiliation with the American Communist Party and participation in popular front causes, their literary contributions, their political activism, and their impact on evolving American society, especially during the Depression and the decade of the 1930s, the Second World War, and the ensuing Cold War. Frances Saunders (1999) exposes the role of U.S. intelligence agencies and their infiltration, influence, and shaping of arts and literature through manipulation of intellectuals to pursue an ideological agenda during the Cold War.

Although I was immersed in the study of Brazil and its intellectual life, my own thinking evolved as the decade of the 1960s ushered in an era of New Left thinking and challenge to mainstream and Old Left ideas alongside an impetus toward participatory democracy, experimentation, and radical leftist tendencies. Yet intellectuals eventually retreated once more as American society turned conservative and consolidated under the right-wing presidencies of Nixon and Reagan. Whereas Russell Jacoby (1987) emphasized the withdrawal of intellectuals, writers, and thinkers from public life after the tumultuous 1960s in his critically significant *The Last Intellectuals* (1987), Eric Lott in *The Disappearing Liberal Intellectual* (2006) traced the decline of the left, especially in the period 1992–2005; he criticizes this left's turn to social democratic reform in the form of identity politics or a cultural left. Carl Boggs (1993) describes this shift in terms of a crisis of modernity. An understanding of these trends evolves in personal accounts and retrospective works on the decade of the 1960s and its aftermath, including those by Todd Gitlin (1987), an early radical and later sociology professor and more moderate social critic at the University of California, Berkeley; Tom Hayden (1988), in his reflection on his experience as a leader of the student movement of the 1960s; James Miller (1987), in a serious retrospective of the 1960s, its understanding of participatory democracy, and the ideas that shaped the movement; and Harvey Terres (1996), drawing on his personal experience during the struggles of the 1960s and as a worker in various industrial jobs and later as an academic in his writing about the New York Intellectuals and their legacy and influence on the New Left during the 1960s and the far right in contemporary times as he traces the evolution of intellectual discourse and action from progressive to conservative discourse with attention to organization, individuals, and publications.

Other useful historical accounts of this rise and decline of intellectuals include those by Anderson (1995), who develops "activism as it unfolded, chronologically, each event building upon another, as the movement became a kaleidoscope of activity and as the sixties expanded in complexity and swelled in emotion"; Berman (1996), who dwells on four moments of 1968 and its implications; and Calvert (1991), who emphasizes the movement during the 1960s and its outlook for participatory democracy and spiritual faith in the goodness of every human being. A younger generation of historians assess the period in Farber (1994);

whereas Isserman (1987) looks at the links between the Old Left of the 1930s and the New Left of the 1960s, and Katsiaficas (1987) revisits the history of the New Left of the 1960s and the social movements associated with it in the United States and around the world. Historian Rorabaugh (1989) writes about the Berkeley movement during the 1960s, while editor Korda (1999) helps us with his impressions of major writers over many years in the New York publishing world. Richard Flacks (1988) explains the weaknesses of the left, especially leftist organizations that insist on conformity to their memory and identity, while sharing resources and information and mutually clarifying vision, strategy and program (277). Levine (1996) responds to the idea, inherent in Bloom (1987), that the contemporary university has closed to the absolute truths of classical writings and argues that we should "be open to the reality that all peoples and societies have cultures that we have to respect to the extent that we take the trouble to understand how they operate and what they believe" (19).

My understanding sees the Gramscian organic intellectual as an ideal type often conspicuous and even admired in traditional society, but today less influential in modern technological society. In my study of twentieth-century Brazilian intellectuals, I am generally concerned with scholars, teachers, journalists, and others rather than with an intelligentsia as distinguished by Gouldner, although the lines of demarcation are not always clear. At various times, some of these intellectuals assumed major roles in the state apparatus, and thus they were in a position to exercise power in dealing with the problems they perceived in their society. I want to know if their cultural production and their political participation influenced Brazil to awaken from its obsession with an inferior colonial past and to bring Brazilians together in common purpose to transcend past difficulties and unite the country in common purpose. Thus, my principal concern is a critical assessment of the production of ideas and knowledge by intellectuals and their impact on economic and political life. I am less interested in intellectuals as a class than in their relations with other classes. To what extent do they empathize with the bourgeoisie or proletariat? How do they identify their class position and class consciousness? I am also interested in their ideas and knowledge in theory and practice. Is their production diffused in abstract or concrete forms? Is their output incorporated into general commodity production, as suggested by Debray, or does it generate critical and creative thinking? Is the content of their ideas and knowledge shaped by bourgeois ideals associated with the emerging capitalist society, or does it serve to counter the bourgeois outlook? Are the intellectuals inspired by positivist and liberal views or by Marxist perspectives, and did this lead to any practical outcomes? Have they simply retreated from their ideals and aspirations and concentrated on their professional careers within university or the state? Finally, are they interested in gradual change and reform, or are they committed to radical solutions? Do they advocate change within an evolving capitalist accumulation, or do they see socialism as an alternative?

Four principal themes run through my study. The first depicts the dramatic struggle of intellectuals to transcend a sense of inferiority based on Brazilian colonialism, backwardness, and dependence on foreign culture. Various intellectual ideas and movements have dominated Brazilian political thought and activity since the recognition, in the late nineteenth and early twentieth centuries, that the nation needed to transcend a colonialism and dependency on culture abroad. This awakening was not widely apparent after Brazilian independence in 1822 and during the imperial period up to the end of slavery and the establishment of the Old Republic in 1891. The rupture with colonialism accompanied the rise of an agrarian capitalism based on coffee production and export, along with oligarchical political domination under the ruling classes of Minas Gerais and São Paulo. Chapter 1 emphasizes the evolution of political thought throughout the twentieth century. This thought is particularly important in Rio de Janeiro, until 1960 the political capital and base for state institutions and political parties; in São Paulo, the burgeoning center for industry in the urban areas and coffee in the countryside and for the immigrant and national workers and their incipient labor movements; and to a more limited extent in the Northeast, especially Salvador (the old capital and locus of slave trade) and Recife, the region of major sugar production and export into world markets as well a center of cultural activity stimulated by many of the nation's major artists, novelists, historians, and social scientists. Chapter 1 introduces various overviews that depict the struggles to transcend cultural manifestations of inferiority and cast off the colonial legacy while introducing new understandings based on pride in nation and national destiny. Major themes such as nationalism, the bourgeois revolution, paths toward development, and alternative conceptions of democracy are introduced by the twentieth-century Brazilians presented in the initial chapter. They are explored in the chapters that follow.

The second theme focuses on the search of intellectuals for a national identity. It evolves for the most part in Chapter 2, which describes the

Rio intellectuals of the Instituto Brasileiro de Economia e Sociologia e Política (IBESP) and the Instituto Superior de Estudos Brasileiros (Superior Institute of Brazilian Studies [ISEB]) from the early 1950s until the 1964 coup and delves into their ideas on nationalism and development. This story is not widely known outside Brazil, but it is a fascinating account of how intellectuals of different political persuasions came together, examined major national problems, and began to evolve a political ideology of national development that would bring consensus to political economic thinking and, through the state, implement solutions to problems and permit Brazil to emerge as a major international power. Their effort accompanied a broad awakening around the belief that Brazil would someday overcome economic underdevelopment, social inequality, and cultural backwardness. There was internal dissension along this path, eventually culminating in a military coup in 1964 that brought down the ISEB but allowed its ideas of nationalism to carry on in different ways.

The third theme revolves around the efforts of São Paulo intellectuals to seek national identity and lead Brazil out of its backwardness through in-depth field studies and empirical work aimed at systematic analysis and understanding of particular problems around racial discrimination, social inequality, class differentiation under a rapidly industrializing region of the country, and the conspicuous problems that accompany early capitalism. Chapter 3 examines these intellectuals, with emphasis on social scientists and historians who gravitated toward Caio Prado Júnior and the Marxist social science journal *Revista Brasiliense* and the Capital Group of graduate students and young professors associated with Florestan Fernandes. Their work is known outside Brazil, but my account delves into their thinking and outlook, their cultural production, and their attempts to change society through new ideas and understandings.

A fourth theme draws out how the national experience of Brazilian intellectuals confronted and challenged ideas and theories that emanated from Eurocentric and North American thinking about development, some of it within prevalent mainstream thinking and some of it within outmoded ideas about backwardness in the dogma of the Third International and the Soviet Communist Party. Chapters 4 and 5 attempt to relate theory and reality by looking, on the one hand, at the important ideas on backwardness and underdevelopment evolving in the work of Caio Prado Júnior and Celso Furtado, on dependency in the writings of Theotônio dos Santos and others, on associated dependent development in the work of Fernando Henrique Cardoso, and on subimperialism in the contributions of Ruy Mauro Marini; and, on the other hand, examining various attempts by Brazilian intellectuals to transform Brazilian society through involvement in the state and representative democratic institutions, in political parties, and in contrast with popular and participatory democratic practices: as proletarians working through urban and rural labor organizations, in social movements to open up society, and in revolutionary and armed struggle in the Brazilian experience.

Intellectuals and Political Thought in Twentieth-Century Brazil

An anonymous writer in the daily *Estado de São Paulo* (September 16, 1984) expressed a Brazilian intellectual's concern that the politicians and leaders of the day were blind to the reality of the country – immersed in politically romantic conceptions, compromised by the struggle for power, and obsessed with demagoguery – and urged them to begin to build democracy and a modern life on the basis of objective progress. This concern was not new. Brazilian intellectuals had long attempted to relate to the problems of society through participation in politics (Miceli, 1979; Reale, 1984; Moraes, Antunes, and Ferrante, 1986). Examples range from Sêrgio Milliet and the modernist vanguard of the twenties; Afonso Arinos de Melo Franco (1933, 1936), who related history to his understanding of culture and nationalism from a position close to the centers of power; Mário de Andrade, whose famous Itamaraty conferences offered a critique of his own activities as an aristocrat and advocated the development of a culture based on an ideology of creative national consciousness; and the participants in the First Brazilian Congress of Writers on January 22, 1945, who called for the redemocratization of Brazil.

Brazilian intellectuals of political persuasions from right to left have occupied political positions. Economist Celso Furtado served the Goulart government as minister of planning. José Sarney, at various times a

This chapter draws heavily from the introduction to a special issue of *Latin American Perspectives* (*LAP*) focused on intellectuals in Brazil (Abu-El-Haj and Chilcote, 2011). I thank *LAP* for permission to reproduce the material and Jawdat Abu-El-Haj, a professor of political science and sociology at the Federal University of Ceará, for his significant contribution to the understanding of Brazilian intellectual life and history.

senator, vice president, and president, published a popular novel while serving the Médici government. Jânio Quadros was president as well as the author of a collection of short stories. The renowned novelist Jorge Amado was a federal deputy representing the Brazilian Communist Party (Partido Comunista Brasileiro [PCB]); Álvaro Lins, a Pernambuco writer, headed the cabinet during the Kubitschek administration. Darcy Ribeiro, a well-known anthropologist and novelist, was vice governor of Rio. The novelist Plínio Salgado was the founder of Ação Integralista Brasileira. The writer and lawyer Francisco Julião was a Socialist deputy (see Couri, 1984, for further examples).

During the 1950s, movements around the political scientist Helio Jaguaribe and the philosopher Roland Corbisier sought to promote an ideology of developmental nationalism and attempted to implement their ideas through direct participation in politics, and the school of intellectuals around the sociologist Florestan Fernandes produced some of the best social science writings on Brazil during the 1960s and promoted an opening in the military dictatorship during the 1970s that allowed some of them to participate directly in politics.

A fundamental theme of my study revolves around how intellectuals strive to break from traditional perspectives and search for new ways to conceptualize and understand their nation, its uniqueness, and its identity, and to promote its development into the modern world. These examples suggest that Brazilian intellectuals historically have fulfilled their role and achieved recognition in the public arena through writing, art, music, and other cultural activities while often engaging society, not only through their cultural production but occasionally by becoming involved in politics, sometimes influencing outcomes, and often being marginalized into ineffective outcomes. This dichotomy appears throughout Brazilian history.

EARLY INTELLECTUALS

Toward the end of the First Republic (1891–1930), the concern among all classes in Brazil was not hegemony but survival in a time of economic and political uncertainty. Slavery had been abolished in 1888, and although traditional practices prevailed in the Northeast, agriculture elsewhere evolved from traditional practices into commercial and industrial enterprise spurred on by the export of coffee, particularly in São Paulo state. Ruling oligarchies in São Paulo and Minas Gerais dominated the national political scene at a time when intellectuals searched for new directions and were inclined to associate with progressively oriented partisan groups opposed to the oligarchies. Anarchism and anarcho-syndicalism, socialism, communism, and Trotskyism were the principal tendencies.

Anarchism, which advocates the replacement of the authoritarian state by some form of cooperation among free individuals, was largely inspired by the writings of Pierre-Joseph Proudhon and later Michael Bakunin and Peter Kropotkin. Spanish, Portuguese, and especially Italian immigrants to Latin America in the nineteenth and early twentieth centuries brought anarchist ideas with them, and they found their voice in the trade unions that evolved with industrialization, with the result that by about 1920 anarcho-syndicalism dominated the workforce and contributed to moderate reforms, including wage increases. Ideological and leadership differences were evident among the various anarchist and anarcho-syndicalist organizations that eventually coalesced around the Brazilian Workers' Confederation (Confederação Operária Brasileira [COB]), founded in 1908, which combined unions from Rio and São Paulo and as far south as Porto Alegre.

Less influential than anarchism but still significant, socialism drew from the thought of Marx and Engels. The first of several early attempts to establish a socialist party, on August 1, 1892, at the first Congresso Socialista Brasileiro in Rio de Janeiro, failed, but it did lead to the formation of several socialist-oriented workers' groups, notably in Rio, São Paulo, and Porto Alegre. Also in 1892, a different assemblage convened the first Congresso Socialista do Brasil, and this led to the founding of the Socialist Party of Brazil (Partido Socialista do Brasil [PSB]). In 1895, some 400 workers and intellectuals established the Partido Socialista Operário in Rio de Janeiro, and from May 28 to June 1, 1902, a second Congresso Socialista Brasileiro met in São Paulo and approved the program and statutes of the Partido Socialista Brasileiro. The Partido Socialista Colectivista was established at the same time, and it was followed by many other splinter socialist groups. A PSB was revived briefly in 1917 under Nestor Peixote de Oliveira, reflecting the influence of the French theorist Jean Juarés. Particularly important was the Clarté Group, whose publication *Clarté* called for a new socialist party that would organize the working masses.

Communism in Brazil owes its origins to Marx and Engels, but Lenin and Stalin also influenced it under the Third International. The PCB was founded March 25–27, 1922, by progressive intellectuals and workers involved in socialism and anarchism (see Chilcote, 1974: 15–26). Throughout most of its first fifty years, the PCB was illegal. Its adherents were generally middle-class intellectuals. From 1922 to 1929, the party concentrated on internal organization and international recognition. It was a time of the revolts of the young *tenentes* (lieutenants) in 1922 and 1924 and the ensuing march through thousands of miles of the hinterland led by Luiz Carlos Prestes, a young army engineer who later became secretary general of the party.

Trotskyism in Brazil, as in Latin America in general, has followed various lines of thinking. An early split occurred in 1928 with the defection from the PCB of intellectuals such as Aristides Lobo, Lívio Xavier, Patricia Galvão, Geraldo Ferraz, Plínio Melo, Mário Pedrosa, Edmundo Moniz, and Febus Gikovate and labor leaders such as João da Costa Pimenta, Joaquim Barbosa, and Hilcar. In 1937–1938, a second division involved Hermínio Sacchetta, who had headed the PCB in São Paulo but left the party to organize the Trotskyist Revolutionary Socialist Party (Partido Socialista Revolucionário [Trotskista] [PSR(T)]) (see Antunes, 1992). Sacchetta took the position that the Soviet Union should receive unconditional support, whereas Pedrosa and Moniz believed that the state bureaucracy there would become a governing class that would interfere with the realization of a workers' or socialist state.

Many of the ideas of intellectuals appeared in books and pamphlets, but it was especially in periodicals that their thinking on nationalism and development evolved. The *Revista do Brasil* has been characterized as "the first nationalist journal to emerge in Brazil" (Dorin, 1963: 52). Launched in São Paulo in January 1916, it was edited by Júlio Mesquita, Luís Pereira Barreto, and Alfred Pujol, with its chief editor initially being Plínio Barreto and later Monteiro Lobato. Many of these early writers continued their analyses four decades later in the progressive *Revista Brasiliense*, and Dorin considered the latter a successor to the former (66).

With anarchist, anarchist-syndicalist, and socialist leanings and a Marxist orientation, the Clarté Group launched the biweekly (later monthly) *Clarté: Revista de Sciencias Sociaes* in September 1921. Originating in Paris and influenced by the French intellectual Henri Barbusse but published in Rio de Janeiro, it was critical of the Brazilian state and its relation to the ruling classes. *Clarté* included Marxists such as Evaristo de Moraes and Evarado Dias and reflected a strong interest in the Soviet Union on the international level and in the "intellectual struggle" on the national level. It published seven numbers, called for the formation of a socialist party, and was influential in the formation of the

PCB in 1922. Clandestinity did not deter progressive intellectuals from affiliating with the PCB, illegal throughout most of its existence, and its ranks included many prominent journalists, novelists, historians, and social scientists.

The ideological formulations of intellectuals in these journals are essential to the mobilization of class interests. As organic intellectuals, they were activist in mobilizing power, usually in counterhegemonic ways, and dedicated to the transformation of class values and beliefs into legitimate and popular outcomes. Most supporters of social classes limit their practices to empirical defense and public debates, but organic intellectuals go a step farther. They transform class interests into the institutionalized assemblages of theories, themes, and scientific standards that are essential to reform. Alfredo Ellis Júnior, Fernando de Azevedo, and Roberto Simonsen performed this role over a span of five decades. They pioneered historical reconstructions, actively participated in paradigmatic debates, and consolidated prestigious intellectual groups.

Fernando de Azevedo led a new fraction of the urban middle classes composed of professionals in alliance with a new urban bourgeoisie made up of merchants and importers. Culturally, they revolved around the newspaper *O Estado de São Paulo*. The founding in February 1926 of the Democratic Party (Partido Democrático [PD]) in opposition to the agrarian São Paulo Republican Party (Partido Republicano Paulista [PRP]) crystallized their class interests into a political program. Although the PD was presided over by Antônio Prado, the president of the Associação Comercial de São Paulo and the patriarch of the São Paulo bourgeoisie, it was class ambiguous. By and large, the new party represented a diversity of elites in transition from rural- to urban-based production and commerce. Under its auspices, Fernando de Azevedo introduced the educational principles of the 1934 Constitution and formulated the proposal for establishing the University of São Paulo (USP).

The formation of an intellectual grouping of the industrial bourgeoisie can be traced to January 1928, when the industrialists George Street, Francisco Matarazzo, and Roberto Simonsen split from the commercial association and organized the Center of São Paulo Industries. Its cultural expression became the School of Sociology and Politics of São Paulo, founded by Simonsen in 1933 as Brazil's first graduate program of social science and modeled on that of the University of Chicago (Fausto, 1983[1970]; Love, 1982).

1930 TO 1945: SEEKING NATIONAL UNITY THROUGH THE STATE

The foremost intellectual of the landed oligarchy was Ellis Júnior. In contrast to Washington Luiz, Basílio de Magalhães, and Afonso Taunay, he personified the unity of wealth, political power, and cultural prestige of the coffee aristocracy. He founded the USP School of Philosophy and Literature in 1931 and went on to publish numerous volumes on the racial superiority of the São Paulo landed aristocracy. In his first book (1934[1924]), sponsored by Afonso Taunay, then director of the São Paulo Museum, Ellis Júnior described the history of Brazil as five centuries of the *bandeirante* (pioneer) expansion. In his second and more influential book (1936[1926]), he drew upon eugenics to justify the planters' political leadership. In his last major work (1937), he retreated from determinism to pragmatism, describing the superiority of the pioneers not as ethnic but as the product of their work ethic, family cohesion, and austerity. In his last work (1944), his focus narrowed further to biographies of the founders of São Paulo, a nostalgic look back at a faded society.

In the same period in which Ellis Júnior abandoned grand historical reconstructions, Azevedo and Simonsen took the opposite path. They initiated their intellectual careers with an empirical defense of their classes, engaged in major public controversies, reconstructed Brazil's history, and founded prestigious educational institutions that introduced new theories, social research, and scientific standards. Azevedo's (1953) choice of public education as a central theme reflected a defense of the new urban middle classes, which adopted liberalism and supported social mobility through competitive labor markets.

Azevedo's advocacy for merit and performance contradicted the interests of the other fraction of the Brazilian middle classes in the rest of the country. Although the transition to modern capitalism in São Paulo had expanded labor markets for the urban middle classes, in the rest of the country, the survival of the middle strata depended on civil service jobs. When the agro-export crisis caused a collapse of state revenues and threatened their welfare, they united under the banner of nationalism in defense of political and administrative centralization. By the mid-1930s, the survival of these public-sector middle classes depended on enhancing the role of the central government in reducing regional disparities, expanding white-collar jobs, and restoring economic growth. Momentarily, during the 1930 revolution, they allied themselves with the private-sector middle classes in their support for the antioligarchic platform, but they parted company with them when the central government decided to reduce the autonomy of São Paulo. Because of economic, political, and cultural centralization in the Southeast, São Paulo projected the interests of the private middle classes, whereas Rio de Janeiro and Minas Gerais manifested the interests of two groups: the pluralists who advocated expanding political representation and the techno-bureaucrats who were focused on modernization and productivity. The techno-bureaucrats eventually converged with the industrial bourgeoisie to advocate development and nationalism.

Azevedo initiated his saga in the mid-1920s, when *O Estado de São Paulo* sponsored a study of the situation of schools and faculties in São Paulo (Azevedo, 1937[1926]). In addition to compiling the opinions of educators, he presented a historical reconstruction of Brazilian intellectual life. His survey exposed the dualism of the traditional educational system, identified with agrarian interests, formulated a concrete conception of educational reform, pointed to the goals of education, and associated them with social change. The dual system, a legacy of colonialism reinforced during the empire and continued into the First Republic, was rigidly stratified. The popular classes received primary and technical education, whereas secondary and higher education was reserved for the agrarian oligarchy. In addition to limiting communication between the elites and the masses, it impeded the dissemination of systematic knowledge about society and its problems. In Azevedo's view, Brazilian higher education had for two centuries sustained a decaying society led by an outdated oligarchy. He believed that an advanced urban-industrial society required an educational system that would eliminate the social barriers between classes and introduce modern science as a standard of excellence. Cultural change would be inevitable when different social classes converged in an integrated, free, and compulsory public educational system from nursery school to the university. Eventually, social stratification would be shaped by new values centered on merit, professionalization, and performance.

Roberto Simonsen followed a similar path, departing from an empirical defense of the industrial bourgeoisie to paradigmatic debates and a grand historical reconstruction that culminated in the founding of the first Brazilian graduate program in the social sciences. His initial pieces, written as manager of the first private construction company in Brazil, attributed low productivity to lack of scientific management, planning, and rational organization of labor. He argued that technical deficiencies caused labor conflicts and perpetuated the class struggle, the principal threats to social peace (Lima, 1976). This perspective guided his defense of modernization as the underlying ideology of the industrial bourgeoisie and its intellectual center in São Paulo, leading to the establishment of the School of Sociology and Politics of São Paulo in 1932 and USP in 1934. Between 1932 and 1937, the former introduced social theories that gave priority to the training of managers and planners, whereas the latter was devoted to academic social science.

The political support of the Paulista urban elite for the 1930 revolution was decisive to the demise of the First Republic. Its political organ, the PD, had negotiated the support of Getúlio Vargas in exchange for control of the state of São Paulo, but the appointment of Lieutenant João Alberto Lins, born in Pernambuco, as interventor (temporary administrator) led to a rebellion known as the Constitutionalist Revolution. The three competing social class segments (coffee planters, the middle classes, and the industrialists) converged in February 1932 in the Frente Paulista Unida (Paulista United Front). Fighting in the same trenches for the autonomy of São Paulo were the historical rivals Mesquita Filho, Simonsen, Ellis Júnior, and Azevedo (Dulles, 1984). However, in 1933, Vargas exchanged the pacification of the São Paulo elites for a constitutional assembly, and the unity of the three classes remained intact when Ellis Júnior, Simonsen, and Mesquita Filho were dispatched to the assembly. In the same accord, Armando de Sales Oliveira, the leader of the rebellion, was appointed interventor. He continued to govern until 1936 and intended to run against Vargas for the presidency, but the elections were canceled when Vargas decreed the Estado Novo.

In the assembly, Azevedo helped to prepare the proposal for the founding of USP and to formulate its educational principles. In the 1934 constitution, the hegemony of the São Paulo middle class reached its peak when it approved the educational objectives of the "New School," a group of educators led by Azevedo and Anísio Teixeira. Public education from primary school to the university became universal and free. The freedom of teaching and research was ensured against political interference, and special funds were set up to finance new public educational facilities. That year, the favorable political climate allowed Azevedo to consolidate the ideological segment of the civil middle classes into Brazil's most prestigious institution of higher education. USP's crest read "Scientia Vinces" (Knowledge Conquers), conveying the message that despite the political and military defeat, São Paulo insisted on Brazil's political leadership through its universities (Cardoso, 1982).

Azevedo's influence was evident in the organization of the new university, which in addition to the traditional School of Law, the Polytechnic, and the School of Medicine, had a School of Philosophy, Letters, and Sciences. This institutional collectivity sought to reconcile the interests of the different social classes. While the old faculties continued to receive the traditional families, the School of Philosophy absorbed the immigrants, the lower middle class, and women. Its mission was interdisciplinary education and research. Its teachers were to enjoy academic freedom to train a new generation of researchers in universal science and empirical research. Thus, Azevedo sought to convert the interests of the São Paulo middle class into institutional practice by linking social mobility to higher education and scientific practice.

Recognizing that without the professionalization of a new generation of researchers who could sustain the new ideology, the founding of USP would have no lasting effect, Azevedo took action on two fronts. First, he introduced sociological functionalism as the guiding science of the private middle class. In 1935, he founded the Brazilian Sociological Society and published the first review of Durkheim-influenced sociological theories (Azevedo, 1939). He also expanded the Brasiliana collection, a project of the Companhia Editora Nacional devoted to the gathering of information on the history of Brazil. Second, he negotiated directly the hiring of European scientists for the School of Philosophy, Letters, and Sciences. The first French mission of social scientists, in 1934, spent a few months and then returned to France after a dispute over wages and working conditions. The second mission, from 1935 to 1938, included Jean Maguer (philosophy and psychology), Fernand Braudel (history of civilization), Claude Lévi-Strauss (politics, sociology, and anthropology), and Pierre Monbeig (geography). The third mission, the smallest but the most influential, brought Roger Bastide (1964; see also Hamburger et al., 1996), who with Azevedo trained a whole new generation of intellectual leaders, among them Florestan Fernandes, Antônio Cândido de Mello Souza, and Maria Isaura Pereira de Queiroz.

Parallel to his efforts to consolidate USP, Azevedo published his historical reconstruction *Cultura Brasileira* as the two introductory volumes to the 1940 general census (Azevedo, 1943/1944[1940]). In it he defended cultural autonomy and free universities as the most effective tool for development. The essence of political independence, he argued, resided in institutions in which scientific autonomy and research were protected. Free, public, and integrated, they offered equal opportunities and challenged rigid social stratification. Social mobility unleashed the potential of a society repressed for centuries by traditional hierarchies. Through its universities, Brazil would finally reconcile social equity, economic progress, and representative democracy and achieve the status of a developed nation.

The military defeat of São Paulo in 1932 had changed the course of the industrial bourgeoisie, which between 1933 and 1937 replaced political with ideological engagement when it directed its funds and intellectuals to establishing a field of its own in the School of Sociology and Politics. In its first phase (1933–1939), the school represented the official ideology of the industrial bourgeoisie and its curriculum centered on administrative modernization, planning techniques, rationalization of labor, and the training of managers for the public and private sectors.

As a professor at the school, Simonsen (1937) sketched the history of Brazil as a series of business cycles leading to a national economy – from sugar to farming and the occupation of the hinterland to mining, cattle raising, and coffee production. For Simonsen, political independence became possible when different productive regions converged to form an integrated whole. São Paulo coffee production was highly complex, ensuring for the first time since colonization the circulation of money and domestic markets. Industry, the successor of coffee production, was even more complex; for the first time in history, Brazil's wealth was wholly centered on local accumulation. Simonsen argued that industrialization began in São Paulo and gradually became a national project led by a national class, the industrial bourgeoisie. That developmentalist project could be advanced only when planning by a centralized state expanded to the rest of the country (Simonsen, 1973[1939]).

In the late 1930s, the academic inspiration for the School of Sociology came from the University of Chicago. The cities of Chicago and São Paulo had gone through similar social changes with the arrival of European immigrants. The school's founders considered community studies such as those conducted by the Chicago sociologists well suited to the measurement of the assimilation of immigrants and the black minority by industrial societies. Simonsen hoped that by combining field research, empirical knowledge, and urban planning the school could train a new generation of public and private managers (Nogueira, 1968). In addition, despite the authoritarianism of the Estado Novo, the two protagonists of its administrative reforms, Luiz Simões Lopes and Moacir Briggs, had also been influenced by Chicago political scientists (Abu-El-Haj, 2005).

Trained by Robert Park in Chicago, Donald Pierson had focused on racial acculturation in his doctoral research, conducted with the physician and anthropologist Thales de Azevedo in Bahia, and he was influenced by Arthur Ramos, the founder of Brazilian anthropology, and by the sociologist Gilberto Freyre. Drawing on community studies, he argued that racial mixing had established a system of values that determined the dynamics of class relations in Brazil (Corrêa, 1987). At the School of Sociology, Pierson turned the city of São Paulo and the small urban agglomerations in its hinterland into field research sites for community studies. Cunha and Cruz das Almas, two isolated communities that had been experiencing changes with the opening of roads and the arrival of Italian immigrants since the late nineteenth century, served as case studies. Pierson hoped that graduate training in community research would advance local development projects and urban planning and that the experience of São Paulo would be replicated in other regions and foster the development of a new generation of planners embedded in Brazilian social life (Nogueira, 1968).

Two social scientists of German origin, Emilio Willems and Herbert Baldus, worked with Pierson in the graduate program and in editing the first social science periodical in Brazil, *Sociologia*. Willems began his association with the School of Sociology in 1936 as a professor of anthropology. In 1941, he left to establish the anthropology program at the USP School of Philosophy and later accepted an invitation from Vanderbilt University. Under his guidance, Gioconda Mussolini and Egon Schaden, the first professional ethnographers in Brazil, earned their graduate degrees. In 1953, Schaden initiated *Revista de Antropologia*, the first journal of its kind in Brazil. Herbert Baldus joined the school the same year as Pierson, and in 1941 he left to become chair of anthropology at the São Paulo Museum. Florestan Fernandes, Sêrgio Buarque de Holanda, and Darcy Ribeiro were his master's-level students.

During those years, the prestige of the School of Sociology was at its peak. It conducted state-of-the-art field research, maintained the only graduate program in social sciences, and enjoyed the financial support of the industrial bourgeoisie. However, its extreme empiricism distinguished it from the line espoused by Azevedo and Bastide at the School of Philosophy. Bastide and Lévi-Strauss, students of Marcel Mauss and participants in the *Année Sociologique* (the journal founded by Durkheim in 1896), argued that ethnographic data should be collected through field research. The establishment of the Estado Novo and the promulgation of its constitution in 1937 were as decisive for the intellectual consolidation of the public middle class as the revolution of 1932 and the 1934 constitution were for that of the private middle class. First, the foundation of a modernizing authoritarianism and a functioning capitalism appeared with the political and administrative centralization of the Estado Novo and an augmentation of public-sector jobs, ensuring the relative autonomy of white-collar workers from state oligarchies. Second, the recruitment of the middle classes from different regions for positions in the federal administration increased their political and intellectual prestige.

Integralists, Catholics, and rebellious young officers or *tenentes* had for decades been in a position to lead the public middle class (Forjaz, 1989), but it was a group of intellectuals organized around the pragmatic Gustavo Capanema, a politician and a writer from Minas Gerais, that now assumed that role. Although São Paulo loomed as Brazil's economic heart and Rio de Janeiro as the center of its political and cultural institutions, Minas Gerais, one of the cradles of independence, was falling into obscurity (Arruda, 1989, 1990). To compensate for its fragility, the state's elites invested in political training. Electoral studies and formal political analysis were included as core courses in its law school, the traditional center of elite formation. Capanema assumed the role of an activist intellectual of the public middle class when he switched his loyalty from local bosses to Vargas. During his tenure as minister of education and health between 1934 and 1945, he implemented the educational project of the Estado Novo, founding the University of Brazil and the National School of Philosophy.

Although the educational program of the Estado Novo retained free and public education, it reversed key ideals of the 1934 constitution. Universal access was to be offered equally by public and private institutions, Catholicism was to be taught in public schools, and coeducation was canceled. By far the program's most controversial aspect, however, was the reorganization of higher education. In a regression to the pre-1934 system, it distinguished scientific, professional, and vocational training and reserved the first two to the elites in universities and traditional schools. Funding for the third would come from union contributions managed and supervised by employers' industrial and commercial confederations through the National Industrial Apprenticeship Service and the National Commercial Apprenticeship Service, respectively (Schwartzman, Bomeny, and Costa, 2000).

Although Azevedo and Capanema agreed that higher education would contribute to development, they clashed on two key issues. First, whereas Capanema considered the university to be an instrument of national unity, recruiting its students from different regions to form a national elite, Azevedo saw education as a promoter of social mobility. Second, since Capanema subordinated higher education to national development goals set by the central government, priority was given to the development of human resources rather than to science, research, and professionalization compatible with international standards. Azevedo (1953) hoped that making scientific research a priority would reduce the distance between Brazil and the rich countries.

With the enactment of the Estado Novo, the standards defended by Azevedo were reversed, and an offensive was launched against the institutions of the private middle class. It started in Rio de Janeiro, after the failure of the National Liberation Alliance (Aliança Nacional Libertadora [ANL]) rebellion, an antifascist movement that united communists, army officers, and anti-imperialist forces. In November 1935, Anísio Teixeira, who had been nominated by Pedro Ernest, the mayor of Rio de Janeiro and an ANL supporter, was replaced by Capanema's ally Francisco Campos as head of the Department of Education. Then Afrânio Peixoto, the rector of the University of the Federal District, lost his job to Alceu Amoroso Lima, the foremost educator of the Dom Vital Center, the historical rival of the New School. In January 1939, Lima officially liquidated the University of the Federal District, and its faculty was transferred to the National School of Philosophy, the ideological core of the University of Brazil.

The National School of Philosophy replicated the organizational structure that Azevedo had established in São Paulo. Alongside the natural sciences, it included the social sciences and philosophy. To secure its prestige as a center of excellence, Capanema hired European researchers to design its new curriculum, but in contrast to the liberal profile promoted by USP, these researchers were all Catholics. In 1939, its first director, after consulting the French Catholic philosopher Jacques Maritain, approved Jacques Lambert (sociology), André Gros (policy), and Maurice Bye (economy) as new professors. In 1940, Lima resigned to establish the Catholic University of Rio de Janeiro and was replaced by Santiago Dantas, a nationalist lawyer. Later, two of his students and protégés, Alberto Guerreiro Ramos and Luís Aguiar Costa Pinto, became the founders of social science education in Rio de Janeiro.

In 1938, on the pretext of submitting state-run public education to the targets of the Ministry of Education, Capanema's offensive reached the USP School of Philosophy. First came the dismissal as political agitators of three historic figures of the traditional Law School. Then the government vetoed the hiring of the graduates of the school, stereotyped as "philosophers," for teaching positions in the Department of Education both in São Paulo and in the interior. Finally, European teachers hired during the administration received notifications of dismissal, their services having been declared incompatible with the economic priorities of a developing nation.

The climax of the offensive came in 1939, with the appointment of Ellis Júnior as director of the School of Philosophy. Adhemar de Barros, his childhood friend and ally in the PRP, instructed him to abolish the school. Ellis Júnior, a son of the coffee aristocracy, although he had spent his political life fighting the Estadão group associated with *O Estado de São Paulo*, in his last historical pieces became obsessed with the autonomy of São Paulo, considering it the last bastion of liberty in a country marred by oligarchies (Ellis Júnior, 1934[1924]). During his tenure, he disobeyed Barros, sympathized with the complaints of the students against the Department of Education, and renegotiated the dismissal of the European teachers. He went on to support an indefinite strike declared by the Law School against the proposed awarding of an *honoris causa* to Getúlio Vargas. Conflicts between supporters of Vargas and his critics spread into the streets of São Paulo. Capanema, along with his young assistant Vítor Nunes Leal, were forced to negotiate directly with the students a truce that included the return of the suspended professors and continuity of the School of Philosophy – a tacit admission of the autonomy of the school (Motoyama, 2005).

With the coming to power of Getúlio Vargas, intellectuals turned toward issues of national and political significance. During 1932 and 1933, a series called the Coleção Azul (Blue Collection, because of the deep blue color of its covers) appeared in Rio under the editorship of Augusto Frederico Schmidt. It included volumes by Martins de Almeida (1932) on the October 1930 revolution and issues such as race and land tenure; by Virginio Santa Rosa (1933) on the rise of the rebellious young *tenentes* and Vargas, arguing that the petty bourgeoisie was capable of bringing about the revolution in Brazil; by Plínio Salgado (1933) on the significance of integralism as an approach to order and equilibrium rather than reform; by Alcindo Sodré (1933) on the overthrow of the empire, the rise of the republic, and the influence of *tenentismo* in the Vargas period; and by Affonso Arinos de Mello Franco (1933) on the role of intellectuals vying for revolutionary changes under fascism or communism.

Writing in several important journals, intellectuals began to focus less on regional and more on national questions and the prospects for a national bourgeoisie. *Cadernos da Hora Presente* represented intellectuals close to Vargas and his corporatist regime. Appearing quarterly with nine numbers from May 1939 to July–August 1940, it was published in Rio, São Paulo, Belo Horizonte, and Recife in an effort to project a national presence. Its first issue included a piece by Plínio Salgado, a renowned integralist, and contributions by such later prominent intellectuals as Rômulo de Almeida (1939), an economist and technocrat influential in the regime, and Alberto Guerreiro Ramos (1939, 1940), a Afro-Brazilian concerned about racism.

The monthly journal *Cultura Política: Revista Mensal de Estudos Brasileiros*, first published in Rio in March 1941, included substantive articles and detailed analysis of themes related to Brazil's national destiny. Each issue focused on the activity and policies of the Vargas government and articles on political and social problems, economy, government activity, and cultural concerns, including intellectual evolution. In his initial mission statement, editor Almir de Andrade (1941) made a plea for national unity and anticipated the transformation of institutional life in the direction of democracy as a means for resolving social and economic crises. The first issue also included a brief segment emphasizing the traditional gap between political people and intellectuals and suggesting that intellectuals had become more conscious of Brazil and its problems and willing to participate in public life. Ensuing issues focused on the national question, nationalism, and Brazil as nation. Toward the end of 1941, more speeches and writings of Vargas and references to his government appeared, and there was a concerted effort to tie government to national development and intellectual life. In celebration of its second year, *Cultura Política* set forth a program of unity in search of a new politics and a revolutionary course for Brazil. Thereafter, it concentrated on Vargas, the state and nationalism, and the themes of politics, economics, and culture that had appeared throughout the earlier numbers. There were occasional essays by prominent writers such as Graciliano Ramos, Luiz da Câmara Cascudo, Ademar Vidal, Hélio Viana, and Djacir Menezes. Curiously, there was also a short article by Lieutenant Colonel Humberto de Castelo Branco, who would emerge as a general and president in the aftermath of the 1964 coup and military rule.

Several contributors later associated with the Higher Institute of Brazilian Studies (Instituto Superior de Estudos Brasileiros [ISEB]) were involved in *Cultura Política*: historian Nelson Werneck Sodré wrote a series of pieces on the issue of national borders (1941a, 1942), on the possibility of revolutionary change within the government and program of Getúlio Vargas (Sodré, 1941b), on economic factors related to regional disparity and internal markets (1941c), and on nationality in Brazilian literature (1943). Rômulo de Almeida (1943) provided a detailed overview of the economy, problems of national integration, and expansion. Celso Furtado (1944) questioned the reality of a modern democracy. This journal published up to the end of the regime, and it was important not only for its reflection of the policies and actions of the Vargas regime but also for its effort to conceptualize and project development in a national context.

1945 TO 1964: ENVISAGING A DEMOCRATIC NATIONAL BOURGEOISIE AND CONFRONTING IMPERIALISM AND DEPENDENCY

After the fall of the Vargas regime in 1945, a successor journal, *Cultura e Política*, appeared in Rio de Janeiro as an irregular quarterly first published in September–December 1948 by the Ministry of Education and Health and directed by José Simão Leal, with sections on art, science, history, literature, documentation, review, and bibliography. The first issue included an article on musical nationalism by Renato Almeida, an essay on culture and ethos by anthropologist Arthur Ramos, and a historical essay by José Honório Rodrigues. The second issue (January–April 1949) contained contributions by major literary and cultural specialists Arthur Ramos, Mário de Andrade, and Manuel Diégues Júnior, whereas essays on race by reputable social scientists L. A. Costa Pinto, Djacir Menezes, Darcy Ribeiro, Sílvio Romero, and Edson Carneiro appeared in later issues. As in the past, the emphasis was on recognizing the significance of Brazilian culture.

In Rio, intellectuals focused on national questions. Leftists writers, many of them affiliated with the PCB, envisaged a democratic and national bourgeoisie as possible in the democratic opening that ensued after Vargas. They saw the shaping of a national consciousness as a means to undermine the colonial obsession of the past. For example, Antônio Cândido de Mello Souza examined the literature on national consciousness and set forth a program for study (1959, 1965, 1968, 1969, 1995). In the revision (1969) of his 1954 doctoral thesis, Dante Moreira Leite attacked studies that promoted a national character as an escape from the past. Roberto Schwarz (1967) criticized the cultural vanguard for reinforcing the capitalist system, and Mota (1980: 247) brought new perspective to thinking about important sectors of "left bourgeois intellectuality." The Maranhão poet and journalist Ferreira Gullar (1979: 77), who addressed themes of nationalism and popular culture in two important works (1965, 1969), was particularly concerned about the alienating influences of foreign culture. He saw Brazil's international relations as characterized by dependency and imperialism and argued that the debate on national problems of the early 1960s had revealed a fundamental contradiction in Brazilian culture: "the separation manifested in painting, theater, cinema, and literature." Intellectuals began to explore every aspect of nationalism, linking the struggle for autonomy and ending backwardness to imperialism and negative consequences of foreign investment and presence in the national political economy.

Whereas the intellectuals of São Paulo saw science itself as a force for social change, the intellectuals of Rio believed that theory should be applied to political practice. In the 1940s, the latter divided into two groups. In the National School of Philosophy, Vítor Nunes Leal focused on political representation and formulated a theory of political development. In 1949, he examined the dilemma of representation during the period of socioeconomic transition from a rural to an urban society. In focusing on the autonomy of politics, he established a theme that continues to be central to intellectual debates. This formulation would not have had the same prestige if Leal had not been in command during the most crucial period of the consolidation of the Brazilian political system.

Moving in the opposite direction, Alberto Guerreiro Ramos tied political and social change to industrialization. His publications formalized the techno-bureaucratic intellectual field by stressing scientific management and planning as instruments of industrial modernization. Although his reputation as a social scientist was enhanced by the debates with Florestan Fernandes on the role of intellectuals, his prestige was derived from his presence in the ISEB at the height of social change in the mid-1950s. Ramos's analysis of the dilemmas of power, intellectuals, and social change influenced the debate about development and how to attain it through economic and social policies.

Having survived Capanema's offensive, the USP School of Philosophy attracted new recruits different from those of the traditional schools of law and medicine, including descendants of immigrants, lower income people, and women. When Egon Schaden (1939), Gioconda Mussolini

(1938), Antônio Cândido de Mello Souza (1939), and Florestan Fernandes (1941) graduated, they were dispatched to the School of Sociology to be trained in social research under Donald Pierson, Herbert Baldus, and Emilio Willems (Pereira, 1994; Ciacchi, 2007). Redemocratization in 1945 strengthened the reputation of USP. During Dutra's presidency, Azevedo became secretary of education for the state of São Paulo, and between 1950 and 1953 he reached the peak of his intellectual prestige when he was elected vice president of the International Sociological Association. He chaired the first doctoral committees of his two assistants, Florestan Fernandes and Antônio Cândido de Mello Souza. Fernandes's doctoral thesis (1970[1951]) and his *livre docência* (required to receive the equivalent to tenure) yielded two theoretical volumes on functionalism in sociology and its empirical application (1953, 1959b). Robert Merton acclaimed them as among the seven most important syntheses of contemporary sociological theories (D'Incao, 1987b; Martins, 1998). His work on the Brazilian black in a class society (Fernandes, 1964), written in defense of his full professorship, was a watershed in Brazilian social thought, presenting race prejudice as a cultural determinant of stratification in class society.

Antônio Cândido de Mello Souza took a similar path. His thesis in 1945 became the classic study on the critical method of Sílvio Romero (Souza, 1963) and served as the basis for his monumental study of Brazilian literature (1959, 1965). His doctoral dissertation (1964), advised by Azevedo and inspired by Roger Bastide, showed a pragmatic and adaptive *caipira* (inhabitants of the interior of São Paulo) very different from their depiction in the traditional literature. Similar pragmatic views on social values were presented in the grand compilation of the history of philosophy in Brazil by João da Cruz Costa (1956[1945]).

Two facts determined the intellectual dominance of the School of Philosophy in São Paulo. First, influenced by French sociology, the new generation of faculty critiqued the "community studies" associated with sociology at the University of Chicago. Second, the empirical studies led by Florestan Fernandes on central themes in contemporary Brazil – the influence of race prejudice on class stratification and the analysis of industrial capitalism – showed that this school had significant potential for continuous renovation. Although in Rio de Janeiro the two intellectual fields of the public middle classes focused on the education of the elite, the School of Philosophy gave priority to professionalization of the intellectual as a researcher trained in formal science and dedicated to field research.

By the late 1940s, the predominance of the School of Philosophy was apparent. The intellectuals of the São Paulo bourgeoisie had switched from hegemony through educational institutions to an institutional presence in the Estado Novo. Furthermore, USP enjoyed the financial resources of the state of São Paulo. Finally, since the School of Sociology and Politics was dedicated primarily to graduate training along the lines of the University of Chicago, student demand there stagnated, while USP, which graduated teachers for public education, grew alongside the expansion of that system.

These factors were reinforced by a methodological critique. Florestan Fernandes (1948) presented what would become the main division of the two traditions in São Paulo. He acknowledged that the study of communities provided valuable research techniques but argued that social research had to focus on social classes, the prime force in capitalism. He went on to distinguish between a school of thought that envisioned cultural continuity through "acculturation" and "assimilation" and one that considered Brazil to be in the process of social change. Similar views appeared in the preface of the doctoral dissertation of Antônio Cândido de Mello Souza, originally inspired by community studies. In 1953, the *Revista de Antropologia*, founded by Egon Schaden, became a critical forum on Chicago sociology. Articles by Maria Sylvia Carvalho Franco, Octávio Ianni, Ruth Cardoso, and Eunice Durham equated empirical ethnography with a loss of purpose in the social sciences (Franco, 1963; Corrêa, 2003; Ciacchi, 2007). In 1959, isolated and lacking local support, Pierson left São Paulo for the Smithsonian.

The methodological entrenchment of the School of Philosophy was followed by empirical investigations on the two most difficult issues of Brazilian society: racial discrimination and the dynamics of social classes in underdeveloped capitalism. First, in 1950, the anthropologist Alfred Métraux included São Paulo in a United Nations Organization for Education, Science and Culture (UNESCO) project (Maio, 1999) conceived by anthropologist and head of the National Museum, Arthur Ramos, as a study of Brazilian miscegenation as a "laboratory of civilization." The proposal suggested the existence of a "racial democracy" that would facilitate peaceful coexistence between social classes under capitalism. Fernandes and his two assistants, Fernando Henrique Cardoso and Octávio Ianni, went beyond the quantitative surveys envisioned by the proposal to include qualitative research on race and social stratification in urban centers. Their findings not only revealed a problem with the project's hypothesis but also challenged important sociological studies of race in Brazil and abroad. They recognized that miscegenation was widespread in all social strata in Brazil, but although they suggested an eventual retreat of race prejudice with the advance of urban industrial society, they documented its intensification parallel to competition in labor markets. They concluded that economic development and competitive labor markets might aggravate rather than alleviate prejudice. These results contradicted the studies of Ramos, which made the integration of blacks contingent on their participation in the nationalist struggle for industrialization. A similar notion had been advanced by Pierson in his doctoral dissertation in 1935, in which he argued that Brazilian prejudice was based on color rather than race. For the first time a group of Brazilian researchers dialogued with social theories, conducted an extensive empirical study, and established a concrete theory of social stratification in Brazil. In addition to the two publications of Fernandes (Bastide and Fernandes, 1955; Fernandes, 1964), the doctoral dissertations of Cardoso (1962a) and Ianni (1962) were based on the results of this project.

The second wave of research followed a proposal by Fernandes for research on modern Brazil in an attempt to predict the future of "industrial civilization," taking the city of São Paulo as a case study. In 1961, with the support of Alain Touraine, director of the Laboratory of Industrial Sociology at the University of Paris and then a visiting professor of sociology at USP, Fernandes established the Center for Research in the Sociology of Industry and Labor (Centro de Sociologia Industrial do Trabalho [CESIT]) to raise research funds from the National Industrial Confederation and the São Paulo State Foundation for Research Support. When the proposal had been approved, Fernandes designated Fernando Henrique Cardoso to collect data, Octávio Ianni to prepare the sample of public and private companies, and Marialice Mencarini Foracci and Maria Sylvia Carvalho Franco to supervise the field research and prepare the reports. The British anthropologist Bertrand Hutchinson helped with the questionnaire on the social values of entrepreneurs. The field research was carried out by USP freshmen Celso de Rui Beisigel, Leôncio Martins Rodrigues, Gabriel Bolaffi, José Carlos Pereira, and Lourdes Sola (Fernandes, 1977).

The survey focused on four themes: the values and work ethic of the industrial entrepreneur, the effect of developmentalism on the growth of the industrial economy, working conditions during the transition from traditional industry to the modern enterprise, and the influence of technology on Brazilian social conditions. The findings were presented by Cardoso (1964) and pointed to the first formulation of the concept of associated dependency. For Cardoso, the alliance between the industrial bourgeoisie, the proletariat, and the middle classes had been made possible by protectionism and state investment in basic industry, but with the advance of industry the multiclass alliance had collapsed, for two reasons. First, the middle class had become intensely nationalistic and demanded the deepening of state ownership. Second, the expansion of industrial labor and its increased organizational capacity permitted greater working-class militancy – demands for better living conditions, higher wages, and more social benefits. Political pressure on the ruling classes was aggravated by the mobilization of the peasant masses for equal rights. Pressured economically by high inflation and weakened politically by social strife, the national bourgeoisie distanced itself from the nationalist social pact and joined international capital as a junior partner. In this study, Cardoso contradicted the positions of the ISEB and developmentalist theorists in general by arguing that industrialization in developing countries would create situations of dependence because of internal social dynamics and class struggle rather than external impositions.

While the new generation at USP was absorbed by academic themes, participated in empirical research, dialogued with social theories, and received international recognition from the international scientific community, in Rio de Janeiro politically engaged intellectuals were forming a parallel assemblage. The emblematic figures Vítor Nunes Leal and Alberto Guerreiro Ramos, both associated with the National School of Philosophy, led its two variants. Although the former focused on the political arena and became the pioneer of political science in Brazil, the latter was involved in public administration and planning institutions.

Leal, born in Minas, was director of the Documentation Service of the Ministry of Education and Health under Capanema in 1939. In 1943, Leal became the political science chair at the National School of Philosophy. Ironically, Santiago Dantas, director of the National School, had chosen Alberto Guerreiro Ramos, who had just completed his degrees in social sciences (1942) and law (1943), but was vetoed because Ramos was a militant in an integralist organization in his home state of Bahia.

Between 1946 and 1949, Leal wrote his thesis for a full professorship in political science at the National School. His research dealt with the way the municipality, the arena of traditional power of the *coronel* or large landowner, accommodated the modern central government established during the First Republic and institutionalized by the political and administrative centralization of the Estado Novo. Despite its theoretical deficiencies, it became a classic of Brazilian political thought (Leal, 1975[1948]). He found that, despite the expansion of territorial representation, the system was far from a typical representative democracy in which political parties mediate between social interests and government institutions. His explanation was *coronelismo*, the exchange of political favors between the centralized authority and an outdated social structure based on the *latifundio*. In 1956, his connections with the Minas elite led him to be designated attorney general and, after eight months, head of the cabinet of the newly elected President Juscelino Kubitschek, charged with the allocation of political allies to managerial positions in state-owned companies. Leal had envisioned difficulties but believed that a reformist government could regulate the political milieu. Those expectations faded when, in August 1959, under pressure from his political allies in the congress, Kubitschek asked him to step down; a year later, he was appointed a judge of the Supreme Court. In Brasília, he joined Darcy Ribeiro and Anísio Teixeira as a founder of the University of Brasília. Together with Hermes Lima and Evandro Lins, he formed a bloc to combat corruption. After the 1964 military coup, they expedited habeas corpus for many political prisoners, but in 1969 the government demanded their resignation.

The work of Raymundo Faoro complemented that of Leal. Of particular importance was his *Os donos do poder* (1975[1957]), an interpretive historical study of Brazil from early Portuguese times to the Old Republic. With emphasis on the bureaucratic patrimonial state in its precapitalist phase as an aristocratic entity, he argued that it was the bureaucracy of high public functionaries or agents of the state that held power. Despite the victory, more apparent than real, of democratic ideas, administrative power was exercised more by functionaries, including the military, than by politicians (263).

Ramos established himself as the major intellectual of the second direction in Rio de Janeiro. His 1945 thesis for tenure was the first comprehensive synthesis of scientific management theories and planning in Brazil (Ramos, 1950). In it, he argued that Weberian bureaucratic rationalization had replaced class struggle as a determinant of social stratification in industrial capitalism. He complemented that theory with Mannheim's assertion of planning as a substitute for markets in large private and public organizations. He concluded that because Brazil was located in an intermediate stage between patrimonialism and rationalization, bureaucratic reform would be required to establish planning as a developmentalist vehicle.

Two events propelled Ramos to leadership in his field. First, the industrial bourgeoisie that had led the modernization tendency since Simonsen's first publications had changed its strategy. During the Estado Novo, it abandoned its political alliances with the private middle class in São Paulo and joined the regime. That shift highlighted its transition from a defensive posture centered on technical modernization and productivity to an offensive posture in favor of protectionism and industrial policy. Second, it relinquished its educational institutions in São Paulo and invested in political activism and agenda setting. Consequently, the Institute for the Development of Rational Labor Organization, founded in 1931 to promote industrial productivity and rational administration in São Paulo, was replaced by the economics department of the São Paulo State Federation of Industries, the first economic research think tank in Brazil, as the main institution of the São Paulo bourgeoisie. This new intellectual endeavor was made up of economists charged with producing studies and surveys to sustain Simonsen's defense of planning within the Estado Novo. Similarly, the School of Sociology lost its importance when Simonsen left his teaching position to represent the industrialists in the influential Council of Industrial and Trade Policy (Bielschowsky, 1988).

After the Second World War, when planning fell out of favor for having been associated with authoritarian practices, Simonsen withdrew from public institutions and devoted himself to economic surveys. His experience in the economics department of the São Paulo State Federation of Industries was transferred to the National Industrial Confederation, which produced the first generation of developmentalist economists. Despite his death in 1948, the new intellectual field became the breeding ground for the Brazilian techno-bureaucracy. Four of its economists held key positions in state economic institutions in the 1950s. Rômulo de Almeida headed the council of economic advisers of the second Vargas government in 1951, became the first president of the Banco do Nordeste in Fortaleza in 1952, and was influential and involved in the formation of the ISEB. Ewaldo Correia Lima and Joaquim Mangia took up positions as senior managers of the National Economic Development Bank. In the middle 1950s, Correa Lima was a founding member of the ISEB and headed its economics department. Ferreira Lima presided over the State Federation's economics department and replaced Simonsen as the main protagonist of the industrial bourgeoisie while publishing biographies and histories of industrial associations (Bielschowsky, 1988).

In 1951, Ramos organized the techno-bureaucratic field founded by the industrial bourgeoisie at the invitation of his old companion in Bahia, Rômulo de Almeida. While Almeida, Ferreira Lima, Mangia, and Correia Lima occupied managerial positions in the state and class-based organizations, Ramos devoted his time to an intellectual defense of techno-bureaucracy. He taught administrative theory to Brazil's bureaucratic elite in the graduate program of the Getúlio Vargas Foundation, founded by his former superior at the Administrative Department of Public Service (Departamento Administrativo do Serviço Público [DASP]), Luiz Simões Lopes, and through the ISEB participated in public debates on industrialization and intellectuals (Oliveira, 1995). His historic exchange with Fernandes was one of the defining moments of Brazilian social science. Between 1954 and 1958, Brazil's two major sociologists debated the role of intellectuals in society, the purpose of social research, and the effect of knowledge on development.

The debate began during the Second Latin American Congress of Sociology in Rio de Janeiro in 1953, when Ramos raised three considerations about the role of intellectuals. The first was that countries like Brazil that had suffered cultural colonization should not continue importing theories, methodologies, and concepts from developed countries. Priority should be given to public debates on the fate of the nation, the constraints on its development, and its relations with other civilizations. Its methodology should be flexible, constantly adapting new cultural representations to the national culture. Brazilian intellectuals should model their works on the publications of Alberto Torres, Oliveira Vianna, and Azevedo Amaral, which focused on an internal revolution seeking a national consciousness and civilizing purpose. The second was that the scarcity of financial resources for economic development and infrastructure required Latin American intellectuals to sacrifice expensive field research for general interpretations and to maximize the public debate at minimum financial cost. The third was that empirical social research derived from refined theories was a luxury appropriate to countries of high culture and beyond the comprehension of ordinary Brazilians (Ramos, 1954).

Fernandes (1958b) rebutted these views, arguing, first, that intellectuals must not confuse science with nationality; although knowledge was rational and universal, nationality was emotional and particular. Second, developing countries had to give scientific development the highest priority to overcome backwardness and internal inequalities. The financial resources spent on scientific research never came at the expense of economic production but usually improved efficiency and quality. Third, the complexity of development, the difficulties of social change, the financial constraints on the universities, and the lack of access to the technologies available to researchers in advanced countries had to be offset by methodological refinement and greater command of theory.

Ramos (1958e) crystallized his vision in a mature work arguing that every country had its own particular rationalization process. The intellectual's role was to adapt new expressions to the main matrix of Brazilian culture by publicly debating obstacles to administrative rationalization and secularization. Although Ramos did not present a precise definition of Brazilian culture, he alluded to the values derived from peaceful ethnic conciliation promoted by Catholicism. Its universalism allowed for a pacific fusion of different races and generated a culture of solidarity. Whereas in Europe class struggle and political revolutions and in the United States racial segregation and racial mistrust had led to a competitive and conflictive stratification, in Brazil miscegenation had created the conditions for peaceful coexistence between social classes. Ramos concluded that the inherent harmony between social classes made Brazil receptive to planning.

By the mid-1950s, three paradigms had been consolidated. USP adopted a Durkheimian functionalism that upheld the sanctity of science, professionalism, and empirical research as instruments of social change. Fernandes, the intellectual heir of Azevedo and Bastide, formulated grand syntheses, engaged in debates, conducted extensive research, and founded the São Paulo School of Sociology at USP. Leal introduced political development, established political science, and confronted Brazil's political dilemmas in the academy and politics. Finally, Ramos synthesized modernization and scientific management theories, defended planning, and formulated the theory of public intellectuals.

The intensity of social conflict, peasant mobilizations, inflationary crisis, the political ambiguity of the industrial bourgeoisie, and the difficulties of party representation were mirrored by internal critiques of the three fields. Fernandes had linked social rights to generational change in values through public education, and when he studied the ordinary person with a functionalist lens, he described a submissive subject dominated by traditional values. His predictions of a new culture of rights achievable only in urban-industrial society fell apart in the period of popular militancy. Whereas Leal limited representation to political institutions, the masses intervened directly in political life, using all means from land invasions to strikes and support of populist leaders. Whereas Ramos insisted that intellectual life, cultural institutions, and social struggles were dependent on a national project of industrialization, the bourgeoisie opted for an obedient association with international capital (Ianni et al., 1965).

In 1958, Fernandes's assistants formed the *Capital* Group, partially in reaction to his excessive sociological formalism, and focused on a critical reading of Marx's *Capital* and other writings (Giannotti, 1998; Bastos, 2006). At about the same time, there was controversy within the ISEB about a book written by its founder, Helio Jaguaribe, defending foreign investment in Brazil's petroleum industry. Jaguaribe eventually resigned, and Ramos followed suit. Roland Corbisier assumed its leadership, then left to become a state representative, and Álvaro Vieira Pinto led the ISEB's final radical phase in the midst of the popular demands for profound reform in the last years of the Goulart administration (Toledo, 1978). A new generation called for a radical revision of its original theses: big business, international capital, and the *latifundio* were identified as obstacles to a nation mobilized by repressed peasants, the superexploited urban proletariat, and small and medium-sized companies involved in the internal economy (Sodré, 1986; Miglioli, 2005; Santos, 2005).

The critique of the institutionalist paradigm was led by Francisco Weffort (in Ianni et al., 1965), who argued that, under the objective conditions of the Brazilian party system inherited from the 1930s, populism was the only form of political expression possible for the Brazilian masses. For Weffort, the origins of representation could be found in the Bonapartist counterrevolution of 1937 and its ensuing corporatism, when the decaying oligarchies and the rising industrial bourgeoisie turned to Vargas as the arbiter of social conflict. The working class was pacified by a combination of state-controlled unionism, the banning of its legitimate representative, the PCB, and open coercion by the political police. In the 1950s, industrialization expanded the ranks of the proletariat, which mobilized in defense of its social rights. Because the party system reflected the interests of political oligarchies, the masses resorted to populism as a vehicle to advance their interests.

Although Fernandes dictated the official social science and determined research topics, it was Caio Prado Júnior who gave the new generation in São Paulo a sense of the purpose of social research. Born into the coffee aristocracy, socialized politically in the PCB, and an adherent of historical materialism, he contested the dominant paradigms of Brazilian historiography. In his first book (1933), he established a research agenda centered on an analysis of the dominant classes from agrarian mercantilism to industrial capitalism. His work would become the history of class struggle in Brazil.

His initial critique centered on the ideology of *bandeirismo* and its glorification of the heroic conqueror depicted in the works of Washington Luiz, Basílio de Magalhães, and Alfredo Ellis Júnior. In showing that the expansion of Brazil's southern frontier was determined by the competition between Spain and England for control of precious metals, Prado Júnior linked the existence of Brazil to European primitive accumulation. His demystification of *bandeirismo* was followed by a historical analysis of the origins of the bourgeoisie comprised of exporters linked to international markets and tied to an alliance with the metropolis to control a vast territory, facilitate the export of wealth, and perpetuate political subordination. When the colonial system isolated the provinces and prohibited the formation of an internal market, it prevented the emergence of dominant classes with aspirations for independence. Although the extraction of wealth was the purpose of colonization, its production was based on slave labor in a vast and sparsely inhabited territory. The colonial model reflected a consistent but unusual early capitalism. The bourgeoisie realized its profits in the international market, the colonial state blocked internal accumulation to sustain its administration, slavery produced wealth for the market, and the administrative system was run by elites uprooted from their social environment.

To sustain a larger dominant class after independence, the colonial system had to be expanded. The commercial bourgeoisie was given more power to export wealth, monoculture was intensified, and the extraction of wealth from the direct producers reached new heights. For half a century, Brazil was in a permanent state of rebellion presented by the elites as separatist movements. For Prado Júnior these regional movements represented the reaction of Brazilian civil society to exploitation. Fragmented into isolated provinces by the colonial system, it could not unite in a national movement. Its suppression in the name of national unity eliminated the possibility of a national capitalism. In its place the commercial bourgeoisie perpetuated dependency, political repression, and rigid social stratification. With this formulation, Prado Júnior established a dichotomy between two capitalist projects in constant competition since independence: a dependent capitalism run by an internationalized bourgeoisie that continued the colonial legacy of underdevelopment and repression and a national capitalism rooted in the general interests of the masses and internal accumulation.

In a subsequent work, Prado Júnior (1942) showed how slavery, monocrop cycles, and regional social relations of production combined to form a coherent colonial economic system. In the 1950s, his attention shifted to industrial capitalism and its class struggles. Civil society now expressed itself no longer in regional rebellions but in urban and rural labor movements. This is the theme that dominated the *Revista Brasiliense*, the most important intellectual forum between 1955 and 1964. His articles concerned agrarian movements, the nature of the industrial bourgeoisie, the meaning of development, and the theoretical inconsistency of the Brazilian left. In his last book (1966), he awakened the new generation of social scientists to a critical and concrete analysis of a national capitalism rooted in Brazilian social history.

1964 TO THE 1980S: FROM MODERNIZING AUTHORITARIANISM TO THE DEMOCRATIC OPENING

The military coup of 1964 shattered the aspirations of progressive Brazilian intellectuals to participate directly in political life. It marginalized them from cultural activities, thus undermining new ideas about shaping the nation and contending with a perceived threat from imperialism and foreign interests. The military regime moved quickly to close down the ISEB, impose censorship, eventually intervene to purge the Congress of opposing members, and harass intellectuals with imprisonment or pressure them to flee into exile. In 1966, Ramos left Brazil permanently to teach at the University of Southern California. In 1968, the military repression affected Fernandes and his assistants, and in 1969 Fernandes, Cardoso, and Ianni were forcibly retired. In January 1969, Leal, Lima, and Evando were removed from the Supreme Court. Fernandes left Brazil for a long exile at the University of Toronto; after his exile in Chile, Cardoso, along with José Arthur Giannotti, Cândido Procopio Ferreira de Camargo, Juárez Rubens Brandão Lopes, Octávio Ianni, Paul Singer, and Elza Salvatori Berquó, founded in São Paulo the Brazilian Center for Analysis and Planning (Centro Brasileiro de Análise e Planejamento [CEBRAP]) (Sorj, 2001). The vast majority had participated in the *Capital* Group and followed Prado Júnior's lead when he advocated a social analysis focused on political practice (Biderman, Coza, and Rego, 1996; Mantega and Rego, 1999; Bastos, 2006).

In the late 1970s, the pluralist turn reached Brazil's left after its failed armed struggle. Its strategy, however, focused on political inclusion rather than political contestation (Sader and Paoli, 1986). Intellectuals assumed the role of catalysts of the popular forces and became involved in social movements. Their theories, public discourse, and political practices shifted from socialism to democracy (Weffort, 1978, 1984; Chauí, 1982; Sader, 1988; Moisés, 1995; Gohn, 1997; Dagnino, Olvera, and Panfichi, 2006). The ideological turn from the state to civil society came from different sources. Under the influence of Eurocommunists expelled from the Communist Party by the Soviet faction, the concept of civil society was introduced into the New Left. Carlos Nelson Coutinho's notion of democracy as a universal value became one of its pillars, necessitating that political democratization be the first step in a long struggle to uproot the autocratic values embedded in Brazilian daily life. Once democratic practices reached the sphere of the means of production, the utopian conciliation of democracy and socialism, liberty and equality, and subject and collectivity would become a viable political practice (Coutinho and Nogueira, 1985; Coutinho, 2006). Paulo Freire's (2005) pedagogical philosophy was another influence on the New Left. The association between adult literacy, popular participation, and empowerment reinforced the option for a grassroots democracy among progressive Brazilian intellectuals, especially during Freire's tenure as the Partido dos Trabalhadores' secretary of education for the city of São Paulo.

Writing in the 1980s, after the return to democracy following nearly twenty years of military rule, Florestan Fernandes, who had lost his academic chair in the late 1960s as a result of political repression, referred to the intellectuals of the dictatorship period as the "lost generation" (1977[1980: 213–252]). At the same time, Sêrgio Miceli's collection of essays (1984) focused on the "cultural elite" of university professors during this period and related their productivity to "state mechanisms of cultural activity" and "markets of capital goods." The state was the provider of resources and the instrument of cultural ideology at a time when cultural production was largely subject to the pressures of state policy and structures of power. The historian José Honório Rodrigues (1984) lamented that twenty years of dictatorship had represented "a history of failures, mistakes, mischievousness, and injustice" and argued that for many intellectuals this "ill-fated" period was accompanied by a loss of cultural identity. The political scientist Maria Helena Moreira Alves (1985: 76) analyzed the state's repressive apparatus under control of the National Security Council and the National Information Service and concluded that the "opening" of the early 1980s represented not a transition to democracy but an attempt to institutionalize the regime through more flexible political mechanisms capable of increasing the support base of the state. Ruben George Oliven (1984) examined the relationship between popular and hegemonic culture, in particular noting the influence of state intervention and the role of mass media, and showed how the ideological apparatus had transformed and assimilated components of popular culture into cultural expressions of the dominant classes. Arguing that intellectuals' allegiances were divided between European and Brazilian culture, he suggested that the modernist movement of 1922 had allowed a reassessment of cultural and artistic movements dependent on foreign influences and permitted a look at Brazilians' cultural roots. In his view Brazilian culture had initially been conceived as emphasizing order and progress and later as "civilization in the tropics," whereas the 1946–1964 period saw the construction of a popular and progressive national project and, after 1954, a penetration of foreign capital that altered the cultural base in a framework of dependency (74–79).

As these scholars were writing about the repressive state and its negative impact on culture, the productivity of intellectuals appeared to be declining. In 1980, Brazil allocated the lowest percentage of its national budget to education of all the countries in Latin America. There were thirty-five million illiterates and eight million children of school age not attending school, and only twenty-eight of every one hundred students finished their first year. Nearly four of every five who entered the universities had been trained in private schools. Marilena Chauí (*Folha de São Paulo*, October 15, 1984) attributed these problems to a state educational apparatus that was "centralized, bureaucratic, vertical, authoritarian, and discredited," based as it was on three ideas that prevailed after 1964: national security, implying "ideological selection and censorship"; "rapid training of semiliterates for the expanding market of work and for a type of consumption requiring a minimum of schooling"; and "the geopolitics of an emerging potential by the year 2000." This dilemma reflected the previous decade of repression and the financial crisis in the universities. In 1984, the professors, employees, and students of the federal universities went on strike for higher salaries and improved working conditions, arguing that government concessions to the International Monetary Fund had brought about "absurd budget cuts with an extremely negative impact on the university" (José Carmine Dianese, in *Folha de São Paulo*, August 28, 1984). Carlos Guilherme Mota characterized the university as "superbureaucratized" (*Folha de São Paulo*, August 29, 1984). Fernando Henrique Cardoso argued for more effective representation, with professors, employees, and students participating in budget decisions on teaching and research (*Folha de São Paulo*, September 20, 1984). Clearly, there was a need for university reform, decentralization, an increase in resources, and greater autonomy.

The philosopher José Arthur Giannotti (1984: 39) attributed the low level of intellectual life at that time to subservience to imported ways of thinking, such as the Anglo-American functionalism that influenced academics in the School of Philosophy at the USP, monolithic Marxism-Leninism based on the Soviet model, and, finally, Gramsci's rejection of Marxist-Leninist orthodoxy in favor of a pluralist perspective, which tended to disperse intellectuals on the left who were not prepared to criticize the Brazilian reality. Fernandes (1977[1980]: 137]) suggested that intellectuals should struggle against the influence of the national bourgeoisie and the authoritarian state, joining in the debate over relations between the civil society and the state, explaining developments in the periphery of the world system, and contending with issues of the distribution of income, social inequality, and participation in power.

Under the direction of Marilena Chauí, a series entitled "The National and the Popular in Brazilian Culture" and built around her introductory overview (Chauí, 1983) and her earlier work on ideology (1980a, 1980b, 1982; see also Chauí and Carvalho, 1978) presented critical studies of the mass media. Critical assessments of the cultural impact of television (Galvão and Bernardet, 1983), fine arts (Zilio and Lafetá, 1983), literature (Lafetá and Leite, 1983), music (Squeff and Wisnik, 1982), and the theater (Arrabal and Lima, 1983) followed.

In the aftermath of the 1964 coup, censorship and repression gradually undermined the tradition of literary and political journals such as *Anhembi*, *Revista Brasiliense*, and *Sociologia* that flourished in the 1950s and early 1960s and the later *Paz e Terra*, *Política Externa Independente* and *Revista Civilização Brasiliera*. *Teoria e Prática* was one of the last attempts by São Paulo radicals to set forth new ideas. Police intervention prevented publication of its fourth issue, and thereafter many of its contributors clandestinely joined the urban struggle or fled into exile. Radical social science writing on societal issues was represented by the CEBRAP journals, *Revista CEBRAP* from 1969 and *Novos Estudos CEBRAP* from 1981. More mainstream views appeared in the

Rio journal *Dados*, published by the Rio de Janeiro University Institute of Research (Instituto Universitário de Pesquisas de Rio de Janeiro [IUPERJ]), founded by Cândido Mendes de Almeida but edited by young Brazilian scholars who had just returned from doctoral study in the United States.

By 1972, the armed struggle had been crushed by the dictatorship, and there were stirrings of an intellectual opposition dedicated to opening a dialogue on cultural and political repression. Weekly opinion magazines such as *Movimento* (the same name as the national student publication during the 1960s), *Argumento*, and *Opinião* flourished with the growing dissatisfaction with the military dictatorship during the early 1970s. With the granting of amnesty, the opening in the direction of electoral democracy, and the awakening of the labor movement and a series of strikes after 1979, there were weeklies and journals reflecting particular political movements, including the Trotskyist *Em Tempo* and *Convergência Social* and the communist *Voz da Unidade*.

The work of several São Paulo scholars illustrates this reassessment. Maria Celia Paoli, a sociologist, focused on the debate in social science over the historical role of urban workers and suggested that all previous premises and theories could now be challenged. In a provocative paper (Paoli, Sader, and da Silva Telles, 1983) she argued that scholarship during the 1950s and 1960s emphasized a particular view and overlooked other perspectives. She pointed to research showing that, contrary to prevailing assumptions, the Brazilian working class had never been backward or irrational, that a strong bourgeoisie existed, and that the peasantry was not the remnant but the product of capitalism. Brazilian society was heterogeneous and did not necessarily conform to the dominant paradigm that characterized past research and writing. Citing Marilena Chauí, she argued that the *fala silenciada* or "unspoken word" in Brazilian intellectual circles was the perspective of the workers themselves. Rather than viewing them as dominated subjects, she demonstrated their self-awareness and struggle as a class. She concluded that at the end of the Vargas period the labor movement was forced to define itself within the bureaucratic structures of the state but that, although labor legislation constrained the activities of some unions, it stimulated others to organize and take action. Paoli, Eder Sader, and Vera da Silva Telles (1983) elaborated on this critique by focusing on past scholarship and the break in intellectual production provoked by the strikes in 1978 and thereafter. Whereas workers had traditionally been viewed as subordinated to the state and incapable of confronting authority, the intellectuals of the 1980s had begun to concentrate on a historical revision.

The 1964 coup brought an end to optimism about a developmental solution within the national democratic project and destroyed illusions about the possibility of a democratic transformation. An important essay by Francisco de Oliveira (1972) exposed the weaknesses of ideas such as marginalization in explaining the poverty, unemployment, and other problems of the urban population and shifted attention to the exploitation of the workforce itself. At the same time, the political silence about the working class was broken by academics such as political scientist Francisco Weffort (1972, 1975), who attempted to revise old thinking about the impotence of the labor movement. Calling attention to a new worker militancy, he showed that workers were active and willing to strike in spite of the constraints imposed by unions and political parties. His thinking was linked with direct political action in the labor movement and through the Workers' Party (Partido dos Trabalhadores [PT]), for which in the mid-1980s he served as secretary general.

During the late 1970s and early 1980s, the political opposition was growing in the face of the dominant national security state imposed by the military. The opposition Brazilian Democratic Movement (Movimento Democrático Brasileiro [MDB]) actually won some elections, and the military under General Figueiredo began to plan for a gradual return to representative democracy. The MDB became the Party of the Brazilian Democratic Movement (Partido do Movimento Democrático Brasileiro [PMDB]), and eventually four major parties in addition to the government party, the National Renovation Alliance (Aliança Renovadora Nacional [ARENA]), were allowed to participate, including the PT, the Brazilian Workers' Party (Partido Trabalhista Brasileiro [PTB]), and the Democratic Labor Party (Partido Democrático Trabalhista [PDT]). In 1979, most ARENA members formed the Social Democratic Party (Partido Democrático Social [PDS]) and then split, with the Liberal Front Party (Partido da Frente Liberal [PFL]) becoming a major party. Fernando Henrique Cardoso became a federal senator under the PMDB in 1982. His mentor, Florestan Fernandes, lamented that his former students and colleagues were abandoning the university for political careers (he himself eventually became a federal deputy from São Paulo). The presidential election in 1984 permitted the candidacy of civilians, with the military presumably controlling the outcome through an electoral college designed to ensure victory for its candidate. The winner was the PMDB candidate, but he died before taking the oath of office and was succeeded by the vice president (José Sarney), the candidate of the PFL. Eventually, a constituent assembly promulgated a new constitution in 1988, and

Fernando Collor became the first freely elected president since the 1964 coup. Collor was impeached for corruption and succeeded by Itamar Franco, who brought then-Senator Cardoso into his government as foreign minister and eventually planning minister. Cardoso astutely implemented a stabilization program and in 1994 was elected president under a new party, the Brazilian Social Democratic Party (Partido da Social Democracia Brasileiro [PSDB]), serving two terms until 2002 and attracting to his government intellectuals such as Bresser-Pereira, José Álvaro Moisés, and Francisco Weffort. His successor, Luiz Inácio da Silva or Lula, won and held the presidency for two terms under the PT. A lathe operator from São Paulo but originally from the Northeast, Lula was knowledgeable and astute, and although his party was influential in labor, both in the cities and countryside, it also included leadership from among prominent intellectuals, including political scientist Marco Aurélio Garcia who also served under the ensuing presidency of Dilma Rousseff.

The political opening was accompanied by a surge of activity among new social movements and a realignment of forces within labor that permitted a break from their dependence on the state. The splintering of the PCB accompanied the emergence of the political parties, with some leftist groupings becoming assimilated into the PMDB, dissident communist and Trotskyist currents joining the PT, and socialists and social democrats constituting the leadership of the PSDB. Intellectuals participated in these movements and parties but also launched new and generally short-lived publications in pursuit of theory. The thought of Gramsci was particularly of interest, especially in the writings of Carlos Nelson Coutinho (1979, 1981), and Fernandes revealed that he had been a Trotskyist. In general, in the shift from authoritarianism into a plethora of political parties and social movements by the end of the twentieth century, this was not a period of great theoretical advance, and indeed, many intellectuals began to retreat from Marxist thought and focus on more empirical and descriptive studies, at the same time becoming less activist in politics.

FROM OLIGARCHY TO REPUBLICANISM AND PARTISAN
IDEOLOGIES: HISTORICAL SYNTHESES AND OVERVIEWS

Our overview alludes to various schools of thought and patterns of intellectual thinking. Table 1.1 reveals major periods of Brazilian twentieth-century history and provides a synthesis of how intellectuals have related

TABLE 1.1 *Major Historical Periods and Perspectives*

Historical Periods	Perspectives
1890s–1930 Abolition of slavery and formulation of national perspective (Cunha, Torres)	Formation of an agro-mercantile bourgeoisie Aspirations for a national or democratic bourgeoisie
1930–1945 Education and reform after 1930 (Oliveira Vianna, Freyre, Prado Júnior, Azevedo)	Bourgeois educational advance Modernizing authoritarianism Functional capitalism Building a national bourgeoisie
1945–1964 Import substitution, infrastructure, and autonomous capitalist development (Furtado, Tavares)	Structuring autonomous national development
Democratic-bourgeois revolution of PCB (Sodré, Guimarães)	Empowering a national bourgeoisie to carry out the revolution against imperialism
Neo-Bismarkism of the ISEB (Jaguaribe, Guerrero Ramos, Mendes de Almeida, Corbisier)	Role of the state in national development under capitalist hegemony
Political sociology of the São Paulo School (Fernandes, Cardoso, Ianni, Rodrigues)	Associated dependent capitalism to confront foreign exploitation
National security and capitalist development of ESG (Golbery Couto e Silva)	National destiny and modernizing authoritarianism
Dependency, capitalist underdevelopment, and associated dependent development (Caio Prado Júnior, Dos Santos, Marini, Cardoso)	Imperialist superexploitation and the new dependency

ESG, Escola Superior da Guerra (Superior War College); ISEB, Instituto Superior de Estudos Brasileiros (Higher Institute of Brazilian Studies); PCB, Partido Comunista Brasileiro (Brazilian Communist Party).
Synthesized from Bresser-Pereira (1984b), Fernandes (1977[1980]), Ianni (1984), Mantega (1984), and Mota (1980).

to these schools of thought and tendencies. The ensuing discussion draws on the analysis of Dante Moreira Leite, Carlos Guilherme Mota, Sêrgio Micelli, Octávio Ianni, Florestan Fernandes, Luiz Carlos Bresser-Pereira, and Guido Mantega.

The dilemmas of Brazilian intellectuals were explored in Dante Moreira Leite's 1954 grand review of Brazilian social thought. The national character ideology had lost its appeal when university intellectuals, driven by the optimism of an industrialized Brazil, began to question its consistency. In literature, sociology, philosophy, and psychology, the inferiority complex that had dominated Brazilian culture since colonialism was abandoned. Criticism of Eurocentrism led the academy to discover Afro-Brazilian, Indian, and folk (caipira, *sertanejo*, and others) as authentic expressions of national culture. Intellectuals turned to a concrete analysis of society, objectively examining industrial capitalism and such phenomena as social mobility and class struggle. Still optimistic, Leite believed that the discovery of Brazil by its intellectuals would eventually extend their critique from a focus on national character to attention to socioeconomic inequalities under industrial capitalism.

Leite (1969[1954]) worked out this position through critical sketches that identified the positive and negative qualities of the major intellectuals who had shaped the Brazilian outlook: Sílvio Romero (1851–1914), who believed that Brazilians could overcome their sense of inferiority and appearance as apathetic, without initiative, and unenthusiastic, along with their tendency to mimic the foreigner in intellectual life (194); Affonso Celso, who despite acknowledging indecisiveness, assumed an optimistic view of the Brazilian as hospitable, orderly, peaceful, patient, charitable, accessible, tolerant, and honorable (200); Euclydes da Cunha, who described the *vaqueiro* or cowboy as brave, fixated on the land, adventurous, and tied to tradition, the Paulista as rebellious and free, and the Indian as inept at work, rebellious, and impulsive (214); Nina Rodrigues, who held that Brazil was inferior because of its black population and its mixed race (220); Francisco José de Oliveira Vianna, whose work, replete with racial distinctions and biases, was appreciated by rural elites in Brazil and whose reformist ideas of the 1920s were associated with the developmentalism of the 1950s (219–220); Alfredo Ellis Júnior, who focused on Paulista nationalism (235) and considered Paulistas different from other Brazilians in their ability to synthesize all elements of the immigrant population (238); Arthur, who like his precursors tended to describe Brazilian culture as primitive and inferior, resulting in an imperfect mix of backward cultures (243); Azevedo Amaral, who believed that the African and Indian cultures negatively reflected on white culture (243–244); Afonso Arinos de Melo Franco, who viewed Indians and Africans as ostentatious and disrespectful of the legal order (249); Manoel Bombim, who transcended the racial predispositions of his predecessors but adhered to notions of a Brazilian psychological character (255) as parasitic, aggressive, resistant, and conservative; Alberto Torres, an abolitionist and republican who believed in the messianic mission of elites in Brazil (257) and could not comprehend an elite that would not permit a change in the nation (257–258); Paulo Prado, who assimilated in his work such national characteristics as sadness, eroticism, romanticism, disorderly individualism, apathy, and imitation (267); Gilberto Freyre, who emphasized a belief in the supernatural, eroticism, and individualism (285); Sêrgio Buarque de Holanda, who saw Brazil as unique in transplanting European culture to a tropical country (287); and Fernando de Azevedo, who emphasized mysticism, sensibility, imagination, resignation, docility, submissiveness, individualism, generosity, and tolerance (303).

In his synthesis of Brazilian social thought, Carlos Guilherme Mota (1980[1974]), writing at the height of political repression, picked up where Leite had left off. Extremely pessimistic, he saw intellectuals as the key to bourgeois hegemony. Using a Gramscian analysis, he depicted the bourgeois counterrevolution as violence engulfed by hegemony. He believed that intellectuals legitimized authoritarianism when they restricted their critique to the domination of the countryside and promoted the illusion that citizenship rights could be attained only under industrial capitalism. However, when their social research touched on inequalities and the universities became involved with popular movements, the bourgeoisie and its allies revealed their true autocratic nature. To legitimize open coercion they had to produce a new definition of Brazilian culture, but their new ideology was but the past renewed. The pragmatic Brazilian who had dominated social science and literature was abandoned in favor of a new version of the national character. Brazilian culture was redefined as emotional, erratic, undisciplined, and thus incompatible with bourgeois democracy and capitalist rationality; only discipline imposed by an authoritarian state could bring about development and progress. When the armed forces silenced the democratic forces, mass communications regimented by large economic groups pacified critical consciousness.

Mota (1980) provided a comprehensive synthesis of the roots of Brazilian thought in terms of several fundamental periods. The first of these was the "rediscovery" of Brazil, from 1933 to 1937, represented by Caio Prado Júnior (1933), whose materialist analysis gave attention to historical popular revolts. In contrast to Oliveira Vianna, who had considered racial miscegenation a problem, Gilberto Freyre (1964[1933]) now exalted it. Sêrgio Buarque de Holanda (1956[1935]) offered a critique of authoritarianism and hierarchy, ever-present themes in explanations of Brazil. The São Paulo businessman Robert Simonsen (1937) offered an economic-historiographical survey, Fernando de Azevedo (1943) wrote on culture, and Nelson Werneck Sodré (1944) on the empire.

The thought of a second period, from 1948 to 1951, reflected the early contributions of the university, especially the USP, and the influences of cultural missions to Brazil led by Fernand Braudel, Claude Lévi-Strauss, Roger Bastide, and others. Among the works that appeared in this period were those of Vítor Nunes Leal (1948), who distinguished rural from urban life and emphasized the politics of the rural *coroneis* or political chieftains of the interior, and João Cruz Costa (1956[1945] 1964), who examined the history of Brazilian thought.

The period from 1957 to 1964 was represented by the school of Florestan Fernandes, especially the classic work on capitalism and slavery of Fernando Henrique Cardoso (1962a); the emphasis on planning in the work of Celso Furtado (1965, 1967b); Holanda's (1956[1935]) focus on culture; the nationalism and dualist theories of national reality in the publications of the ISEB; the orthodox Marxism of Nelson Werneck Sodré, Wanderley Guilherme dos Santos (1963c), and Inácio Rangel (1975); the nationalist modernization and historiography of the revisionist José Honório Rodrigues (1963, 1965); and the study of the power structure of Raymundo Faoro (1975[1957]). This was the period influenced by Fernandes that produced a new generation of scholars including Ianni (1971), Cardoso (1971), Schwarz (1967), and Giannotti (1983). Schwarz, for example, defended his doctoral thesis on the relationship between literature and society and offered a truly new historical perspective on literature and its decisive moments.

From the 1964 coup until about 1969, many important works were influenced by that earlier period, including those of Prado Júnior (1966), Ianni (1968), Fernandes (1965a, 1968, 1969), and Leite (1954, 1969 [1954]). Ianni examined the end of Getulismo and populism, and Fernandes related the dependency of Brazil to a class analysis. Leite looked at the character of the Brazilian and the ideological lines in the interpretations of Freyre, Holanda, Azevedo, Vianna, Cruz Costa, and Prado Júnior. This period represented a shift in emphasis to the systematic study of dependency on the economic, cultural, and intellectual levels.

Finally, the period of 1969 to 1974 saw dependency theory at an impasse. The role of the traditional schools of philosophy was questioned as the university was restructured on the U.S. model and an independent CEBRAP was founded with an interdisciplinary focus.

Countering Mota's pessimistic evaluation of intellectual life, Sêrgio Miceli (1979) initiated a series of diametrically opposite syntheses coinciding with the democratic struggle, the growing prestige of the CEBRAP, and the public presence of intellectuals in mass communications. It began in 1978 with his doctoral dissertation and included the publications of Maria Arminda Arruda do Nascimento on Paulista culture, Simon Schwartzman on the scientific community, and others on intellectuals' thematic and regional diversity. The composition of Miceli's doctoral committee was a reaffirmation of the São Paulo intellectual field, articulating universal social theory with concrete analysis of Brazilian realities. Alongside the French sociologists Pierre Bourdieu, Pierre Ansart, and Louis Marin sat Antônio Cândido de Mello Souza, Leôncio Martins Rodrigues, Gabriel Cohn, Luiz Carlos Bresser-Pereira, and Maria do Carmo Campelo de Souza. In the audience were two USP icons: Fernando Henrique Cardoso and Boris Fausto. Miceli argued that the period between 1920 and 1945 was essential to understanding the transition of Brazilian intellectuals from dependence on the oligarchies to autonomy and diversity compatible with international standards. Before the university system and the adoption of modern social science, the oligarchic origins of intellectuals, the primitive cultural labor market, the monopoly of education by the traditional law and medical faculties, and the predominance of romance and literature publishers impeded a lively intellectual life. Division within the dominant classes in the 1920s, however, offered an opportunity to consolidate the intellectual field. The emphasis on literature during Modern Arts Week was supplemented by stress on architecture and the fine arts. All this expanded after the political polarization of the urban and rural factions of the São Paulo elite. However, as the legacies of Mário de Andrade and Oswald de Andrade had shown, intellectuals were still imprisoned by this attention to literature. By 1932, the politically disarmed São Paulo elites returned to academic life as a last resort to preserve their power resources. Universities were established, autonomy was achieved, and new intellectual groups emerged. Diversification advanced when intellectuals were polarized between adherents and antagonists of the Estado Novo. When democracy was reimposed in 1945, Brazilian intellectuals had firmly established themselves as an autonomous and highly diversified group. Miceli's analysis followed Cardoso's pluralist lead; when elites fragmented into competing interest groups, those excluded tended to advance and consolidate autonomous arenas. After inclusion came autonomy, defended by professionals versed in social theories and involved in concrete research.

Two collections organized by Miceli (1989, 1999) reveal the extent of the disciplinary, methodological, thematic, and regional diversity of Brazilian intellectual production. The second of these volumes is devoted to refuting the work of the French researcher Daniel Pécaut (1990). Miceli (1989) had shown that intellectuals gained autonomy from the oligarchies when they were shielded by the university system. Pécaut agreed that intellectuals had gained significant autonomy since the 1930s but held that their worth was determined more by their embeddedness in political institutions than by their academic credentials. This tendency had, he suggested, been exacerbated by industrial capitalism. By commanding social theories, coherent language, planning, and managerial skills, they had formed a corporatist group that occupied leadership positions in the state. For Pécaut, after industrialization in the 1950s, Brazilian intellectuals projected themselves as a new ruling elite. Miceli's rebuttal of Pécaut was complemented by Arruda's (2001) studies of the cultural institutions of São Paulo, designated as "the cultural complex," in the 1950s. By examining the new poetic, visual arts, drama, and sociological vocabulary introduced by intellectuals in São Paulo, she showed how new cultural traditions had taken root in metropolitan São Paulo. Historical personalities such as Fernandes and the dramatist Jorge Almeida had nationalized global trends and led struggles to establish a new "culture of participation" that secured intellectual freedom of speech. Although the military coup suppressed culture, the universities, insisting on professionalism, sustained the new intellectual position. For Arruda, the quality of knowledge could not be separated from its institutional setting, theories, debates, methodologies, and standards.

In an overview of the intellectual currents of the postdictatorship period, Octávio Ianni (1984) identified three models. In the model of the democratic bourgeois revolution advocated by the PCB, political and economic development was based on the growth of national capitalism, and the nation was considered dependent but with the potential to become autonomous and self-sustaining, with centers of national decision making. This development would come about through the alliance of the urban and rural classes under the vanguard of a national bourgeoisie in the struggle against *latifundismo* and imperialism. A popular democratic regime would bring about the bourgeois democratic revolution through an alliance of the proletariat with the bourgeoisie and the support of the peasants and other subservient classes. The Neo-Bismarckian model, advocated by the ISEB and first elaborated by Helio Jaguaribe (1968), viewed Brazil as largely archaic and in need of modernization through the efforts of industrialists and intellectuals in conjunction with the state in promoting capitalist economic development. According to this conception, the elites, principally industrialists, would advance their ideas, intellectuals and technocrats would put them into practice, and capitalist economic development would be carried out under the authoritarian state. Finally, the security and development model, represented by the Superior War College (Escola Superior da Guerra [ESG]), was implemented as the doctrine of national security with emphasis on "associated capitalist development" after the coup of 1964.

Florestan Fernandes (1977) reflected on the political thought of his time in an overview of Brazilian sociology. He noted that one of the intellectual products of the breakdown of slave society was the work of Euclydes da Cunha, whose *Os Sertões* was "the first sociographic description and historical-geographical interpretation of the physical setting, human types, and conditions in Brazil" (35). Later, Alberto Torres (1933) assumed the pioneering role in the pragmatic formation of sociological thought in Brazil. After 1930, there was an effort to institutionalize teaching and develop new bases for sociology. Historical-sociological analysis adopted the positivist approach characteristic of the contributions of F. J. Oliveira Vianna (1933, 1949), Gilberto Freyre (1964[1933]), Caio Prado Júnior (1933, 1942), Fernando Azevedo (1943), Sérgio Buarque de Holanda (1956[1935]), and Nelson Werneck Sodré (1944). Sociological investigation was stimulated through such institutions as the USP's School of Sociology and Politics, established in 1933, and the School of Philosophy, Science, and Letters, established in 1934. Fernandes identified the influence on his own thinking of foreigners such as Herbert Baldus, Donald Pierson, and Roger Bastide and national thinkers such as Fernando de Azevedo and Alberto Guerreiro Ramos. Among the contributions of his followers, initially at USP and after 1964 in CESIT, he listed that of Maria Isaura Pereira de Queiroz on local power and messianism (1965), Fernando Henrique Cardoso on capitalism and slavery (1962a) and industrialists (1964), Octávio Ianni on the failure of populism (1968), Marialice Mencarini Foracchi on ideology, Luiz Pereira on the labor movement (1965), Leôncio Martins Rodrigues Netto on industrial conflict and labor (1966), José de Souza Martins on the precapitalist social formation (1978), and Gabriel Cohn on petroleum and nationalism (1968).

In his syntheses of the major directions of Brazilian thought since about 1930, Luiz Carlos Bresser-Pereira (1982b, 1984b) identified six interpretations of the Brazilian reality and offered his own formulation: (1) the agro-mercantilist bourgeois perspectives of Oliveira Vianna (1958), Paulo Duarte (1950), Euclydes da Cunha (1944), Alberto Torres (1933), and Sílvio Romero; (2) the national-bourgeois view of the 1950s and early 1960s, represented by the PCB and the ISEB and writers such as Helio Jaguaribe (1957a, 1957b, 1958a, 1958b), Inácio Rangel (1957, 1960), Alberto Guerreiro Ramos (1957d, 1958c), and Celso Furtado (1959a, 1959b), of a more nationalist bent, and Nelson Werneck Sodré (1944, 1958, 1959, 1961a) and Alberto Passos Guimarães (1963, 1964), who combined their nationalism with a Marxist framework; (3) the modernizing authoritarian line represented by the ESG, which emerged to contend with the influence of the PCB and the ISEB and to prevail in the period after 1964 through the thought of Golbery do Couto e Silva (1955, 1957, 1967), Roberto Campos (1964a), and Eugênio Gudin; (4) the functional capitalist orientation of Caio Prado Júnior (1966), João Manuel Cardoso de Mello (1982), Fernando Novais (1983b), Boris Fausto (1983), Francisco Oliveira (1977a, 1977b), and Leôncio Martins Rodrigues Netto (1970); (5) the new dependency school of Fernando Henrique Cardoso (with Faletto, 1969, 1970, 1979), Celso Furtado (1961, 1964), Paul Singer (1968, 1981), and others; (6) the idea of the hegemony of industrial capital, as set forth by Eli Diniz (1978); and (7) Bresser-Pereira's own interpretation, which emphasized the role of an emerging techno-bureaucracy.

In contrast, Guido Mantega (1982, 1984) examined five models: (1) developmental nationalism, (2) import substitution, (3) bourgeois democracy, (4) Marxist socialism, and (5) capitalist underdevelopment. His central argument departed from the controversy over the direction of economic development: on the one hand, the defense of economic liberalism and a preoccupation with growth in the agricultural sector and, on the other, the developmentalist current that preached the intervention of the state in the economy as the means to bring about industrialization. Mantega saw the Brazilian intelligentsia as tending to polarize around these two positions during the 1940s and 1950s. In contrast to this debate was the developmentalist ideology advocated by most of the Brazilian left during the 1950s. This movement included the PCB, which insisted on the necessity of industrialization as the path to development, and the ISEB. Furtado of the ISEB emphasized import substitution and the need for a transition from the coffee economy to industrial accumulation, whereas Rangel was concerned about the oligopolistic character of the Brazilian economy both in commercial agriculture and in industrialization. The two men proposed similar strategies of development and adopted certain neoclasical and Keynesian propositions.

As Mantega described the situation, the PCB, drawing on Lenin's analysis of czarist Russia and his proposal of a bourgeois democratic revolution and applying the theses of the Third International to the backward colonies, emphasized the semifeudal character of Brazilian agriculture and the export of primary products as impeding the development of the industrial productive forces (see Chilcote, 1974, for an overview). These theses were elaborated in the Fifth and Sixth Congresses of the PCB and in the writings of Nelson Werneck Sodré (1958) and Alberto Passos Guimarães (1964) toward the end of the 1950s. Their position was not radically different from the import-substitution model, since both incorporated a strategy of industrialization through the national bourgeoisie and the state, but adherents of the import-substitution model tended to follow the policies advocated by the Economic Commission for Latin America (ECLA). In the middle of the 1960s, both currents were under attack by thinkers advocating new ideas. The ISEB suffered from internal dissension, and the PCB began to splinter into several factions, with the formation of the Communist Party of Brazil (Partido Comunista do Brasil [PC do B]) and its advocacy of armed struggle and rejection of the PCB's main line of conciliation with the bourgeoisie and a peaceful road to capitalist development. The principal attack was presented by historian Caio Prado Júnior (1966), who attempted to show that Brazilian agriculture was essentially capitalist and indeed had never been feudal. He ridiculed the party for its reformism and discussed capitalist underdevelopment as a form developed through imperialist exploitation of the country, a pattern that he believed was typical of capitalist expansion throughout the developing world. At about this time, André Gunder Frank (1966, 1967) began to publish his thesis of capitalist development of underdevelopment, including some articles (1963, 1964) in *Revista Brasiliense* (published by Prado Júnior) in which he elaborated on the theses of Paul Baran. Ruy Mauro Marini (1969, 1973b, 1978b) offered a variant of this view with the elaboration of the theory of superexploitation of peripheral workers. According to his concept of subimperialism, the development of the Brazilian forces of production was tied to surplus extraction from neighboring countries. Mantega pointed to the similarity of the ideas of Theotônio dos Santos and the theory of dependency to Trotsky's views, reproduced in the theses of the Fourth International, and cited the contributions of Singer, Oliveira (1977a), and Cardoso (1971). In his opinion, all these various positions except dependency indicated the need for structural change. Furtado and Rangel indicted the monopolistic character of Brazilian industrial structure, the PCB and Sodré blamed the semifeudal agrarian structure, whereas Prado Júnior attributed underdevelopment to the difficulties of a country in conditions of semicolonialism and imperialist exploitation, and Frank and Marini focused on capitalist domination. Although some writers advocated change through reforms, others looked to the socialist revolution.

The ambitious overviews of Bresser, Fernandes, Mantega, Mota, and others help sort out the trends in Brazilian political thought (see Table 1.1) since the opening to electoral democracy in 1945. By 1974, the economic "miracle" had collapsed in the face of the international petroleum crisis, rising prices on imports of foreign oil, and the subsequent recession in Brazil. At the same time, the military regime had crushed the diverse urban movements of armed struggle that had challenged its hegemony from about 1969 to 1972. Thereafter, Brazil had evolved toward another opening in which the opposition emerged victorious in the congressional elections of 1982 and the indirect elections for president in 1985. The gradual relaxation of controls over the society involved an amnesty for political dissidents and exiles and the participation of many intellectuals in political parties and the electoral process. This process was spurred by strikes beginning in 1978 and the emergence of popular social movements throughout the country. These developments were accompanied by some reassessment of the perspective and role of intellectuals in interpreting change in Brazilian history.

This chapter has examined intellectual activity through historical periods during the twentieth century, beginning with the struggle to transcend a colonial mentality and resist foreign influence and throughout emphasizing the search for a national identity and culture. It shows the formation of major university and research organizations and the proliferation of national journals, accompanied by different tendencies, debates, and contrasting impacts on Brazilian society. It also relates intellectuals and their ideological and theoretical preferences to major political parties and emerging social movements. It summarizes other overviews that synthesize intellectual thinking over time and how it relates to major patterns of thought. It identifies the role and the significance of major intellectuals, both in public political life and in private endeavors, who were influential and contributed to various lines of thinking and traditions that led Rio intellectuals generally to envisage the nation as evolving through the apparatuses of the state and the São Paulo intellectuals to shape an image of the nation based on a national capitalism or socialism uniquely Brazilian in character. This leads us to the ISEB movement in Rio and the *Capital* Group in São Paulo whose origins, evolution, and importance are elaborated in Chapters 2 and 3.

2

Developmental Nationalism and the Rio Movement

Nationalism has been a prevailing sentiment in Brazil since independence in 1822 and throughout the imperial period of the nineteenth century; however, during the Old Republic, a colonial mentality persisted, especially among intellectuals. Two nationalist movements evolved from the rapid changes emanating from the break with colonialism and empire. On the left, the Jacobins of the 1890s coalesced middle- and working-class segments opposed to the dominant *latifundistas* in pursuit of a more open national government and society. On the right, the Nationalist Social Action (Ação Social Nacionalista [ASN]) advocated a return to agrarian society while opposing materialism and individualism; they ultimately sided with the dominant class, "the same upper class that the Jacobins had opposed in order to suppress a possible socialist revolution," with the result that "nationalism was converted from a progressive force to a defensive regressive one" (Topik, 1978: 101).

The dilemma of transcending a colonial mentality was still evident when Getúlio Vargas was ushered into power in 1930, bringing an end to the regional oligarchical rule of the Old Republic (1891–1930). With the central government in Rio, he sought to integrate and consolidate the disparate geographical regions of Brazil into a nation. Throughout the state, he also focused on national concerns over energy, petroleum, and other natural resources. At issue was whether capitalism would evolve autonomously through domestic investment, depend on foreign investment, or both. The end of the Vargas regime in 1945 and the opening of politics to an array of political parties and interests accompanied an awakening as Brazilians began to reach a deeper national consciousness. Intellectuals, both conservative and progressive, searched for ways to overcome the sense of inferiority and alienation shared by most Brazilians. One concern was rethinking Brazilian dependency on the outside world and another was overcoming backwardness and pursuing autonomous development.

Darcy Ribeiro (1980: 154–166) exposed the essential problem by addressing the question of a national consciousness and the prospects for intellectuals' breaking through with new understandings. Up until the middle of the twentieth century, he argued, with the exception of the work of Sílvio Romero and Euclydes da Cunha, political thought was devoted to alien influences. A reformulation of social consciousness at that time had critically exposed Brazilian culture as a remnant of colonial times and opened it up to new ideas. Working such themes as creativity, alienation, consciousness, and revolution into a class analysis, he contrasted colonial Brazil with contemporary Brazil; whereas formerly the dominant classes had ruled over a population divided into free workers and slaves, in contemporary Brazil they ruled over peasants and workers, with marginal peoples below them (88). Against the background of an examination of different national university systems, he proposed the National Project of Brazilian Intellectuality (1968) that led to the establishment of the University of Brasília, with himself as first chancellor.

This preoccupation with a national consciousness was associated with populism, as elaborated in a revealing synthesis by Francisco Weffort (1978) and an analysis of the role of the university in building a populist movement by Luiz Antônio Cunha (1983). Populism also manifested itself through the state, with broad segments of the bourgeoisie supporting it during this period and up until the 1964 coup (Andrade, 1979: 41–86). The national bourgeoisie, however, was a weak link to the statist economy because national firms during the 1960s faced challenges, even under conditions of import substitution (Boshi, 1979: 103–111).

With the suicide of Vargas in 1954, Brazil moved toward what Álvaro Vieira Pinto called a *tomada de conciência*, a self-awareness made possible when the bonds of dependency were broken and people could envision the possibility of economic development. Brazilian intellectual movements awakened to the possibility of change and national identity. This early nationalist sentiment appeared in a 1960s survey of politicians, educators, churchmen, social scientists, and military, who expressed their desire for planned action in the direction of "a highly productive economy of self-sustained growth controlled by Brazilians, higher standards of living for all, an independent foreign policy, and an end to the alienation and discontent born of prolonged inferior status" (Bonilla, 1963: 234–235).

The Superior Institute of Brazilian Studies (Instituto Superior de Estudos Brasileiros [ISEB]) was established as an independent institute for study and research at the graduate level in Rio de Janeiro in 1955. Its purposes were to seek findings in the social sciences for the development of a general theory of national development and to formulate a national ideology of development through the study of Brazilian economic, social, and political life. It arose from the discussions of Brazil's problems among the young intellectuals of the Itatiaia Group (named for the national park located between São Paulo and Rio de Janeiro where they met on weekends for study and discussion), which had earlier led to the establishment of the Brazilian Institute of Economy, Sociology, and Politics (Instituto Brasileiro de Economia, Sociologia e Política [IBESP]) and to the publication of the journal *Cadernos de Nosso Tempo: Revista de Cultura e Informação Política*. Helio Jaguaribe was the IBESP's administrator, and Roland Corbisier, Rômulo de Almeida, Alberto Guerreiro Ramos, and Ewaldo Correia Lima constituted the journal's executive committee. Published in Rio and edited by Lima, the journal had an editorial board that included Cândido Mendes de Almeida and Inácio Rangel.

Five issues of the *Cadernos* appeared from 1953 to 1956. Its mission, as described in the first issue (October–November 1953 [1–2]), involved "interpreting and debating the problems of our times in Brazil" so that the nation could cast off its colonial mentality and prefabricated ideas. The first two issues featured essays by Jaguaribe (1953) on the Brazilian "crisis" and its possible solutions. Arguing that the national ideology, which had once reflected optimism about progress and values related to the individual and equality, had, under liberal democracy and capitalism, declined and become discredited (143), he called for a new national ideology and a system within which it could function (148). The third issue (January–March 1955) focused on the presidential succession, featuring an analysis by Jaguaribe (unsigned but with his initials in the table of contents) and contained analyses (also unsigned but probably by Mendes de Almeida and Ramos) on political events, including the implications of the death of Vargas. In the fourth issue (April–August 1955), Hermes Lima (1955) offered a conceptualization of nationalism as a cultural-political value based on the political-social conditions of the people or the state. For a people subjected to foreign influences, he argued, nationalism required a struggle for liberation. He used oil as an example of what the nation had to fight for and defend, and he called for a struggle against capitalism: "The nationalist position . . . is the only policy compatible with the vision of a Brazil conscious of its historical destiny" (100). Ramos followed with an incisive analysis (1955) of the 1930 revolution as a historical turning point in the building of the nation and went on to attack the utopian thought of Jackson de Figueiredo, Alberto Torres, Alceu Amoroso Lima, and others who sought to move the Brazilian intelligentsia toward an idealistic sense of the nation. Ramos argued that they were spending more time reading prescriptive texts than experiencing objective conditions (107). Instead, they should be interpreting problems in terms of a national psychology, envisioning the salvation of the nation by intellectuals and elites, and reducing political problems to moral problems (108).

In the final issue (January–March 1956), Ramos (1956b) continued his critical appraisal of Brazilian intellectuals who had shaped anthropology and sociology with a broad understanding of Brazil, such as João Ribeiro, Sílvio Romero, Euclydes da Cunha, Alberto Torres, and especially Virginio Santa Rosa and Azevado Amaral. This issue also included a very detailed plan (47–188) for a policy of national development that suggested the Brazilian crisis could be resolved through "struggle and cooperation among classes" (124) to promote development for all in a nation in which all would sacrifice equally. It demanded freedom for labor, a minimum wage, and welfare benefits. It called for the development of "a progressively national structure" (136) and an evolution from semicolonial mercantilism to industrialism. It argued for the liberation of the bourgeoisie from its semicolonial and underdeveloped mentality to one that was oriented to the country's development (136–137). It referred to Brazil's dependence on the United States as a "dependency that presently exists on a grand scale ... a product of satellitism with North America" (169) that could not be completely transcended because "the United States is the great imperialist power of the century" (169) but that economic development of Brazil along the lines outlined would mitigate this.

The ISEB set out to examine questions of national development, formulate a Brazilian ideology of development, and share its findings with the public. It took shape around a core of intellectuals representing various disciplines and an interesting program of graduate study using their writings as texts. It offered both general and specialized courses in sociology, economics, history, philosophy, and economics. The people I talked with felt that it had set a standard for nationalist theorizing that strongly influenced subsequent writing on nationalism both in content and in style. It shaped the outlook of a substantial number of students over the course of its existence: in 1960, for example, thirty-eight students completed a year-long graduate course available to middle-level government functionaries and military officers, and during the summer break of January–February 1961, a hundred students attended twenty-five evening lectures on topics such as colonialism, development, and imperialism. In one of his courses, Cândido Mendes de Almeida (1958) lectured on "the intellectual in the face of historical process." The lecture was concerned with development in the direction of some positive outcome in which the intellectual is autonomous from government and power and serves as the conscience of groups and classes, and not merely as an elite, in the search for a better society. A course by Vieira Pinto (1958b) reviewed philosophers from ancient Greece to the nineteenth century; one dealt with "transcendental consciousness" and the philosophy of Kant, and another turned to Hegel. A commemorative booklet on the ISEB's progress in 1956 included a keynote address in which President Juscelino Kubitschek asserted that "nationalism has its objective in these decisive years to work for development" (Kubitschek et al., 1957: 48) and a list of student theses, many of them devoted to nationalism and development.

Within two months of the ISEB's establishment under President João Café Filho's Ministry of Education in July 1955,[1] the *Revista Brasiliense*, based in São Paulo, launched its first issue. Their political lines may have overlapped, but there were few ties between the organizers of the two groups, regional differences were apparent, and the São Paulo group expressed skepticism about the ISEB and its formal ties to the government, as well as about its allegedly "right" nationalism in contrast to the "left" nationalism of the *Revista Brasiliense*. Divisions within the ISEB were evident in the perception of its "fascist" and "communist" origins, represented in the early ties of Roland Corbisier and Alberto Guerreiro Ramos to integralism under Vargas and to the affiliation of Nelson Werneck Sodré with the Brazilian Communist Party (Partido Comunista Brasileiro [PCB]). Furthermore, two personalities were

---

[1] See the bylaws and official designation of ISEB in *Diário Oficial* 94, no. 161 (July 15, 1955), 13641–13642, Decreto of December no. 37,608 (July 14, 1955), signed by President João Café Filho. Alteration relating to financial matters in *Diário Oficial* 96, no. 110 (May 15, 1957), 12131, Decreto 41, 500 (May 15, 1957), signed by President Juscelino Kubitschek. Restructuring in *Diário Oficial* 98, no. 85 (April 15, 1959), 8457–8458, Decreto no. 45,811 (April 15, 1959), signed by President Juscelino Kubitschek. Abolition in *Diário Oficial* 102, no. 68 (April 10, 1964), 3217–3218, and Decreto 53,884 in *Diário Oficial* 102, no. 70 (April 13, 1964), 3281.

conspicuous for their contrasting orientations to national problems – Helio Jaguaribe in the early years and Álvaro Vieira Pinto in the later years – and their perspectives shaped an ideological and personal struggle over what was appropriate for national development. Early differences appeared in the prefatory notes to a comprehensive analysis of Brazilian problems and in an outline of a policy for national development (most likely set forth by Helio Jaguaribe) that favored capitalist modernization but doubted the prospects for socializing the means of production without mature economic conditions. This skepticism was a sign of ideological differences and eventually led to an open dispute in 1958 with the publication of Jaguaribe's treatise (1958b) on the petroleum question and the state monopoly by Petroleo Brasileiro (Petrobrás), formed in October 1953. The split over Jaguaribe's treatise culminated in the departure of Jaguaribe and his conservative colleagues, including Roberto de Oliveira Campos and Anísio Teixeira. A transitional period under Corbisier was followed by a period of political activism under Vieira Pinto that ended with the 1964 coup.

The fifteen profiles of participants in the ISEB that follow are drawn from semistructured informal interviews[2] conducted several years after the ISEB was dismantled following the military coup. Many of those I talked with had been arrested and imprisoned and lived in fear. All but one of the interviews took place in Rio de Janeiro. All of them had

---

[2] The interviews were all tape-recorded over the course of one and a half to three hours. The interview schedule was divided into two parts. The first dealt with biographical information, including educational level attained, occupation, political participation, extent of travel abroad, and identification of Brazilians and non-Brazilians who had influenced the respondents' thinking about nationalism and development. The second part delved into the respondents' activities prior to the establishment of the ISEB, including intellectual currents under Vargas and the integralist period, the Itatiaia Group, the IBESP, and *Cadernos de Nosso Tempo*; I was interested in their impressions of Vargas, the establishment of the national steel company, Volta Redonda, Petrobrás, and the era of Juscelino Kubitschek and the building of Brasília as the capital during the late 1950s. I asked how they perceived the objectives of the ISEB and its structure and how they understood its influence on the political and economic ruling classes, the military, cultural sectors, and the masses. I inquired about their understanding of nationalism and development, as well as their views on foreign capital, petroleum, heavy industry, national resources, the industrial and agrarian sectors, and imperialism. I questioned how they felt about Brazilian thinkers who had contributed to a Brazilian ideology of nationalism and development, in particular Oliveira Vianna, Alberto Torres, Gilberto Freyre, and José Honório Rodrigues, and about contemporary popular personalities such as João Goulart, Miguel Arraes, Leonel Brizola, and Carlos Lacerda. I asked them to identify the major obstacles to the development of a Brazilian nationalism and how they envisioned the possibility of an ideology of Brazilian nationalism and development.

achieved recognition within intellectual circles. The youngest were Martins and Santos, the oldest Pereira and Sodré, with the others ranging between thirty-five and fifty years of age. All resided in Rio, although Corbisier's roots were in São Paulo, Rangel's in Maranhão, Campos's in Sergipe, and Barbosa's in Minas Gerais. All but Sodré, a respected historian who claimed to be self-taught through his years in the military, had university training. All of them were involved in academic endeavors, most as teachers, several as editors, and three (Rômulo de Almeida, Corbisier, and Ramos) in elected office. Most claimed not to be politically active, except Santos, who acknowledged his student activism. Most had not traveled outside Brazil, but Ramos became a professor at the University of Southern California, and Jaguaribe and Mendes de Almeida lectured at the University of California (Los Angeles and Riverside). Most claimed to have been influenced by colleagues within the ISEB, especially Furtado, Rangel, and Vieira Pinto, whereas three referred to Alberto Torres as an important Brazilian thinker, four to Marx, and one to Max Weber. Two of them had been influenced by integralism under Vargas, whereas four considered themselves Marxists.[3]

Further information on these intellectuals is available in the writings of Caio Navarro de Toledo (1978, 1986, 1995b, 1998), who also organized an anthology (Toledo, 2005) on the movement a half century after its founding. In his brief introduction to the anthology, Toledo notes that the ISEB was, for the most part, made up of nonacademics of various ideological tendencies who met frequently to debate "crucial problems of the Brazilian reality" (7) and to engage with the political and social life of the country. Initially, it was a grand intellectual and political front that included liberals, communists, social democrats, progressive Catholics, and others. Its participants followed various theoretical lines, among them Marxism, existentialism, and other philosophical tendencies,

---

[3] Marie Zentai assisted in synthesizing the content of the interviews. She noted internal struggle among the ISEB intellectuals, different perspectives, incompatibility among their ideas about one theme or another, ideological radicalism, and different preferences as to whether their activity was to promote political direction, steer clear of Marxism, or dissociate themselves from the left. She felt that Jaguaribe's response was articulate, Ramos's verbose, and Corbisier's weak in substance. In general, respondents were unenthusiastic about their progress in understanding the idea of development. They were divided over the 1958 ideological crisis, with some seeing it as relating to an internal power struggle, others as leading to a radicalization of thinking. They saw ignorance among left intellectuals, property relations, and U.S. imperialism as obstacles to building an ideology of developmental nationalism. They believed that a national bourgeoisie must lead the developmental process but that a nationalist project need not be tied to socialism.

and its objective was to formulate an ideology for national development. During its nine years of existence, it moved from a theorizing phase to a militant leftist phase, but throughout, it maintained a continuity in its defense of national sovereignty and democratic politics.

Toledo's invaluable collection assesses how intellectuals conceived and implemented ideas by working with, influencing, and shaping traditional and new institutions. Memoir combines with description and analysis to provide a deep understanding of a failed experiment that struggled with questions of nationalism and development, questions that have permeated the theoretical literature and caught the attention of less-developed countries in Latin America and elsewhere. Brief memoirs by founders Cândido Mendes de Almeida and Helio Jaguaribe identify the origins of the ISEB and describe the evolution of its pursuit of a national developmental path for Brazil. Joel Rufino dos Santos and Jorge Miglioli concentrate on the experience of the last phase of the ISEB, the period of the "new history" and the experimental programs of the Ministry of Education. Here, ISEB people, usually affiliated with government or the private sector, are contrasted with the academics of the University of São Paulo [USP]) in that their ideas emerged from practical experience, whereas those of the academics evolved through theoretical thinking on campus. These contributors argued that the ISEB did not represent a socialist alternative but was concerned principally with nationalist autonomy and development. Alzira Alves Abreu (who wrote a doctoral dissertation on the ISEB [1975] and, provides [2001] additional background) discusses the new technocracy that emerged from the Vargas period: "The ISEB intellectual can be thought of as an intellectual in transition, corresponding to the passing of an agrarian society, in which the intellectual formation was valued as an instrument for maintaining the traditional cultural values and standards, to a modern industrial society with its dominance of technology" (103). She reveals that early ISEB intellectuals, such as Jaguaribe, Mendes de Almeida, Ramos, and Rangel, had published in military journals and that some of them had emerged from the integralist movement of the 1930s. Alexandro Eugênio Pereira looks at the origins of some of the early participants, including Rangel, who was involved in the armed struggle of peasants in Maranhão during the 1930s. Toledo provides a comparative analysis of the ISEB and its adversary, the Institute for Research and Social Studies, which was involved ideologically in the 1964 coup. Gérard Lebrun offers a critical assessment of the work of Álvaro Vieira Pinto, originally published in 1963. Finally, Luiz Carlos

Bresser-Pereira identifies the influences of the Economic Commission for Latin America (ECLA) on the ISEB and compares the two institutions during the late 1950s and early 1960s.

PROFILES OF ISEB INTELLECTUALS

The following profiles are presented in two segments: first, a group of ten prominent intellectuals, many of them founders of the ISEB movement and especially active in the early and transitional period (Cândido Mendes de Almeida, Rômulo de Almeida, Júlio Barbosa, Domar Campos, Roland Corbisier, Alberto Guerreiro Ramos, Helio Jaguaribe, Gilberto Paim, Inácio Rangel, and Nelson Werneck Sodré), and second, a group of five who were active in the late period, all reputable scholars (Michel Debrun, Carlos Estevem Martins, Osny Duarte Pereira, Wanderley Guilherme dos Santos, and Álvaro Vieira Pinto). The interviews paraphrase and directly quote in a manner intended to let the respondent reveal his own experiences and feelings about his ISEB experience, share impressions of colleagues and their behavior, and assess the successes and failings of an unusual collective effort to mobilize a backward nation along a path to development.

Cândido Mendes de Almeida, born in Rio, is the author of works in history and political science. He was active and influential in the early years of the Rio movement, serving as a founding member of both the IBESP and the ISEB. In 1961, he was deeply involved in the Instituto de Estudos Afro-Asiáticos, and he was an advisor to the Quadros government. In 1963, he was a founder of the University Research Institute of Rio de Janeiro (Instituto Universitário de Pesquisas do Rio de Janeiro [IUPERJ]), which became one of Brazil's important research institutions. He identified Brazilian nationalism as developmental nationalism: "Since 1946 we can call it an ideology of developmental nationalism. Along came issues such as petroleum that shaped our nationalism." He also mentioned other issues, such as the construction of power plants that led to a program to supply electricity throughout the country, the opening of Brazilian commerce to the socialist countries of the Soviet Union and Eastern Europe, and agrarian reform that gave land titles to peasants: "Today there is a discrepancy between reality and these desires. The nationalist program is far from implementation."

He felt that Vargas was a great Brazilian nationalist: "In the first Vargas period there were important ideas and plans. In the second period many things were accomplished. The state and its organization must be capable of pursuing these objectives." He went on to characterize Juscelino Kubitschek as "a promoter of nationalism, not necessarily a great nationalist ... more a facilitator than a great nationalist." He believed Jânio Quadros was a surprise. Until his final moments, he was a nationalist: "He was a precursor to the idea of an independent foreign policy. He pushed the modernization of Brazil, all with a minimum of parliamentary support." João Goulart "did not have a very clearly defined program and was inclined to economic development but lacked a plan. He sought a plan through Celso Furtado, but it was not realistic." Leonel Brizola, an intelligent former mayor and governor, envisaged a national plan. In Almeida's view, Miguel Arraes "lived on another planet and did not understand Brazil."

Among Almeida's ISEB colleagues, Rômulo de Almeida was a nationalist in practice more than a theoretician. Ewaldo Correio was very intelligent, moderate, cold, progressive. Ramos was a great promoter. Inácio Rangel was very intelligent. Jaguaribe was important for his contributions. Nelson Werneck Sodré was a great teacher, and Álvaro Vieira Pinto was effective in 1963.[4]

As to nationalist thought, in Almeida's words: "One of the great problems is its complexity and everything that must be constructed. There is no institution capable of implementing nationalism to bring about substantial change." Almeida felt that his extensive reading of classical thought and foreign works, including socialism, was "insufficient to understand the Brazilian economic reality. There is a need to study deeply in order to formulate an ideology of national development for Brazil" (interview, Rio de Janeiro, May 17, 1967).

The ISEB experience appears to have provided a basis for his understanding of nationalism. Like Jaguaribe, he dwelt on the Modern Art Week of 1922 and described it as "a reaction not only against the typical *belle epoque* metropolitan mannerism but also against an attitude that produced the everlasting exile of the national intellectual elites from

---

[4] The ensuing analysis is based on previously unreported interviews and encounters with former participants in the ISEB conducted during 1966 and 1967, three of them in Los Angeles and Riverside and the rest in Rio. I also talked with Álvaro Vieira Pinto, a major figure during the ISEB's radical phase, but I was unable to obtain an extensive interview because he was living in seclusion and in fear of being arrested. With the help of Marie Zentai, during the late 1960s, the data were organized around the themes covered in ten of the fifteen interviews conducted. All of the interviews are available as part of my archive in the Special Collections of the Tomás Rivera Library of the University of California, Riverside.

their own surroundings" (Almeida, 1968: 17). Almeida showed how these moments were transformed into a profound search for national identity, culminating in the Vargas period and accompanied by the integralism of Plínio Salgado. His insights into the rise of nationalism foreshadowed his assessment of the ISEB movement and its intellectual contributions, which he identified as a break with the colonial view and a projection of "the socio-historical totality of development," an element of critical consciousness in sociohistorical reality and nationalism as the political force in the development process (25–28).

Most important was Almeida's (1963) detailed overview of nationalism and development in the periphery, in which he drew on historical examples; generalized about nationalism and development; and described the economic, sociological, cultural, and political aspects of these terms in general and speculative ways. He focused on the developing nations of Africa, Asia, and Latin America and identified national revolutions oriented toward development. Turning to leftist perspectives on development, he offered an interesting discussion (124–154) of the content and meaning of nationalism for various social classes. He treated development as a social and economic system, departing from a structural-functional approach but interestingly offering a synthesis of ideas on capital, state intervention, autonomous development, bourgeois democracy, infrastructure, import substitution, risk and the contradictions of development, and the challenge of development for the left in Brazil (for his retrospectives on the ISEB experience and the 1964 authoritarian period, see 1980 and 2005).

Rômulo de Almeida, born in Bahia, studied law and social sciences, paying scant attention to economics even though he became known as an economist. In an early report (1943), he provided a detailed overview of the economy, identified problems of national integration, and assessed the prospects for expansion. In an interview, he said that his work with Vargas helped to shape various national plans involving energy (particularly petroleum), electrification, forest resources, and the establishment of the Banco do Nordeste, along with national projects on agriculture and rural credit. He headed the Banco do Nordeste in Fortaleza in 1954, the year Vargas committed suicide. He did not continue in this role under Café Filho but instead ran successfully for federal deputy under the Brazilian Workers' Party (Partido Trabahalhista Brasileiro [PTB]). Later, he became secretary of state in Bahia and coordinated regional planning there. He served briefly under Quadros in 1961 but declined to coordinate national planning. With the Organization of American States, he pondered ways of forming a

Latin American common market and unifying regional economies, and he assessed the contradiction between nationalism and foreign capital. Among nationalists, he argued, there were various groups of the left and right dating back to independence, but the most recent movements involved the struggle for development and national mobilization while fighting paternalism. Since the 1930s, integralists, individuals from many different currents (including social Catholics) that were not necessarily fascist, had supported Vargas's nationalist tendencies. The communists also supported nationalist causes. Almeida chose to give nationalism a positive thrust: "In my activism I wanted to warn of dangers and to foment nationalism as an ideology of national development with solidarity, autonomy, and an alliance of positive and progressive groups to overcome social conflict, as well as to study nationalism as a means of opening attitudes and ideas throughout the world" (interview, Rio de Janeiro, October 8, 1967).

Rômulo de Almeida envisaged his role in the Grupo de Itatiaia as one that combined different elements. He was also involved with the IBESP, even though he was outside Rio for much of the period of the IBESP's ascendancy. He observed that the majority of these groups desired autonomy and nationalism and were leftist, but some participants had been integralists, among them Roland Corbisier, who was very rightist at the time but shifted his outlook. He acknowledged as influential in this movement Celso Furtado and Correia Lima, Guerreiro Ramos, Bishop Dom Helder Câmara, and Corbisier. He believed that ISEB studies were both good and bad and that their influence was uneven: "influential among students and technocrats within the government, minimally among the military, and negligibly among the elites and the masses, during a time when I was abroad" (interview, Rio de Janeiro, 1967).

Júlio Barbosa, born in Patrocinio, Minas Gerais, studied in Belo Horizonte, graduated in law, and taught and chaired the department of political sociology at the Universidade de Minas Gerais. In 1959–1961, he was affiliated with the ISEB, taking the place of Guerreiro Ramos, who had left after his altercation with Jaguaribe. He taught courses on development and on a theory of Brazilian nationalism but was unable to remain because the institute did not have funds to sustain a transfer to Rio. He felt that Furtado, Jaguaribe, Guerreiro Ramos, and Vieira Pinto were the most important writers on the problem of nationalism and national ideology oriented to development at a time when the country was embroiled in partisan activity on both the right and the left. Barbosa considered Vieira Pinto an extraordinary intellectual, interested in psychology and probably the only Brazilian philosopher to incorporate the concept of development into his outlook while building a new Marxist category focused on the underdeveloped nation. He thought of the Itatiaia group as made up of competent intellectuals who ensured continuity with the ISEB. Their thinking on nationalism identified the country as autonomously capable of elaborating a theory of development. The Superior War College (Escola Superior de Guerra [ESG]) and the ISEB contrasted in perspectives. The ISEB evolved as an "incomplete expression" of the political system. Its closure may have been unjustified, but it was unable to sustain itself. He felt that the ESG was also important but that there was no relationship with the ISEB even though some military attended ISEB courses (interview, Belo Horizonte, June 12, 1967).

Domar Campos, who was born in Sergipe and studied in Santa Catarina, lived most his life in Rio, except for four years in Uruguay and a year in Argentina. He studied chemistry, was a journalist for two Rio newspapers, and eventually joined Roberto Campos, Rangel, and Gudin as "Brazilian economists without economic training." His credentials were based on a course with the ECLA, work with Roberto Campos from 1950 to 1953, and involvement with the Central Bank and Itamaraty. A technocrat who published in economic journals, he was not affiliated with any political party, but he did participate in the Grupo de Itatiaia and later in the ISEB in its second phase, when he was an assistant to Rangel and taught a course on economic development. He withdrew from the ISEB in December 1963, just before the coup.

As a nationalist leaning toward socialism, Campos favored an ideology of nationalism and a rationalization of the same. He envisaged capitalism as a necessary stage of development and, given scarce capital, believed that investment of foreign capital might be necessary. Brazil's problem, however, was that its national bourgeoisie and its proletariat both lacked class consciousness. Although many in the Grupo de Itatiaia and the IBESP had been integralists, they were able to reach understanding with intellectuals on the left, such as Rangel, Vieira Pinto, and Nelson Werneck Sodré. Campos considered Celso Furtado a nationalist whose writings were important. Marx was influential, as was Sartre; yet had Jaguaribe remained, he would have restrained populism and the tendency toward communist influence within the ISEB (interview, Rio de Janeiro, June 8, 1967).

Roland Corbisier, a philosopher with roots in São Paulo and who moved to Rio in March 1954, participated early in the Grupo de Itatiaia, the IBESP, and the ISEB.[5] He proclaimed himself a socialist in a country not ready for socialism. He acknowledged that he had been an admirer of Plínio Salgado in his youth and that, initially, he had felt that integralism was a true form of nationalism, although later he understood it to be impressionistic, sentimental, intuitive, and lacking a rational scientific base. He believed that Alberto Torres's *O problema nacional brasileiro* (1933) was an intuitive understanding of the Brazilian national problem, in particular its economic dependence and cultural alienation. He considered the Grupo de Itatiaia as having come together without any ideological position, whereas the ISEB promoted a national conscience that was necessary to confront the country's problems of industrialization and development. Through conferences and sophisticated publications aimed at the dominant classes, the ISEB aimed "to form an informed elite leadership capable of under-standing and solving the problems of the nation." Rebutting the allegation that the ISEB was Marxist or communist, he argued that it functioned as a government institution whose council was appointed and its professors contracted by the Ministry of Education. Its work was focused on nationalism and development, and it addressed a bourgeoisie aware of its role in the struggle against the tendency of imperialism to absorb the internal market.

Although the reactionary press confused awareness of nationalism with communism, Corbisier explained that the crisis within the ISEB related to Jaguaribe's advocacy of foreign capital as a means to advance the petroleum industry's development in the country. Initially, a majority, including Roberto de Oliveira Campos and Anísio Teixeira, supported Jaguaribe, but shortly thereafter, while he was traveling in Europe, the consulting council of some fifty persons was disbanded and the central council assumed fiscal responsibility. On his return, Jaguaribe, together with Campos and Teixeira, appealed these administrative decisions by the Ministry of Education, but they were

---

[5] An autobiography of his life, ideas, and actions traces his trajectory from integralism to Marxism (1978) and includes a preface by Nelson Werneck Sodré. This essential work recounts the founding, in 1948, with Vicente Ferreira da Silva, Almeida Salles, Paulo Edmur de Souza Queiroz, Francisco Brasileiro, and Inácio da Silva Telles of *Colegio* and its five issues that he describes as a philosophical journal of culture and art, and one ideologically oriented to the right while assuming an existentialist position (48). He recounts his experiences in São Paulo, the Grupo de Itatiaia, and the ISEB. In a book (1980) dedicated to Lenin, with references to the Greek philosophers and to Engels, Marx, and Lenin, Corbisier offers a somewhat general and abstract discussion of intellectuals and revolution that does not focus on Brazil.

not reconsidered, and the three resigned. Corbisier felt that Campos was antinationalist and that, with his resignation, the ISEB unequivocally adopted a nationalist position.

Corbisier assumed a major administrative role thereafter at a time when the ISEB was interested in nationalism as a global ideology of development sustained by the working class, proletariat, middle classes, peasantry, and industrial bourgeoisie. He argued that the ISEB stance favored a bourgeois democratic revolution similar to the French Revolution. The development of Brazilian capitalism, the formation of a national entrepreneurial class, and the industrialization of the country would lead to the emergence of a national bourgeoisie: "Nationalism and socialism are two enemies of imperialism." In 1960, he was elected as a state deputy from Guanabara, resigned from the ISEB, and served as a federal deputy from August 1963 until April 10, 1964, when he was ousted by the military after its coup. He felt that the ISEB had had little influence on the military or with the masses but was influential within the student movement. The ISEB was nationalist, not socialist, and not influenced by the Partido Comunista Português (PCP) (interview, Rio de Janeiro, May 29, 1967; see also Penha, 1982, for a brief overview of Corbisier's work in philosophy).

This emphasis on a progressive nationalism not driven by socialism or communism is evident both in Corbisier's shift from his earlier integralism and in his role in shaping an ISEB in pursuit of an agenda of nationalism and development. His writings also reflect this direction, especially early on, in a collection of journalistic pieces (1950) on consciousness and the nation, including an essay on the bourgeoisie: "Perhaps the bourgeoisie has lost its great opportunity to anticipate history and assume its initiative and command of the revolution. Its great error will have been an error of consciousness" (63). He called on Brazilians (88–95) to struggle against contradictions, to be conscious of the need for a new Brazil and its reality, and to join in the common struggle (111).

His work dwelt on the emergence of Brazil from its colonial past and the prospects of an underdeveloped and semicolonial nation in the face of imperialism. His ambitious work on the alternatives of reform and revolution (1968) invoked Alberto Torres's call for awareness of exploitation under imperialism, in particular economic dependence, and cultural alienation. He also alluded to the works of Euclydes da Cunha and Oliveira Vianna who had contributed "immensely in raising consciousness about our reality and the formation of the national problem" (22). His analysis of events up until the coup of 1964 examined internal and external contradictions, contrasted the efforts toward reform or revolution and elaborated on the peaceful or violent road to change. He argued for a change in attitude and for a struggle against dependency and semicolonialism: "on a cultural level, this opposition of an intelligentsia must evolve as an organ of national conscience – on the political level in the struggle of nationalist parties and movements with interests in national development; and on the economic level carried out by the actions of independent industrialists and an industrial proletariat with a technological base" (1960a: 40).[6]

Corbisier identified nationalist lines of thinking and linked philosophy to criticism (1976a), and in an interview (1976b), he elaborated about the ISEB as an "experiment of planning or projecting national development as a means of scientifically knowing our national reality" (18). He argued that nationalism was possible when there was a national bourgeoisie independent of rural oligarchies and foreign capital: "Nationalism consists of the formulation of a project that implies the adoption of an ideology and the recognition of a national reality in two respects: natural and human" (21).

Helio Jaguaribe. In his youth, Jaguaribe was a member of the Vanguarda Socialista. He was involved in a publication of the same name in Rio under the direction of Mário Pedrosa, a student of Marxism and a militant in a Trotskyist current that brought progressive intellectuals together: "I participated in this group, and it was a phase of Marxist criticism that in large measure shaped my understanding of Marxism: Marxism was the first line of ideas that shaped my university studies. I withdrew eventually because of my concern with an orthodox Marxism and also because of my doubts about Trotskyism. I left the movement during the Dutra government."

Jaguaribe was also interested in the political currents and personalities that preceded the Grupo de Itatiaia and the ISEB, in particular two lines of literary nationalism during the 1930s: Graciliano Ramos and the regionalism of writers of the Northeast on the left, and Federico Schmidt who moved rightward with integralism but later pulled away from a nationalist stance and joined with Francisco Campos in a position favorable to foreign capital. All this literary nationalism emanating from the right and left had little influence on the Grupo de Itatiaia because it was not involved in literature. Other nationalist lines were more influential

---

[6] See his related study of the problems of culture (1958, 1966b), cultural alternatives (1956b), pedagogy (1952), responsibilities of elites (1956a), and nationalism (1957, 1966b) as Brazil evolved into a modern era symbolized in the construction of Brasília (1960a). His published work through the ISEB included two short monographs (1960a and 1960b).

with the group: the industrial nationalist line of Roberto Simonsen; the line of social science intellectuals of university and academic origins; the labor union line within the General Command of Workers (Comando Geral dos Trabalhadores [CGT]); the communist line emanating from the PCB; the nationalist line opposed to the communist position; and the nationalist line of Christian Catholic origins that, in earlier times, vacillated between right and left and that led to the popular action position of Jackson de Figueredo (in his time marked by a rightist tendency) and the progressive Catholic nationalist position of Alceu Amoroso Lima.

The Grupo de Itatiaia included people representing many of these positions. Some were influenced by Spengler and German culturalism, and some were impressed with the Spanish philosopher Ortega y Gassett, who was influenced by Kant but very original and creative in his thinking: "We were completely caught up with Ortega and his ideas. We were intellectually influenced by Kant, phenomenology, and existentialism." The Paulistas in the group were led by Miguel Real, who evolved from integralism, as had Corbisier; these Paulistas combined their past criticism of liberalism with an anti-imperialist perspective.

Jaguaribe explained that the Rio group was split, with Rômulo de Almeida and others bringing with them their past integralism, whereas others like himself came to it with Marxist and Stalinist influences. There were two currents: "the Paulista, founded on cultural idealism, and the Carioca or Rio one, which opposed capitalism and was influenced by Marxism." Almeida, an integralist during the early Vargas period, later turned to the left: believing that the second Vargas government would favor popular action, he became an economic adviser to Vargas. In this, Almeida was influenced by Evaldo Correia Lima, through Roberto Simonsen and his Confederação Nacional da Indústria, which attracted some very capable men of that time.

Briefly summarizing the accomplishments of the Grupo de Itatiaia, Jaguaribe said that it made a theoretical and practical effort to bring together diverse groups in the social sciences to analyze the Brazilian situation. It wanted to influence the Vargas government through Almeida, who sought "an ideological consistency in the government." Its deliberations resulted in the publication of its ideas; for instance, an important analysis on the Brazilian crisis and about which there was much discussion (Jaguaribe 1953, 1954, 1981). Despite their differing integralist and Marxist lines, the group initially was characterized by both unity and differences: "first, in the shift from philosophical discussion to social concerns, and ultimately there was a rupture." The Grupo de Itatiaia had evolved into the IBESP, which was financially supported by its own funds and through a project established with Anísio Teixeira, a reformer who had long argued that the educational system was archaic and favored the privileged (1957). Later attention turned to the ISEB and its evolution during the Café Filho government. A central theme continued to be educational reform and national development (Geraldo Bastos Silva, 1957). Its emphasis on interpreting Brazilian reality was similar to the mission of the ESG but distinctly different ideologically: "We wished to neutralize this difference by reaching out to the ESG (Guerreiro gave three lectures, I gave one, and so, too, did Ewaldo Correia and Rômulo de Almeida). We never reached any consensus, since the ESG was led by generals who emanated from the 1930 revolution and assumed anticommunist positions."

In Jaguaribe's view, Kubitschek helped transform Brazil from an agrarian society into an industrial one. Conditions allowed his government to support the ISEB as an institution at work on a national ideology of development until 1958, which was a transitional year: "In that moment some of our group became aware that we were in the moment of a profound revolution and that they were part of a leadership group." Yet there were two negative aspects: "first, a propensity for a doctrinaire and dogmatic approach; and second, a tendency for scholars to be overly activist." Jaguaribe seemed uninterested in the role of a public intellectual and felt that the ISEB as an institution should not be involved in politics, and he was critical of later changes under Álvaro Vieira Pinto – the turn toward activist politics and policy and what he saw as the influence of the PCB (interview, Riverside, California, October 17, 1966).

While the ISEB evolved in Rio, in São Paulo, intellectuals were associated with the USP and influenced by French intellectuals and the building of a sociology with a Paulista foundation and Marxist tendencies. According to Jaguaribe, Caio Prado Júnior and "his position of Marxist humanism" was also important: "It is my impression that major strands of thought came together and eventually assimilated into the CEBRAP [Centro Brasileiro de Análise e Planejamento (Brazilian Center for Analysis and Planning)] under Fernando Henrique Cardoso." The Paulista left was hostile to Corbisier, but the ISEB assumed a critical stance under his administration: "The difference between our institutions today and the ISEB is evident in that the ISEB deliberately contributed to thought oriented to action and a message to the people to become politically involved. In my view, ISEB contributed in a relevant way until it became contaminated with relevant Marxism" (interview, Rio de Janeiro, July 23, 1994).[7]

Reflecting on the experience a generation later, Jaguaribe felt that the nationalist vision of the 1950s was no longer useful and suggested instead a liberal approach with limited protectionism for the economy. He was optimistic about the Cardoso presidency, which he characterized as liberal and social democratic rather than neoliberal. He was impressed with Cardoso's influence in São Paulo and with CEBRAP, and he believed that the most modern thought was in the group formed around Bolivar Lamounier and his liberal social-democratic perspective. He saw the PSDB as an outcome of the crisis of Marxism and the drift of intellectuals away from Marxist philosophy. He felt that intellectuals linked with the Workers' Party (Partido dos Trabalhadores [PT]), lacked theoretical vision and simply depended on slogans to make a difference in contemporary Brazil (interview, Rio de Janeiro, July 23, 1994).

When I asked Jaguaribe to comment on intellectuals who had either advocated nationalism or were influential in this movement over the years, he mentioned Euclydes da Cunha, "a hero who introduced Marxist thought to Brazil"; Monteiro Lobato, a figure of importance in nationalist thought early in the twentieth century and "the first to demand a national approach to the control of oil"; Fernando de Azevedo, a pioneer in education and "a member of our council but not active"; Gilberto

---

[7] Although *Revista Brasiliense* generally reflected the views of São Paulo intellectuals, it also was attentive to ideas emanating from the Rio intellectuals associated with the ISEB. Guerreiro Ramos (1958d), for instance, discussed the idea of a center (south) and a periphery (west and north) in Brazil, and he related historical changes in the economy to different export crops (e.g., coffee in the recent period). His work was reviewed somewhat favorably by Teotônio Júnior (1958) and Bastos Filho (1960). Another reviewer (XXX, 1959) examined Jaguaribe's *O nacionalismo na atualidade brasileira* and the debate within the ISEB over Petrobrás, emphasizing the author's preference for "a bourgeois solution" in the face of capitalist and socialist alternatives and criticizing him for believing that foreign capital should be part of Brazilian national development. Cunha Xavier critically reviewed Celso Furtado's *Formação econômica do Brasil* (1959a), identifying problems with historical references and conceptual distortions and comparing its analysis to that of Caio Prado Júnior. Finally, Dorian Jorge Freire (1960) contributed a note in defense of the ISEB against the campaign by business and conservative leaders to close it down. Herbert José de Sousa (1962) focused on "violence as a characteristic of an underdeveloped country" (164) and turned to the ISEB for an understanding of violence (165). Michel Debrun (1963) reviewed the ideological thought of Vieira Pinto, Jaguaribe, and Ramos within the ISEB and argued that one of the institute's important advances was its focus on development (93). A speech by Osny Duarte Pereira (1963) to students of the ISEB and a description of its courses and approaches included a discussion of reform measures to ensure development.

Freyre, a renowned sociologist "involved in IBESP with criticism and ideas"; and Sêrgio Buarque de Holanda, a "historian who supported our efforts." His list of principal figures also included Rômulo de Almeida. Jaguaribe saw Almeida as a man of importance in Brazilian history who published little and who, influenced by Roberto Simonsen, systemized Vargas's ideas on nationalism, evolved a line of programmatic nationalism, and tried to convince Vargas to adopt a systematic approach to development within economic nationalism. Almeida was instrumental in plans that established Petrobrás, Electobrás, the Carvão Nacional, the Banco do Nordeste, and the plan for reorganizing the national railway system. He inspired the formation of the Coordination for the Improvement of Higher Education Personnel (Coordenação de Aperfeiçoamento de Pessoal de Nível Superior [CAPES]) foundation and was influential in the naming of Anísio Teixeira as its first director. He was interested in popular housing, which led to establishment of a national housing bank (interview, Rio de Janeiro, October 27, 1967). Jaguaribe singled out Roberto Campos for favoring foreign capital as a means of overcoming underdevelopment and for being the first Brazilian economist to propose economic planning in Brazil and especially to incorporate the use of national resources: "Initially his position toward nationalism was uncertain; later he championed foreign capital but within a nationalist line." Campos administered the Banco de Desenvolvimento but was wary of the role of the state in the economy. Michel Debrun was a "brilliant" French intellectual interested in Brazilian affairs who gave courses, did research on politics and ideology, and published an interesting book with the ISEB (1957). Celso Furtado was drawn to the IBESP but was more involved in the ISEB: "one of the first to focus on the Brazilian economy with vision and a perspective on economic development." Ewaldo Correia, an economist, "contributed immensely to ISEB theory" and brought in Lima Rocha, an economist and specialist with Petrobrás who coordinated many studies of the petroleum industry; also economists Domar Campos and Gilberto Paim. Hermes Lima of the Partido Socialista do Brasil (PSB) and "a left progressive" significantly helped with ISEB theory. In Jaguaribe's view, Guerreiro Ramos "gave enormously to Brazilian studies and sociology," linking "our Brazilian traditions and past understandings to philosophical and sociological positions" such as the thought of Alberto Torres and Oliveira Vianna. Ramos introduced the group to Nelson Werneck Sodré and also brought in Paulo de Castro, who marginally participated but gave lectures at the ISEB. Inácio Rangel, "an economist with major participation in the ISEB," developed the concept of duality in the Brazilian economy. Vieira Pinto, a neo-Kantian later attracted to Marxism and who became "a scholastic and schematic Marxist," was very active during the final phase and headed the philosophy department (interviews, Riverside, California, October 17, 1966; October 27, 1967; Rio de Janeiro, July 23, 1994).

Jaguaribe published three studies through the ISEB: a superficial survey of Brazilian philosophers and their ideas (1957a); a series of lectures on the national political situation and institutional conditions of development that referred to the need for an ideological line and consciousness (1958a); and a lengthy treatise on nationalism in Brazil (1958b) so controversial that it led to his departure from the ISEB. He coordinated early volumes (IBESP Plan 1956; ISEB 1956) identifying Brazilian problems. All his later writing on the topic drew on this comprehensive work, placing emphasis theoretically and conceptually first on Brazilian nationalism and, second, on specific issues such as petroleum, foreign capital, and foreign policy. He suggested integrative and imperialist types of nationalism and argued that Brazilian nationalism must be examined in a dialectical way: "For the long term, it leads us to supernational forms that now may be premature to conceive of; in the short term, the dialectical conception of Brazilian nationalism should lead to an understanding of how to transform our traditional structures" (1958b: 55). On the controversial question of oil, he disagreed with the basic thesis that national capital should be solely responsible for exploration, and he did not support the idea of a state monopoly. He argued that foreign private capital was possible in a free market not dominated by a state monopoly (117–121). His preference was for a national bourgeoisie to lead this process (213).

After resigning from the ISEB, Jaguaribe published many studies on nationalism and development, focusing on Brazil but also examining Latin America in general. In 1961, he examined the bourgeoisie and proletariat, focusing attention on nationalism as "a social historical phenomenon" and on its economic, social, cultural, and political contradictions, and on ideology and the distinction between the state and private enterprise in the promotion of development. In 1962, he produced a major synthesis that used the Brazilian state and the evolution of its economy as a case study on economic development and political organization. Building on these two monographs, Jaguaribe published essays abroad (1966a, 1966b, 1967, 1967–1968, 1968) that emphasized three stages in Brazilian development (colonialism, semicolonialism, and transition to the republic), and he examined planning under Vargas, the structural crisis, and populist experiments up to the coup of 1964. All this work culminated in a monograph, *Economic and Political Development* (1968), that was an updated and revised translation of his 1962 book. He argued that national capitalism was the most suitable model for Brazilian development, and he called for a pact between the national bourgeoisie and labor, strengthening of the state, and political and economic integration with "the Atlantic community under U.S. leadership." Later, he looked back (1979, 2005) at the ISEB movement and its early roots in integralism and attempted to place the successes and failures of the ISEB within a historical context.[8]

Gilberto Paim, born in Rio, described himself as self-taught, having served in the military and then "become an intellectual." Paim believed that nationalists in the military felt obligated to turn to politics: "I was influenced by various ideas but not caught up in the thought of any particular one. I have a Marxist formation as well. I read a lot."

As he saw it, the ISEB idea began with the Vargas government. The central theme was to study development as both theory and practice. There were different tendencies, but all were oriented to development and all had the objective of awakening Brazil from its colonial and backward mentality: "It was a psychological contribution." He felt that the Grupo de Itatiaia reached some consensus over the concept of development and critical thinking about it. The group was technocratic in orientation; its second meeting included Corbisier and others and discussed how Brazil could move forward, with the idea of seeking an intellectual strategy lying outside the political parties: "It was an effort to formulate an ideology, even incorporating Marxist perspectives and analysis about development, colonialism, and imperialism." In his view, the IBESP was an effort to reformulate an intelligentsia interested in

[8] The relevance of his Brazilian case to Latin America is in his attention to imperialism (1977a), to a historical overview of underdevelopment in Latin America (1967, 1970a), and to issues such as foreign development and foreign technical assistance. Interestingly, he assessed the impact of Marx on Latin American intellectuals. He identified Tobias Barreto as the first Brazilian to write about Marx, reviewed Marxist influences up to the formation of the ECLA, and asserted that "the new intelligentsia" offered hope for development (134–135). Subsequent writing reflected on these themes: a political model of the Brazilian socioeconomic structure (1970b, 1978); an analysis of alternatives (1990) in light of the weakness of the public administration, the failure of development, the problems impeding modernization, hyperinflation, and governing impasse; a retrospective (1982) on populism over the past half century and its potential in the democratic opening; and an argument (2000[1986]) for a new social pact to resolve the problems of inequality and poverty in Brazil.

reaching power. It published a journal that was concerned with national issues: "a journal of the intelligentsia and the major themes of the times."

Paim joined the ISEB in 1956 and taught history – this, despite the fact that he was known as an economist, probably because of his book (1957) on industrialization and natural economy (a study of manufacturing activities within agriculture in early Brazil, including changes under a coffee economy in rural areas, early industrialization, early agrarian reforms, and the limits of industrialization) and because of a 1960 journal article on foreign enterprise. He defined development "as a process of material advance and a shift from an agrarian to industrial society to the building of a new class of the bourgeoisie. Development should be based on national interests with its profits distributed within the nation." Nationalism was a term "derived from the German experience and associated with capitalism and the bourgeoisie. In Brazil, it was developed in the work of Alberto Torres and later in the ideas of contemporary politicians."

Paim observed that Kubitschek and his political party had emerged within a new environment of widespread nationalism, even within the armed forces that provided support for his government. There were two currents in the government and the ISEB, one to the right (*entreguista*) in favor of foreign investment, especially U.S. capital, and the other to the left (*nacionalista*) in favor of national capital. With the demise of the advisory council, its members, including the conservative economist Roberto Campos, were marginalized: power shifted from the council to the staff and to the left, thus provoking dissension within the ISEB and debate nationally.

As the ISEB staked out a progressive direction, financial support for its activities diminished: "The ISEB never had the conditions to implement serious long-term research, but its influence was significant among the public at large as it was sought out by parliamentarians, labor unions, and other groups." Paim saw Jaguaribe as a precursor, one who provided the inspiration for a movement, and Corbisier and his group in São Paulo as representing a different perspective, while Rangel associated with intellectual advisers to Vargas and "as a Marxist, not only represented the traditional elite but was of a technocratic bent." In Paim's view, although different people headed various disciplinary directions, the ISEB mission involved, first, setting forth a project for conquest of national power; second, formulating a critical view of the national situation; third, building a movement of intellectuals with the idea of establishing an ideology for development; fourth, departing from a global analysis and interpretation; and fifth, realizing a vision of the future through a structured approach to understanding Brazilian reality. Organizationally, two councils of prominent figures linked the main group and the government in power and were "oriented to the cultural trends of the country while drawing intellectuals from the major urban areas of São Paulo and Rio."

Manifestations of nationalism, Paim argued, could be found throughout Brazilian history: "I examined nationalism as a means to push the social struggle, and I envisaged Vargas as the major nationalist figure, representative of the bourgeoisie whose image carried on through other personalities, Kubitschek as a conciliator, reconciling imperialist interests with the national course, João Goulart as a populist with a program of reform, and Brizola as an agitator. I remained with ISEB until it was terminated by the military after the coup. In a dialectical process, it was reaching out with its courses and politicizing the popular sectors" (interview Rio de Janeiro, May 22, 1967; May 25, 1967).

Alberto Guerreiro Ramos emphasized his accomplishments and was critical of others. In a rambling interview, he talked about French writers who influenced him, such as Jean-Paul Sartre, and of the Brazilian Alberto Torres. He felt that Vargas could have done much more for the nation. Ramos believed that the Grupo de Itatiaia awakened interest among the youth, politicians, and intellectuals, and he credited Jaguaribe as being "the one who inspired us, he wrote most of the material."

Ramos talked about his desire to build a reputable department of sociology, instead of one that, he believed, was "absorbing all the funds for its own projects, while other departments were not doing anything so that when Jaguaribe took funds from sociology, he lacked intellectual honesty, and I took the matter to the group in 1958, just as he published his book on petroleum, and we and others attacked the thesis of the book."

Believing that Jaguaribe, Rangel, and he had produced the only important work of the ISEB, Ramos went on to attack Corbisier, affirming that he had emerged as director because of his close ties with the Ministry of Education and was "incompetent and an opportunist" while the emotional and intelligent Vieira Pinto was "absorbed in romanticism and mystical ideas" (interview, Riverside, California, November 18, 1966).

A prolific writer, Ramos initially published several essays (1939, 1940) in the integralist literary journal *Cadernos da Nossa Hora*. His early work looked at industrial sociology (1952), appealed for a national sociology (1954), explored Brazilian politics (1956a), and dwelt on the sociology of power (1957a, 1957b, 1958a). He edited and introduced an important anthology of essays (1958e), originally presented to an ISEB course in late 1955, that included economic-social analysis by Alexandre Kafka, Ewaldo Corrêa Lima, and Rômulo de Almeida; political social analysis by Djacir Menezes (1972) and Themistocles Cavalcanti; and cultural analysis by Nelson Werneck Sodré, Roland Corbisier, and Roberto Campos. This assessment of Brazilian problems reflected the dilemma of a colonial legacy; in it, Ramos reflected on such terms as "duplicity" (identified by Rangel as "a basic law of our formation"; Ramos 1958e: 22); "heteromony," explained not as Brazilian national reality but as the reality of other countries (25); "alienation" as opposed to self-determination; and "inauthenticity" or the assimilation of values that do not correspond to national reality. Among the essayists, Lima drew heavily on ECLA policy that could lead Brazil to dynamic and autonomous economic development; Almeida argued (105) that agricultural production could serve as a foundation for "a program of economic development that is integral and unitary" (105); and Corbisier (187–218) looked at culture within Brazilian colonial structure, outlined options for an underdeveloped and semicolonial country in the face of imperialism, and showed that "peasants and merchants unconsciously remain tied to the interests of underdevelopment and semicolonialism" (215).

In other ISEB works, Ramos published a paper on national power and the emancipation of Brazil from threatening forces (1957a) and another paper on ideology and national security (1957c) in which he argued that "every system of national security necessarily has ideological content" (15), that "the ideology of national security ... is the same as Brazilian capitalism in formation" (50), and that national strategy had to be vigilant about the economic penetration of foreign capital (33). The ISEB also published his important *A redução sociológica* (1958e), which drew heavily from his ISEB courses and his writing and thinking outside Brazil, although it makes comparisons with Brazil. This work offered general propositions for finding a path to national development, and the notion of "a sociological reduction" involving a systematic critical and collective approach (44–47). Leite (1983) emphasizes its importance as a concept for Brazilian sociology.

During the interview, Ramos (1957d) delved into nationalism and xenophobia in the early thinking of Alberto Torres, whom he said did not understand that "Brazil could evolve within Brazilian capitalism" (32). Ramos's study focused on different interpretations of race in the thought of Sílvio Romero, Euclydes da Cunha, Alberto Torres, Oliveira Vianna, and Nina Rodrigues. This effort to raise awareness of racial issues about Afro-Brazilians included a piece on the pathology of the "white" Brazilian, his own perspective as a black Brazilian, his manifesto on race relations in Brazil, and an interview on the crisis of Brazilian sociology.

Ramos devoted considerable attention to the Brazilian "problem" of nationalism (1959d,), examining the replacement of landowner influence with that of the industrial bourgeoisie, whose interests depend on internal consumption and the working class (1960: 23), and arguing that modernization was necessary and helped by intellectuals whose "critical consciousness" raised awareness of national reality and the development of a new Brazilian society. In a volume on power (1961), probably based on his personal experience in politics, he offered a sober assessment of the PCB, especially its dependence on the Soviet Union, and of the ISEB's role in influencing nationalism in Brazil (119–137). In a critical assessment (1961) of revolutionary prospects in Brazil, including a critical review of the work of Vieira Pinto, for whom "nationalism was a doctrine of war" (197), he revealed how he tried to convince Brizzola to moderate his leftist position before Goulart's fall (1963). Finally, Ramos offered a very interesting and critical overview of nationalism (1968) as a social movement originating in the mid-1950s. He identified a typology of nationalisms: (1) the nation as a closed system, (2) operational or strategic nationalism (exemplified by the ISEB), (3) co-optive nationalism (represented by communists within the ISEB during the Goulart government who used nationalism to further their goals and saw it as a bourgeois ideology), (4) populist nationalism (used by politicians to mobilize sentiments and emotions along with theoretical elements of Marxism), and (5) naïve nationalism (the belief that everything Brazilian was good and everything foreign was bad, represented in the thought of Álvaro Vieira Pinto and his *Cadernos do Povo Brasileiro*). Ramos attributed the decline of Brazilian nationalism to the ISEB crisis, the rise and fall of Quadros as a national leader, and the chaos around Goulart. He criticized (14–17) Wanderley Guilherme dos Santos for assuming, rather than empirically demonstrating, that history was a sequence of class struggles; Celso Furtado for believing that only nationalism would integrate the antagonistic interests of classes; Octávio Ianni for arguing that the industrial bourgeoisie could not destroy the archaic structure without tactically aligning itself with the proletariat (15); Sodré for not recognizing the contradictions in his belief that the middle class helped solidify the dominant strata of society; and Paula Beiguelman and her work on politics (1967) for relying on the individual origins of military leaders while neglecting the role of the army and its institutional challenge in moments of political crisis. He attacked Francisco Weffort for exaggerating the importance of a national bourgeoisie and Wanderley Guilherme dos Santos for pejorative connotations of such terms as "equilibrium," "compromise," and "conciliation," which "are always suspicious in radical nationalist approaches" (19). He argued that most discussion of imperialism was "distorted," as exemplified by Sodré's argument that the role of the nationalist movement should be to "resist imperialism" and Jaguaribe's association of imperialism with the United States (20–21). He condemned these and other writers for their emphasis on the "vanguards of workers" in leading the way out of the colonial condition and achieving "socialism" and "the proletarian revolution" (23–25). In particular, he singled out Vieira Pinto for saying that "the authentic elite relies always on the mass as a whole" and that "only what is popular is national." He characterized many nationalist intellectuals for being "people's militants" and suggested that it was "not accidental that Vieira Pinto had called for the popularization of the Brazilian university" and that the Ministry of Education and Culture had given "a group of Marxist-Leninists the task of rewriting Brasilian history" (26).

Ramos felt that the interdisciplinary approach emphasized by Jaguaribe was important, given the limitations of academic disciplines, especially in an underdeveloped country; all the movement founders agreed that "theories and methods produced in developed countries could not be literally observed or followed in developing countries," and they were all concerned about relevant problems in Brazil (54–59). Nevertheless, the ISEB crisis led to a prevalence of Marxist-Leninist values in the leadership after 1958 (59).[9]

[9] Ramos clarified that he had resigned in December 1958 over Jaguaribe's efforts to distribute research funds evenly among the institute's various departments, and he criticized Bonilla and Skidmore for attributing the crisis to a dispute between moderate and radical nationalists. Jaguaribe, Campos, and Teixeira had resigned over a structural reform that limited the powers of an advisory committee of which they were members. Thereafter, the absence of this advisory committee was of no consequence. Mendes de Almeida left in 1960, at a time when he wanted to succeed Corbisier as director (Ramos 1968: 52–53n). Rangel was "a very competent Marxist, but a Marxist usually in disagreement with the positions and policies of the Brazilian Marxists and Marxist-Leninist groups" (53). Isolated in Los Angeles, Ramos lamented that "nationalism is no more a heuristically fruitful perspective. In fact, nationalism is a dead issue" (93).

After the military coup in 1964, Ramos moved to California and a professorship at the University of Southern California. His contributions included a review of literature about sociology and development in the field of public administration (1966); this work focused attention on formalism in Brazil as a strategy for social change and cited Inácio Rangel for the distinction between external to internal conditions in a dialectical process (422). In his attention to national development, Ramos focused on the dichotomy of center and periphery and compared the imperialist domination of foreign countries over Brazil with discrepancies within Brazil (152–153).[10]

Inácio Rangel established his roots in Rio, although he was born in Maranhão, studied law in Brasília, served as an economic adviser to Vargas (1952–1954), and participated in an ECLA course in Chile in 1954. He observed that, before the Second World War, intellectuals turned left toward progressive currents and right toward integralism and fascism; after the war, these divergent tendencies worked toward consensus on the resolution of concrete problems. Consequently, earlier tendencies were mitigated and some even shifted orientations from right to left and from left to right. Thus, the IBESP and the ISEB were born without allegiances to previous ideologies, and the journal *Cadernos de Nossos Tempos* was based on intense dialogue in a time of new conditions in which communism and fascism were no longer essential: "The Itatiaia group served to bring together intellectuals of diverse perspectives in a time of need to resolve national problems and a responsibility beyond our means. The country expected from us something that was not possible. We could launch the journal, but our work was modest."

Rangel characterized the ISEB as being founded during the Café Filho government, whose antinationalism evolved into a nationalist program; thereafter, the ISEB correspondingly shifted its focus on national problems each year in line with changes in the country: "It is curious that we were perceived as united when in fact we did not feel this unity. There were in fact three ISEBs: the first, based on the Itatiaia experience and the thought that evolved through the IBESP under the influence of Jaguaribe

---

[10] His final work (1984[1981]) argued that a market-centered theory of organizations was not applicable to all contemporary situations and that a new model was needed to deal with questions of human existence. An entire issue of *Revista da Administração Pública* (1983) was dedicated to Ramos after his death, including two additional articles of his own, an appraisal of his work by Jaguaribe (Ramos, 1983) and Rangel (Ramos, 1983; see also 1995), and a review of the literature on modernization and a critique of nineteenth-century influences and reductionism in sociological approaches.

and a preoccupation with research; the second, the ISEB that was more representative of what we were and in search of a response to our national problems; and finally, an ISEB whose consciousness was exaggerated outside with hatred and sympathy but did not correspond to the reality inside, and it came to an end because it no longer was able to grow, and its ideas were exhausted in a time of economic and ideological crisis." By 1960, with the original group diminished: "I refused to be nominated to carry out my duties under the new regime, so I left. I did not believe it possible to establish a research institute as Jaguaribe and Guerreiro Ramos wished."

Rangel believed that Brazilian nationalism was always of military inspiration: "Thus we sought to influence military officers of a positivist bent who had an interest in industrializing the country. Likewise, the students were in the vanguard of revolutionary nationalist organizations." He came to realize that the notion of nationalism was somewhat limited and closed, with its emphasis on nationalization: "The idea began well before we were conscious of it, and now as an ideology it has a specific meaning." He understood development as not simply an economic conception but as taking many forms. Rangel dwelt on the idea of nationalism within communism and its affinity to industrialization, and he was attracted to the ideas of ECLA that Luiz Carlos Prestes also had emphasized. The issue of petroleum and the destiny of the petroleum industry was one focus of attention to nationalism, but it was manifested well before the ISEB could study and theorize such issues. He identified Goulart, Quadros, Kubitschek, Vargas, and Arraes as nationalist politicians willing to bring about change in the country and Jaguaribe, Mendes de Almeida, and Rômulo de Almeida as persons who had contributed significantly to the shaping of the ISEB (interview, Rio de Janeiro, May 25, 1967).

Rangel's most important theoretical work (1957) revolved around the concept of duality. He argued that when America was discovered, Europe's overproduction was a duality of feudalism with traces of capitalism or a mercantile capitalism and thus that it incorporated feudalism into foreign expansion of the precapitalist and the pre-slave regimes. The feudalism established by the Portuguese king in Brazil was not purely feudal: relations of a feudal character were established between the king and those granted land titles, but the grantees established relations typical of other modes of production and that reflected a primitive stage of development: "The Brazilian fiefdom was not internally feudal, that is, it was not yet feudal. Brazil evolved with a feudal formation that was associated in dialectical union with one side being feudal and the other prefeudal" (8). The crown, directly or through a public service concession, sold to the European market the products or tributes received from its vassals. With the opening of its ports and the appearance in Brazil of a mercantile intermediary different from the old public service, the crown conceded to an enterprise, and a new element appeared, one constituting "a second duality" tied to the outside and to an emerging industrial capitalism. Describing the Brazilian duality, Rangel distinguished "internal" and "external" poles. With the opening of the ports in 1808, a new mercantile capitalism appeared along with a new class of merchants; until 1889, the internal pole consisted of (internal) slavery and (external) feudalism whereas the external pole consisted of (internal) mercantile capital and (external) industrial capital. This duality evolved into other dualities thereafter.

His major ISEB study also looked at duality in the Brazilian economy. His duality distinguished between prosperity and depression, ancient and modern, precapitalism and capitalism, domestic and foreign, colonialism and postcolonialism, and internal and external relations of production. Rangel argued that: "it is not enough to say that the *latifundio* is a mixed feudal-capitalist entity; it is internally feudal and externally capitalist" (1957: 30). He identified duality as fundamental for understanding the Brazilian economy and focused on internal and external relations of production, each with its own laws and each pressuring the other "in permanent conflict" (32). Elaborating on the duality of the national economy and its development, he described how Brazil had passed through phases: "mercantilism discovered us, industrialism gave us independence, and financial capitalism led to the republic" (37). Duality was also a theme running through his other work (1978a, 1980a, 1981).[11]

Nelson Werneck Sodré, born in the interior of Bahia, worked as a journalist, writing for communist publications and eventually serving as

---

[11] Rangel's other ISEB studies focused on resources in the national economy. One (1960) examined monetary and financial problems in an effort to address the question of expansion and the availability of goods and services in the economy. It looked at the theory and practice of programming, the role of the state and capital in economic growth, and the problems of planning related to inflation and external debt. Another study (1963a) examined inflation, agrarian structure and crisis, oligopoly in agriculture, and the role of budget and capital. Other writings delved into the issue of reform during the Goulart government (1963b), power and politics under authoritarianism (1978b), and economic development (1975). A study of the national question (1980b) identified shifting capitalist relations of production, national integration under Vargas, and agrarian reform and emerging capitalism in the countryside.

editor of *Correio da Manhã*. He was affiliated with the PCB until 1953, and he encouraged me to write about the party: "This would be important for Brazil and a way to explain the marginalization of the left throughout its twenty-century history" (see Chilcote, 1974). He described the establishment of the ISEB as an effort to break with the legacy of backwardness and inferiority that had long pervaded Brazilian thinking. The PCB had posed the question of whether to pursue a new direction or to remain as a (semifeudal) agricultural nation. The Grupo de Itatiaia aggregated people with political backgrounds – both those to the left with communist influence and those to the right with integralist experience – under the first Vargas period. This mix of progressive and more conservative official elements, itself a paradox, represented "a common uneasiness with prevailing Brazilian problems and a consensus that the obstacles of the past had to be overcome and a national destiny had to be identified."

Between 1956 and 1958, Sodré said, the ISEB united around its mission of promoting industrialization as a way out of Brazilian backwardness. However, differences surfaced in 1958 with the rupture developing over Jaguaribe's book defending foreign investment in the petroleum sector: "I was against the ideas of Jaguaribe at a time when the ISEB had a great prestige with its courses and writings." He remembered Cândido Mendes de Almeida as erudite and Guerreiro Ramos as the most practical collaborator in sociology and research, one who, in Rio, was emerging as an intellectual counterforce to Florestan Fernandes in São Paulo.

By 1963, the ISEB continued to function but without adequate resources: "Under João Goulart, we received some resources and were able to carry on. To our left, were more radical tendencies, including the parliament and its left nationalism," but, he affirmed: "I am certain that Goulart did not want to take Brazil to communism as Roberto Campos and others alleged."

Sodré believed that the problem of nationalism was secondary to development, both themes defined by the right and left. The ISEB published occasional analysis in *O Semanário*, while *Revista Brasiliense* was "always a friend of ISEB, and Caio Prado Júnior was significant for us." The pamphlet series *Cadernos do Povo* was "a radical and brilliant idea, with elaboration of nationalism and development, including my study in the series [1975] that distinguished between rich and poor and called upon the poor to participate in strikes" (interview, Rio de Janeiro, May 29, 1967; see also a memoir, 1988).

Sodré was a prolific and respected writer on many themes. Early work focused on a history of Brazilian literature and its economic significance (1943). A series of articles in *Cultura Política* looked to problems of national unity (1941a, 1941c, 1941d) and to large agricultural properties and landowners (1941b) in Mato Grosso, the push west, poverty, family clans, and the rural and urban dispersion of the population in the region. In 1942, he offered brief biographical sketches of major early twentieth-century Brazilian thinkers: Azevedo Amaral, Gilberto Freyre, Oliveira Vianna, Fernando de Azevedo, Graciliano Ramos, José Lins do Rêgo, Jorge Amado, and Lúcio Cardoso. His examination of the formation of Brazilian society (1944) concentrated on the role of Portugal in early commerce and settlement in Brazil. Six of his writings were published by the ISEB, including a study (1957b) of cultural influences that historically have shaped a colonial outlook in Brazil; an early and somewhat superficial class analysis of Brazilian development (1957a), from mercantile capitalism to the Industrial Revolution, with emphasis on the national bourgeoisie (1964b) and the proletariat and their antagonism in the period of industrialization; an essay (1957c) on the origins and significance of the Treaty of Methuen of 1703, resulting in Portugal's dependency on England, decline in industry, shift to vineyard lands, and transfer of gold to England; a treatise (1959) that explains nationalism as a response "to external economic forces, the most powerful obstacle to our development" (35) and as a means "to transcend the contradiction between the national bourgeoisie and the working class" (37); a work on the ideology of colonialism (1961a) with essays on Brazilian thinkers rooted in colonialism (Azeredo Coutinho, José de Alencar, Sílvio Romero, Euclydes da Cunha, and Oliveira Vianna); and a history of Brazilian nationalism, its roots, and evolution (1962). In 1968, he elaborated on nationalism and national consciousness as an outgrowth of the colonial period and a search for national identity, looked at the duality of development and underdevelopment in relation to social structure, and set forth a program of nationalism oriented toward solving problems of underdevelopment.

Sodré influenced the activities of the ISEB, especially in its late phase. After its demise, he assessed its importance through a series of studies (1976/ 1978/1979) that recount (1978a and 1978b) how Guerreiro Ramos invited him in 1954 to join with the group as a specialist in Brazilian history at a time when he held the rank of lieutenant colonel in the army and was accused of being a communist; that focus on the crisis within the ISEB over Jaguaribe's book on petroleum and foreign capital in Brazil; and that examine the role of intellectuals and their influence on the ISEB. A book (1964a) on the historical formation of Brazil departs from feudalism, mercantilism, and early capitalism in Portugal and turns to Portuguese colonization and expansion, the republic, and empire, and ends with the theme of revolution and a look at the contradictions within a country that remains colonial and dependent yet, despite a weak national bourgeoisie, must transcend imperialism.

This work led to a series of studies on the role of the national bourgeoisie and the Brazilian revolution. In the absence of a viable national bourgeoisie, Sodré advocated national development to overcome the colonial legacy and allow for national development. He elaborated a class analysis of the high, middle, and petty bourgeoisie, and the peasantry, the proletariat, and the semi-proletariat (1963b: 226). His serious study of the Brazilian bourgeoisie (1964b) examined feudalism and slavery; identified the roots of commerce and mercantile capitalism; and analyzed the challenge of imperialism, the end of slavery, the evolution of an export economy, the decline of the *latifundio*, and the consolidation of the bourgeoisie with the 1930 revolution. He argued that the Brazilian revolution involves a process in which the national bourgeoisie must play a role, either pacific or violent, in seeking power and that neither the proletariat nor the peasantry is in play while the bourgeoisie is deciding its own destiny.[12]

THE LATE GENERATION OF ISEB ACTIVISTS

The diverse founders and thinkers who came together to establish the ISEB and shape its direction in the early years sometimes leaned on graduate students as research assistants, especially in the period under Álvaro Vieira Pinto when such promising participants as Michel Debrun, Carlos Estevem Martins, Osny Duarte Pereira, and Wanderley Guilherme dos Santos contributed significantly.

[12] Other works by Sodré include a military history of Brazil (1965a), beginning with its colonial origins and the influence of *tenentismo* in the national phase represented by the 1930 revolution; a history of the Brazilian press (1966) from colonial times to about 1960, reviewing hundreds of periodicals and with attention to left socialist, communist, and working-class sources; and a history of Brazilian culture (1970, 1990). He also explored the origins of independence (1965b) and the aftermath dominated by the *latifundio*, the challenge of liberalism, and the ensuing repression of the left. He contributed a brief interpretative history of the Prestes Column during the 1920s (1980), essays on the history of the PCB (1980–1981, 1984a), a short study of twenty years of military dictatorship (1984b), and an analysis of the reactionary offensive to Brazilian politics (1992).

Michel Debrun, a French philosopher who studied in Paris and taught briefly in Toulouse, reached Brazil in 1956 and taught courses in the ISEB. He also taught philosophy at the USP and, after 1970, at the Universidade Estadual de Campinas (UNICAMP). In 1982, he wrote his thesis on Gramsci's philosophy and politics. This theme runs through another book, published in 1983. His book on ideology and reality (1957) evolved from his political science course and appeared under the ISEB imprint; it departed from Karl Mannheim's work on ideology and relied on Álvaro Vieira Pinto's thesis that, without an ideology of development, there can be no national development (15). It examined philosophers from Marx to Mannheim and Sartre while analyzing ideology and its significance. While teaching at the USP and in the Brazilian School of Administration of the Fundação Getúlio Vargas, Debrun (1962) turned to "raising consciousness of the political dimension and relations between political life and total social life" (11). His ranging discussion related politics to national societies by examining praxis as political consciousness and political action in relation to cultural, religious, economic, military, electoral, and partisan "phenomena." He argued that as violence diminishes, future societies will become less political (139). His essay on the ideological understanding of history appeared in *Revista Brasiliense* (1963).

In another study, Debrun (1964) looked at an ideology of nationalism and development through the theses of Celso Furtado and the influence of ECLA, identifying strategies for how Brazil could emerge from authoritarian rule by initially reconciling European values with African and native Indian values, resolving differences between authoritarian elites in power with dissident elites, and rationalizing strategies to mitigate inequalities. He believed that authoritarianism undermined the ISEB, yet the ISEB and its intellectuals inspired an analysis of Brazilian society, its history, its potential, and its weakness (36). He referred to the Gramcian distinction between organic and traditional intellectuals (93–99), suggesting that organic intellectuals do not affiliate with political parties. Debrun believed that history could be understood as a disequilibrium between dominant and dominated classes whose differences would, in time, be mitigated through conciliation (128–129). He felt that in its early attention to the national bourgeoisie, the ISEB was able to transcend the "spontaneous development" of the Kutitschek period and deepen an understanding of development (109).

Carlos Estevem Martins was associated with the ISEB during two distinct periods: during 1961, as a researcher, and during its final months after organizing the *Centro Popular de Cultura* (CPC) of the União

Nacional dos Estudantes (UNE). His intensive six-month sociology course for graduate students was designed to revitalize the institution with more theoretical and empirical research: "The ISEB failed to capture the historical process experienced by the institution." Martins was active in student unions, including the União Metropolitano dos Estudantes (UME) and its newspaper, *Metropolitano*. Together with Wanderley Guilherme dos Santos, they wrote several articles under the name of Carlos Guilherme: "I was Carlos and he was Guilherme." Unaffiliated with any political party, "we taught university classes but once our activities were banned, we couldn't stay at the university and then Vieira Pinto brought us to the ISEB." Martins emphasized how the intense political struggle was reflected in an ISEB that kept changing as the founders were all replaced by others "whose project was more elitist-technocratic." They espoused a nationalist ideology while at the same time seeking a power base in the government's executive agencies via "technological prestige." However, their project was stifled by popular sentiment and a popular-nationalist movement. The increase of union activity and the politicization of other popular social classes influenced the ISEB as its technocratic elite began to lose control of the project and were replaced by younger staff. At the same time, activist intellectuals such as Paulo Freire became widely known in Rio because of their contacts and activities with the ISEB, and it is clear that the theme of developmental nationalism interested Freire (Paiva, 1980, 1986). Likewise, Francisco Julião first appeared in Rio through lectures at the ISEB well before his notoriety in Recife on behalf of the peasant leagues. Thus, these popular figures were introduced and their political positions became widely known because of their participation in the ISEB. The election of Miguel Arraes as governor in Pernambuco coincided with the election of Carlos Lacerda in Rio, thus signifying a shift to the conservative right in Rio and a turn toward progressive politics in Pernambuco. Freire, Arraes, and Julião had frequent contacts with the ISEB: "The institute had tremendous influence on the intellectual elite in the Northeast, especially in Pernambuco. Paulo Freire acknowledged that his work was inspired by Vieira Pinto. ISEB publications were widely distributed in the Northeast and in the rest of the country."[13]

[13] In an extensive interview (1985), Freire speaks of his participation in the ISEB and believed that people did not understand its significance. He had come to know several Isebianos before the coup, including Álvaro Vieira Pinto who he felt was unjustly treated: "Álvaro was a great intellectual, but a timid man ... who spoke, in theoretical terms, mostly of a critical consciousness." Exiled to Chile in 1964, he spent time with Pinto there, returning to Brazil in 1967.

Martins lamented that his research at the ISEB on the evolution of Brazilian political thought from the time of independence to the present was lost in the 1964 coup, when the police confiscated all materials from the ISEB: "My research defended the central ISEB premise that Brazilian political thought was very much influenced by external fads and was a type of *cultural dependency.*" Later, this idea of dependency in the work of Fernando Henrique Cardoso and others was very popular in São Paulo, but "for me it was a kind of déjà-vu, because at ISEB this was our central idea." He felt that the work of Celso Furtado, Guerreiro Ramos, and others was a denunciation of this situation of dependency: "Thus, our research was enormous, done with great difficulty at the National Library. At the outset we had to find all original material dating from nineteenth-century Brazilian thought. When we were about to begin the twentieth century, the research was halted and confiscated by the police."

The younger staff of the ISEB, in particular Pedro Celso Cavalcanti, Pedro Alcântara, and Joel Bergaman, were all trained in history and influenced by Nelson Werneck Sodré. They wrote the new version of the *Manual da história do Brasil (A nova história)* as an initiative to publish and disseminate work for general consumption. Whereas in the early years Helio Jaguaribe and Guerreiro Ramos held the belief that ISEB courses were only to be offered to high public officials of the government, with the aim of training a technocratic elite of public officials and providing them with scientific, political, and ideological training, toward the end there was a great change at the ISEB. The regular courses remained structurally the same, but the specialized courses were open to graduate students, union activists, and lower officers (sergeants) of the Armed Forces. With its new audience, ISEB publications also changed in format and distribution, moving from the official government press to the pamphlets of the *Cadernos do Povo Brasileiro* and booklets called *História Nova*. These were geared toward the general public and were, in particular, distributed through the CPC and its projects in literature, theater, cinema, and record production: "There was an influence of the ISEB upon the CPC, but we had no formal joint project, even though we also formed CPCs in Recife, Bahia, Minas Gerais, and São Paulo."

The coup of 1964 and the closure of the ISEB was in part a reaction to its outreach to lower ranking army officers. The ISEB and the ESG were in constant competition. Although the ISEB had a larger audience than the ESG, the forms of nationalism espoused by the ISEB and the ESG were totally different: "Whereas the ESG notion of nationalism was very influenced by Western thinking on interdependence and alliance with the international bourgeoisie, the ISEB understanding of nationalism was influenced by the idea of an alliance between the State and the national bourgeoisie. The ISEB drew heavily from ECLA and its mainstream thinking through the work of Celso and others."

Martins believed that the ISEB contributed very little intellectually because it was not a scientific-academic school; it was much more a political-ideological movement. He believed that if it had survived in 1964, it would have developed more empirical research because the younger staff were trained political scientists, and they wanted to do more empirical work. He recalled that, in São Paulo, there was great resistance to the ISEB and that Paulista intellectuals refused to participate in any joint projects. The Rio group wanted to form a new journal and include Paul Singer and Fernando Henrique Cardoso on a joint editorial board, but the São Paulo group refused because they thought that the ISEB was too political and less academic.

In 1963, Martins worked with the Arraes government in Pernambuco, mainly due to his experience at the CPC. He developed a training course for municipal officials: "I invited Carlos Lessa, Fernando Henrique, and Caio Prado Júnior to develop the six-month course with me. Wanderley Guilherme dos Santos taught sociology, Caio Prado Júnior history, Carlos Lessa economics, and I political science." After the coup of 1964, he participated in the founding of the IUPERJ with Wanderley Guilherme and Cândido Mendes de Almeida. In 1966, he went to Chile for master studies, then to the University of Essex for further work. He returned to Rio in 1969 and joined the CEBRAP group in São Paulo (interview, São Paulo, September 19, 1983).

One of Martins's earliest writings focused on the question of a popular culture (1963), in which he identified his vision of revolutionary culture and cultural reform through his activities in the CPC with attention paid to such questions as cultural alienation, popular culture, false consciousness, and organization of popular culture. He also contributed an important work (1977) on the capitalist state, emphasizing its three forms (capitalism of the bourgeois state, capitalism of the transition state, capitalism of the autonomous state), an analysis of change through crisis in the political model, and an assessment of external politics through the 1964–1974 period of the military dictatorship. Finally, he looked (n.d.) at U.S. and Brazilian relations before and after the 1964 coup and argued that the power structure tends to generate a "moderate" nationalist tendency with an emphasis on exports subject to national control and that this power structure is also associated with a "moderate" populism under the dominant coalition of the exporting industrial bourgeoisie and most of the nonexporting *latifundio* sector. He believed that the cause of the downfall of this coalition was "the failure to build a new power structure to bring about a revolutionary socialist movement" (3). He argued that the domestic bourgeoisie defined the limits and goals of the nationalist movement and that the alliances behind the movement tended to exaggerate the importance of the national bourgeoisie. Similar to the subimperialist model described by Ruy Mauro Marini after the coup (12), the liberal imperialism of an internationalist bourgeoisie under Castelo Branco and his national authoritarianism model were based on "the joint expansion and centralization shared by the State and foreign capital" (41).

Osny Duarte Pereira, a journalist and progressive jurist during the later years of the ISEB, wrote several books about the legal aspects related to foreign domination and imperialism. He believed that the ISEB was founded largely by *integalistas* who awakened to their earlier positions and opposed imperialism. He characterized the crisis within the ISEB as a personal dispute rather than one motivated by ideological differences, but felt that it also reflected a shift from an *integralista* position to an anti-latifundist and anti-imperialist stance. He believed that, in its infancy, the ISEB manifested only fascist tendencies but later became nationalist in its outlook.

He joined the ISEB in 1961, replacing Cândido Mendes de Almeida as head of the department of political science. He and others lectured on national problems and national development at a time when funding was scarce due to a congressional campaign against the ISEB. Influential among students, he felt that the ISEB had had little impact on the military except for some officers who attended courses and that it certainly did not hold sway among the elites. Among its publications, those of Vieira Pinto he held as being most important, with the writings of Corbisier and Guerreiro Ramos also playing an essential role. Although *Cadernos de Nosso Tempo* was not widely known, the *Cadernos do Povo* series was especially influential, while the Editora Brasiliense "was important and represented some communist thinking."

He defined nationalism as "a political manifestation within the economy that stirs the nation to struggle against the forces of imperialism and *latifundia*." According to Pereira, nationalism in Brazil could be understood through Petrobrás, Volta Redonda, and the State. Vargas was important for nationalism, he argued, despite his vacillation, errors, ambivalence, and compromises with imperialism; Kubitschek was a developmentalist, not a nationalist, who encouraged foreign capital; Quadros was ambivalent and his nationalism contributed to his popularity; and Goulart was a great nationalist, as demonstrated by his intervention in the iron and steel industry (interview, Rio de Janeiro, May 31, 1967).

Pereira's writings focused on nationalism and constitutional law (1960, 1962), resistance against multinationals (1975), a case study (1967) on the iron and steel industry, and his experience in the ISEB (1963, 1995).

Wanderley Guilherme dos Santos, born in Rio and educated in philosophy from 1955 to 1958, was intensely interested in politics, eventually obtaining his doctorate in political science at Stanford University. During the early 1960s, he taught philosophy at the ISEB, focusing on three great influences: Vargas, Marx, and Ortega y Gassett. He taught the history of nationalism in Brazil and dated underdevelopment to redemocratization after the fall of Vargas in 1945 and a frustrating period of legalization for the PCB in which efforts were made to form a popular university. About 1950, there was a clamor in defense of petroleum, and a Centro de Estudos de Defesa do Petroleo was formed. In particular, the Clube Militar promoted nationalism at a time coinciding with the activities of the Grupo de Itatiaia, while at the USP a more academically oriented movement emerged within the school of philosophy, where French professors were recruited in the social sciences. Santos believed that the first cultural movement of any consequence was the Grupo de Itatiaia and the aggregation of intellectuals such as Corbisier, Ramos, and Vieira Pinto who shifted from integralism to a progressive and popular position: "Any characterization of these people as fascists, however, could not hold up in an examination of their intellectual activity."

He described the beginnings of the ISEB as homogeneous despite different perspectives on development, nationalism, and cultural independence. Once attention shifted from agrarian development to industrial development, the major question was to determine the type of development and the role that foreign capital would play. Santos believed that Jaguaribe's book was a first attempt to answer that question, yet the debate that followed its publication and especially student reaction to it led to Jaguaribe's marginalization and resignation, thus allowing the ISEB to elaborate a progressive line of research and thought. When it was necessary to distribute funding more equitably among the departments, Ramos also resigned, under the pretext that funds had dried up and impacted his ability to move projects along. Cândido Mendes de Almeida opted to join the government of Jânio Quadros in

1960, at a time when the government considered terminating the ISEB altogether. During 1960 to 1962, there were no factions within the ISEB because everyone struggled to survive. In 1963 and 1964, there were differences, for example, between the younger group and those who carried on from the past. Representatives of the UNE frequently visited the ISEB as it turned toward student radicalism. Vieira Pinto reached out not only to students, but also to labor leaders and members of the parliamentary nationalist front, but no formal accords were reached with them: "It is my sense that the student leadership and the parliamentary front leaders were more influential with the ISEB than vice versa, but that the ISEB was influential in the political arena. Under Goulart relations between the government and the ISEB improved immensely."

Santos felt that the ISEB outreach and its intellectual production were substantial: "The influence of the ISEB on the Brazilian elite was enormous and remains with us until today. All this effort to modernize Brazil is a product of the ISEB." While Jaguaribe "coalesced" the intellectual groups, Guerreiro Ramos and Vieira Pinto were "theorists who most advanced an ideology of nationalism," and Nelson Werneck was "an organizer of nationalism." The ISEB represented "an effort to discover Brazilian political social thought, to transcend alienated culture, to direct culture toward national interests, and to build on social thought reaching back to the last century."

According to Santos, the ISEB mission was facilitated partially by other cultural influences, including O Semanário, which was "polemical"; Editora Fulgor, "journalistic and nationalist but not necessarily doctrinaire"; the Revista Brasiliense, "broad in its view, very open, in assimilating multiple progressive positions within nationalism"; and the pamphlets of the Universdade de Povo, which he characterized as "not very influential." Politicians contributed in varying ways: Vargas "ushered in a nationalist political style that was influential to 1964"; Kubitschek "was a developmentalist, not a nationalist, but willing to accept nationalism"; Quadros was nationalist during his brief tenure and "obsessive about absorbing total power"; while Goulart "simply desired more power," Arraes "did not believe that he had the power to carry out his nationalist policies," Brizzola "radicalized nationalism as he sought changes in the structure of the country," and Lacerda was "permanently radical in all the sense of nationalism."

Santos believed that "nationalism lacked a coherent political program and must be tied to socialism" (interview Rio de Janeiro, May 5, 9, 19, 1967). In a book (1962a) published by the ISEB, he identified contradictions within Brazilian capitalism through a class analysis of the bourgeoisie, workers, and peasants and the role of imperialism while arguing that the rapid advance of capitalism after 1930 was due to a dominant alliance of the bourgeoisie with the exporting *latifundist* class. Similar to Boris Fausto, he interpreted the 1930 revolution as "a coup of the bourgeoisie."

Pessimistic about the prospects for reforms (1963c), Santos argued that the national bourgeoisie could not lead capitalist development in Brazil because it would not relinquish its own interests. He also was concerned with the politics of compromise and the ideological constraints of the national bourgeoisie in its ties with imperialism. He analyzed the limits for structural reform during the Goulart regime, the nationalist criticism of foreign capital, and the problem of agrarian reform. He revealed why the national bourgeoisie, in following a populist road, was unable to lead a struggle against imperialism. Skeptical about populism as a reformist way to incrementally achieve structural change, he called on progressive militants to "seize the hegemony of Brazilian society" (90). He argued (1962b, 1963a, 1963b, 1986) that the 1964 coup emanated from a political crisis within the coalition of the PSD and PTB that had sustained Vargas and his successors in power (1966: 57).

Santos looked at various forms of liberalism (1978a and 1978b) and traced (1977, 1978a, 1978b) its role in Brazil since colonial times. This historical analysis drew from Oliveira Vianna's notion that "the building of a liberal society demands a state strong enough to break the bonds and linkages of the family-based society prevailing in Brazil" (32). Politicians and intellectuals actually pursued this idea through the Vargas revolution of 1930.

In an analysis (1978b) of the Geisel military regime, Santos questioned whether an authoritarian political regime could bring about change through conventional political means, and he was concerned with how authoritarianism can be superseded by democracy and the necessity of dealing with social justice, arguing that "the conversion of an authoritarian system to a stable democratic regime depends on the existence of a strong social democratic party" (16).

He offered observations (1988) on the political chaos of the democratic opening. Later, as a co-author with Jaguaribe and others (Jaguaribe et al., 2000[1986]), he advocated a structural approach to solving the problem of poverty in Brazil. Having once been critical of Jaguaribe, the two collaborated a generation later.

Álvaro Vieira Pinto was a philosophy professor of Plato and Kant and, in the view of Carlos Estevem Martins, entered the ISEB "without any notion of political life or of political conjuncture." Yet, in a very short time, he was "politicized" and assumed the leadership of the ISEB, bringing with him with an academic orientation very different from that of Jaguaribe. Initially, he was not a Marxist, but "through the ISEB he came into contact with Marx and Mao." He was attracted to the Marxist sector of the ISEB under Nelson Werneck Sodré. He also learned from the writings of Mao Zedong, because "Mao was very much read at ISEB, particularly his law of the hierarchy of contradictions (principal and secondary contradictions)," and he had "incredible intellectual baggage, and was a true scholar." Vieira Pinto had a scientific-academic knowledge of medicine, mathematics, physics, history, and philosophy. He was a professor of the history of philosophy at the Universidade de Estado do Rio de Janeiro; spoke several languages, including Latin, French, German, English, and Russian; and also was a musician who played the violin. He attracted younger researchers to the ISEB, including Martins and Wanderley Guilherme dos Santos who "were prohibited from teaching at the university because of our political activism, even prohibited from entering the building of the university" (interview, Carlos Estevem Martins, São Paulo, September 19, 1983).

Vieira Pinto published important work, although his writings were not prolific and often tended to be philosophical, abstract, and sometimes difficult to understand. His early work with the ISEB included a volume on ideology and national development (1956) arguing that backward development in Brazil is due to "lack of objective consciousness of our reality" (14) and that "without an ideology of development there can be no national development" (29), although he makes clear that an ideology of development must not be confused with partisan politics (44). The ISEB also published his brief early essay on ideology and national development (1960[1956]) and a mimeographed anthology of philosophical texts for teaching (1959).

His activism sprang from his major ISEB study on conscience and national reality (1960). Motivated by the activism of the UNE, he argued (1962?) that university reform was linked to the reform of Brazilian society. He felt that students, not professors, should lead this social struggle for reform (13–14), believing that a professor represents the dominant groups in society and thus contributes to the shaping of an elitist culture that works to the detriment of the mass of workers: "A university of an underdeveloped country lacks the ideological conditions that the people need to produce an authentic culture" (48). He also believed that development was not possible in a country dependent on foreign capital, where professors are material agents of this relationship, and where their culture does not allow them to overcome the collective alienation of the university (55). He criticized Brazilian education: "it was always a function of the interests of the dominant classes" (135) to oppose any deep university reform because a solution does not lie with leaving intact "the dominant social apparatus" but in "reforming the relations of the university with the reality of the country" (146). Thus, a student committee could plan for reform, engage in intense political struggle, and pressure higher authority for change, not only in the university but also in society at large (152–155). Both students and professors may share equally in the governance of the university, one that must become a university of the people and open to all those qualified to study there (157–162). He also wrote (1963) on methodological considerations for a definition of underdevelopment, as well as a text in the *Universidade do Povo* series (1975) on why the wealthy do not participate in labor strikes. Educational reform permeated the UNE during the early 1960s, and there was a clear relationship with the ISEB. For example, economist José Serra (1980: 23–30) was UNE president from 1963 to 1964 and Jacob Gorender, a communist, was involved in its popular mobilization.

THE ISEB AND THE ESG

Our interviews touched on the relationship of the ISEB and the ESG. Although various ISEB people lectured at the ESG, Cândido Mendes de Almeida (1957) and Alberto Guerreiro Ramos (1957b) published in the *Revista de Clube Militar*, and lower ranking military personnel attended ISEB courses and lectures, there is little evidence to suggest that the ISEB influenced the military. Clearly, its outreach aimed at drawing lower ranking and younger officers into its thinking about nationalism and development. René Dreifus, who has written on the coup (1981), felt that among the military officers purged by the coup, none was influenced by the ISEB, although some of them may have used it as a means for reaching out to the universities. Furthermore, the ISEB was closed down, partially due to its being ineffective or inoperative (Dreifus interview, Rio de Janeiro, July 6, 1995). Certainly, the ESG was caught up in the idea of nationalism through modernizing the country, building its infrastructure, and bringing together disparate geographical regions. Like the ISEB, its theoretical vision incorporated the nation into its outlook, as attested to in the thought of General Golbery do Couto e Silva, whose military planning for Brazil mapped out the country and its regions (1955) and elaborated strategical considerations related to national security (1957). He was influential in the early years after the 1964 coup when he guided the imposition of a national security state as the *eminence gris* of the regime. The principal tenets of this doctrine included the belief that Brazil must serve as a junior partner of the United States in the struggle against communist subversion in Latin America and that this subversion must be countered from within, thus necessitating a large repressive network of intelligence agencies operating under the military. There ensued fifteen years of repression, constraints on freedoms, censorship, disappearances, and torture.

The 1964 coup abruptly closed the ISEB, which was seen as subversive[14] to a military whose own progressive roots traced back to *tenentismo* in the 1920s (Rios, 1966) but whose authoritarian tendencies conflicted with civil society (Martins Filho, 1987, 1995). The foundation for military rule can be traced to 1949 and U.S. influence and attention to the national security state; this considerably influenced emerging doctrine, the role of the military, and the national objectives that evolved within the ESG (Peregrino, 1966). Further light was shed on this theme by Bolivar Meirelles (1990) who delved into the ideological groups and conflict within the armed forces from 1945 to 1964, in particular focusing on the ESG and its advocacy of the doctrine of national security while showing how nationalist groups were oriented toward the country's economic independence, an expansion of democratic liberties, and the formation of a peasant–workers alliance with both petty and national bourgeoisie in an effort to represent anti-imperialist forces within the armed forces. Meirelles identified ideological confrontations within the armed forces and the difficulty of the ESG (with its nationalist ideology) to confront and transcend the systematization of U.S. imperialism in Brazil. The link of militarism to imperialism is identifiable before and after the 1964 coup (Cannabrava Filho, 1970). This link relates to a

---

[14] *O Globo* dedicated a supplement to the ISEB and its history (see Editors O Globo, 1960) that identified communists within the ISEB: Milton Coelho da Graça, administrator in charge of ISEB courses who allegedly organized a faction of the PCB within the ISEB; Antônio Ferreira Paim, ISEB researcher who participated in a training course in the Soviet Union and worked two years for Radio Moscow and married a Russian; and Moacir Paixão e Silva, an ISEB instructor and member of the PCB and an editor of *Estudos Sociais*. This historical account also emphasized integralist roots, including the participation of Almeida Salles and Roland Corbisier, and affirmed that Corbisier wanted to make the ISEB into a partisan group and a rival to the ESG.

theoretical discussion (Burgess and Wolf, 1979) about the power and dominance of the military through the ideas of the ESG; particularly those concepts that guide military thinking and affirm that the state serves international capital in addition to national capital linked to foreign capital (19). This is a theme that Philippe Faucher explored in his serious study (1981) of the military from 1962 to 1977, which identified the state as exceptional within a dependent capitalist society. Journalist Ana Lagôa (1983) revealed how the Sistema Nacional de Informações (SNI) operated under military rule, together with diagrams and data about a propaganda agency originally modeled after the National Security Agency in the United States, while Maria Helena Alves (1985) incisively analyzed the national security state in Brazil after 1964 and how 700,000 persons were organized into a network of intelligence agencies operating under the military executive to implement an exploitative model of capitalist development, repression over politics, and manipulative control over the labor unions.

NATIONALISM AND THE RIO LEFT PRESS

The conscious effort to build an ideology of nationalism and development through the ISEB in Rio after Vargas's suicide influenced efforts to tie politics to the sentiments of nationalism through the political parties and the ensuing governments. With its policies of promoting nationalism and democracy, opposing imperialism, and anticipating the evolution of a genuine national bourgeoisie that could build the means and forces of production to a level that would benefit the urban and rural working classes, the PCB was particularly active in arousing public interest in national causes. Yet the PCB faced internal unrest. Its secretary general, Luiz Carlos Prestes, was a popular figure whose fame stemmed from the revolts of army *tenentes* (lieutenants) in 1922 and 1924 and his ensuing march through the backlands (1924–1927) in defiance of the ruling oligarchies of São Paulo and Minas Gerais. Banned and censored as a party for most of the years since the PCB's founding in 1922 and until the middle 1980s, when political parties were able to achieve legitimacy, the party experienced a brief period of legitimacy when, in December 1945, Prestes was elected a federal senator along with a dozen party federal deputies. In May 1947, the party was again outlawed. The debate within party circles was reflected in its monthly theoretical journal, *Novos Tempos*, first published in September 1957 with a mission statement that Marxism would guide its analysis. A schism appeared within the party in August 1954, when it opted for a program of national salvation after the death of Stalin in 1953 and the attacks on cult of personality. Thereafter, the party dedicated attention to Brazilian nationalism (Peralva, 1957a; Peralva et al., 1957b), while one of its leading intellectuals, Nelson Werneck Sodré, became influential in debates and writings within the ISEB. *Novos Tempos* included an attack by Calvino Filho (1957) on renowned historian Caio Prado Júnior, a prestigious party member who had criticized a Soviet manual on political economy.

The PCP also launched a monthly *Novos Rumos* that focused on national questions and issues. Edited by Osvaldo Peralva, Leôncio Basbaum, Roberto Morena, and others, it appeared in six numbers from September 1957 to April 1958. It aimed to promote debates within the party after Stalin's death while aligning itself with outside currents oriented toward forming a nationalist front for the bourgeoisie and working class. In the initial issue, Teixeira (1957) outlined conditions aimed at helping a national bourgeoisie evolve as a progressive movement in the first phase of revolution: dependency on North American imperialism, allegiance of the *latifundio* to imperialist exploitation, impoverished people living in a wealthy country, problematic industrial development, and an urban working class with a tradition of struggle existing alongside rural workers who have little experience with struggle. In an effort to reach beyond party circles, *Novos Rumos* published weekly from 1958 to early 1964, shifting its attention from theory to themes of nationalism within the party and in the emerging broad nationalist movement that sought more autonomy and changes through radical reform.

A broad coalition of progressive activists, intellectuals, and journalists clustered around another weekly, *O Semanário*, dedicated to elaborate polemics, analysis, and the theoretical explanation of nationalism. Edited in Rio de Janeiro under Oswaldo Costa and an editorial committee that included Hermano Alves and collaborators such as Newton Carlos and Milton Campos, *O Semanário* first appeared on April 5–12, 1956, and closed with the coup (no. 376 March 19–April 1, 1964). It published an array of themes on national interests and foreign threats (see Table 2.1). With the announcement of a new phase, *O Semanário* (no. 26, September 27–October 4, 1956) identified its mission as a defense of the Brazilian national interests and people, especially against foreign "trusts" who exploit and oppress 85 percent of the Brazilian press. Thereafter, it defined nationalism and its tenets, with Oswaldo Costa identifying nationalism as a historical process (1956) and Pedro Dantas laying out his concerns with the struggle against imperialism and exploitation. A manifesto presented by Oswaldo Lima Filho (1956) to the Chamber of Deputies included the platform of the Frente Parlamentar Nacionalista, which called for struggle on behalf of the national economy, revision of treaties to protect national interests, building the industrial base, intervention by the state to accelerate the development of the country, defense of national resources, controls on excessive profits, nationalization of publicity agencies, resistance to private monopolies, improvement of work conditions in the countryside and implementation of an agrarian reform, balancing of income and development among regions of the country, and defense of the cultural riches of the nation. Jorge Zarifhetto (1957) attempted to characterize nationalism as a spontaneous phenomenon that surges, sometimes without a leader, through nationalists who oppose U.S. imperialist policy and advocate that the state explore for petroleum, minerals, and hydroelectric power. David Serra (1957) described nationalism as opposing colonizing capital but channeling investment toward national development.

Nationalism is the prominent theme in O *Semanário*, as shown in Table 2.1. Nearly 22 percent of the themes identified in the weekly publication over its eight-year existence pertain specifically to nationalism and its manifestations; this intensifies to nearly a third of all content in 1959–1960. There was occasional reference made to nationalization of foreign enterprise, and national security was a concern. The petroleum issue dominated attention, sparked in part by Jaguaribe's policy recommendation that foreign capital be involved. Attention to agricultural issues was prominent, often referring to the need for agrarian reform in the countryside but more frequently looking at commodities on the world market such as coffee, cotton, rubber, and wheat. These and other commodities were seen as being manipulated by the United States and other world powers in the global market, including trade arrangements that benefit outside business and investments in Brazil. Coffee usually was discussed in relation to its growing regions (São Paulo and Paraná), wheat to the south, and rubber in the Amazon. There was enormous concern about banking and the influence of the World Bank and the International Monetary Fund (IMF) and their financial ties with Brazil, as well as about foreign capital and investment and control over domestic manufacturing. Feature stories emphasized sharp differences between classes, alluding to an ongoing class struggle among the peasantry in the countryside, the working class in the large cities,

TABLE 2.1   O Semanário *Thematic Content 1956–1964*

Volumes Numbers	1 (1–38)	2 (39–89)	3 (90–141)	4 (142–191)	5 (192–241)	6 (243–278)	7 (279–293)	8 (332–373)	Totals:
Agriculture	21	36	44	60	39	70	40	28	338
	8.54%	4.41%	5.03%	4.48%	5.39%	8.87%	16.95%	10.04%	6.38%
Banking	16	48	36	97	27	42	10	36	312
	6.50%	5.88%	4.12%	7.25%	3.73%	5.32%	4.24%	12.90%	5.89%
Class	3	1	0	12	21	26	22	5	90
	1.22%	0.12%	0.00%	0.90%	2.90%	3.30%	9.32%	1.79%	1.70%
Colonialism	12	64	73	73	40	25	19	11	317
& Imperialism	4.88%	7.84%	8.35%	5.46%	5.53%	3.17%	8.05%	3.94%	5.98%
Culture	2	8	18	4	13	17	0	1	63
	0.81%	0.98%	2.06%	0.30%	1.80%	2.15%	0.00%	1.11%	1.19%
Democracy	2	1	2	4	0	3	1	2	15
	0.81%	0.12%	0.23%	0.30%	0.00%	0.38%	0.42%	1.06%	0.28%
Economy	75	292	275	359	231	176	41	56	1505
	30.49%	35.78%	31.46%	26.83%	31.95%	22.31%	17.37%	20.07%	28.39%
Intellectuals	0	3	12	56	12	26	0	3	112
	0.00%	0.37%	1.37%	4.19%	1.66%	3.30%	0.00%	1.08%	2.11%
International	14	19	29	41	46	58	14	24	245
Influence	5.69%	2.33%	3.32%	3.06%	6.36%	7.35%	5.93%	8.60%	4.62%
Labor	8	12	10	55	32	62	27	11	217
	3.25%	1.47%	1.14%	4.11%	4.43%	7.86%	11.44%	3.94%	4.09%
Local &	3	13	28	15	24	32	10	12	137
Regional	1.22%	1.59%	3.20%	1.12%	3.32%	4.06%	4.24%	6.35%	2.58%
Military	4	21	20	52	3	25	2	21	148
	1.63%	2.57%	2.29%	3.89%	0.41%	3.17%	0.85%	7.53%	2.79%
Nationalism	44	224	258	304	167	101	27	40	1165
	17.89%	27.45%	29.52%	22.72%	23.10%	12.80%	11.44%	14.34%	21.98%
Politics	14	40	28	140	47	78	2	13	362
	5.69%	4.90%	3.20%	10.46%	6.50%	9.89%	0.85%	4.66%	6.83%
Revolution	2	1	2	5	2	9	2	6	29
	0.81%	0.12%	0.23%	0.37%	0.28%	1.14%	0.85%	2.15%	0.55%
Social	15	25	31	47	19	35	16	9	197
	6.10%	3.06%	3.55%	3.51%	2.63%	4.44%	6.78%	3.23%	3.72%
Socialism	3	2	2	3	0	4	3	1	18
	1.22%	0.25%	0.23%	0.22%	0.00%	0.51%	1.27%	0.53%	0.34%
State	8	6	6	11	0	0	0	0	31
	3.25%	0.74%	0.69%	0.82%	0.00%	0.00%	0.00%	0.00%	
Collection Totals:	246	816	874	1338	723	789	236	279	5301
	100.00.%	100.00%	100.00%	100.00%	100.00%	100.00%	100.00%	100.00%	100.00%

O Semanário issue numbers by year:
1. No. 1 (April 5–12, 1956) to No. 38 (December 2–27, 1956)
2. No. 39 (December 27, 1956–January 3, 1957) to No. 89 (December 19–26, 1957)
3. No. 90 (December 26, 1957–January 2, 1958) to No. 141 (December 25–31, 1958)
4. No. 142 (January 8–14, 1959) to No. 191 (December 26–January 1, 1960)
5. No. 192 (January 9–15, 1960) to No. 241 (December 26–January 1, 1961)
6. No. 243 (January 1–7, 1961) to No. 278 (September 26–October 2, 1961)
7. No. 279 (May 3, 1962) to No. 293 (August 9, 1962)
8. No. 332 (May 9–15, 1963) to 373 (February 27–March 4, 1964)

and the oligarchy and ruling classes located primarily in the center and south of the country.

Historical themes of colonialism and postcolonialism appeared frequently, along with fervent anticolonialism and anti-imperialism themes emphasizing selling out (*entreguismo*) and co-optation through dependency on foreign credit and investment, resulting in local and international exploitation. In the cultural sphere, there was frequent focus on foreign and domestic cinema, with a demand for national production and emphasis on national values; the press was often taken to task for its conservative stance, attributable to foreign control and influence over telecommunications. Democracy was associated with nationalism but with little effort made to elaborate any conceptualization of its meaning within Brazilian society.

The economy and all its issues was a major topic, with attention focusing on the national debt, national development, industrialization, trade, and finance and the key issues being the nationalization and control of energy and power, iron and steel, mineral resources, nuclear power, and petroleum. Inflation was of great concern, and poverty was identified everywhere in Brazil. Foreign and domestic "trusts" were blamed for many of these economic problems. Labor was also topical, with a focus on work strikes, trade unions, and syndical affairs and on segments of the labor force, such as metalworkers. Reports appeared on workers and their problems throughout the country and on peasant unions in the Northeast.

It was not surprising that, in late 1959, conservatives attacked the ISEB for its progressive and leftist leanings. Roland Corbisier (1959) responded to this "conspiracy against Brazilian nationalism," arguing that the ISEB was neither a center of subversive propaganda nor of communist orientation, that it did not oppose private capital nor advocate class struggle, and that it supported nationalism as a global ideology of development, representing the interests of national capital, the middle class, and the urban and rural proletariat. He affirmed that the ISEB did not advocate the socialization of the means of production but supported state intervention in the planning of the economy and the implementation of an economic infrastructure in the country. It did not defend proletarian internationalism but looked for national solutions to national problems, nor did it favor ultranationalism. It supported state control of petroleum, energy, and petrochemicals and restrictions on foreign investment. Nelson Werneck Sodré argued (1959) that nationalism was compatible with military organization, and he provided historical examples to support his thesis; even as he and others worked to establish close ties with the ESG, it was clear that the two organizations were incompatible (after May 1963, *O Semanário* reported left- and right-wing maneuvers within the armed forces, as well as the threat of right-wing activities of the Inter-American Development Bank and the possibility of a military coup). Occasional stories did not take seriously the "Sorbonne group" within the ESG and its fear of a populist left and the radical reforms under the Goulart regime. On the surface, the struggle appeared to be between the government and popular sectors, including labor, peasants, and students who favored some sort of revolutionary change, on the one hand, and a military aligned with conservative and ultraconservative groups who promoted a counter-revolution and repression of progressive forces, on the other. As the ESG evolved its approach and consolidated its resolve, the nationalists lacked unity, and the Goulart government found itself weak in the face of a strongly ideological and unified military group largely identified with the army.

Through local and regional coverage of the political parties, especially the PCB and leading communist personalities, attention was focused on civil rights since the 1930s under Vargas. The state was seen as a force for change, with development and nationalism mobilizing the broader population. Revolution as a theme appeared in historical examples such as Russia, China, Algeria, and Cuba but was not mixed with the polemics over nationalist issues nor elaborated in conceptual efforts to explain the meaning of nationalism. Among social issues covered were the struggle for a higher minimum salary and eradicating poverty and improving the welfare of the population. Themes of nationalism also became associated with the student movement as a force for reform and change alongside the emerging social movements of the times.

The role of Rio intellectuals was of concern, especially as reflected in differing perspectives, ideologies, and personalities within the ISEB, yet there was little reference made to Paulista intellectuals. Early content related to the debate around petroleum, some of it stimulated by the crisis within the ISEB over Helio Jaguaribe's controversial book (see Commentary 1958a, 1958b, 1958c, 1958d). Jaguaribe was seen as having sold out to foreign interests and willing to sacrifice national control of Petrobrás.[15] *O Semanário* covered the dispute between Jaguaribe and

[15] Later (Commentary, 1959a), there is a discussion of the resignation of the ISEB president, Roberto Saturnino Braga, related to a fervent attack by the UNE against the ISEB and Jaguaribe's book, accusing the ISEB of siding with Standard Oil and against Petrobrás.

Guerreiro Ramos that led eventually to the resignations of Jaguaribe and Roberto Campos, while Corbisier accused Ramos of abandoning the ISEB mission, becoming a martyr of nationalism, and leaving the ISEB for opportunistic reasons. This newspaper also was favorable to Guerreiro Ramos, first in a review (no. 46, February 14–21, 1957, 4) of his critical assessment of Brazilian sociology (1957d) and later of his ideas for a detailed economic plan, including attention to national bases, national ideology, development, and natural resources (Ramos, 1958a, 1958b, 1958c). Ramos argued (1959a) that nationalism was a means for solving problems because the elite lacked a national consciousness. Thus, development would occur through capitalist means, the working class needed more consciousness, the state had to organize the economy because private capital was limited, peripheral peoples would achieve full sovereignty through nationalism, and socialism was inevitable. Later, Ramos (1959b) focused on a typology of nationalism, portraying the Brazilian people as utilizing national resources to resolve problems. He also argued (Ramos, 1959c) that nationalism is necessary for those who lead when the masses lack consciousness.[16]

CADERNOS DO POVO AND OTHER POPULAR PAMPHLETS

In her doctoral dissertation, Angélica Lovato focused on the twenty-eight *Cadernos do Povo Brasileiro* pamphlets published from 1962 to 1964 by Énio Silveira and his publishing house, Editora Civilização Brasileira, and the series organizer, Álvaro Vieira Pinto. She emphasized (Lovato, 2009)

---

[16] Other ISEB intellectuals occasionally published in this paper, including Josué de Castro (1956) and Osny Duarte Pereira (1956) in defense of Petrobrás; later, Pereira (1959a) optimistically affirmed that nationalism would evolve with various tendencies and eventually supplant imperialism, while in another piece (1959b) he analyzed the impact of nationalism on the judicial system. Celso Furtado was reported as giving a talk at the ISEB in defense of the Northeast (*O Semanário*, no. 185 [November 14–20, 1959], 4) that later was published as *A operação nordeste* (1959). Issue 186 (November 21–26, 1959) provided support for the ISEB and Furtado, whereas no. 188 (December 5–11, 1959) contained elaborate discussion of the ISEB, its ideology, its courses of study, and its research. Sodré (1961b) argued for a realistic literature that favored human interests and needs rather than serving as a romantic instrument of the bourgeoisie, while Corbisier (1961) called for an alliance of socialists and workers. A favorable review (no. 273, August 26–September 2, 1961) of Vieira Pinto's book (1960) on conscience and national reality emphasized two types of consciences: one that ignores social conditions and consequently is subject to the material objectives it serves and leads to nationalist action; and the other that is able to recognize its objective conditions and is able to analyze objectively, resulting in revolutionary action.

the relationship between Silveira and the ISEB and the CPC under the UNE.[17] She also examined the influence and thought of Nelson Werneck Sodré.

Marilena Chauí analyzed discourse around national and popular movements of the 1960s. Not wanting to show the veracity or falseness of this early effort nor provide a social history of the period, she studied (1983) the rhetoric of a dynamic time while examining the *Cadernos do Povo Brasileiro* to show how themes such as nation-national and people-popular appear throughout. She characterized the pamphlets as heterogeneous, some as informative, others doctrinaire and pragmatic, and others calling for direct struggle. All are presented around four central ideas: the people and its vanguard, definition of nation and the anti-imperialist struggle, definition of the place of the state as promoter of a historical transformation initiated by the masses, and the idea of revolution. All the pamphlets are built upon dichotomies, antinomies, and antitheses that are presented as contradictions. The people are presented as good, orderly, peaceful, based on justice and disposed to organize collectively. The nation is presented as national sentiment and autodeterministic in the face of powerful evil forces. The politics of this period are distinguished between aspiration toward socialist revolution and bourgeois democracy (Chauí, 1983: 74). Antagonisms in the texts are evident between localism and cosmopolitanism, nationalism and internationalism, and localism and cosmopolitanism (96–101).[18]

---

[17] Barcellos (1994) has organized thirty-two essays by participants in the CPC and UNE, including Carlos Estevam Martins, Herbert de Souza, and José Serra.

[18] See the *Cadernos do Povo* series published in Rio by Editora Civilização Brasileira: no. 1, 1962, Francisco Julião, *Que são ligas camponesas?*; no. 2, 1962, Nelson Werneck Sodré, *Quem é o povo no Brasil?*; no. 3, 1962, Osny Duarte Pereira, *Quem faz as leis no Brasil?*; no. 4, 1962, Álvaro Vieira Pinto, *Por que os ricos não fazem greve?*; no. 5, 1962, Wanderley Guilherme, *Quem dará o golpe no Brasil?*; no. 6, 1962, Theotônio Júnior, *Quais são os inimigos do povo?*; no. 7, 1962, Bolivar Costa, *Quem pode fazer a revolução no Brasil?*; no. 8, 1963, Nestor de Holanda, *Como seria o Brasil socialista?*; no. 9, 1963, Franklin de Oliveira, *Que é a revolução brasileira?*; no. 10, 1963, Paulo R. Shilling, *Que é reforma agraria?*; no. 11, 1963, Maria Augusta Tibiricá Miranda, *Vamos nacionalizar a indústria farmacêutica?*; no. 12, 1963, Sylvio Monteiro, *Como atua o imperialismo ianque?*; no. 13, 1963, Jorge Miglioli, *Como são feitas as greves no Brasil?*; no. 14, 1963, Helga Hoffmann, *Como planejar nosso desenvolvimento?*; no. 15, 1963, Padre Aloisio Guerra, *A igreja está com o povo?*; no. 16, 1963, Aguinaldo Marques, *De que morre o nosso povo?*; no. 17, 1963, Edouard Bailby, *Que é o imperialismo?*; no. 18, Duarte Sérgio Guerra, *Por que existem analfabetos no Brasil?*; no. 19, 1963, João Pinheiro Neto, *Salário é causa de inflação?*; no. 20, 1963, Plínio de Abreu Ramos, *Como agem os grupos de pressão?*; no. 21, 1963, Vamireh Chacón, *Qual é a política externa conveniente*

Several popular pamphlet series appeared alongside the *Cadernos do Povo* during the early 1960s, such as the *Universidade do Povo* series (1963–1964), edited by Gondin da Fonseca, José Rêgo, and João Cunha Andrade and published by Editora Fulgor in São Paulo. This series stated its mission as one "to diffuse exact information and give the Brazilian people cultural bases that allow them to exercise their rights and duties."[19] The content of these pamphlets included such themes as guerrilla struggle, the Cuban Revolution, U.S. imperialism, poverty, agrarian reform, class struggle, and basic reforms under João Goulart. The *Coleção História Nova* series,[20] edited by Roberto Pontual and published in early 1964 in Rio, had as its intent to "reformulate in essence and method the study and teaching of our history" or to revise history. Authors included Joel Rufino dos Santos, Maurício Martins de Mello, Nelson Werneck Sodré,

ao Brasil?; no. 22, 1963, Virginio Santa Rosa, *Que foi o tenentismo?*; no. 23, 1964, Osny Duarte Pereira, *Que é a constituição?*; Extra, 1963, Barbosa Lima Sobrinho, *Deste quando somos nacionalistas?*; Extra, 1962, Franklin de Oliveira, *Revolução e contra-revolução no Brasil?*; Extra, 1962–1963, Affonso Romano de Sant'Anna et al., *Violão de rua*. 19, 3 vols.

[19] *Universidade do Povo* series Edited by Gondin da Fonseca, José Rêgo, and João Cunha Andrade. Published by Editora Fulgor in São Paulo; first published in 1963. The mission of this series was "to diffuse exact information and give the Brazilian people cultural bases that allow them to exercise their rights and duties." Volumes in order: no. 1, 1963, Gondin da Fonseca, *Guerra de Guerrilhas*, São Paulo: Editora Fulgor; no. 2, 1963, José Eêgo and Je. E. Estrêla, *Ianques contra Cuba (David enfrenta Gorilas)*; no. 3, 1963, Gondin da Fonseca, *A miséria é nossa!!!*; no. 4, 1961, Herculano Neves, *321 perguntas a um brasileiro*; no. 5, 1963, Esequiel Matinez Estrada e Siné, *A verdadeira história do tio sam*; no. 6, 1963, Eduardo Portella, *Política externa e povo livre*; no. 7, 1963, Gondin da Fonsca, *Jango fala a nação*; no. 8, 1963, Gondin da Fonseca, *Os gorilas, o povo e a reforma agraria. Manifesto dos bispos do Brasil*; no. 9, 1963, Jamil Alamansur Haddad, *Romance do rio da guarda*; no. 10, 1963, Barbosa Lima Sobrinho, *Máquinas para transformar cruzeiros em dólares*; no. 11, 1963, Brasil Bandecchi, *Origem do latifundio no Brasil*; no. 12, 1963, Miguel Arraes, *O povo no poder (discurso)*; no. 13, 1963, Luiz Osiris da Silva, *O que são as reformas de base?* no. 14, 1963, Unírio Machado, *A indústria da doença*; no. 15, 1963, Cid Franco, *Negrinho do viaduto e as classes conservadoras*; no. 16, 1963, Pompilio Diniz, *Canto da liberdade*; no. 17, 1963, Padre Aloísio Guerra, *O catolicismo ainda é cristão*; no. 18, 1963, Lenina Pomeranz, *Que é o salário?* no. 19, 1963, Arlindo A. Lucena, *"Bagrinhos" e tubarões*; no. 20, 1964, Sylvio Monteiro, *A ideologia do imperialismo*.

[20] *Coleção História Nova* edited by Roberto Pontual. Its mission is to "reformulate in essence and method the study and teaching of our history." Published in Rio de Janeiro in early 1964 as an effort to reinterpret aspects of Brazilian history. Authors include Joel Rufino dos Santos, Maurício Martins de Mello, Nelson Werneck Sodré, Pedro de Alcântara Figueira, Pedro Celso Uchôa Cavalcanate Neto, and Rubem César Fernandes. The titles of volumes in order: vol. 1, *O descobrimento do Brasil*; vol. 2, *A sociedade do açucar*; vol. 3, *As invasões holandesas*; vol. 4, *A expansão territorial*; vol. 5, *A decadência do regime colonial*; vol. 6, *A independência a República*; vol. 7, *Da independência de 1822*; vol. 8, *O sentido do abolição*; vol. 9, *O advento da república*; vol. 10, *O significado do Floreicnismo*.

Pedro de Alcântara Figueira, Pedro Celso Uchôa Cavalcante Neto, and Rubem César Fernandes, and the subject matter focused on the discovery of Brazil, sugar, the Dutch invasions, territorial expansion, the decadence of the colonial regime, independence and the republic, and abolition. Another series, *Cadernos de História*, appeared in São Paulo, published by Livraria Oblisco under the editorship of Brasil Bandecchi. Eleven titles appeared in 1964.[21]

LATER RIO INTELLECTUALS

Intellectual life may have diminished with the demise of the ISEB and the imposition of a military dictatorship after 1964, but despite repression, censorship, imprisonment, and exile, Rio intellectuals carried on with writing in newspapers, journals, and books. Eventually, with democratic opening in the early 1980s, they became visible in opposition politics. Among them were Carlos Nelson Coutinho and Leondor Kondor, as well as others activists.

Carlos Nelson Coutinho studied law and later philosophy in Bahia; upon his graduation from the university, he moved to Rio after the ISEB was closed down. But some of its ideas prevailed, particularly the notion that Brazil was in a stage of consolidating national capitalism against feudal agrarian society and imperialism. These ideas emanated from the PCB and were similar to ISEB thinking at a time when it was believed that Brazil was not fully capitalist. Coutinho felt that the Paulistas had an advantage, however, in that, from the beginning, they considered Brazil as capitalist. This position was evident in Caio Prado's *A revolução brasileira* (1966), which criticized the notion of stages that stated Brazil had to pass through a democratic national stage and later arrive at socialism: "I was a member of the PCB but disagreed with much of the party line and never was supportive of the ISEB ideas because they underestimated the question of class. I knew and sympathized with the work of Nelson Werneck Sodré. In 1964–1965 there were non-Soviet

---

[21] *Cadernos de História*, under the editorship of Brasil Bandecchi. Published in São Paulo by Livraria Oblisco. All titles published in 1964: no. 1, Memórias de Martin Afonso de Sousa; no. 2, Pêro de Magilhães Gandavo, *História da província Santa Cruz tratado da terra do Brasil*; no. 3, José Anchieta, *Informações do Brasil e suas cpitanias* (1584); no. 4, Brasil Bandecchi, *Origem do latifúndio no Brasil*; no. 5, André João Antonil, *Cultura e opulência do Brasil pelas minas do ouro*; no. 6, Pêro Lopes de Sousa, *Diário da navaegação*; no. 7, José Bonifácio de Andreda e Silva, *Escritos políticos*; no. 8, Perdigão Malheiro, *A escravidão Africana no Brasil*.

Marxist writers published in Brazil, for example Lukács, Gramsci, and Marcuse – writers that Perry Anderson called Western Marxists."

Coutinho felt that the "ISEB was absolutely fundamental because it formed a Brazilian cultural agenda on nationalism with its project of developmental nationalism and a popular base. A good share of leftist Brazilian thinking ran through the ISEB. Clearly, it was internally contradictory, yet what unified the ISEB was its advocacy of an ideology of developmental nationalism that at that moment was hegemonic in Brazil: developmental nationalism." He emphasized that sociologists at the USP known as Paulista Marxists introduced the question of populism, giving social class more importance than did the ISEB. The Paulista group was more correct in its view of what was happening in Brazil at the time. The ISEB was more an instrument of legitimizing a populist policy, whereas the Paulista group characterized the question of populism in the structural terms of that period and assumed a more critical stance in relation to that period. The Paulistas were tied to the university, whereas the ISEB clearly had a political purpose.

Coutinho knew Roberto Schwarz well, and we talked about Cândido Mendes de Almeida and his sympathy for the PT in 1994. He referred to the journal *Civilização Brasileiro* in Rio that included articles from both Rio and São Paulo intellectuals and ceased after the repression in 1968: "This journal was very important because it gives you an overview of intellectual life and ideas. One of its early essays by Cardoso on the Brazilian political model helps to understand his outlook after the 1964 coup. Celso Furtado's analysis at the time was also important." I discussed my interview with Fernando Henrique Cardoso in 1984, when he insisted at the time that he was a Marxist. Coutinho believed the work of Cardoso was not Marxist, yet at that time the influence of Marxism on his thinking was indisputable. He also felt that Giannotti (1985) had an important role in the *Capital* Group with his interesting emphasis on the young Marx.

Coutinho left the PCB in 1980 and, with Leondro Kondor and Armênio Guedes, founded a new group, although he was sympathetic to the PT after 1986 and, with Leondro, joined the party two years later: "My dissidence within the PCB was reflected in my writing on democracy as a universal value [1980] that was an effort to reformulate thinking within the party based on Eurocommunism and the idea that socialism without democracy was not viable. Our group within the PCB represented dissidence and opposed Luiz Carlos Prestes." The divergence was over the question of democracy: "We actually for a short time controlled the *Voz da Unidade*, the organ of the PCB after the return of the exiles. It was an attempt to convert the party to Eurocommunism along Italian lines. Part of our group left for the PMDB [Partido do Movimento Democrático], including Marco Aurélio Garcia, Luís Werneck Viana, and others, while I, Leondor, Davi Capistrano, and others turned to the PT."

He worked on the theories of Gramsci in 1966 and translated the first Gramscian book to Portuguese with a preface from Leondro: "His thought was influential, but I was more interested in Lukács, although later Gramsci definitely influenced my thinking and his influence as "the Marxist author who has most influenced the social thought of Brazil." Marxism has declined everywhere, he affirmed, but during the dictatorship, it was evident everywhere. Many of the writers of that period were inadequate, including Poulantzas and Marta Harnacker, whose book on historical materialism was "a schematic, full of errors, a bad introduction to Marxism." He believed *Crítica Marxista* to be an important journal and although he was encouraged to participate by Celso Frederico, Armando Boito opposed him (interview, Rio de Janeiro, July 27, 1994).[22]

Leondor Kondor joined the Communist Youth movement in 1951 and was a member of the PCB until 1981, his formation evolving from the influence of a father who was a medical doctor, a member of the PCB, taught him Marxism, and was imprisoned more than twenty times. During the 1970s, he studied for a doctorate in Germany and spent time in France. Influenced by Nelson Werneck Sodré, as a student, he participated in the ISEB, but in our interview he implied that Sodré may not have been a member of the PCB although he remained close to it. He studied with Vieira Pinto, who showed him how philosophers understood the reality

---

[22] Carlos Nelson's early writing focused largely on Gramsci, including an essay on cultural life in Brazil (1979) and the impact of the Prussian Road on intellectuals that argues that a national-popular culture would enhance intellectual life and free it from its weaknesses; a book (1980) on democracy, with an emphasis on Gramsci and the relevance of these ideas to Brazil; and an article (1981) on intellectuals and culture in Brazil. With Marco Aurélio Nogueira (1985), he edited an anthology on Gramsci and Latin America, including essays by José Arico, Juan Carlos Portantiero, and Arnaldo Córdava on Gramscian influence in Latin America; and an anthology (1986) of his writings on culture and ideology in Brazil. His important work on Gramsci (1989) covers his life, his theory of the state, socialist strategy, and the role of the political party and explores the universality of his concepts and their relevance to Brazil. An anthology of his essays (1990) includes work on intellectuals, cultural life in Brazil, an interpretative analysis of the thought of Caio Prado Júnior (167–185), and an overview of the importance of Gramsci in Brazil (199–213). His 1992 text on democracy, socialism, revolution, and Marxism appeared in the series *Polêmicas do Nosso Tempo*.

of society and could engage in political struggle, but he acknowledged that very few students attended Vieira Pinto's courses and understood his ideas and complicated political language. He also studied with Paulo de Castro, an exiled Portuguese in Brazil, and with Corbisier, "a curious figure" politically involved in the PT and an old-line Marxist of somewhat rigid views and originally involved in integralist politics. He was critical of Inácio Rangel, arguing that his views were confused.

Overall, he was skeptical of the ISEB model of developmental nationalism. He was closest to Carlos Nelson Coutinho in Rio after the 1964 coup. He felt that Marxism in Rio reflected the general crisis of Marxism: "There is a need to revise and renew, not only a Leninist model but recognition that Marx has helped us a great deal. Marx himself would have had difficulty understanding many of the currents." According to Kondor, there are few Marxists of importance in Rio, and the profile of the Carioca intellectual is different from that of São Paulo: "The Carioca improvises. History is marked by improvisation and lack of organization. A greater liberty and more specialization, less solidarity.... The Paulista is more organized, disciplined, industrious." He believed that Caio Prado Júnior and his "classical Marxism" had some influence over Rio intellectuals, especially Carlos Nelson.

The problem of the intellectual and the state, Kondor asserted, is that intellectuals tend not to be organic or sympathetic to the proletariat. He felt that Fernando Henrique was a supporter of liberalism, Roberto Schwarz was a militant, Michael Löwy a combative Trotskyist and Marxist, and Florestan Fernandes began his career as a conciliator and ended as a convinced radical. He identified as important Paulista intellectuals Fernando Novaes, Mário de Andrade, and Sêrgio Buarque de Holanda who were not really Marxists, but important intellectuals. He believed that Antônio Cândido first knew Marxism in 1963 and thereafter was recognized as culturally more Marxist than other Marxists, and that Ciro Cardoso was a historian who applied Marxist method with care (interview, Rio de Janeiro, July 29, 1991).[23]

Márcio Moreira Alves, as a journalist, political scientist trained at the University of Paris, and politician, criticized (1964) the military and its

---

[23] Among Kondor's work is a study on Brazilian intellectuals and Marxism (1991) that includes brief profiles of Nélson Werneck Sodré (75–78), Antônio Cândido (79–85), Roberto Schwarz (95–101), and Ciro Flamarion S. Cardoso (111–115). His anthology on Marx (1983) comprises essays by Brazilian progressive intellectuals José Arthur Giannotti, Maria da Conceição Tavares, Marilena Chauí, Moniz Bandeira, and Nelson Werneck Sodré.

handling of internal and external affairs. His exposé (1966) of authoritarian rule resulted in his expulsion from congress. Inspired by the urban guerrilla movements and the prospects for a Brazilian struggle against imperialism and the military, Alves published an overview of revolutionary Brazil (1973) and in Lisbon an account (1975) of the April 25, 1974, Portuguese revolution that toppled the old dictatorship. He also wrote (1978) on the progressive wing of the Catholic Church in Brazil. He believed that the alliance between the big bourgeoisie and the techno-bureaucracy of the state and between the techno-bureaucracy and the middle-level bourgeois elements of the state bureaucracy (such as Banco do Brasil and Petrobrás) were beginning to break down. These alliances were exacerbated by IMF demands to cut the funds for investment and maintenance of the state enterprises (interview, Rio de Janeiro, July 20, 1983).

Marcos Arruda, coordinator of the Políticas Alternativas para o Cono Sul (PACS) in Rio de Janeiro, economist, and "popular" educator, worked closely with Brazilian labor and cooperatives and was active early in the PT, particularly in social movements and issues around socioeconomic solidarity, sustainable development, and participatory democracy. His study of praxis and economic solidarity (2003) emanated from his close association with Paulo Friere and his literacy program during the 1970s. In my talk with him in the midst of the democratic opening, he felt that the financial sector and the government had created an "artificial crisis," so that inflation, recession, and unemployment were "deliberate policies intended as solutions to the crisis.... that we are facing an insurmountable conflict between the logic of capital and the logic of the people." His analysis emphasized a duality of power: "At the political level there is the duality between the military-technocratic power and the power of transnational capital that is hegemonic." At the time, he was pessimistic about forming a socialist party: "Each leftist party wants its own power bloc, and there is no desire to unify in order to defeat the immediate enemy. The PT has potential in the future, but today it lacks a clear direction" (interview, Rio de Janeiro, August 2, 1983). His criticism of the PT did not subside, as attested to in his famous letters to President Lula. Years later, Angela Mendes de Almeida, a Rio academic, concurred with this sentiment: "Brazilian intellectuals today are dispersed, there is no unity, no utility, no creativity. Life is complicated, everyone tends to their own affairs and problems" (interview, Rio de Janeiro, July 5, 1995).

Associated with the ISEB were prominent people from the Northeast, such as Celso Furtado (1958), but also *Miguel Arraes*, who was known not only for his progressive politics and three terms as governor of the Northeast state of Pernambuco, but also for his involvement with the ISEB during the early 1960s. Elected mayor of Recife in 1959, he represented a loose coalition of liberals, socialists, communists, progressive Catholics, students, and intellectuals. Arraes's overview of the economy (1971, 1974) emphasized dependence on foreign capital, the ruling elite and their domination, popular movements, the 1964 coup and the military regime, and the unity of the masses and the new stage of struggle. He was seen as a complex man who knew his way around the "old politics," yet "rode the crest of a new wave, which many thought would sweep the country" (Page, 1972: 52). When I talked with Arraes years after the coup, he was pessimistic about the world, and he was not optimistic about the democratic opening and its contradictions in Brazil (1982). He despaired the lack of a "people's spirit" such as existed before 1964, when the Brazilian system was emerging within capitalism. The present stage, he believed, had destroyed all the traditional roots of the people: "Humanity is in the process of destruction, the masses dispersed. Man has no basis for reaction. The rural farmer cannot be proletarianized. Motivation is lost. The state is manipulated by the state for the benefit of capitalists" (interview, Recife, July 30, 1983).

Manoel Correia de Andrade, a Recife intellectual committed to agrarian reform and the author of studies on the land and people of the Northeast (1964, 1968) was known for his work on development (1970) and was recognized in my interviews as sympathetic to the ISEB. *Josué de Castro* became known internationally for his work on hunger, especially in the Northeast and the Amazon, but also throughout the world (1961).

Luiz Carlos Bresser-Pereira (interview, Rio de Janeiro, June 11, 2009) placed himself alongside other developmental economists, such as the "conservative but intelligent" Delfim Netto and the "progressive" Maria da Conceição Tavares, a combative intellectual committed to ideas. Bresser revealed his early exposure to ideas on the left through conversations with Hermínio Sacchetta, a Marxist involved in Leftist activities and the editor of the newspaper *O Tempo* that was owned by Bresser's father. He considered the ISEB unique in its fundamental idea of development and its roots dating to the 1930s and the rise of a state bureaucracy and industrialization accompanied by a populist pact between the bourgeoisie and labor. ISEB's great contribution was its realization that Vargas was leading a developmental political pact, together with the industrial (national) bourgeoisie, the urban workers, the public bureaucracy, and non-exporting sectors of the old oligarchy that successfully brought about the national and industrial revolution of Brazil. Ideologically, he said, the ISEB was aligned with the idea that a national bourgeoisie could foment development. The alliance with labor served industrialization and the export of manufactured goods in the mid-1950s. The crisis was the consequence of the collapse of this alliance, which led to the defeat of Lott and the victory of Quadros. Lott was a conservative supported by the left, including the communists, because he favored nationalism: "The *fatos novos* or new facts were the consolidation of the national bourgeoisie and the continued dominance of the oligarchy at the end of the 1950s. Another fact was the emergence of movements of industrialists and the formation of various pacts. The ISEB appears as the workers were organizing. A domestic market surges. International industrial groups invest, and thus nationalist sentiment arises and anti-imperialist sentiment arises as a consequence."

Bresser believed that, after 1964, the social scientists of the USP and, indeed, almost all of the left in Brazil were also active: Prado Júnior published his important work criticizing the national bourgeoisie, and Cardoso and others shifted their analyses along a new path. At the same time, they were critical of the ISEB: "Its historical role was shaped by Jaguaribe, who showed his understanding of earlier influences and carried the movement forward. Rangel was a student of Marx and focused on the dialectic within Marx. Ramos went to Los Angeles and shifted his interests. He was an important person with his *A reducção sociológica* and was a great critic of North American functionalism, even before C. Wright Mills. Jaguaribe wrote his book on structural-functonalism but was not so influential."

Bresser acknowledged little contact with the ISEB: "I knew Mendes de Almeida a little because of our affiliation with Catholicism. I knew Inácio Rangel, and Guerreiro Ramos was a friend. After 1964, I paid more attention." Nor did he have much contact with São Paulo intellectuals because of his studies abroad. After his return, he turned to economic issues and eventually to the CEBRAP. "By the 1970s, there was a critique of these past ideas. We began to focus on authoritarianism. Generally, there was a lack of global analysis as we considered democracy and a search for a new pact between the national bourgeoisie and the working class" (interview, Fortaleza, May 29, 1984). Although he thought of himself as a political economist and published with CEBRAP, he was outside its circle of intellectuals. In fact, he considered his outlook rather close to the ISEB, but he did not engage with that group. His work included a general overview of the Brazilian economy (1982a) and a detailed look at accumulation (1986) and stagnation (2007). Other works dealt with populism and democracy (1985), the Collor government (1991), Brazilian development (1968, 1973, 1977, 1984a), the ISEB experiment in Rio (2004a, 2005), and Brazilian political economic theory (1982b, 1984b, 2011). Another theme of great interest in his work was the role of the state in Brazilian society, including a major work favoring the republican state (2004b) and theoretical perspectives (1984a, 1997) drawn from his experience as a minister of administration in the Cardoso government, in which he argued that, although neoliberalism might lead to trimming of the state's excessive bureaucracy, a proper approach would be to strengthen the state by making it more efficient. An example of his creative approaches was an early work on the state and technocracy (1981), in which he points to the emergence, in a time of the decline of the capitalist mode of production, of a technocratic or state mode of production and a new social class, the techno-bureaucracy, one different from those envisaged by Marx (interview, Rio de Janeiro, June 11, 2009).

His seminal essay on developmental theories and currents in Brazil (1982b, 1984) was a useful synthesis of various interpretations of national development in Brazil. While serving as a minister in the Cardoso government, he published (1993) an interesting essay, arguing that the State could be strengthened through administrative reform. In a 2011 work, he compares the views of the ECLA and ISEB intellectuals with those of the São Paulo sociology school and the national-dependent perspective with Marini's idea that dependency in Latin America is characterized by superexploitation. An extensive and sympathetic understanding of Bresser's accomplishments has been produced by Nakano, Rêgo, and Furquim (2004).

OTHER CULTURAL OUTLETS

The evolution of intellectual thinking in Rio de Janeiro was influenced by the *Cadernos da Hora Presente* (Rio de Janeiro, São Paulo, Belo Horizonte, and Recife), an integralist quarterly published from 1939 to 1940 (its initial issue included a piece by Plínio Salgado). Generally philosophical and literary, its content emanated among intellectuals close to Vargas, including Rômulo de Almeida (1939), who wrote on education and democracy, while Guerreiro Ramos (1939, 1940) examined contemporary poetry. On the left, the Communist monthly *Problemas: Revista Mensal de Cultura Política* published seventy-three issues from August 1947 to 1956 under the editorship of Carlos Marighella (issues 1–15) and Diógenes Arruda (issues 16–73). Issue content generally consisted of articles by Soviet and international communist figures, interspersed with writings by Prestes, Diógenes Arruda, and other Brazilian communists; there were frequent introductory notes on politics by the editor and occasional analysis on national issues, such as petroleum, although most of the content emanated from the Third International and its affiliates. Astrogildo Pereira, Jacob Gorender, and other intellectuals contributed to its content. The biweekly *Divulgação Marxista* was edited by Calvino

Filho and S. O. Hersen and also published in Rio de Janeiro from July 1, 1946 to January 10, 1947. In its initial mission statement, the editors emphasized the need to build understanding of Marxist theory that strongly supported the PCB, with special attention paid to the Soviet Union. Edited by communist intellectual and party activist Astrojildo Pereira from 1958 to 1964, *Estudos Sociais* first appeared in May–June 1958, with its mission statement describing it as "a journal of Marxist tendency trying to intervene democratically alongside other currents of thought in the debate on questions about our economic, social, and political reality." A tradition of Marxism had prevailed in the country since well before the founding of the PCB in 1922, but the party's clandestinity throughout much of its history had inhibited dissemination of its thought, and Marxist debates were clearly limited to closed meetings. Thus, *Estudos* sought to provoke Marxist debate and controversy.[24] For example, Jacob Gorender (1958) criticized Ramos and his *A redução sociológica* for arguing that an eclectic approach combining outside sociological work with Brazilian sociology cannot lead to an ideology of development and a national sociology (347).[25]

In what is perceived as an important conjuncture, the *Síntese Política Econômica Social* (SPES) was launched under editor Fernando Bastos de Avila, SJ, as a progressive Catholic journal with concern for national issues. Founded by a group of Catholic thinkers who offered a message of hope in a time of pessimism and sought new thinking and ideas about changing structures through dialectical thinking, each issue set forth a brief viewpoint followed by articles and analyses organized along political,

---

[24] Its first issue consisted of articles by Moacyr Paz on the problems of economic development, by Carlos Marighella on land income in Brazil, by Fragmon Carlos Borges on the historical origins of landed property, and by Miguel Costa Filho on work in Minas Gerais. Filling out the issue was a section "Problems in Debate" with a Marxist analysis on economic fundamentals and policy, and book reviews, including one by Ruy Facó on Leôncio Basbaum's *História sincera da república*. The second issue (July–August 1958) included a piece by Jacob Gorender on the crisis of foreign policy, an article by Edison Carneiro, and the first of a series by Herminio Linhares on resistance movements of the past. The ensuing issue (September–December 1958) included useful material on national questions, with attention paid by Mário Alves (1958) to the nationalist movement and the fragility of national capital. Later (1962), he returned to an analysis of the national bourgeoisie and its crisis.

[25] Other ISEB personalities in our study appeared in *Estudos Sociais*, including a favorable review by Fabio Lucas (1958) of Sodré's perspective on the Brazilian revolution (1963b), an essay by Gilberto Paim (1960) on foreign enterprise and capital, a review by Renato Guimarães (1962) of Celso Furtado's analysis of development and underdevelopment (1961), and Santos Guilherme's (1963) anticipation of the 1964 coup.

economic, and social questions. Its first issue of January–March 1959 offered a mission statement on structural change. The second proclaimed that the journal offered "synthesis and hope" to accompany the emergence of "a new national" thrust. It related Marxism to problems of national security, agrarian reform, and the ecological bases of industrialization. A particular emphasis on nationalism runs through its material, including an analysis by Bishop D. Agnello Rossi (1960) that Brazil faced a crisis of nationalism within its political party configuration and conjuncture.[26]

Edited in Rio by Lourival Coutinho, *Panfleto* appeared with a single number in June 1958, emphasizing three goals: nationalist action, nonpartisanship, and economic autonomy. Its goals included struggle against international colonizing capital, defense of national interests, and support for labor. It called for a return to the streets over questions of the nation and petroleum.

As a political and cultural journal edited by Eduardo Portella, *Tempo Brasileiro: Revista de Cultura* initially appeared September 1962 as a Rio quarterly and later published twice yearly. Its mission statement called on Brazilian intellectuals to confront and solve social problems. Its first issue included essays by Cândido Mendes de Almeida on international affairs, Vamireh Chacon on politics in the evolution of Brazilian development, and Jorge Amado on the struggle in Angola, whereas the second issue (September 1962) included essays by Wanderley Guilherme dos Santos, Helio Jaguaribe, and Inácio Rangel, and its last issue (no. 30–31 July–December 1972) turned to debates in Althusser, Balibar, and other Marxist writers.

From March 1965 to September 1968, the influential bimonthly *Revista Civilização Brasileiro* appeared in Rio, published by Editora Civilização Brasileira, with Ênio Silveira as editor, Roland Corbisier as secretary, and an advisory committee including Ferreira Gullar, Nelson Werneck Sodré, Octávio Ianni, and Oswaldo Gusmão. Its mission desired to be neither partisan nor sectarian, yet it expressed concern over foreign

---

[26] A progressive Catholic tendency within the ISEB manifested itself through the SPES, including a piece on state and education by Alceo Amoroso Lima (1958) and an analysis of clientelism, politics, and capitalism in an era of developmental hopes by Cândido Mendes de Almeida (1962). After examining revolutionary possibilities (5 no. 20, October–December 1963: 3–5 and 6 no. 21, January–March 1964: 3–7) and despite the 1964 coup, the journal continued to publish, with its focus on religious themes, some problems, and occasionally a philosophical interest, such as the relevance of historical materialism and Marx's treatment of history (Freire, 1966). In its final issue (10, no. 39–40 (July–December 1968) and in the face of military repression, it announced that the ten-year project of publishing the journal had come to an end.

influences and sought a path toward nationalism. The first issue included articles by Osny Duarte Pereira, Francisco de Oliveira, Celso Furtado, Nelson Werneck Sodré, and Roberto Schwarz. An essay by Florestan Fernandes (1965b) proclaimed that a bourgeois revolution had yet to mature in Brazil and that intellectuals committed to it had a role to play.

With the dictatorship intact, it was somewhat surprising that intellectuals continued to debate important questions about the ruling military. Sodré (1965a), for example, brought a revisionist understanding of history through the celebrated *História Nova* series of booklets, while Corbisier (1966a, 1966b) refined his conception of culture around the national problem, Kondor (1967) examined the role of intellectuals among a rebellious youth, and Lima Sobrinho (1966) reflected on Alberto Torres's understanding of imperialism in the late nineteenth century and nationalism in the twentieth century. The presence of São Paulo intellectuals is also prominent, including such writers as Oliveira and Schwarz. Weffort analyzed the state and masses in Brazil (1966), while Caio Prado Júnior (1967a) elaborated on the prospects for the Brazilian revolution (reviewed exhaustively by Cid Silveira 1966) and Fernando Henrique Cardoso focused on dynamic industrial sectors of the national bourgeoisie, exploring this theme back to Vargas and Dutra and into the Goulart government and delving into class conflict (national bourgeoisie with the *latifundistas*) and class interests when caught up in popular struggles that threaten to undermine financial-industrial bourgeois interests.

Described in its mission statement by its editor Ênio Silveira (1978) as a collection of books open to all tendencies concerned with humanity and published in a monthly series, *Encontros com a Civilização Brasileira* (Rio de Janeiro) both complemented and continued the tradition of the *Revista Civilização Brasileira*. It reflected views and investigation of "the national intelligentsia" and engaged intellectuals in debate against the military dictatorship and for democratic liberties. This new series comprised 29 issues from July 1978 to 1982. Its consulting council included a mix of Carioca and Paulista intellectuals: Arthur Giannotti, Barbosa Lima Sobrinho, Carlos Nelson Coutinho, Fernando Henrique Cardoso, Frei Betto, Helio Jaguaribe, Leandro Konder, Leonardo Boff, Octávio Ianni, and Roland Corbisier.[27]

---

[27] Important debates appear in these volumes, for example, on the national question in no. 24 (June 1980), 23–101 and another in the same volume on socialism, freedom, and democracy (105–161); one on agrarian reform in no. 22 (April 1980), 157–232; on the Cuban revolution in no. 18 (December 1979), 153–207; on intellectual activity in the university in

Other journals reflecting intellectual and academic thinking included *Polítca Externa Independente*, a quarterly focused on international problems and published in Rio by Editora Civilização Brasileira under Ênio Silveira with a consulting council comprised of Barbosa Lima Sobrinho, Celso Furtado, Hermano Alves, Josué de Castro, Márcio Moreira Alves, and others. Its first three issues (May 1965, August 1965, and January 1966) included articles by leftist and mainstream commentators on various issues, including the U.S. invasion of the Dominican Republic and the crisis of Pan Americanism.

A journal with a religious bent that was bimonthly in Rio by Editora Paz e Terra and edited by Waldo A. César, *Paz e Terra* first appeared in July 1966 with an essay by Nestor Raúl García on Latin American intellectuals and a documentary section on the martyred Colombian priest, Camilo Torres. Its editorial board of liberal progressives comprised prominent historian José Honório Rodrigues and progressive Catholics such as Dom Helder Câmera. Its pages included an essay by Celso Furtado (1967a) on development.

More mainstream social science views appeared in the Rio journal *Dados*, founded in 1964 by Cândido Mendes de Almeida and first published by the IUPERJ, and after 1969, part of a center for graduate study and research initially led by young Brazilian scholars who had returned from doctoral study in the United States. Secluded in Botafogo, IUPERJ was unable to sustain itself financially; in June 2010, all its professors resigned, their salaries unpaid for the previous six months, and joined the Universidade do Estado do Rio de Janeiro as visiting professors. There, they established a graduate program for some two hundred students who joined them. Over the years, IUPERJ had granted 281 doctoral and 471 master's degrees. Its professorial ranks had included Eli Diniz, Wanderley Guilherme dos Santos, Bolivar Lamounier, Simon

no. 16 (October 1979), 77–102; on intellectuality in no. 12 (June 1979), 172–247; on agrarian reform in no. 7 (January 1979), 172–221; and on the bourgeois revolution in no. 4 (October 1978), 175–207, which complements the ideas of Florestan Fernandes (1979) who sees a continuing revolution since the early sixties, interrupted by the military coup, but now advancing and in need of intellectual involvement. Octávio Ianni (1978) delved into examples of repression of cultural life and intellectuals after 1964, dwelling specifically on the imprisonment of Sodré and colleagues associated with the História Nova project. In search of roots in the bourgeois revolution, Rangel (1978a) turned back to dualities during colonial slavery, while Viotti da Costa et al. (1978) studied when and how the revolution came about. The national question was taken up by Rangel (1980b), with a focus on the 1930s and 1960s, whereas Rosa (1980) synthesized and drew out its implications and Cerqueira (1980), drawing upon Gramsci, looked at the role of intellectuals within popular sectors and Coutinho (1979) at culture and democracy.

Schwartzman, Amaury de Souza, and Luiz Werneck Vianna (*Folha de São Paulo*, June 22, 2010).[28]

In my interview with Diniz, she envisaged the IUPERJ as the major intellectual institution in Rio, one where intellectual life flourishes (in contrast to the universities) and resources are limited. Most of her work (1978) was focused on private industrial enterprises or firms during the 1970s and 1980s. During the postauthoritarian and military period, the transition to representative democracy was smooth, and the private business sector influenced a large share of the congress. She felt that the Cardoso government had moved in a neoliberal direction, that forms of representation within the state were "disarticulated," and clientist lines persisted. Consequently, the entrepreneurs gained influence and labor weakened. She saw Cardoso as aligned with entrepreneurs while using social pacts with labor, and Lula as somewhat effective in his approach (Diniz, 2011) (interview, Botafogo, Rio de Janeiro, July 6, 1995).

More of a progressive influence within IUPERJ, Luiz Werneck Vianna examined the PCB and its relations with and influence on the intelligentsia: "It had effective representation in the workers' movement and attracted the intelligentsia" (1984a: 56). His analysis emphasized the expansion of the capitalist economy that brought changes in the professional ranks and "transformed the intellectuals into a social stratum separated from the popular classes" (60, note 1). He also looked at the problems of organizing intellectuals (1983) and produced a useful study on social scientists and public life (1994).

How to assess this innovative and unique experience? As life in Rio prospered during the second half of the twentieth century, intellectuals from different backgrounds came together to discuss the prospects for growth in a way unseen in previous decades. The ISEB provided an outlet for intellectual expression and a space for constructive debate among social scientists aimed at changing the political, social, and economic state of Brazil. It was not my purpose to distinguish an ideological framework to differentiate among the three periods of ISEB history, but it is very clear that the early period is less ideological as the founders, in spite of their diverse perspectives, came together in search of a national ideology. In the transitional period, by contrast, they

---

[28] The mainstream *Revista de Ciências Sociais*, *Revista Brasilieria de Estudos Políticos*, and *Revista de Ciência Política* carried on with a more academic tradition and generally did not touch on important contemporary issues.

confront a major issue in Jaguaribe's advocacy of foreign capital as a means to develop the petroleum industry, and it is around this position that they deeply disagree. In the third period, the division plays out in intellectual circles outside the ISEB and under Vieira Pinto and his acceptance of more progressive views, including Marxism, and the ISEB intellectuals assume more activist roles inside and outside the ISEB. This is a period in which state support, certainly under Quadros, lessens, and although there is affinity between many ISEB intellectuals and the nationalism promoted by Goulart, resources for the ISEB remain scarce.

From the interviews, we can see that ISEB intellectuals had differing opinions, but it is important not to lose sight of the fact that, although there were internal differences within the group, they were all possessed of a national consciousness aimed at attaining the same thing – national development. According to Rangel, "The one thing that all ISEB intellectuals had in common was the desire to industrialize." They understood it as necessary for Brazilian progress, and intellectual life in Rio was shaped by this underlying unity of idea.

From 1953 to 1958, Jaguaribe identified essential practical and theoretical issues from social science in the face of the limitations of traditional academic disciplines around which the ISEB eventually organized. Lucas (1983) believed that the consensus among the founders was that "the theories and methods produced in developed countries could not be literally observed or followed in developing countries" and that the focus should be on Brazilian problems. The leadership crisis "was less rooted in doctrinaire disagreements than in personal rivalries and ambitions which could not be harmonized" (59). Rangel, for instance, was "a very competent Marxist, but Marxist usually in disagreement with the positions and policies of Brazilian Marxists" (53). "The dominant values of Marxism-Leninism permeated the leadership of the ISEB after 1958. Once seized by a group of Marxist-Leninists, the ISEB lost its possibility to succeed as a respected agency of social science.... Had the ISEB continued to practice a more objective form of social science, perhaps nationalism would have moved in another direction" (59–60). This somewhat dubious assertion overlooks that the institutional stability and survival of a progressive ISEB depended on continuing state resources, which in turn were impacted by political instability and the political preferences of different governments.

Cultural life flourished during the ISEB period prior to 1964, as attested to by intellectual writing in progressive journals and a plethora of pamphlets aimed at transcending a colonial mentality, raising consciousness, formulating an ideology of national development, and mobilizing the population to break from external dependency. Its momentum carried on in the face of military control, censorship, and repression. Indeed, the resistance to the authoritarian regime ultimately pressured the military to permit an opening toward democracy. This opening led to a dispersion of political parties and the formation of various social movements around particular issues and causes. In this process, cultural life dissipated, intellectuals turned from activism to the academic enterprise, and their production declined in Rio and elsewhere.[29]

This chapter on Rio intellectuals has focused on the influence of the ISEB and the nationalist movement with roots dating to the nineteenth century, the *tenentismo* that ushered Vargas into power in 1930, and the populist momentum culminating in the 1964 military coup. Throughout this history, intellectuals have maintained ties with the state and its policies and participated in projects for change, especially during periods of opening and electoral democracy that offer a link between a relatively autonomous civil society and the state. Helio Jaguaribe has reminded us that intellectuals such as José de Alencar, a renowned novelist but also a politician with close ties to the Old Republic, did not present projects to change the existing order. Sêrgio Miceli showed us how writers of the 1922 Modernist Movement were recruited within the circle of families tied to the dominant class that tended to co-opt their activism in

---

[29] This decline was due also to changing conditions globally and a transition under Fernando Henrique Cardoso and Inácio Lula da Silva, in which political life splintered into many groups but remained stable under formal representative democracy and the domestic economy began to grow as Brazil emerged as a player in the international scene. René Dreifuss observed that intellectuals, past and present, constitute small groups; they are regionally based, have little contact with the Northeast and Rio Grande de Sul, are ideological, and tend to be self-serving: "Rio intellectuals are part of a small intellectual current, unlike groups of intellectuals elsewhere. They tend to be paternalistic with constraints and sometimes cutting off access, even to the universities." This draws from a past legacy of elitism and personalism: "they rarely look inwardly. Intellectuals comprise a great mystery. Today the incapacity of intellectuals to understand what is happening is a problem. The Brazilian intellectual is ignorant, full of presumptions" (interview, Rio de Janeiro, July 6, 1995). Newspapers have provided a platform for intellectuals to engage with the issues of society, but, as David Fleischer writes, several of the important daily newspapers closed, including the Rio *Jornal do Brasil*, in September 2010 (founded in April 1891); the *Correio da Manhã* in July 2010 (founded in 1891), once progressive but closed down by the military government in 1968; the *Tribuna da Imprensa* in December 2008 (founded in 1949) and used by Carlos Lacerda to attack Getúlio Vargas and Juscelino Kubitschek during the 1950s; and in São Paulo the *Gazeta Mercantil*, founded by the Herbert Levy family, which ceased publication in May 2009 (*Brazil Focus*, July 10–16, 2010).

politics or public service. After 1937, censorship and repressive measures under the New State, for example, tended to mold intellectuals to a dependency on the state. Many intellectuals (Graciliano Ramos, for example) obtained positions within the bureaucracy, but few were able to support themselves on earnings from their cultural production. Intellectuals of various persuasions have occupied political positions of high order, including Jânio Quadros and José Sarnay on the right and Jorge Amado, Celso Furtado, Francisco Julião, and Darcy Ribeiro on the left. Although intellectuals may too often be co-opted, some of them were committed to change, such as Sêrgio Milliet, who led the modernist vanguard during the 1920s; Afonso Arinos de Melo Franco, who wrote about cultural nationalism in the 1930s; and Jaguaribe, Guerreiro Ramos, and others who advocated a national ideology of developmental nationalism in the 1950s. It is not surprising that, into the 1950s, many intellectuals sought refuge in the PCB, such as the artist Cândido Portinari and historians Caio Prado Júnior and Nelson Werneck Sodré. Nor is it surprising that after the splintering of the PCB and the military suppression after 1968 intellectual production began to decline as many intellectuals retreated to their universities or fled to exile. In the face of a political and economic crisis and with dependent ties to the international financial community and a large foreign debt, many Brazilian intellectuals carried on within academic institutions oriented to the transmission of routine intellectual work.

3

Nationalism and Marxism in the São Paulo Movement

Two Paulista intellectuals contributed significantly to a break with a colonial mentality and to a search for new understandings as Brazil abolished slavery and established a republic while capital flowed into agriculture, commerce, and industry. Outside university circles, Caio Prado Júnior influenced intellectuals through a new nationalist and Marxist interpretation of historical changes, while Florestan Fernandes helped transform academic life and sociology in particular. How did these two prominent São Paulo scholars shape new thinking in the twentieth century, and what was their connection to public life and political involvement, on the one hand, and to the academy, on the other? Did their profound investigations lead not only to shifts in academic perspectives, methodology, and theory, but also to reforms of society at large?

The Escola de Sociologia e Política de São Paulo (São Paulo School of Sociology and Politics), founded in the 1930s, served as a progressive center for early social science training and writing and was important in the development of sociology as a discipline. Its journal, *Sociologia*, published quarterly from about 1938 to 1964, was influential among São Paulo intellectuals.[1] *Anhembi*, first published in São Paulo in December

---

[1] Cyro Berlinck (1964) reviews the history of the initial thirty years of the school's activity and refers to early visiting American teachers, including Horace B. Davis, a prominent Marxist who contrasted classical political economy with the dialectical method and whose radical perspective initially provoked "a great educational problem" (283). During 1963 and 1964, *Sociologia* published a favorable review by José Pastore of Celso Furtado's *Pre-revolução brasileira*, a review of Florestan Fernandes's *A sociologia numa revolução social* by J. V. Freitas Marcondes, and an essay by Fernando Henrique Cardoso on industrialization and mass society.

1950, dealt with politics, culture, and literature. In its mission statement, editor Paulo Duarte (1950) argued that socialism and collective action would lead to social justice. Early issues tended to focus on cultural rather than political and social themes, although a section on contemporary events covered political developments and occasionally mentioned Portuguese intellectuals in exile in Brazil. At the end of its first decade, an issue on oil criticized two extreme positions: capitalism driven by free enterprise and nationalism inspired by patriotism and resistance to imperialism (see 39 [no. 116], July 1960). Issues devoted to industry, agriculture, and education followed. The journal featured early writings by major Paulista intellectuals including Florestan Fernandes and his students Fernando Henrique Cardoso and Octávio Ianni.

Another progressive Paulista journal of tremendous influence, *Revista Brasiliense* and its publishing house Editora Brasiliense, appeared in September–October 1955 as a bimonthly with a promise to be open to all views. Edited by Elias Chaves Neto, it had a distinguished editorial board that included Sérgio Milliet, Caio Prado Júnior, Edgard Cavalheiro, Sérgio Buarque de Hollanda, João Cruz Costa, E. L. Berlinck, Álvaro de Faria, and Nabor Caires de Brito. Other founders were Fernando de Azevedo, Florestan Fernandes, Heitor Ferreira Lima, and Josué de Castro. Its initial mission statement of August 1955, signed by forty-four founders, was dedicated to the memory of Monteiro Lobato, the founder of Editora Brasiliense, and attributed Brazil's backwardness to foreign dependence.

The contributions to *Revista Brasiliense* asserted the need to address national, not regional problems (no. 6, July–August 1956: 2–3). Under Chaves and Prado Júnior, the journal focused on essential questions in history and social science, debate to draw out differences, and openness to progressive perspectives. Both men were affiliated with the Brazilian Communist Party (Partido Comunista Brasileiro [PCB]), and, during a brief period in which it was not clandestine (1945–1947), Prado Júnior was elected federal deputy. In its early issues, they wrote on nationalism and theoretical questions of Marxism, while the renowned socialist Evarardo Dias wrote on labor and socialism and Heitor Ferreira Lima on the evolution of Brazilian socioeconomic thought.

At the outset, Chaves (1955) set the tone for a strong emphasis on nationalism, pointing to "the nationalist solution" as "resolving the problems of misery and backwardness" rather than "submitting our economy to the interests of North American trusts" (60–61). The solution, he believed, lay in developing infrastructure and a national industry, resolving problems of transportation, and taking advantage of the country's abundant resources. Chaves later (1956, 1960) reviewed the way Marxism shaped culture, illustrating his views with the Soviet example.

Commenting on nationalism in Brazil as "a temperamental phenomenon without roots in the intelligentsia" and "an emotional stimulus without rational content," Prado Júnior (1955) described it as neither negative nor xenophobic. As political thought, it expressed public opinion about "the dependent and subordinate situation the country faces in relation to the large financial and capitalist centers of the contemporary world. . . . This situation is that of a peripheral country within the capitalist system, a country marginalized but complementary to it and thus dependent and not properly integrated with it . . . [a country] in a subordinate position, suffering from the unfavorable contingencies of that system" (81–82). He identified Brazil as a peripheral and dependent country that needed to transcend its conditions in order to realize its national identity (1959: 9). Industrialization, he believed, was essential to this process, and it would have to be accompanied by a nationalist policy based on economic development (15), and that development would require state intervention. In a lengthy analysis of the agrarian question (1960a, 1960c) based on statistical detail and historical understanding within a Marxist framework, he argued for agrarian reform. Claudio Tavares (1960) responded with questions about whether agricultural labor was salaried or based on exchange, while Michael Löwy (1960) drew upon Karl Kautsky, Rosa Luxemburg, and José Carlos Mariátegui to argue for a socialist and agrarian revolution in Brazil and the liberation of all Brazilian workers. In a later article, Prado Júnior (1962a) continued the dialogue on agrarian reform.

In an effort to expand these views, Hermes Lima (1958) conceptualized nationalism as political and cultural, the essence of a nation: "There is no nation without nationalism" (8). Among its manifestations, he identified a call for political independence and economic freedom. He called attention to Alberto Torres's insistence that Brazil not abandon its resources and peoples to domination by outside forces (14) and went on to suggest that state leadership and popular mobilization would be necessary to realize a national consciousness and a developmental project (16). Brazilian nationalism in its political and cultural form had to become an expression of the power of the people in defense of a national personality (24). Earlier he had written (1945) about how Brazil could move from monarchical and traditional politics to something uniquely Brazilian. With an analysis grounded in the work of early Brazilian thinkers such as Tobias Barreto and Ruy Barbosa, he drew upon the work of Caio Prado Júnior. Later

(1954), he argued that although Vargas lacked a popular organizational base for confronting backwardness (13), he nevertheless "became a symbol of the nationalist ideals of this country" (18). The Vargas period, in his view, was an awakening (*tomada de conciência*) in which the promotion of the iron and steel and petroleum industries became a symbol of the nation. Interestingly, Lima's views on nationalism first appeared in *Cadernos de Nosso Tempo* (1955), the precursor journal to Higher Institute of Brazilian Studies (Instituto Superior de Estudos Brasileiros [ISEB]), and in writings emanating from the discussions of the Itatiaia Group. Similarly, João Cruz Costa (1962) moved from an early concern with colonialism to an exploration of the meaning of nationalism for a dependent country like Brazil.

Approaches to nationalism and development abounded in the journal. Florestan Fernandes (1956, 1960) offered an overview of science since the sixteenth century in his search for a rational and scientific explanation of Brazilian society (see Bittencourt, Rabinovitch, and Goldenberg, 1961, for a critique). Fabrício Soares (1959) defined nationalism and imperialism as two ideologies in dialectical opposition. He suggested that nationalism served both to accelerate the process of development and as an anti-imperialist force (89). Octávio Ianni (1957) explored the features of Brazilian nationalism, whereas Fernando Henrique Cardoso (1958) argued that educational reform was necessary for economic development. Paulo Fernando Lago discussed nationalism and its various manifestations in connection with secondary education. Fernandes (1962) argued for popular education in Brazil as a means of assimilating the population into the system of national production, enhancing its culture and fostering economic development and social progress.

The journal also drew attention to labor and popular movements. Prado Júnior (1961a) linked Marxist theory with practice in this area and, in an examination of the 1960 elections, drew from Marx by emphasizing various concepts and the design of his work and showed how to understand and relate it to theory and practice. In his theoretical discussion of capitalization within economic development, with some reference to Brazil, Prado Júnior analyzed the October 3, 1960, elections with a criticism of the PCP for having "abandoned the popular masses by insufficiently and inadequately organizing the base" (1960b: 14–15). Ridiculing the populist demagoguery of the campaign, he argued for direct contact with the people through their own unions and class organizations (17). The tasks for Brazilians, he said, were pursuing economic freedom, stimulating the forces of production, implementing financial stabilization, and controlling inflation (1961a, 1961b). Ianni (1961) offered a class analysis of workers and their prospects under the agrarian and industrial bourgeoisies.

The journal brought together early writings of a younger generation of Paulista scholars who belonged to a study group on Marx's *Capital*. José Arthur Giannotti (1960) published notes drawn from the group's discussions. Löwy (1962b) was especially interested in the young Marx and his writings on alienation and the individual in capitalist society. He also elaborated (1962a) on the ideas of Marx, Lenin, Luxemburg, and Gramsci with regard to class consciousness and the revolutionary party. Cardoso (1962b) presented an analysis of the working class in Brazil and the degree to which it was cohesive as a class. José de Souza Martins (1963) argued that the government's three-year plan would overcome precapitalist tendencies and conditions in Brazil and allow for a bourgeois revolution. The early writing of André Gunder Frank (1963) on economic integration in Latin America and (1964) on Brazilian agrarian capitalism and the myth of feudalism appears in the journal and predates his popular writing in the United States (1966, 1967) on capitalist underdevelopment that was especially influential on North American thinking about Latin America. Frank argued that capitalism, not feudalism, was the cause of backwardness in Brazil and drew upon the work of Paul Singer for some of his discussion. This last issue of *Revista Brasiliense* also included an article by Prado Júnior (1964) on the agrarian question in Brazil.[2]

---

[2] Many of these prominent intellectuals also wrote for the mainstream but respected *Revista Brasileira de Ciências Sociais*, a publication of the Escola de Ciências Econômicas (School of Economic Sciences) at the University of Minas Gerais that first appeared November 1961 with essays by Giannotti on formal thought, Ianni on the crisis of sociological thought, and Jaguaribe on the impact of the resignation of President Jânio Quadros, while L. A. Costa Pinto opened with an essay on social change. The second issue included pieces by Florestan Fernandes, Celso Furtado, Fernando Henrique Cardoso, and Aníbal Pinto on sociological and economic questions, with Cardoso dwelling on the dialectical method in sociological analysis and Furtado on the aftermath of a Brazilian revolution. The third issue included essays by Francisco Iglésias (from Minas), Octávio Ianni and Francisco Weffort (from São Paulo), and Josué de Castro, Inácio Rangel, and Michel Debrun (from Rio). The fourth issue included an extensive analysis by Raúl Prebisch on obstacles to development and the escape from underdevelopment, Costa Pinto on social classes, and Simon Schwartzman on economic and political development, while Ianni looked at the way capitalism spawned radical activity on the extreme right and left. Castro, with Gilberto Paim, examined the changes in the Brazilian economy after the Second World War and argued that the Brazilian left was politically conservative in its defense of representative democracy and economically revolutionary in its struggle against imperialism and underdevelopment. Rangel wrote about Brazilian duality, with an external pole represented by the advance of capitalism

CAIO PRADO JÚNIOR AND A NEW UNDERSTANDING

Caio Prado Júnior was born of a wealthy family in São Paulo in 1907, graduated with a degree in law, and studied for a year in England. As we have seen, he was a member of the PCB from 1931 on, and, after the Second World War, when the party was briefly legal, he was elected to Congress. His work, however, challenged the traditional and sometimes intransigent positions of his party; for example, its position on semifeudalism as an explanation for backwardness. He looked to socialism as a way of overcoming the dependency and imperialism that had afflicted the periphery since colonial times. Specifically, he argued that monopoly capitalism and foreign investment were responsible for the deformation of the periphery. His class analysis distinguished the ruling classes from the working class and the subsistence masses. He questioned the idea of a dual society, arguing that feudalism and semifeudalism were not evident in Brazil as the PCB claimed, and he was suspicious of interpretations advocating the confrontation of international capital by a progressive national bourgeoisie. Indeed, he rejected the bourgeois-democratic revolution as a solution to the crisis of capitalism in the developing world. Near the end of his life, I spent three hours with him in a review of his life and work. He affirmed that he had remained in the PCB in spite of his criticisms and that early on within the party he had defended his thesis that Brazilian backwardness was attributable to capitalism and not feudalism (interview, São Paulo, August 25, 1982).

The essence of his thought is found in several volumes on these themes: one (1933) on the politics of the colonial period in Brazil, the revolution of independence and the organization of the state thereafter, and the imperial period of the late nineteenth century; a second (1942) on Brazil since the colonial period; and a third (1963) on the economic history of Brazil since 1500. His history of the colonial period, translated into English as *The Colonial Background of Modern Brazil* (1967b[1969]), was perhaps his most important book. It focused on colonization as a "commercial enterprise" in which "the foremost objective [was] the exploitation of the natural resources of a virgin land for the benefit of European commerce"

and an internal pole attempting to eliminate backwardness. He contrasted industrial capitalism with mercantile and more primitive capitalism, with one form dependent on the other. Michel Debrun (1963) suggested that Álvaro Vieira Pinto's *Consciência e realidade nacional* provided a synthetic view of history in terms of the relations between dominant and dominated, a method for evaluating political thought, and a political program for countries on the path to development.

(20). He argued that the colonial economy's agrarianization of production influenced the development of the Brazilian economy and the entire complex of social relations. Because the colonial economy was cyclical and based on an external foundation, "it did not create the foundation needed to support it and maintain a population dependent on such a structure: an organized system of production and distribution of resources for the material subsistence of the population. Instead it created a 'mechanism' for which the population was nothing but the element of propulsion, designed to function safely for the benefit of completely extraneous objectives" (45). The colonial system incorporated structural contradictions that impeded the transformation of Brazil. It was deeply rooted in the Portuguese monarchy, of which the colony was an integral part (423): "The strongest ties that bind them into some kind of social whole are the most primitive and rudimentary human links, stemming directly and immediately from the relationships established in labor and production, particularly the subjection of the slave or semi-slave to his master" (400).

Ultimately, Prado Júnior argued, Brazil's economic and social unrest had deep historical roots in the colonial system, which was based on the exploitation of both labor and natural resources for the realization of commercial value and was therefore inadequate as a foundation for social structure. The system was fraught with contradictions, and these were the driving force in the restructuring of colonial economic and social institutions. Class contradictions, such as those between landowners and merchants, and contradictions due to the ethnic composition of the country (prejudice and the degradation of slaves and Indians) combined with the illegitimacy of the government to contribute to the exhaustion and replacement of the colonial system. Ideas about change were mere reflections of the objective external situations that structured everyday individual relationships.[3]

---

[3] The thought of Caio Prado Júnior in *Revista Brasiliense* can be synthesized through his comment on political issues (1960b, 1961b, 1962b), nationalism and development (1955, 1959, 1961a), and agrarian reform (1960a, 1960c, 1962a, 1964a); see Iglésias (1982) for a brief sketch of Caio Prado Júnior and selections from his major works on politics, economy, colonialism, agrarianism, and development, including biographical notes that situate his work on political life during the colonial period in terms of key moments shaped by the left. Araújo (1977) provided a useful overview of Prado's thought, and D'Incao (1987a) brought together appreciative essays by Heitor Ferreira Lima, Antônio Cândido, Florestan Fernandes, Octávio Ianni, Carlos Nelson Coutinho, Leondor Kondor, Inácio Rangel, Jacob Gorender, Marco Aurélio Garcia, and many others, while Fernando Novais (1983a) incisively examined Caio's trajectory as historian.

After the 1964 coup and its repercussions on the left, Prado Júnior published a major assessment (1966) of what had occurred, coupled with an attack on the PCB and its misleading policies. His controversial essay was not only an indictment of the 1964 coup, but also an affirmation that the Brazilian revolution had to be socialist. At the same time, while remaining a member of the party, he criticized the PCB for its "sectarianism," its "opportunistic policies," and its adherence to an "outmoded" theory of revolution drawn from antiquated Soviet and Third International perspectives. He argued that Marxism and the dialectical method should guide an understanding of history (41).[4]

FLORESTAN FERNANDES, SOCIOLOGY, AND ACADEMIC TRANSFORMATION

Florestan Fernandes was undoubtedly impressed by the many prominent visiting scholars whose lectures and research gave prominence to Emile Durkheim and Max Weber, thinkers whose methodologies and ideas not only influenced his studies but later his teaching as a professor in São Paulo. It is unlikely that the methodology or thinking of Karl Marx shaped their outlook, and Fernandes appears to have followed this direction in his teaching during the late 1950s and early 1960s. Indeed, his students turned to Marx through an informal seminar they organized on *Capital* in the tradition of progressive graduate students in Europe and North America.

Thus, it was something of a surprise that on his sixtieth birthday he elaborated on his early interest in Marx and Trotsky. In interviews with J. Chasin, Heleieth Saffioti, and others, he offered a retrospective (1981a) on his early years. Although he was attracted to the PCB and its famous leader, Luiz Carlos Prestes, the radical youth of the time tended not to join the party. After Vargas came to power, communists moved toward groups supporting him, but Fernandes joined an extreme left Trotskyist group, the Coligação Democrática Radical, that he was involved with from 1943 to 1950: "I always maintained contact with other groups, for example, the anarchists and the PS and the old militants who were not

---

[4] Assis Tavares (1966–1967) produced a useful review and critique of this work to which Prado Júnior responded (1967a). Earlier, Claudio Tavares (1960) had criticized his analysis of agrarian issues. Rocha (1980) criticized the work of both Prado Júnior and Frank. See Novais (1983a) for a sympathetic appraisal.

of my generation. I circulated with left people, except for the PCB ... but was known for my Trotskyist orientation. Many of my activist student colleagues knew little about Marxism" (1981a: 18–19). During the 1950s, he was involved in intellectual activities rather than politics: "I wanted to join the PCB, but their positions were often negative, and I remained outside and instead worked hard as an intellectual." He believed that political parties did not offer solutions and that the intellectual could not fill this space, nor could intellectuals form their own movement in a class society in which workers could not mature politically and develop as an independent class (23). He published an anthology of writings by Marx and Engels (1983) as if to affirm his interest in their thought.

Fernandes completed his undergraduate studies in 1943 and a teaching degree in 1944, and he undertook doctoral work in 1945–1946 at the private Escola de Sociologia Política (School of Political Sociology). In 1946, he translated Marx's *Contribution to a Critique of Political Economy*, which, with a lengthy introduction, was published by Editora Flama, a small publishing house affiliated with the (Trotskyist) Fourth International. He opposed the PCB's Stalinist line and eventually left the Trotskyist movement, arguing that, like other leftist parties in Brazil, it failed to provide political roles for intellectuals and involved few workers: "I was a militant, an activist, but I separated political activity from intellectual life." He attributed this stance to the "eclectic educational orientation of USP [the University of São Paulo]," implying that, at the time, professors were not very political; he added that, after 1969, he had abandoned "eclectic sociology" to become a militant teacher. He mentioned that in his work he referred to Marx and Weber and that he had studied Marxism as a current in social science. In his major work on sociology [1977/1980], he called on intellectuals "to contest" and build "a critical and militant sociology," and he devoted a chapter to alternative historical sociology and its Marxist influence. Pushed out of the USP by the military after the 1964 coup, he taught in Canada and was offered tenure there but returned to Brazil in 1972 because his family would not join him. Back in Brazil, he wrote books and essays but was not allowed to teach, even though he was absolved by a military trial: "In 1975, I began to teach again openly as a Marxist because I had lost hope that there would be a party that could utilize my work. At the PUC [Pontifícia Universidade Católica], I give courses openly, according to my ideas and positions. Since 1977, nobody has ever told me not to give Marxist courses." He described his interest in functionalism but denied being a functionalist: "I have used functionalism but at the same time I was a militant, a Trotskyist, and I could not have been a functionalist" (interview, São Paulo, September 26, 1983).

Fernandes wrote extensively about education and the role of intellectuals (1956, 1960, 1961, 1962), and his major work (1966) assessed education in Brazil, including the contributions of Fernando de Azevedo and Anísio Teixeira. He believed that authoritarian rule in Latin America after the Second World War forced Latin American Marxist intellectuals to examine Latin American reality and conclude that a revolutionary class party was needed to allow the intellectual to assume different roles. If the intellectual worked at a university, he was associated with an institution that would naturally limit his production. In a university setting, he did not have the freedom to produce a theory of revolution and was not involved in class struggle. As a member of the petty bourgeoisie, the intellectual was limited: "We cannot place the intellectual above the class movement. Thus the confusion through which we must live: the low level of proletarianization and the fact that the intellectual accommodates very easily to his lifestyle as a petty bourgeois" (interview, São Paulo, September 26, 1983).

His research and writing were wide-ranging, including an extensive series of journal articles on folklore (1959a) and culminating in a book (1978) that included journal articles written since 1945 that related folklore studies to positivism and empiricism and argued that they reflected bourgeois interest in the study of popular culture. His major study of race relations challenged nearly universal views of racial democracy (1965a, 1969), such as that of Recife sociologist Gilberto Freyre, who had studied in the United States and emphasized racial equality in his classic studies of Brazil (Maio, 2011) and whose perspective was also adopted by Donald Pierson, Charles Wagley, and Carl Degler until the 1950s. This dichotomy is profiled in the work of Edward Telles (2004), who argues that although racial democracy was challenged by São Paulo academics beginning in the 1950s, some form of it continued to be defended by U.S. academics until the 1990s.

Fernandes devoted considerable attention to the role of intellectuals in the revolution (1965b), the tasks for the intellectual in the democratic revolution (1979), the bourgeois revolution (1970[1951], 1974, 1975, 1981c), and the concept of revolution itself (1981b). *A sociologia no Brasil* (1977[1951]) drew on earlier writings in *Sociologia* and *Anhembi* and chapter 4 of a book on ethnology and sociology in Brazil (1958a). It began with the intellectual consequences of the breakdown of slave society as reflected in such classic works as Euclydes da Cunha's *Os Sertões*.

Fernandes describes this as a moment of transition and as Brazil's "first sociographical and historical-geographical interpretation." Thereafter, sociology in Brazil became "a technique of consciousness and explanation of the world" (1977[1980]: 35). Alberto Torres (1933), he said, had "assumed a pioneering role in the 'pragmatic' formation of sociological thought in Brazil" by focusing on the Brazilian national problem with "analysis that ties history to pragmatic efforts both pragmatic and ideological" (35). He saw the intellectual contributions of F. J. de Oliveira Vianna (1933) as "positive investigation" or "social psychology" (Vianna, 1949) and identified as important to sociology the work of Gilberto Freyre, Caio Prado Júnior, Fernando de Azevedo, Sêrgio Buarque de Holanda, and Nelson Werneck Sodré, as well as that of outsiders such as Donald Pierson, Roger Bastide, Jacques Lambert, Herbert Baldus, and Charles Wagley.

He considered his students his collaborators, placing Cardoso and Ianni first among them and Marialice Mencarini Foracchi, Maria Sylvia Carvalho Franco, Luiz Pereira, Leôncio Rodrigues, and others just behind them. Their contributions from 1960 to 1965, he believed, "stimulated a reformulation of theories that explain capitalism, class structure, and the state in the imperial centers of industrial civilization" (1977[1980]: 201). He wrote extensively on "the lost generation" under the military dictatorship of the late 1960s and early 1970s (213–252) and the contradiction of the intellectual who may be radical on an external level but is confronted by conservative control internally and faced with "a rupture that separates official duty from ideological option" (228). He suggested (229) that the intellectual had to work on three levels: first within the institution dedicated to teaching and research; second, in opposition to special interests within the establishment and in favor of egalitarian society; and third, in solidarity with the workers' movement and socialism. After having complained that many of his students had left academia for political life (Fernando Henrique Cardoso being the most conspicuous among them), he later, in 1986, joined the Workers' Party (Partido dos Trabalhadores [PT]) and was elected a federal deputy from São Paulo, and his thinking evolved in the direction of possible socialism (Fernandes, 1989; see also Arruda, 2011; Ricupero, 2011). In a book of essays (1989) drawn from a column in daily newspapers, he criticized the party for its reformism but was optimistic about its destiny: "As a proletarian party it only can represent and defend proletarian socialism. . . . The working classes and the destitute popular masses will convert the PT into a party of the New Left that Brazil urgently needs"

(226). D'Incao and others (1987b) have written appreciatively about his "knowledgeable militancy."

ANTÔNIO CÂNDIDO AND THE SEARCH FOR NATIONAL IDENTITY IN LITERATURE

Fernandes's dilemma of being a Trotskyist activist and striving to attain recognition as an intellectual was a problem that he often discussed with Antônio Cândido de Mello Sousa, who had opted for revolutionary socialism but encouraged him to dedicate himself to an academic career (Fernandes, 1981a: 19). Antônio Cândido taught both sociology and comparative literature and as a literary critic he frequently wrote analytically on historical and political questions. Long active as a socialist, he was deeply interested in the national consciousness and the evolution of Brazilian literature from a colonial mentality of inferiority and dependence on culture outside the country to a national identity. His approach is evident in a two-volume work on decisive moments in the formation of Brazilian literature (1959) and in an early journal article (1968) on literature and the emergence of a Brazilian identity in which he looked dialectically at four themes: cultural imposition and cultural adaptation, the transfiguration of reality and a sense of the concrete, the ideological use of the past, and the general and the particular in forms of expression. His ideas on literature and society culminated in a major collection of essays (1995), in one of which, reminiscent of the work of Ferreira Gullar (1979), he set out to identify "the literary characteristics of the mild phase of backwardness, corresponding to the ideology of 'the new country'; and of the phase of catastrophic consciousness of backwardness, corresponding to the notion of 'underdeveloped country'" (Cândido, 1995: 121). His view of Marxism, militancy, and the role of the intellectual appeared in a leftist journal (1996), and he also assessed the place of Brazilian intellectuals in Latin American literature (1981). Antônio Cândido emphasized three Brazilian masters whose intellectual formation or development took place in the 1930s: Gilberto Freyre, Sêrgio Buarque de Holanda, and Caio Prado Júnior. He saw Celso Furtado's *Formação econômica do Brasil* and Roberto Simonsen's *História econômica do Brasil* as building on the work of Prado Júnior who, in contrast to Holanda, remained outside the university and was unable to establish a tradition among the historians he trained but who nevertheless left a legacy that persists to this day.

THE CAPITAL GROUP: CONFRONTATION WITH MAINSTREAM SOCIAL SCIENCE

Philosopher José Arthur Giannotti was the inspiration for the formation of the *Capital* Group. After his return in June 1958 from two years of study in France, where he had encountered much interest in Marx, he met with Fernando Henrique Cardoso, Ruth Cardoso, Octávio Ianni, and Fernando Novais and proposed that they organize an informal seminar. Novais suggested reading Marx's *Capital*. Shortly thereafter, the group began to meet every other week. The founders were teaching assistants at the USP, where the young teachers and students wanted to supplement their traditional university courses with study of Marx, whose work was only touched on in formal classes. Although they were becoming interested in politics, only Paul Singer had any political experience through his participation in the labor movement, leadership of a factory committee, and activism in the Partido Socialista do Brasil (PSB) during the early 1950s. With the death of Stalin in 1953 and the dissension within the international communist movement, the young Paulista intellectuals were critical of the irrelevant and intransigent positions of the PCB on national questions, among them its adherence to a dogmatic understanding of Brazilian backwardness as essentially feudal or semifeudal and its optimism about the emergence of a national bourgeoisie to overcome the old order.

From 1958 until 1964, the group studied *Capital* and other works. Its approach was systematic, with each meeting covering a chapter and led by one of the core group of teachers who would give a summary followed by questions and debate. Giannotti was the principal organizer, and his training in philosophy was useful to the seminar. Singer was the militant activist in the group and had previous knowledge of Marx, and his background in economics was essential. Cardoso was trained in functionalism, and he and Ianni were students of Florestan Fernandes, who at the time was drawn to the new American sociology and Talcott Parsons in particular. Novais was the historian. The participants also included Roberto Schwarz, Michael Löwy, Leôncio Martins Rodrigues, and, in the early period, Juárez Brandão Lopes, all of them later important in intellectual circles. Michel Debrun, who had been active in the ISEB after arriving in Brazil from France in the late 1950s, attended as a friend of Giannotti.[5]

---

[5] This description of the *Capital* Group is drawn both from interviews and from my recordings and summary of a panel discussion I attended at UNICAMP (Colóquio sobre Marx, 1983), which included an introduction by Marco Aurélio Garcia and presentations by

In an interview in Brasília on September 26, 1983, Cardoso provided a retrospective on the seminar. He considered it extremely useful for bringing together people of diverse intellectual backgrounds, Marxists and otherwise ("Giannotti was not a Marxist but offered a phenomenological critique of Marx"). In addition to the participants just mentioned, he recalled Bento Prado, Michel Legrand, Otávio Mendes, Ruth Cardoso, Paul Singer, Sebastião da Cunha, and Ruy Fausto, and he went on to say, "Our group was exclusively dedicated to academic studies and the university without any partisan political activities.... We were very critical of the ISEB because of its affiliation with the state. We regarded the ISEB people as ideologues and state nationalists without any critical analytical background." He was especially critical of their concept of a progressive revolutionary bourgeoisie: "In my interviews, I found their views to be liberal, not progressive. I criticized the PCB position of close alliance with the national bourgeoisie. This work influenced my later writings on dependency.... I never was close with Caio Prado, but the seminar group greatly admired and respected him and his nationalist Marxism." Before the seminar, thanks to Fernandes, he had become familiar with Parsons, Weber, and Durkheim, translating Parsons into Portuguese and teaching courses on his work. He believed that the seminar reoriented participants' thinking and directly influenced their theses. Before, there were no courses in Marxism at the universities, and afterward participants began to teach Marxist courses.

André Gunder Frank, he said, never participated in the *Capital* Group and totally misinterpreted its analyses. Frank was a close friend and read Cardoso's thesis in 1960, but most of Cardoso's theoretical work came before Frank's 1966 book. In 1964, Cardoso attended a seminar by Celso Furtado in Chile, and it was during that seminar that he began to formulate his ideas on dependency. Theotônio dos Santos, Vânia Bambirra, Ruy Mauro Marini, and Enzo Faletto all attended seminars on dependency together: "I argued constantly with Dos Santos because he was interested in developing a theory of dependency, while I wanted to focus only on situations of dependency. I never wanted to create a theory of dependency. I have been criticized as being a Weberian, but my methodology is not typological. I focused on the analysis of historical and cultural processes."

He observed that Sartre opened Brazilian scholars to critical analysis and that Gramsci was a greater influence in Argentina than in Brazil. In

Novais, Giannotti, Singer, and Schwarz. On the program but not participating were Cardoso, Ianni, and Rodrigues.

1960, and especially after 1964, Marxism became vulgarized in Brazil; there was too much structural analysis and little political analysis: "Today Marxism is blended with Catholicism (national liberation theology) and other popular orientations. It is politically rich but conceptually poor. The *Capital* seminar was politically poor but conceptually rich."

The idea of the bourgeois revolution, he said, originated with Fernandes's studies of Brazilian slave society, in which he argued that it was impossible to have capitalist development in Brazil without such a revolution: "I differed from Florestan because I tended to focus on political analysis while he focused on social analysis." In 1964, there was an economic revolution to foster the forces of production, but there was no bourgeois-democratic revolution: "I believe that Marxism has weak political theses because it has failed to adjust to changing political, social, and worldwide realities" (interview, Brasília, September 26, 1983).

Other participants also reflected on their experience. For Giannotti, the *Capital* Group represented a new direction, a break with North American functionalism, Weberian influence, and sectarian Marxism. He noted that Sebastião da Cunha brought news and data on the Brazilian economy to the seminar. For Singer, the seminar undermined the limitations of the specialized education in different fields of a group of talented young people and allowed for the assimilation of the perspectives of other disciplines into an interdisciplinary mode of work. It also facilitated the development of original Marxist thought. Singer also observed that participants had read the work of Caio Prado Júnior and that, although they portrayed themselves as far from his thinking, many of them published in his *Revista Brasiliense*. He compared the intellectual with the manual worker, arguing that the intellectual had an advantage in access to a wider body of information. The problem was translating all this information into data that would be useful to the masses that wanted to change society: "We often end up generating theories only for ourselves.... We are beginning to recognize the problem and how to engage in a meaningful dialogue with the masses of rural and industrial workers, how to communicate to them what we have had the privilege to learn. More important, we need to listen and allow them to teach us also; we need to learn from them" (interview, São Paulo, September 26, 1983).

Although André Gunder Frank, who was in Brazil during the early sixties, apparently did not attend the seminar, he was in touch with many of the participants, and some of the ideas emanating from the seminar were relevant to his early writings on capitalism and under-development (1967), which itself received the seminar's critical attention.

Singer confirmed that there emerged an idea, not new to the Marxist tradition but rarely discussed at that time, that the "underdevelopment" of Brazil was imposed by the requirements of imperialism and therefore could not be overcome gradually: "This analysis, later advanced by André Gunder Frank, appeared in the seminar prior to Frank's book.... The intellectual repercussions of this analysis were immense, because we felt intellectually part of the current international events of the moment.... While we felt isolated from Europe and the United States, the seminar's Marxist analysis made us feel that we were an integral part and absolute victim of modern capitalism" (Colóquio Sobre Marx, 1983).

Among those in the seminar who became noted as scholars and were later affiliated with the research institution Brazilian Center for Analysis and Planning (Centro Brasileiro de Análise e Planejamento [CEBRAP]) were Cardoso, Giannotti, Ianni, Novais, Oliveira, and Singer.

Fernando Henrique Cardoso achieved fame as both an academician and a politician. He studied with Florestan Fernandes in sociology at the USP and, at the time, was close to Octávio Ianni and Luiz Pereira. His early research on slavery in southern Brazil was published in a doctoral dissertation and a book (1962a). He also studied the industrial entrepreneur and economic development in Brazil (1964). In this early work he was interested in the dialectical method and Marx's thought[6] and therefore has been "regarded as a 'Marxist' ever since" (2006: 63).[7] He continued: "Marx's works did inspire me, but more for their rigorous method of analysis than for his dogmatic, nineteenth-century view on capitalism and revolution" (63; see Chilcote, 2007, for a review). He also drew on the functionalism and structuralism of sociologists such as Robert Merton and Claude Lévi-Strauss. Structuralism was paramount in the approach to problems of underdevelopment and dependency that

---

[6] Describing events that had impacted his life and outlook, Cardoso mentioned the independence and feminism of his mother, the exploits of Luiz Carlos Prestes as a rebellious army officer and later head of the PCB, and the success of his father, a liberal who, supported by the party, successfully ran for Congress in 1954. Impressed by the party's intellectuals and leaders, he wrote for *Fundamentos*, a PCB-backed publication, and even considered joining the party. However, along with many other young intellectuals, he became disillusioned with it after the death of Stalin. Of the "Marx Seminar" he writes: "We chose to study Marx not only because his works spoke to the problems of transforming an undeveloped society, but also because we felt his views had been distorted by the Communists in Brazil" (Cardoso, 2006: 63).

[7] Vânia Bambirra recalled her time in Chile with Fernando Henrique: "He never was Marxist. He knew Marxism, but he was always Weberian, and he never talked politics, and later nobody thought his government would be so neoliberal" (interview with Jorge Pereira Filho, *Brasil do Fato*, February 2, 2008).

evolved during his stay in Chile at the Latin American Institute for Economic Planning (Instituto Latinoamericano para Planejamiento Económico), where his colleagues included Celso Furtado and Francisco Weffort, and he became friends with Chilean socialists Salvador Allende and Clodomiro Almeyda. This led to his popular study with Enzo Faletto, *Dependency and Development in Latin America* (1969, 1979, which, he argues, "was widely interpreted as leftist because of its worldview – our delineation of the divisions between rich and poor nations ... however, the conclusions were not very leftist at all" (2006: 97). The book opened up an opportunity for him to lecture in France during the protests of 1968. He also wrote for opposition journals such as *Opinião* and *Argumento* that were closed down by the military regime.

As a politician, he first became a senator and then headed the planning and foreign ministries. His success in bringing high inflation under control, which provided the basis for his election to the presidency,[8] which he described as an effort to bring stability to Brazil by setting rules and following them. Capitalism, he says, is "little more than a system of rules. If these rules were respected, then we could build the foundations for lasting prosperity" (2006: 204–205). The left-leaning new leaders in Latin America have all "in practice, demonstrated strong loyalty to capitalism. This is not by accident; they are all smart enough to know that no other path exists in today's world. Even the most extreme leaders recognize this" (226).[9]

---

[8] In describing the policies and practices of his presidency, he says that the statement during his first presidential campaign, celebrated in the press, that everything he had written in the past should be forgotten was a fabrication (Cardoso, 2006: 206).

[9] Cardoso (2006) gives us a brief autobiography, whereas admirers have published sympathetic but useful accounts of his life as scholar and politician. René Dreifus (interview, São Paulo, July 6, 1995) summed up Cardoso's accomplishments by pointing out that he came from traditional families and operated within a Brazilian elite. He was always sheltered by Paulista academics, even when he left the country. He managed to teach abroad and establish a consulting network. He had to be creative to carry out research and to build a protective network around his activities. He can be characterized as " a very able player," "very informed and intelligent," and "interested in understanding change." Mauricio Font (2001) has written a brief biography as an introduction to Cardoso's writings on Brazilian society, dependency and development, authoritarianism and democracy, and other themes. Ted C. Goertzel (1999) offers a sympathetic profile of Cardoso along with a list of his writings, interviews, and writings about him and his work. Joseph A. Kahl (1976: 129–194) focused on his early academic work, whereas Brigitte Hersant Leoni (1997) presents a biography drawn from her years (1994–1996) as a French journalist living in Brazil and during Cardoso's first presidential term. Susan Kaufman Purcell and Riordan Roett (1997) assemble conservative perspectives on Cardoso's early years as president, including

José Arthur Giannotti graduated from the USP in 1953 with a degree in philosophy and embarked on a thesis on phenomenology. In about 1956, he went to France to study and participate in meetings of the radical group Socialisme ou Barbarie, which was made up of intellectuals and workers and included French dissident Trotskyists such as Claude Lefort and Cornelius Castoriadis. The group opposed the bureaucracies that governed modern capitalism. Giannotti studied for a year in Rheims and another in Paris and returned to Brazil "to study Marxism politically and systematically" through the study group focusing on the reading of *Capital* that Fernando Novais had suggested: "We were eclectic, because we read Marx, Keynes, and Hilferding. I read *Capital* in the German version. We read Keynes's *General Theory*, and we read Hilferding in Spanish. We studied how Keynesianism worked and later attempted to critique it." At that time, Paul Singer attempted to make Keynes compatible with Marx, and Fernando Henrique wanted to make Weber compatible with Marx. Florestan Fernandes was more eclectic with his theory and insisted on the study of synchronism through a study of Durkheim, Marx, and Weber: "This theory was absolutely absurd" (interview, São Paulo, October 26, 1984).

Giannotti's major work (1983) included analyses of primitive accumulation, power and the state, capitalism and social classes, and history and revolution. In the transition from authoritarian rule to democracy, he suggested, the new generation was neither very militant nor very much influenced by politics, but it did break from traditional patterns. Influenced by writings like those of Florestan Fernandes, a plethora of national writings emerged. He mentioned his own 1983 book, a lengthy and difficult work that went out of print within four months, as an example of this interest in national questions, along with Marilena Chauí's work on ideology, which sold nearly 200,000 copies. Marxism in Brazil developed as a petit-bourgeois ideology, and, especially in the university, it served to rally resistance against the dictatorship; but in Giannotti's view, very little good work after 1964 was influenced by it. At the time of the democratic opening, the new generation of students was struggling to open up space while his own generation was "suffering from an enormous atrophy, with very few new ideas and a lot of repetition of old ones." There was no national theater, and Brazilian cinema was in ruins. Members of the

cautiously optimistic essays by Albert Fishlow on stabilization and Amaury de Souza on inequality. Hoge (1995) offers some very useful interviews from the beginning of his presidency, whereas Sorj and Fausto (2011) show how he incorporated intellectuals into his government and their influence or lack of it.

generation that had gone abroad and returned in the 1970s faced serious problems because they had become accustomed to a European or an American standard of work, and it was impossible to do intellectual work in the same way in Brazil, without libraries or resources. In the social sciences, people like Bolivar Lamounier and Omar Faria had learned foreign research techniques but here found it hard to move forward. In view of limited national resources, he said, these scholars had to be more flexible and audacious.

Giannotti explained that the purpose of the CEBRAP was to create a new generation of intellectuals and that his role as a philosopher was to facilitate high-level studies.

He believed that the ISEB represented an important ideological moment in Brazilian history. Although its intellectual production was undoubtedly inferior to that of the São Paulo group in critical rigor, it raised the fundamental question of the role of the state in Brazilian society and attended more closely to Brazilian reality. Ianni, Cardoso, and Singer studied Brazilian reality but from a European perspective.

Giannotti felt that in the 1970s affiliation with the CEBRAP offered intellectual survival within Brazil or in exile. As a center of intellectual resistance, it raised essential questions about the nature of primitive capitalism and the concentration of income. "We were identified simply as Marxists even though as Marxists we were reading other works and seeing other realities. In the beginning of the opening in 1973, we were the 'official Marxists' at conferences. It was a false ideological view. Our group gave several seminars for the PMDB [Partido do Movimento Democrático Brasileiro (Brazilian Democratic Movement Party)] that were huge successes and showed politicians how we could be useful. Fernando Henrique led the first seminar in the legislative assembly of Porto Alegre before thirteen hundred people; I led the second on 'The Intellectual and the Context' before a thousand people, and Francisco de Oliveira gave the third. These conferences contributed to the struggle for an intellectual opening. Our leftist friends criticized us for collaborating with an opposition tacitly accepted by the military regime. We also did not contribute to the guerrilla movement; we felt that the conditions did not exist for the establishment of a rural or urban guerrilla movement in Brazil. We traveled all over the country, giving seminars. We criticized the regime as well as orthodox Marxism, and in this way the CEBRAP contributed to the opening. The idea was to seek a new Marxism. We also held important monthly internal seminars during 1975–1976, and this brought diverse people together. Thus, the CEBRAP's intellectual production was important because it raised new questions, introduced new methods. However, it did not accomplish the intellectual renovation that we hoped it would achieve. In this sense we were more conservative than we wanted to be" (interview, São Paulo, October 26, 1984; see also Giannotti, 1984, 1989, 1999).

Octávio Ianni studied with Cardoso and others under the tutelage of Florestan Fernandes. He was an early contributor to *Revista Brasiliense* with a piece on Brazilian nationalism (1957) and an analysis of workers' behavior (1961). He frequently offered a Marxist understanding of the political situation in his country; for example, in 1964, a class analysis of economic development since the end of slavery that emphasized the decline of the agrarian-commercial bourgeoisie in the Old Republic and the push toward industrialization after 1930. He suggested that it was in this period, which saw an increase in the productive forces, wage labor, and protectionism and an ensuing struggle between the agrarian-commercial bourgeoisie in decline and the rising industrial bourgeoisie, that capitalism took hold: "The nascent industrial bourgeoisie found that the economic, political, administrative, and educational institutions it inherited from a predominantly agrarian-colonial past were incompatible with the kind of democracy indispensable for the definitive victory of an industrial and capitalist mode of production" (49). He showed that the industrial bourgeoisie used nationalism and an ideology of development to draw the exploited middle classes and the proletariat into reformist campaigns (51). Elsewhere, he wrote on class and social tensions, the formation of the working class, and education and social classes (1963) and, with Paul Singer, Gabriel Cohn, and Francisco Weffort, he explored the politics of social revolution in Brazil (1965). He went on to discuss the state and planning from 1930 to 1970 (1965), the collapse of populism after the 1964 coup (1968), the role of the state in Brazilian capitalism (1971), the state and its organization of culture (1978), and the crisis of the nation-state (1986); in the latter article, he argued that nationalism inspired a national capitalism incapable of resisting the dynamism of the international economy, one that would eventually succumb to that dynamism (44–45). He also argued (1981) that weakened dominant classes coalesced to defend the bourgeois state in the face of the advance of worker, peasant, and urban social movements. His work touched on revolution and culture (1983) and imperialism and globalization (1995). Finally, he devoted two books (1975, 1989) to an assessment of sociology and society in Brazil.

Fernando Antônio Novais graduated in history from the USP, where his doctoral dissertation (1983b) focused on Portugal and Brazil during the colonial period. He taught there from 1961 to 1985 and later at the Universidade Estadual de Campinas (UNICAMP) and at the University of Texas, the Sorbonne, and universities in Coimbra and Lisbon. His work was noteworthy for its innovative analysis of colonial trade and administration and for its understanding of relations between the metropole and the colony. It was, as we have seen, Novais who pushed the *Capital* Group toward the study of Marx. His work changed the perception of the history of Brazil from a Marxist perspective. The *Capital* seminar avoided an orthodox stage view of history and sought a new system of categories for rewriting Brazil's history. Novais considered it necessary to transcend dogmatism and reductionism in historical analysis because Latin America's social tensions, dependency, and struggle for democracy made Marxism a valuable perspective: "Our intellectuals are not more intelligent than others, but our historical condition leads us to such an approach. Europe and other countries will have to follow our lead in creative Marxism." He observed that whereas in the United States and Europe Marxism was only one among many theories in the social sciences, in Latin America it was an essential point of reference. Mariátegui and Prado Júnior were important Marxist thinkers, and while they matured in what he described as the first of two moments in the history of Marxism in Latin America, one that was extremely reductionist, simplistic, dogmatic, and economistic, they were also representative of the second moment, which was creative, original, and critical. Curiously, he identified the ECLA as being responsible for "the passage from one moment to the other" and its political economy as "an effort to renovate Marxism in Latin America." He felt that the *Capital* seminars "reflected a transition to a more creative and critical Marxism." He referred to other readings, such as György Lukács's work on history and class consciousness, and we recall that Giannotti mentioned that the group had delved into Keynes and Hilferding (Colóquio Sobre Marx, 1983).

Francisco de Oliveira was a sociologist from Recife, a prominent professor at the USP, and a scholar and researcher at the CEBRAP. He considered the Brazilian economy too complex for a classical solution: "Its most significant characteristic could be monopoly regulation. Yet through all the cycles of monopolistic regulation, the Brazilian economy has not brought about a change in the social relations within capitalism that would suggest a stage of well-being.... For this reason we can call this process one of savage capitalism ... internal autonomy converted into a powerful force of external dependency." A transition to democracy characterized by new rules under a new government would, he felt, be difficult because the old groups allied with the authoritarian regime would remain in place and the agendas of the past would compromise the new government. Thus, the negation of the interests of conservative groups would mean not its extinction but its expansion. He saw both an economic and a political crisis as complicating any transition to a new government and substantial change (interview, Aguas de São Pedro, São Paulo, October 24, 1984).

Oliveira's major writings included a critique of dualistic reasoning (1976); a Marxist analysis of mercantilism in the Old Republic, accumulation, oligopolies, and the Brazilian state (1977a); an impassioned study of the Northeast (1977b); an incisive analysis of the recession and unemployment (1983); and an anthology on the economist Celso Furtado (1983).

Paul Singer, after finishing his undergraduate studies at the USP in 1959, taught there until the coup. Under Florestan Fernandes, he carried out a study of five cities that became his doctoral thesis in 1966. He was familiar with the work of Paul Baran on backwardness and noted that André Gunder Frank argued similarly to Caio Prado Júnior that Brazilian agriculture had always been capitalist. He had discussed agrarian reform and feudalism with Frank in Brasília in 1962: "He criticized several of us, including myself and Fernando Henrique, in an article published in *Revista Brasiliense* [Frank, 1964]. During the seminar we discussed his criticism of us. I took the position that it was clear that the process of capitalist penetration in Brazilian agriculture was still under way because the agriculture sector was backward and there were still pre-capitalist formations" (interviews, São Paulo, September 26, 1983, and June 10, 1995).

The Marxist intelligentsia in Brazil, he said, was always redefining Brazilian reality and reacting to events: "We were wrong in our analysis of the 1964 movement, and it forced us to analyze our reality in deeper ways." He argued that the repression of the 1960s and 1970s forced most militant intellectuals to retreat from political activism and, as a consequence, many books were written during that period. With the opening, many intellectuals became politically active again, and their writing declined drastically. He himself had become involved in the PT, "the realization of a dream of having workers, peasants, and intellectuals actively involved in one party." Its expression in the labor movement was, he felt, "much more important and impressive than its electoral success." He despaired of the divergences between the Unified Workers' Central (Central Única dos Trabalhadores ([CUT]) and the Coordenação Nacional da Classe Trabalhadora (CONCLAT) in the labor movement and called for unification of the different factions of the working class (interview, São Paulo, September 26, 1983).

Asked about the meaning of socialism, Singer responded that it evolved out of contradictions within capitalism, led to the socialization of the means of production, and aimed toward an egalitarian society and the abolition of social classes. Francisco Weffort, he said, discounted forms of socialism that he considered negative, such as bureaucratic socialism, authoritarian socialism, and social democracy in which big capital exercised control; he believed that socialism involved the socialization of the means of production within a radical form of participatory democracy. José Arthur Giannotti argued that, ideally, socialism meant the appropriation by workers of the means of production and the elimination of alienation in the work process. All three of these observers looked to the possibility of a socialism in Brazil, Singer seeing it as a result of class struggle with workers gaining control over the means of production, Weffort believing that it would evolve through a progressive political party, and Giannotti insisting that it would require going beyond authoritarianism, on the one hand, and populism promoted by the bourgeoisie, on the other (Singer, Weffort, and Giannotti, 1986).

The seminars of the *Capital* Group, Singer recalls, lasted four years. "There was no economist, so Fernando Novais, a professor of economic history, introduced me to the group. We met every two weeks, generally Saturday afternoon in our homes. We studied *Capital* chapter by chapter from 3 to 5 p.m. and then turned to the political situation and ended with dinner. The reading and study of *Capital* was particularly interesting because it opened itself to all disciplines. Nobody dominated the group. It was an open group that led to two or three other study groups. For instance, Weffort's included Leôncio Rodrigues and Bento Prado. We also studied Keynes, Rosa Luxemburg, and Max Weber. Florestan had nothing to do with the group and worked through the Centro de Sociologia Industrial do Trabalho [CESIT]. The *Capital* Group was important. It showed us that interdisciplinary work was important in contrast to a narrow focus. The group lasted from 1958 to 1965. Fernando Henrique left for exile in 1964 because of the coup, and the experience later led to the formation of the CEBRAP. It was not all the same people, but it served us because we had been thrown out of the university. Of them only Fernando and Octávio had worked with Florestan" (interview, São Paulo, June 19, 1995).

"The richness of *Capital* allowed for a review of the essentials of all the different scientific disciplines. In accordance with our readings of the text, we would focus on anthropology, methodology, historical problems. Therefore I gained an overall education from the seminar. I believe that all of us changed as a result of the experience. The seminar expanded our knowledge and perception of society. Another attraction of the seminar was the discussions of contemporary events in Brazil and globally. We were pioneers in the reading of *Capital*. After the seminar, there was a multitude of Marxist seminars; today there are several groups reading *Capital* here and abroad. In 1975, I was a visiting professor in Germany, and it was almost obligatory for social science students to attend a *Capital* seminar.

"It is interesting to ask why our group started some years earlier. I think it has a lot to do with the history of Marxism. For some fifty years Marxism went through a period of dogmatism and sterility. Between the beginning of the Second International and the early 1960s there were very few critical Marxist scholars. . . . It was not by chance that our seminar began after 1956, that is, after Stalin, the Khrushchev declaration, and the Hungarian revolt, which effectively permitted Marxists to view the doctrine with critical eyes. Today, it is difficult for this generation to understand that at that time to be a Marxist was a decision of an almost 'religious' character. There were only orthodox Marxists, and for them the word 'revisionism' was blasphemy. But the essence of Marxism is revisionism; it is impossible to be a Marxist without being a revisionist. Marx was a revisionist himself; he revised many of his earlier writings in later years. When he said that he was not a Marxist, he was being truthful and authentic, because for him being a 'Marxist' was stopping in time. . . . The reemergence of Marxism as a cultural and political phenomenon in the 1960s was a 'recovery' of Marx. In Brazil, the UK, and Germany people began to read the original Marx as a rejection of dogmatic Marxism. We did just that in our seminar. Giannotti remembers the influence of *Socialisme et Barbarisme* in his position on Marxism. I was influenced by several former Trotskyist intellectuals who shared their dogmatism through Marxism.

"I believe that the *Capital* seminar was successful because the conditions were ripe for it. The seminar was productive in our individual careers and in the CEBRAP. The intellectual work of the CEBRAP was marked by the experience of those who had participated in the seminar [five of the original eight members worked together in the CEBRAP]. In this way, I think we were participating in a wider movement, nationally and internationally, without realizing it at the time. If, in 1958, someone had predicted that twenty-five years later we would be sitting here talking to you, the idea would have been considered ridiculous and pretentious" (Colóquio Sobre Marx, 1983).

As an economist, Singer addressed Brazilian problems such as development (1968), inflation and the cost of living (1980), and inequality in income distribution and social structure (1981). It is not surprising, in light of his practical experience, that he offered a brief treatise (1982; and with others in 1986) on socialism and its implications for unequal and combined development and the possibility of attaining an egalitarian society. He also published a memoir (1996) on his service as an advisor to the São Paulo municipal government of Luiza Erundina.

THE SECOND CAPITAL GROUP

Many of the scholars of the *Capital* Group were forced into clandestinity and exile, and a second line of graduate students carried on in the face of censorship and repression. Among them were Marilena Chauí, Michael Löwy, Leôncio Martins Rodrigues, Emir Sader, Roberto Schwarz, and Francisco Weffort. Chauí was a philosopher deeply involved in cultural affairs. Löwy, who had left Brazil before the coup, had settled in Paris and became renowned internationally as a teacher and scholar. Rodrigues pursued important studies of the labor movement. Sader emerged as a critic of the evolving political scene. Schwarz established himself as a literary critic and appears to have been responsible for what many participants called the Second *Capital* Group, which met sporadically after the coup until about 1966 or 1967. Weffort became immersed in questions of underdevelopment, dependency, populism, and democracy.

Marilena Chauí was known less for her interest in Marx than for her scholarly work on Baruch Spinosa and Maurice Merleau-Ponty, but in one of her weekly newspaper columns she portrayed herself as an activist involved in issues of civil rights and freedom. Her book *O que é ideologia* (1980b) sold more than a 100,000 copies in the Brazilian market. In fact, this popular work built on her focus on ideology (1978, 1980a, 1982) and was concerned with the way ideology could be useful in popular mobilization (with Carvalho Franco, 1978). Affiliated with the PT, during 1988 to 1992, she served as municipal secretary of culture under São Paulo Mayor Luiza Erundina. This was an opportunity to implement reforms aimed at involving greater numbers of people in local and national problems. Although the PT administered the municipal government, it held only fifteen of thirty-three seats on the city council, yet she was able to expand cultural activities, including the refurbishing of theaters, the expansion of libraries, and the establishment of art centers and historical archives (interview, São Paulo, August 21, 1992).

In the important series *Seminários*, Chauí (1983) argued that projects of national popular culture were concerned with national identity and turned to Gramsci, for whom a national perspective offered the possibility of rescuing the cultural history that was the patrimony of the popular classes. According to Chauí, Gramsci thought of the "national" and the "popular" as synonymous and as signifying the capacity of an intellectual or an artist to present ideas, sentiments, and passions for people to recognize and understand and to awaken popular consciousness. The term "national," however, is associated with the dominant class and the term "popular" with the people, and therefore Gramsci's concept of "national popular culture," although of pedagogical value, is not a panacea. It may become a strategy in the class struggle or a way of glossing over social divisions to focus on the national state.[10]

Michael Löwy was a respected French-Brazilian Marxist sociologist and philosopher. Prior to his departure for doctoral studies at the Sorbonne, he studied at the USP with Antônio Cândido, Florestan Fernandes, Octávio Ianni, and Paul Singer and, upon finishing, taught for a year in Rio Preto. In Paris, he studied with Lucien Goldman, receiving a doctorate in 1964 and then teaching political philosophy at the University of Tel Aviv until 1968 and thereafter at the University of Paris, where he was associated with Nicos Poulantzas. He wrote on Karl Marx, György Lukács, Franz Kafka, and Che Guevara (1973); on class consciousness and the revolutionary party (1962a); and on the young Marx (1962b) (the subject of his dissertation). His perceptive critical appraisals (1975, 1981) of combined and uneven development and the theory of permanent revolution were significant contributions. Over the years, Löwy maintained his contacts with Trotskyist movements in France and with leftist currents within the PT in Brazil (interview, Paris, October 18, 1985).

---

[10] Chauí distinguishes between an affirmative and negative image of national popular. In the first case, there is identification between the national sovereignty and the popular sovereignty. In the second, the expression national-cultural resides in an internal division of classes: either the expression national popular is conserved as a strategy or tactic in the class struggle, or it obscures social division and focuses on the national state (1983: 22). Alongside the state, nationalist ideology develops as policy of the state. Alongside society, nationalism develops as a patriotic ideology of a middle class (31). Society may be conflictual or harmonious under a state that is national with its territory, popular because of its sovereignty, and self-determined.

Leôncio Martins Rodrigues had been involved in political militancy for many years before graduating from the USP in 1962. He was affiliated with the Trotskyist Revolutionary Socialist Party (Partido Socialista Revolucionário [PSR]) and in 1954 represented the party at the Fourth International. At the USP he studied with Fernando Henrique and Ruth Cardoso. In his third year, Fernandes invited him to work at the CESIT: "I had not read *Capital*, although I was well read in Marxism and for the most part in Trotsky, Lenin, Luxemburg, and other texts. By the time I entered the university I had left the Trotskyist movement and was not much interested in Marxism, and involvement with the *Capital* Group did not make much sense at the time. Fernando Henrique was associated with the intellectuals around the journal *Fundamentos* but did not talk about Marx. Marxism hardly existed at USP, although I think Ianni gave a course once on *Capital* at a time when it was essential in one's intellectual development.... My situation was ambiguous; Singer and others were Marxist, Juárez Brandão Lopes was not, and I was leaving Marxism behind."

Rodrigues finished his undergraduate studies in 1962 and his master's degree under Fernandes in 1964 with a focus on strikes in São Paulo industries. He took Cardoso's place at the CESIT after the coup. Beginning work on his doctorate, he became involved in a survey of three hundred businesses of varying size in and around São Paulo (1966, 1970). "Later I also had to leave Brazil, given my six or seven years in the Trotskyist movement and that I was working in the 'most subversive' field. Others such as Boris Fausto had no background of militancy but were investigated, probably because of anti-Semitism. I knew people associated with the resistance, and so I left with an invitation to Belgium in 1969." Soon thereafter, the CEBRAP was established, and Rodrigues resolved to return to his position in the university. Being a friend of Cardoso, he participated in the CEBRAP in 1971–1972 but not as a formal member: "In sociology I disagreed with Luiz Pereira and most others who were Marxist. Thus I left sociology for political science, an old discipline in which Fernando Henrique had passed the exams for the chair in political science. He had studied and taught sociology with Fernandes, but in 1964 he was at risk of being imprisoned and fled to Chile, returning to São Paulo in 1968 after a brief visit to France. Fernando de Azevedo was in charge of another course in sociology, but he retired and Fernando Henrique was expected to compete with Rui Coelho for the position. His *livre docência* [a degree beyond the doctorate] was a study of businessmen. Along came the coup of 1964, and Fernando Henrique went to Chile. Ianni competed for the position but lost, mostly because Azevedo supported his assistant, Rui."

While Cardoso was in Europe, political science at the USP was under the direction of Lourival Gomes Machado, but he was not really a political scientist and he left to direct the School of Architecture, leaving in charge Paulo Benjamin, who died in Paris soon thereafter. Cardoso was named to the position, then forcibly retired along with other professors who lost their right to work in a public institution. Francisco Weffort assumed the leadership, and Rodrigues remained with political science at the USP until his retirement in 1985, when he moved to UNICAMP: "I supported Fernando Henrique because I had been a liberal (not neoliberal) since the time I left Marxism and opposed socialism. The problem of Brazilian society is corporatism, bureaucracy, a Lusitanian culture tied to authoritarianism, and the use of the state for private benefit" (interview, Pinheiros, São Paulo, July 11, 1995).

Emir Sader worked on his master's degree at the USP with Ruy Fausto, Giannotti, and Bento Prado. He recalls the visit of Perry Anderson, who "worked with us in Rio and was supportive of our journal *Teoria e Prática*." He left Brazil in 1970, joined Santos in Chile, then moved to Argentina and later to Cuba for six or seven years. He felt that his time in Cuba allowed him to transcend his limited experience in Brazil, whereas Chile served as a laboratory: "When I returned in 1983, I was more into Latin America, since most of the others had sought exile in Europe. There was a schism, as Marco Aurélio and others, influenced by political trends, went to Paris. In contrast to the Soviet influence that prevailed to a certain extent in Europe, what was going on in Central America and Latin America was more influenced by Maoism or Fidel." Sader was referring here to the Política Operária (POLOP), founded by Marini, Moniz Bandeira, and Theotônio dos Santos. Erick Sacks, an Austrian Marxist influenced by Heidegger, was very important in this group and was involved in the PSB in Rio. In addition, there was a current in Minas led by Santos and associated with the Partido Trabalhista Brasileiro (PTB) and a Chamista group that included Chauí in São Paulo and in which Sader participated. He attended many Trotskyist activities and was influenced by Trotsky and Gramsci because of their criticisms of the Soviet Union. Marini, who had worked to organize a propagandist arm to mobilize military people, especially in Rio, was imprisoned in 1964 and left Brazil a year later. Santos had gone to Chile, and the movement became clandestine (interview, Rio de Janeiro, January 29, 1991).

Sader was a prolific writer, a national commentator on political trends, and a sociologist deeply concerned with change in Brazil. He had joined the PT early and organized a volume of essays on the party by militants and intellectuals (1986). A more in-depth study (1988) looked at the working class in São Paulo, the Christian base communities, leftist Marxism, and the new social movements. A lengthy essay (1990) offered a brief overview and political analysis of the period since Vargas. Another (1995) explored the role of the leftist intellectual in Brazil. Focusing on the struggle of the PCB to build a worker–peasant alliance and seize power through a revolution similar to the Russian Revolution, Sader emphasized the party's opportunism; for example, its failure to join the opposition to Vargas in favor of political democracy and its willingness to work within the labor movement controlled by Vargas and the state. Eventually, he became disillusioned with the PT and edited a volume of critical essays on world capitalism and neoliberalism, with particular attention paid to Brazil during the first Lula administration (2003), but later he reconciled with the PT. He also became the executive director of the Latin American Social Science Council (Consejo Latinoamericano de Ciencias Sociales [CLACSO]), an umbrella organization of universities and research centers throughout Latin America.

Roberto Schwarz was associated early in his studies with distinguished São Paulo intellectuals, participated in the *Capital* Group, and emerged as a leading literary theorist and critic of Brazilian culture (1978). Born in Vienna in 1938 but raised in Brazil, he was particularly influenced (Abrantes, 1992) by the literary historian Antônio Cândido de Mello Sousa. He is best known for his attention to the Brazilian novelist Machado de Assis (1990, 2001b) and occasional essays (1967, 2001a) and for his work on culture (1992). In the latter, searching for the nation's roots, he argued that critical ideas of Sílvio Romero, Mário de Andrade, and Antônio Cândido served as a foundation for building a genuine national culture (3). He was particularly concerned with and pointed to the tendency to imitate cultural traits outside the country and with the "fatal consequence of our cultural dependency that we are always interpreting our reality with conceptual systems created somewhere else" (39). He referred to the "organic" nature of Brazilian culture and, in the aftermath of the 1964 coup, the failure of the military to suppress the cultural presence of the left. Despite a right-wing dictatorship, he said, "the works produced by the left dominated the cultural scene" (127).

In 1958, during his second year of undergraduate studies, Schwarz attended the *Capital* seminar meetings but did not participate extensively. Its importance, in his view, was reflected in the innovative theses that it generated. Prior to the seminar, sociology had focused on community studies and racial prejudice. After the seminar, the participants wrote theses in which local problems were linked to world history and the general development of capitalism in Brazil. The principal effect of this new orientation was to show that local history was part of a global historical movement. This attention to world history became part of Cardoso's writings on dependency, whereas Frank's scheme of a center monopoly and a peripheral satellite was formal and universalistic. Although both writers sought to understand the Latin American political problem as a function of the general movement of capitalism, Cardoso's work, in Schwarz's view, was the more realistic.

Perry Anderson joined the Second *Capital* Group while living in Brazil for six months doing research on the 1930 Revolution. He gave three lectures about his research, and, although it was not published, it influenced Boris Fausto. Anderson's contribution inspired the launching of *Teoria e Prática*, of which three issues appeared before the police closed it down. "The second seminar was organized in a similar way as the first. We read *Capital* systematically, and we met every two weeks. Many participants were actively involved in the events of 1968 and were either imprisoned or had to leave the country. In comparing the two seminars, the first was intellectually stronger and produced a more original study of Marx, yet in both instances the participants were convinced that Marxism was important for an understanding of the social sciences and the world situation. In the first seminar, many participants were sociologists for whom Weber had been the major influence, and thus the seminar took on the character of a debate between Marx and Weber. Most of the participants in the second seminar were Marxists and political activists; Weber had no influence whatsoever, and the seminar was less academically oriented. The participants generally thought that the PCB was not really Marxist and only by studying Marx could a true Marxist movement be created. During the second seminar, the climate was very antinationalist, and the leftist nationalistic tradition was considered unrealistic in focusing on anti-Americanism and ignoring the Brazilian class structure. Moreover, the nationalist tradition emerging from Getúlio Vargas was considered xenophobic. The participants of the second seminar took issue with this irrational nationalism" (interview, São Paulo, September 20, 1983).

According to Schwarz, there was no connection between the Rio and São Paulo groups: "The Rio group did not even know we existed in São Paulo, but in our minds they were rivals, and we wanted to show that we were the better group." Because of the repression, Schwarz left Brazil in 1969 and lived in France until 1978. As a literature professor, he participated in the CEBRAP, contributing to its publications on cultural affairs and political economy: "It was the most influential intellectual center of our times; it preserved intellectual freedom." Its publications were for internal consumption, but some of the same topics were presented in the newspaper *Opinião* in 1973–1974 and the journal *Argumento*, both widely circulated outside the CEBRAP, "which had a tacit agreement with the police not to circulate its material."

He described the Marxist intelligentsia as divided and having produced very little substantively: "There is a kind of simple Marxism for intellectuals who are not producing theoretical work. There is a lack of new ideas within the intelligentsia, and Marxism has lost the intellectual initiative in Brazil." During the Goulart regime, the left in São Paulo wanted to participate actively in the regime's populism, and after the fall of the regime it was strongly influenced by the Cuban strategy of armed revolution. With the democratic opening, it became active in the political parties and the legal apparatus of the government (interview, São Paulo, September 20, 1983).

Francisco Weffort was an undergraduate in social sciences at the USP when he participated in the *Capital* seminar. "The seminar made a strong intellectual impression on all of us.... This experience of intellectual formation was perhaps the most important any of us has ever had." He explained that the group did not ignore nationalism as the central issue of the 1960s, but they were critical of the nationalistic ideology of the ISEB that they felt obscured the real problems facing Brazilian society. "The seminar participants valued academic rigor, scientific logic, methodology. The central issue was autonomous economic development or dependent development." In Weffort's opinion, the *Revista Brasiliense* gave Cardoso, Singer, Ianni, and others an opportunity to publish articles and expose their ideas but was not a major intellectual influence in academic circles. It was more influential in militant circles. The major concern of the *Capital* Group was a systematic understanding of the logic of Marx's thinking; there was little discussion of concrete contemporary issues. Caio Prado Júnior was the major influence on Marxist thinking in Brazil, and Cuban influence was important around 1964 and dominated militant intellectual circles. Marxist thought lost its dynamic in the 1970s and 1980s (interview, São Paulo, September 26, 1983).

SCHOLARLY ENDEAVORS UNDER MILITARY RULE: THE CEBRAP AND THE CEDEC

Some of the Paulistas who remained in Brazil after 1964 or returned from abroad encountered a really significant development in the founding in 1969 of an independent research institution, the CEBRAP in São Paulo with funding from the Ford Foundation. According to Giannotti, the foundation had wanted to support three intellectual centers – in Minas Gerais, Rio Grande do Sul, and São Paulo – but only the São Paulo group was able to sustain its activities at the time. He attributed the CEBRAP's success to the *Capital* seminars.

The CEBRAP's activities revolved around research, lectures, and the publication of a journal. Its participants, marginalized from university life, moved toward a social science oriented to praxis, a concept adopted by the *Capital* Group and defended by Caio Prado Júnior. Their attention shifted from themes such as race relations, social stratification, and cultural dynamics to the political analysis of authoritarian regimes, social exclusion, and economic models. Politically, the CEBRAP evolved as an intellectual forum for the democratic opposition. In 1974, Cardoso and Singer wrote the platform of the Brazilian Democratic Movement (Movimento Democrático Brasileiro [MDB]), emphasizing better income distribution, free labor unions, participatory social movements, and economic development. With its books on the best-sellers' list, the CEBRAP had become the most prestigious intellectual forum in the country.

Functioning as a private institution, the CEBRAP aroused public interest in its academic debates. One brought together Maria da Conceição Tavares, José Serra, Luiz Belluzo, Edmar Bacha, and Fernando Henrique Cardoso to challenge the conservative logic of the military regime's technocracy, demonstrating that in periods of democracy there would be compatibility among economic growth, controllable inflation, and improvement in income (a position in contrast to the authoritarian economic policies advocated by the economists Delfin Neto and Mário Henrique Simonsen). Another debate involved Cardoso and Francisco de Oliveira in rebuttals on a stance about urban marginalization set forth by the Argentine political scientist José Nun and the Peruvian sociologist Aníbal Quijano. Nun argued that capitalism tended to create a marginalized mass that did not participate in production, lived on the periphery of society, and was dispensable to capital accumulation. Oliveira (1972) drew on Prado's analysis of the use of slave labor in production for the market to argue that it was common for peripheral capitalism to recreate the productive relations predominant in precapitalist societies; thus, urban marginalization reflected the dependent and technical backwardness of the national bourgeoisie, which, unable to compete with the multinationals, concentrated on low-wage labor-intensive traditional industries, thereby sustaining the underdeveloped capitalism of the authoritarian regime (Abu-El-Haj and Chilcote, 2011: 26–27).

The CEBRAP served as an academic buffer to military intervention during the repressive era of authoritarianism. In 1973, it published *Estudos CEBRAP* as a quarterly edited by Juárez Rubens Brandão Lopes,[11] with an editorial board made up of José Arthur Giannotti, Carlos Estevam Martins, and Francisco de Oliveira. Edições CEBRAP published several monographs on its own and several others with Editora Brasiliense, along with a series called *Cadernos* of which twenty-eight issues had appeared by July–September 1977. The first series of issues of the quarterly tended to include papers that were of theoretical interest but generally not grounded in Brazilian experience. A new phase began with a new title, *Novos Estudos CEBRAP*, in December 1981 and was intended to contain shorter, more timely, and more popular articles. Brandão Lopes continued as editor with an expanded editorial board, including Roberto Schwarz, who offered an introductory note to the first issue attributing the marginalization of intellectuals to the dictatorship and to the growth of capitalism and suggesting that the pessimism of the day provided an opening for a new journal. Schwarz's call for a new direction at this point was backed by Giannotti, who in an overview of the first twenty years of the CEBRAP (1989) said that, having been founded to preserve the spirit of academic life outside the university and to be independent of public funds, with the return of its members to the university it needed to return to its role as an organ of resistance. Brandão Lopes edited the new series until February 1986. Francisco de Oliveira assumed the editorship in September 1987, when the journal offered a formal cover, fewer graphics within, and a clearly more academic orientation. This phase reflected pessimism, preoccupation about the future of the institute and its journal, and a search for a new generation of intellectuals. Many of the articles were translations of debates outside Brazil.

---

[11] Brandão Lopes was a key administrator of the CEBRAP's affairs during its early years. His important publications include a study of industrial development in São Paulo and the interior of Bahia (1964) and a community study of two neighboring cities in Minas Gerais (1967) with attention to patrimonialism, industrial relations, workforces, and social organization.

Among the important contributions were a critique of the idea of dependency by José Serra and Fernando Henrique Cardoso (1978), a discussion of the importance of Brazilians in Latin American literature by Antônio Cândido (1981), a review of the working class and the industrial bourgeoisie through the transition marked by the revolution of 1930 by Boris Fausto (1976, 1988), and an analysis of debt and the deterioration of the economy by Celso Furtado (2000).

Although many intellectuals rallied to the CEBRAP and its optimism for a democratic outcome, at least three divergent tendencies were evident in intellectual circles (Abu-El-Haj and Chilcote, 2011: 29–31). Inspired by the work of Vítor Nunes Leal, a group of political scientists with roots in Minas Gerais and led by Bolivar Lamounier, Olavo Brasil de Lima Júnior, Fábio Wanderley, Maria Campelo de Souza, and Sêrgio Abranches believed that institutional stability would prevail under both dictatorship and democracy. Only political reform, reorganization of political parties, and issue-based political representation would permit the people to be truly represented and eventually lead to economic development and social equality. A second group, including Fernando Limongi, José Cheibub, and Argelina Figueiredo, assumed a pluralist stance and argued that legislative elections were competitive and that the political system reflected stability, democratization, and inclusion. A third group favored mass inclusion over political competitiveness and argued that political parties, influenced by traditional oligarchies, tended to suppress popular participation.

Led by Francisco Weffort, this third group founded the Center for Studies of Contemporary Culture (Centro de Cultura Contemporânea [CEDEC]) in 1976 as an effort to represent the intellectual core of the Brazilian New Left. Its line revived Weffort's earlier critique of party representation in Brazil as suppressing popular participation. It also attracted political scientists and sociologists of social movements, followers of Gramsci's analysis of culture. Although the CEBRAP continued allied with the MDB, the CEDEC became the PT's think tank. Founded during the democratic struggle and developing in the period of the demise of "real existing socialism," the Brazilian New Left abandoned socialism for representative democracy, embraced non-Marxist thinkers such as Arendt and Habermas, and gave up class in favor of social movements (Dagnino, 1994; Alvárez, Dagnino, and Escobar, 2000). Political mobilization of the masses was replaced by education, deliberation, and participatory practice. PT theorists believed that through public deliberations they could erase traditional social values and instill new beliefs. Experiments with participatory budgeting, local councils, and the progressive initiatives of the World Social Forum became its main political practices (Avritzer and Santos, 2002).

As did the CEBRAP, the CEDEC built its activities around research and publication through its first journal, *Revista de Cultura e Política*, published by Editora Paz e Terra in Rio with an editorial board including the philosopher Marilena Chauí, the publisher Fernando Gasparian, and the labor specialist and political scientist José Álvaro Moisés. It appeared as a quarterly from about May 1980 until June 1982. Fernando Henrique Cardoso (1980–1981) contributed an interesting analysis on the political opening and the prospects for democracy that identified several paths – liberal democracy, socialism, and anarchism – and assessed the importance of political parties as opposed to social movements in the evolution of Brazil's political system. The article, drawn from the thinking of the time (including that of Althusser and Foucault), appeared with commentary by Carlos Estevam Martins and others. The CEDEC also published annual volumes of documentation organized by its researchers beginning in May 1981.

Under the editorship of Moisés, in April–June 1984, the CEDEC reshaped its journal into a new quarterly, *Lua Nova*, that engaged with issues of the times. Articles by researchers associated with the center tended to be written in a popular style and were brief, with critical appraisal that attempted to appeal to a broader audience of intellectuals and beyond to parties, unions, universities, factories, cultural institutions, religious communities, and social movements. Its lead editorial focused on the need for democracy and called for its pages to reflect a pluralistic reality and a diversity of views. Its editorial board included Caio Graco Prado, Carlos Takaoka, Joelmir Betting, Aurélio Nogueira, Maria Victória de Mesquita Benevides, Marilena Chauí, Paulo José Krischke, and Pedro Roberto Jocobi. Its collaborators, including Amaury de Souza, Bolivar Lamounier, Boris Fausto, Carlos Hasenbalg, Carlos Brandão, Carlos Estevam Martins, Fernando Gasparian, Francisco de Oliveira, Francisco Weffort, Helio Jaguaribe, Herbert José de Souza, José Honório Rodrigues, José de Souza Martins, Juárez Brandão Lopes, Luiz Jorge Werneck Vianna, Manuel Castells, Paul Singer, Raimundo Pereira, Regis de Castro Andrade, Simon Schwartzmann, and Wanderley Guilherme dos Santos, represented a variety of perspectives.

Later, *Lua Nova* was edited by Gabriel Cohn, the author of an important work on nationalism and the petroleum issue (1968), and its editorial committee included Moisés, Leôncio Martins Rodrigues, and Maria Victoria de Mesquita Benevides. The journal devoted an issue edited by Amélia Cohen (2001) to a review of the first quarter-century of CEDEC activities. Major participants included Jorge Luiz Werneck Vianna, Octávio Ianni, Marco Aurélio Garcia, Carlos Nelson Coutinho, and Francisco de Oliveira. An interesting piece by Oliveira identified three radical thinkers who represented the generation of 1930: Gilberto Freyre, who vigorously denounced slavery; Sêrgio Buarque de Holanda, who criticized patrimonial society; and Caio Prado Júnior, who advanced a new historiography of Brazil.

Moisés had focused on labor and the new unionism early in his career and now turned to political parties and social movements. He felt that the social movements had an important role during the 1970s but more or less disappeared, absorbed by the emerging political parties, in the democratic transition. He considered the influence of the theology of liberation exaggerated. Inspired by De Toqueville, his conception of democracy had economic, social, and political dimensions. He saw intellectuals as divided into two currents, one within the universities, the other outside among artists, journalists, and others. Intellectuals could be organic and active both in society and in a party, but parties were weak: "Today, we do not have parties of any substance in the sense of parties with programs and with ideologies with which they can identify with issues. We are a society of personalities." He criticized some intellectuals for an inability to relate to fundamental issues: "Take the case of Lamounier: he writes about Brazilian democratization, but he is mistaken because he does not take into consideration the question of inequality." Yet he felt that sympathy for the PT and Lula was common among intellectuals (interview, São Paulo, May 31, 1994).

Moisés and Weffort were two of the CEDEC's leading scholars and activists. Weffort focused on labor (1972, 1975) and the politics of the masses (1978). He also wrote about political participation (1980) and produced a widely read volume on democracy (1984) arguing that "Brazil in its 160 years of independent history has not had an opportunity to analyze the thesis of democracy" and that democracy should be understood as "a form of popular rebellion." Moisés published on labor but also turned to the problems of consolidating democracy in Brazil (with Albuquerque, 1989) and produced an empirical study of democracy and culture in Brazil (1995). Both were friends of Cardoso and joined his first government as high officials in the Ministry of Culture. Weffort had served as secretary general of the PT, so his joining the center-right coalition under Cardoso was something of a surprise. However, Emir Sader pointed out that "the intellectual wants power. The intellectual writes rather than transforming reality." He suggested that Weffort was "analytical but inconsistent in his ideological formation" and that neither he nor Moisés would have any impact (interview, Rio de Janeiro, July 7, 1995). René Dreifus shared this view of Weffort: "Weffort and Cardoso were able to perceive great changes as they focused on the prospects of gaining power. They understood that great changes were in the making and that the old formulas were not working as Brazil became part of the global context. Along with most Brazilians, Weffort became bored with the PT, perhaps disillusioned, and was in search of an alternative. Cardoso wants to remain in power into the twenty-first century. He wants to write an autobiography. He is cognizant of his limitations and may solve social problems, but one must not confuse state power with solving social problems" (interview, Rio de Janeiro, July 6, 1995).

PROGRESSIVE PAULISTA JOURNALS IN THE DEMOCRATIC OPENING

The end of the New State under Vargas in 1945 was accompanied by a promising awakening of Paulista intellectuals up until the 1964 coup. Military rule disrupted the universities and their advances and abruptly brought closure to the prolific and polemical writing represented by such popular publishing houses as Editora Fulgor on the left and the progressive Editora Brasiliense that represented many serious scholars within and outside the USP. Nevertheless, resistance to a long decade of censorship and repression after 1964 spurred a renaissance of activity with the political opening in the late 1970s as many leftist intellectuals became involved in politics, sacrificing commitment to ideals and principles for compromise with colleagues. The left, seeking outlets for the expressions of ideas, found space in a host of progressive journals, many of them short-lived and most of them published in São Paulo. Their editorial boards comprised renowned intellectuals as well as younger scholars whose writing revisited past themes of nationalism and development but now also questioned the meaning and implications for the progressive left of representative democracy in a period of more open politics, social movements, and popular mobilization. The quarterly *Debate & Crítica: Revista Quadrimestral de Ciências Sociais* published three issues from July 1973 to July 1974 and was edited by Florestan Fernandes, Jaime Pinsky, and José de Souza Martins with an editorial board including Cardoso, Weffort, Correia de Andrade, Ianni, and Singer. Later, the views of prominent writers appeared in *Socialismo e Democracia*, a quarterly edited by Jacob Bazarian and Daniel Fresnot beginning in January 1984 and describing itself as "independent and pluralist and open to currents that struggle for socialism." It claimed to be independent of any political party, but in fact it included the views of the São Paulo branch of the PCB. Its first issue, reflecting the views of dissident communists still influenced by Marxism and socialism, focused on revolutionary consciousness, unionism in São Paulo, and Luiz Carlos Prestes. Of particular importance was the debate about an alliance of the left, which related the popular front of the 1930s to the existing situation and involved former communists such as Heitor Ferreira Lima, contemporary communists such as David Capistrano Filho, and Christian Socialists such as Frei Betto.

Another São Paulo journal, *Presença: Revista de Política e Cultura*, first appeared in November 1983 with an editorial staff including David Capistrano Filho, João Quartim de Moraes, Luiz Werneck Vianna, and Marco Aurélio Nogueira and an editorial board made up of Bolivar Lamounier, Carlos Lessa, Carlos Nelson Coutinho, Fernando Henrique Cardoso, Leondro Konder, Moisés Vinhas, and Roberto Freire. Probably backed by the PCB and published by Editora Caetes, it was a serious journal; its third issue, focused on the crisis of democracy and transition, was particularly noteworthy with contributions by Kondor, Moraes, and Wanderley Guilherme dos Santos. Vianna published two useful articles, one on problems in mobilizing intellectuals (1983, Vianna et al., 1984b) and the other on the importance of workers in the recent history of the PCB (1984a), whereas Maria Lúcia Vianna (1984) wrote on the role of the nationalist in Brazil.

The independent leftist *Desvios* initiated publication in November 1982. Organized by a collective of São Paulo intellectuals active in the PT and other leftist political movements, it began with an analysis of the labor movement in the São Paulo area. It proposed eleven theses on autonomy for the labor movement, arguing that the moment had arrived to create a labor party and assimilate the important mass movements such as neighborhood associations and women's organizations. The theses were critical of socialist models and despaired of the "crisis of the left" and the lack of theoretical advances. They attacked new forms of dogmatism and tendencies toward bureaucratization and called for new forms of organization and struggle.

In 1984, a group of philosophers associated with UNICAMP organized the journal *Filosofia e Política*, the first issue of which consisted of papers presented at a conference a year earlier commemorating the centenary of

Marx's death (1986). The views on socialism of Paul Singer, Francisco Weffort, José Ibrahim, and José Arthur Giannotti appeared in its pages. *Temas de Ciências Humanas* was published by Editorial Grijalbo in São Paulo under the editorial direction of Marco Aurélio Nogueira, Gildo Marçal Brandão, J. Chasin, and Nelson Werneck Sodré. In 1976, it began to publish a series of annual anthologies of diverse material on Marxist themes, including the occasional reprinting of texts from Lenin and other Marxists. In an interview, Marco Aurélio Nogueira (1978) called it a journal of debate, criticism, and politics that attempted to relate politics to theory. Its eighth issue included analyses by Sodré of the history of the PCB and Konder of the PCP during 1945–1946 and an essay by Manuel Correia de Andrade on the Ligas Componesas from 1957 to 1964. Subsequent issues contained a continuation of Sodré's PCB study (1980, 1980–1981). Sodré also published a memoir of his experience with the ISEB (1976/1977/1978). Other important articles included those of Coutinho (1981) on Brazilian intellectuals and Ianni (1981) on the cycle of bourgeois revolution in Brazil.

Other progressive journals in São Paulo included the quarterly *Problemas: Publicação Teórica e Informativa*, edited by Henrique Cordeiro and first appearing in April 1982 as a publication of the PCB with contributions by Giocondo Dias and communists outside Brazil. *Teoria Política* published seven issues from 1980 to 1985, with an editorial board including Caio Navarro Toledo, Daniel Aarão Reis, and Dêcio Saes. As a journal of theoretical debate, it held that Marxist theory was vital to the situation of Brazil as it moved from dictatorship to democracy. It warned against revisionism and suggested that the themes of concern should be Brazilian social formation, the historical experience of the Brazilian workers and the popular movement, economic and political changes within the capitalist system, socialist transformations, and the strategy and tactics of the proletarian struggle on a world scale and within Brazil. Three essays stand out: those of Ronald de Oliveira Rocha (1980) on the mercantile capitalist emphasis in the thought of André Gunder Frank and Caio Prado Júnior; Wladimir Pomar on tactics of struggle against the dictatorship (1982); and Dêcio Saes on Marx's early conception of the state (1984).

Argumento appeared under the editorship of Barbosa Lima Sobrinho with an editorial board including Helio Jaguaribe and Florestan Fernandes. Published by Editora Paz e Terra, its first issue appeared about 1972. Edited by J. Chassin, the journal *Ensaio (Filosifia/Política/ Ciência de História)* appeared during the 1980s with a focus on the left in the democratic opening and the impact of capital on reformist policies. Its board consisted of Florestan Fernandes, Heitor Ferreira Lima, Dêcio Saes, Edgar Carone, Clovis Moura, Moniz Bandeira, and others. The first and perhaps only issue of *Praga: Revista de Estudos Marxistas*, dated September–December 1996, was published in São Paulo with an editorial board consisting of Caio Navarro de Toledo, Carlos Nelson Coutinho, Emir Sader, Celso Frederico, Fernando Novais, Leondro Konder, Marilena Chauí, Ricardo Antunes, and Roberto Schwarz. It included an interview with Antônio Cândido (1996) that analyzed Marxist ideas and recorded his political activity as part of the Esquerda Democrática, dominated by the PSB, during the 1930s and 1940s.

São Paulo also hosts the *Revista de Economia Política*, a serious academic quarterly once published by Editora Brasiliense and now Editora 34 and edited by Luiz Carlos Bresser-Pereira. Initially appearing in January 1981, its sponsors were and remain Caio Prado Júnior, Celso Furtado, and Inácio Rangel. An organ of the Centro de Economia Política, its early editorial board consisted of such progressive intellectuals as André Franco Montoro Filho, Alberto Passos Guimarães, Clovis Cavalcanti, Edmar Bacha, Eduardo Suplicy, Fernando Homem de Mello, Guido Mantega, Ivan Ribeiro, José Graziano da Silva, José Serra, Luiz Gonzaga de Mello Belluzzo, Manoel Correia de Andrade, Wilson Cano, Francisco de Oliveira, Maria da Conceição Tavares, Paul Singer, and Yoshiaki Nakano. Today, none of these intellectuals serves on its editorial board, which comprises generally liberal and mainstream economists, but it is open to progressive manuscripts. With its attention devoted to political economy, together with many articles focused on developmental issues, it now appeals to political economists everywhere. Its editorial statement welcomes papers with a Keynesian, structuralist, or institutionalist approach, as well as those on development economics and critical of economic theory.

MORE RECENT INTELLECTUAL ENDEAVORS

Campinas and São Paulo intellectuals on the left shaped two journals that today publish and debate controversial issues on important theoretical themes: the *Revista Crítica Marxista* and *Lutas Sociais*. A group associated with UNICAMP launched a journal of theoretical and substantive content, *Revista Crítica Marxista*, in 1995. Published originally in São Paulo by Editora Brasiliense, it has appeared sporadically, with thirty-three numbers through 2011. Its initial nine-person editorial board consisted of Armando Boito Júnior, Caio Navarro de Toledo, Celso Frederico, João Quartim de Moraes, João Roberto Martins Filho, Juárez Guimarães, Marcijo Bilharinho Neves, Ricardo Antunes, and Sêrgio Lessa. Boito, Quartim, and Lessa continue to serve today. It is backed by an editorial council of 137 progressive intellectuals, many of them prominent scholars interested in Marxism. Its content occasionally includes material from abroad. Among its important articles are a piece by Toledo (1995a) on bourgeois and revolutionary strategies useful for implementing democracy on the left, one by Dêcio Saes (1995) on Althusserian ideas in the context of past Marxist theory, one by Tânia Pelligrini (1995) on cultural production and capitalism, and a debate coordinated by Octávio Ianni (1995) on imperialism and globalization. A favorable review by Sêrgio Braga of an important book by Toledo (2005) on the historical importance of the ISEB appeared in issue 23 (2006).

The ensuing discussion focuses on contemporary progressive intellectuals, all of them associated with universities, active in public forums and debates, and continuously publishing on theoretical questions and issues in the political economy.

Ricardo Antunes, in an interview in Washington, DC, on September 28, 1995, said that the work of Roberto Schwarz was perhaps the most sophisticated of the contributions of the *Capital* Group; he was also impressed with the writing of Fernando Novais – inspired by Caio Prado Júnior – on colonial slavery, which used Marx's notion of primitive accumulation to show how Brazil in the colonial world evolved in the mercantile phase of capitalism. The Marxist influence of Nelson Werneck Sodré and Álvaro Vieira Pinto within the left of the ISEB was, he felt, more problematic with its attention to nationalism but was nevertheless an important influence on Marxism. Antunes studied political science at UNICAMP, including a course with Michel Debrun. Among the concepts dominant in political science at the time were populism and dependency (both of which proved mistaken), the latter of which was picked up by the group at the USP that evolved into the CEBRAP and was seen as an advance on the theory of imperialism. In his opinion, Novais took his ideas of dependency from Frank but was more influenced by Cardoso, as was Schwarz. The theory of dependency was a critical revision, an effort to incorporate elements of Marxism without being a Marxist analysis. Whereas Novais and Schwarz represented an original Marxism, Cardoso's Marxism was, he felt, superficial. Cardoso was highly visible in intellectual life, but intellectuals did not necessarily follow him. Weffort and Moisés followed him but by different paths, offering a subtle criticism of Marxism and rejecting the Marxism of the PCB. Eventually, they left the PT to work in Cardoso's government and in pursuit of a social democratic party and the benefits of serving in a government ministry. Caio Prado Júnior worked his ideas through a Marxist perspective, as did Gorender, who had a different conception of Marxism. The influence of Florestan Fernandes, especially since his book on the bourgeois revolution, was as important for the left as it was for sociology. Although he was an intellectual with a Marxist posture, he was influenced by Durkheim, Weber, and Marx and combined elements of their thought.

Antunes described *Crítica Marxista* as an attempt to fill a void in university life and resolve the problem of the turning of leftist elements toward neoliberalism: "It opens up the debate, creates space for people like Gorender, who was affiliated with the PT but criticized it for moving rightward." The journal *Praxis* was a precursor and lesser project in São Paulo, reflecting diverse Marxisms, especially the thought of Lukács and Gramsci but also that of Mao, Marx, and Lenin. It evolved among young students of *Capital* at the USP in the late 1980s and had a run of about a thousand copies.

Armando Boito Júnior, interviewed in São Paulo on July 14, 1995, was critical of USP intellectuals, some of whom were part of the *Capital* Group. Many of them, he felt, were traditional in the sense that they did research and taught at the university but were not party activists in social life. Fernandes differed from the others because he was of popular origin; the others were middle-class and from liberal families not well-situated socially in São Paulo. Through the reading of *Capital*, however, they began to undertake research inspired by Marxism; Weffort criticized populism, and Cardoso showed that entrepreneurs had a limited political universe and were not interested in building a democratic national capitalism. At the same time, the ISEB evolved with Jaguaribe as its principal activist, initially alongside some researchers who were also Marxist at the time, such as Sodré and Wanderley Guilherme dos Santos. The origins of the Rio group were more popular than those of São Paulo. Its members were less academic and more involved in politics alongside the institutions of the state.

When the São Paulo intellectuals began to write on political issues, Boito said, they adopted a critical analysis of populism and developmentalism and criticized the ideas that the Rio intellectuals defended. Whereas the ISEB intellectuals were associated not with a university but with the state, the Paulistas were affiliated with universities under French influence. Weffort and Cardoso criticized the ideas of the PCB and began to support many liberal theses. Weffort correctly attacked the PCB's notion of an alliance with the national bourgeoisie and the idea that the national bourgeoisie was not anti-imperialist. Caio Prado criticized the party's alliance with the national bourgeoisie and its proposal for agrarian reform. With the national question marginalized, the Paulista liberal middle class became more conservative and did not support agrarian reform. The upshot was popular mobilization in the countryside by the landless peasant movement. Once the CEBRAP was founded, this liberal tendency became more pronounced. This group had creatively appropriated the thinking of Marx, but it became more conservative and incapable of reflecting on alternatives for Brazil.

Attempting to explain this shift, Boito pointed to two transitions, in the first of which it abandoned Marxism and turned in a liberal direction. The basic references for this transition were Cardoso's views on authoritarianism and democratization (1970 and 1972), which show Marxist influence but is liberal in its political proposals, and Weffort's *Cultura e Democracia*, the CEDEC journal during the late 1970s and his book on democracy (1984). The second transition was the shift to neoliberalism, Cardoso's through the Brazilian Social Democratic Party (Partido da Social Democracia Brasileiro [PSDB]) in the late 1980s, and Weffort's through his participation in the government.

Asked whether there was an intellectual left at the time, Boito responded that most leftist intellectuals had all but abandoned party activity, including many in the *Revista Crítica Marxista*. Wilson Cano (1977) and Conçeição Tavares (1972) were, in his opinion, not Marxists but critical intellectuals of the left: "I believe that since the 1970s this intellectual left has been marginalized and has no ties to the labor movement. It had its most influence in the resistance to the dictatorship during the early 1980s, especially in their contacts and writings on labor, peasantry, popular movements, and so on. During the 1990s and the Collar, Itamar, and Fernando Henrique governments, many pulled back. Many intellectuals turned toward neoliberal reforms and the privatization of state enterprise, going over to the neoliberal side. The organs of the mainstream press closed their pages to the left intellectual, and the universities were even more closed. My outlook is pessimistic as to the CUT, the PT, and the intellectual left." As for *Crítica Marxista*, "it is Marxist and left and capable of an important role in Brazil. Made up of a group of intellectuals, it is not sufficiently well organized to ensure its growth and expansion." Boito considered himself unusual among intellectuals in that he came from the countryside. His doctoral dissertation was an important study of unionism in Brazil (1991).

Marco Aurélio Garcia, interviewed in São Paulo July 12, 1995, had had no contact with the *Capital* Group because he was from the South, but he was familiar with the debates at UNICAMP in 1984–1985 and had attended a follow-up meeting in São Paulo that included Novais, Giannotti, Singer, and Schwarz. His contacts came later because he was in exile in Chile, where he worked with the dependency theorists at the Center for Socioeconomic Studies (Centro de Estudos Socioeconómico [CESO]) in Santiago under Theotônio dos Santos, Ruy Mauro Marini, and others from 1970 to 1973. In his opinion, this was "the most important period for their study on dependency. I had little contact with the CEBRAP because of my exile. I did not know much about Caio Prado and *Revista Brasiliense*. We were all readers of the journal. It was one of the few on the left, the other being *Estudos Sociais*, a PCB journal. Caio always was an 'outsider' to the left. His vision in *A revolução brasileira* was distinctly different from that of the left. His journal opened up to others, including foreigners like André Gunder Frank, who exposed readers to his thesis on the myth of feudalism." Because Fernandes was a functionalist, he said, the major personalities of the *Capital* Group learned their Marxism mostly outside the university, as did the ISEB in Rio. The *Capital* Group, however, made it clear that it constituted a counterpoint to the ISEB. The universities were not very professional before the dictatorship, the exception being the University of Brasília because its initial faculty members were younger. He felt that the ISEB was influential in its time and established a hegemony of thought about developmental nationalism. Its personalities still had some influence: Celso Furtado, Sodré, Cândido Mendes, and some who participated in politics (Corbisier and Vieira Pinto, who aspired to be minister of education; Furtado, who became minister of culture; and Jaguaribe, who held a post in the Collor government). The relationship of intellectuals to the state had changed, he said, probably because of the professionalization of the universities. Marxism, for example, was influential during this period when the regime was unable to co-opt the intelligentsia. This intelligentsia, many of the members of which were imprisoned, was able to reemerge after 1974 and participate through the MDB and the CEBRAP, which reflected the thinking of the MDB and later the PMDB. An alternative press, including *Opinião*, *Movimento*, and *Em Tempo*, appeared because intellectuals were unable to write in the mainstream press. "Once we began to write memoirs, the press became interested, and many of us became involved in writing for *Folha de São Paulo* and *Journal do Brasil*. The important intellectuals wrote in the alternative press, which had twenty thousand readers." However, they split between those favoring the radical reforms of the PT and those preferring traditional ways of bringing about incremental change through the PMDB and later the PSDB. Although the latter party was aligned with the moderate right, he considered Cardoso not as an *entregista* (sellout) aligned with Washington but as someone who had Brazilian interests at heart. As a leader of the PT, Garcia (1992) later joined the Lula government as a foreign affairs advisor who helped shape a foreign policy independent of the United States and engaged with Cuba and the progressive governments of Venezuelan President Hugo Chávez and Bolivian President Evo Morales.

João Quartim Moraes, a professor of philosophy at UNICAMP, not only was involved in the armed urban struggle but wrote about his experience as a militant in the Popular Revolutionary Vanguard (Vanguardia Popular Revolucionária [VPR]), an urban guerrilla group that emerged in March 1968 out of a POLOP faction in São Paulo that favored armed struggle. Critical of Régis Debray in the leftist press (1970), Quartim synthesized his ideas and experience in a book published by Monthly Review Press and the *New Left Review* (1971). He also organized an anthology of writing on Marxist thought (1995).

Caio Navarro Toledo, interviewed in São Paulo July 12, 1995, compared the Paulista movement to the ISEB experience. He saw the ISEB as a counterpoint to the ESG, recalling that Cândido Mendes de Almeida had even proposed the name "Escola Superior da Paz" for it. The ISEB intellectuals codified a vision of national development or a nationalism that would support a developmentalist ideology. Jaguaribe uncritically advocated a nationalism of ends rather than means that involved both national and foreign capital, whereas the group on the left led by Vieira Pinto viewed foreign capital and imperialism as obstacles to national development. Thus, there were two nationalisms, one pragmatic and the other orthodox. The Paulista intellectuals considered the ISEB "a factory of ideologies" (see Toledo, 1978). Florestan Fernandes, he said, took the position that the role of the intellectual was to develop objective theory and distance himself from politics, whereas Guerreiro Ramos, influenced by Sartre, focused on the need for the intellectual to engage with social causes. Yet, ironically, Fernandes became politically active in the PT and in society in search of solutions to people's problems. The Paulista intellectuals did not initially recognize the ideas of the ISEB intellectuals as valid, but later some reconsidered. Cardoso justified his political involvement, according to Toledo, by rehabilitating the ISEB project as a way of implementing his idea of development leading toward industrial progress in a somewhat dependent state.

Toledo's politicization had begun with the student movement and his participation as a Methodist in the World Federation of Christian Students and its ties to the World Council of Churches and within Brazil aligned with the Catholic youth movement. As a progressive, he had become active in the move toward social transformation and revolution (interview, July 12, 1995, São Paulo). Most of his research and writing revolved around a study of the ISEB (1978, 1995b) and critical essays on intellectuals and Marxism (1986, 1998). He organized a useful anthology of original essays on the ISEB experiment (2005) and a collection of retrospective analyses of the 1964 coup and the fragility of democracy and populism (1997). Optimistic about the prospects for *Revista Crítica Marxista*, he reflected on its effort to move political science toward Marxism, which he argued should not be seen as dogma. However, at an editorial board meeting of the journal on March 26, 2011, he was expelled from the editorial committee, and he accused João Quartim and Armando Boito of turning the journal from a pluralism of theoretical perspectives within a nondogmatic Marxism to an organ of "academic Marxism." He revealed that Dêcio Saes also was ousted from the board and that among others who withdrew in protest were Isabel Loureiro, Virgínia Fontes, Patrícia Trópia, and Luciano Martorano. Their testimonials appear on the blog Amigos da Crítica Marxista (see http://amigosdacritica.blogspot .com/). (Communication from Toledo, February 5, 2012.)

Under the sponsorship of the Núcleo de Estudos de Ideologias e Lutas Sociais in the graduate school of social sciences of the PUC, *Lutas Sociais* celebrated its fifteenth year of publication in 2010. Published twice a year, it is guided by an eight-person editorial board that functions as a collective under the direction of Lúcio Flávio de Almeida (1995). It is nonpartisan and engages issues on the left, with each number consisting of a half-dozen articles, a section of theoretical perspectives, and usually an interview, along with several book reviews. Its editorial council numbers more than eighty academics, younger scholars scattered across the state of São Paulo and elsewhere in Brazil, including Ricardo Antunes, and a few living abroad, such as Michael Löwy. Its initial issue included a provocative article by Pablo Rieznik (1995) on the crisis of power for progressive intellectuals in their transition to the center of government, where, instead of leading their nations against imperialism and toward autonomous development, they were collaborating with foreign capital.

This overview has noted the shift from a "colonial" outlook to modern thinking about Brazil that accompanied the end of slavery, the capitalization of the countryside in the era of coffee as a key export, the rise of industrialization in the towns and cities, and the emergence of the city of São Paulo as a major economic and political center. The thought of two prominent intellectuals, Caio Prado Júnior and Florestan Fernandes, stimulated writing that engaged the public with debate and critical assessment, on the one hand, and led to academic investigation and scholarship, on the other. A new generation of creative intellectuals, initially inspired by Marx and *Capital*, confronted traditional understanding, applied new methodologies, and published monographs of analysis and data drawn from surveys, interviews, and fieldwork related to theoretical advances. The 1964 coup and the ensuing military dictatorship obstructed their work and forced them into clandestinity or exile. Their unity in opposition and resistance to authoritarianism, however, spurred them to form dynamic centers of intellectual activity culminating in a democratic opening that led many intellectuals to find a place in politics and an alternative to the increasingly restrictive demands of the university. This juxtaposition of public and university endeavors stimulated intellectual activity and cultural production, and the essential question today is whether it will be intellectuals or technocrats who produce the ideas for a rapidly developing Brazil and its Paulista core.

4

Capitalism and the Bourgeois Revolution

Understanding Development and Underdevelopment

Brazilian intellectuals have contributed significantly to the understanding of development and underdevelopment. Since early in the twentieth century, they have debated whether capitalism or socialism would lead their nation to development. Their theories have revolved around backwardness, feudalism and semifeudalism, agrarian and mercantile capitalism, industrial capitalism, and socialism. In particular, they have focused on the differences between large landed estates and smallholdings, the prospects for a national bourgeoisie, the history of capitalism in Brazil, and the way in which a less-developed country can bring about a socialist revolution. In so doing, they have challenged prevailing Eurocentric and North American understandings, and their perceptions and insights have influenced those understandings. Along the way, they have asked about when their nation became capitalist and whether a national bourgeoisie was involved. If a dynamic national bourgeoisie were not to emerge, then what role would the state and civil society play in development?

THE BOURGEOIS REVOLUTION AND THE ADVENT OF CAPITALISM IN BRAZIL

The early literature on when capitalism reached Brazil emphasized two Brazils, with feudal backwardness in the countryside and commercial development in urban areas. Jacques Lambert (1967), for example, saw Brazilian society as divided between the old colonial and agrarian nation and a modern industrialized one. Later work questioned the prospects for a bourgeois revolution similar to those in the advanced capitalist world. Capitalism had emerged, it was argued, without the decisive leadership of a strong national bourgeoisie, and intellectuals turned their attention to the time of its emergence and the evolution of its various forms (mercantile, competitive, industrial, and monopoly). Studies focused on determining whether the transition to capitalism had occurred at the time of independence in 1822, with its aftermath of liberal ideology; at the end of slavery under the empire and the rise of the republic in 1889; with the Vargas revolution of 1930 and the consolidation of the state; with industrialization after the Second World War; or with the authoritarian consolidation after 1964.

In his early work on colonialism and later a controversial book (1966) on the bourgeois democratic revolution, Caio Prado Júnior exposed the illusion that a progressive national bourgeoisie could lead the anti-imperialist struggle and usher in a deep capitalist transformation in Brazil. Florestan Fernandes also wrote (1974) about the Brazilian bourgeois revolution, arguing that there was no bourgeoisie during the colonial period, although a bourgeoisie did eventually become established, albeit belatedly and emerging not from a transition with feudalism, as in Europe, but from artisan activities tied to the internal market and commerce. He explained that capital goods were introduced to Brazil along with colonization. The plantations were tied to the commercial base and the external circuit of mercantilization, but they quickly became distorted in three ways: first, part of the income generated by internal economic agents was diverted from the crown through financial agents; second, commercial activities were not typically capitalist, given that the plantation bosses were torn between controlling slavery, on the one hand, and economic activities on behalf of the crown, on the other; and third, generally, the colonial system drained internal riches for consumption abroad (23–24).

Fernandes associated the rise of capitalism with a break with the agrarian aristocracy and the appearance of new types of economic activity: independence and its socioeconomic implications, the coffee plantation owner and the immigrant, the impact of changes in the international market on the internal economy, and the expansion of the competitive social order (1974: 30). He showed that independence allowed the emergence of a bourgeoisie through a liberal ideology that affected political conditions and institutions, in particular, but had economic consequences, especially for the rural landowner. Liberalism destroyed the colonial order and ushered in the national state as a means of preserving slavery. The state bureaucratized the dominant estates, and, with the opening of the ports, a new economic foundation was established that led to a tendency to export and toward dependent capitalism (90).

Although the coffee planter and the immigrant were key protagonists – "both identified with a rupture with the agrarian aristocracy" (103) – slavery did not readily respond to the requirements of capitalism. The emergence of the social competitive order evolved alongside the disintegration of the slave social order. The consolidation of bourgeois power and bourgeois domination occurred at the end of the empire and the beginning of the republic and the beginning of a "modernity" marked by a convergence of internal and external bourgeois interests that brought some stability to the new order. The path of dependent capitalism was difficult, he argued. Instead of experiencing a "national and democratic revolution," Brazil saw "a dependent capitalist transformation" under a bourgeoisie that flourished with that transformation (214).

Capitalist development, according to Fernandes, evolved through three stages that retained the character of a peripheral society because there was no rupture with dependency and because the precapitalist forces of production and underdevelopment had yet to be overcome. First, there was the phase of neocolonial transition to a modern capitalist market, marked in the sixth decade of the nineteenth century by the opening of the ports to the outside world. Second was a phase of consolidation of urban commerce and the expansion of a competitive capitalist economy from the 1860s to the 1950s. Third was a phase of monopoly capitalism, beginning in the 1950s and especially prominent after 1964, represented by the reorganization of the market and the system of production by large corporations, primarily foreign ones (1974: 223). The bourgeoisie had difficulty maintaining power in the face of the collapse of populism with the 1964 coup and the challenge to its hegemony posed by the counter-revolution (342).

Offering his own understanding of the bourgeois revolution, Paul Singer (interview, São Paulo, July 19, 1984) focused on the implementation of capitalism as the mode of production in Brazil, as if whatever existed before had not been capitalist: "In a certain way I agree with the theory that the slave system was not capitalist and that abolition of slavery and the immigration of European workers were part of the process of installing capitalist relations of production and the establishment of an internal market. Abolition and the ensuing two decades of the Old Republic could constitute the bourgeois revolution." He argued that these events did not constitute a revolution and that the revolution of 1930 was much more institutionally revolutionary, occurring at a moment in which an emerging capitalism appeared in certain sectors of the economy even though the majority of economic activities were still precapitalist in nature: "The Revolution of 1930 accelerated the capitalist transformation of the economy. Therefore, when talking about the bourgeois revolution, we would have to start with the abolition and include the events leading to the Revolution of 1930. An agrarian transition to industrialization was under way, and the bourgeois process was completed with the installation of representative democracy in 1945 and with the national unification of the territory under the dominance of São Paulo."

Jacob Gorender's book on the Brazilian bourgeoisie (1982[1974]) offered a clear overview of capitalism and the rise of the bourgeoisie. Gorender, born in Salvador of poor working-class immigrant Jewish parents, had joined the Brazilian Communist Party (Partido Comunista Brasileiro [PCB]), edited the party newspaper in Rio, *Classe Operária*, and then worked with the state party in São Paulo. In 1958, together with Mário Alves and Giocondo Dias, he had formed the Bahia Group, which opposed the Stalinist faction within the party that had aligned itself with President Kubitschek in support of an alliance with the national bourgeoisie. Depicted as "a left minority" within the party central committee, the Bahia Group was eventually ousted, its members dispersing to other political groups during the urban guerrilla struggle, and Gorender was arrested and imprisoned in 1970. Thereafter, he abandoned activism and devoted his attention to the study of the bourgeoisie and slavery during the colonial period.

Gorender identified two influences on Prado Júnior's classical study: Roberto Simonsen, who characterized Brazil's colonial economy as capitalist, and Sérgio Bagú, who clearly presented a view of colonial capitalism within a Marxist perspective. He agreed with Prado that Brazil had never experienced feudalism, but he advanced a different view – that during the colonial period Portugal did not absorb all of Brazil's capital accumulation. The Brazilian mode of production was mercantile capitalist and based on slavery until its abolition. It was, however, the expansion of the coffee industry and the establishment of textiles and other industries that led to the rise of an industrial bourgeoisie within a form of capitalism that evolved from the First Republic to the 1964 coup; he saw this as a project of the dominant bourgeoisie while the *latifundistas* occupied a secondary position in the class structure. In his important book on colonial slavery (1978), he argued that Brazil was a commercial economy designed to provide resources for European capital, that a special colonial "slavery" regime with mercantilist characteristics prevailed, and that this formed the basis for understanding how Brazil had become a capitalist country with a powerful bourgeoisie in control of the state and society without having passed through a bourgeois revolution.

In an interview in São Paulo on August 28, 1982, Gorender argued that the Brazilian left was a "rather combative, militant movement" and theoretically weak: "Its poor conceptualization does not correspond to Brazilian reality of an industrial country with a substantial proletariat." The universities had produced a tremendous body of work that was indispensable for an understanding of the Brazilian reality, but this work also displayed biases and limitations: "The professors lack revolutionary experience, and their work is inadequate to revolutionary organization. I believe that this theoretical work cannot be the privilege of university professors; those with militant experience can develop their own theoretical perspective."

Arguing that most understandings of industrialization in the state of São Paulo had concentrated on the coffee economy and the large estate, Mauricio Font (1992) pointed out that Furtado (1963b) and Tavares (1972) considered industrialization an uneven process, responsive "to exogenous interruptions in international trade" dating to the 1930s, import substitution during the Great Depression, and the new political conditions associated with the 1930 Revolution – in other words, that world crises had allowed for autonomous growth and the transition to industrialization in Brazil. In contrast, Cardoso de Mello (1982) and Cano (1977) saw industrialization as a positive outgrowth of the expansion of the coffee export sector. Cardoso de Mello explained delayed or late capitalism as due largely to a shift from a colonial to an export economy and from an economy under slavery to mercantilism and wage labor. The capital accumulation of the large coffee growers served as a foundation for industrialization: there was "a direct relationship between periods of export expansion and industry." Cano, for his part, held that subordination to the export sector resulted in "retarded industrialization." Thus, by the 1930s, coffee production was a driving force in the formation of capital. Finally, Font suggested, on the basis of his own study, that the earliest stages of industrialization in São Paulo may have occurred autonomously before the 1880s: "Rather than forming a well-integrated social system with the export economy controlled by land-based elites, industrialization is seen as representing a differentiated structural alternative" (1992: 28). "Dynamic, independent agriculturalists provided conditions favoring industrialization in several instances, while their absence has been accompanied by industrial retardation in others" (48).

Yet another approach to the emergence of industrialization focused on state intervention and the rise of monopoly capital in Brazilian agriculture. Eliete Silva (1985) saw the intervention of the state in agriculture as a tool of the dominant classes and the representatives of big capital. Silva examined Portuguese mercantilism in the colonial period, the end of slavery, and the reformulation by the state of new relations of production, which involved the proletarianization of the workforce and the hegemony of the city over the countryside. Before 1930, she argued, and under the oligarchical state, the dominant class was able to use mechanisms leading to the formation of dependent capitalism. From 1930 to 1945, under the modern interventionist state, exports of raw materials served to finance industrialization in an era of authoritarianism and nationalism serving national capitalism. The transition and crisis in the formation of the monopolist state from 1946 to 1964 was marked by periods of relative political freedom from 1930 to 1934, 1945 to 1950, and 1961 to 1964. During this period, state intervention shielded nationalist policy and urban-industrial activities. During the Dutra period from 1946 to 1950, the state provided stimulus to industry; during 1951–1954 the state redefined itself through national entities managed under the state (such as Petrobrás). Under Kubitschek, from 1955 to 1960, the Superintendency of Northeast Development (Superintendência do Desenvolvimento do Nordeste [SUDENE]) dealt with agrarian reform and a developmental strategy, whereas development policy favored the formation of national capital and opposition to dependent capitalism (Silva, 1985: 209). From 1964 and thereafter, there was a consolidation of the monopolistic state. The economic model evolved through a preparatory phase (1964–1968) in favor of the *latifundio*, foreign interests, and a bourgeoisie associated with the petty bourgeoisie, and after 1968 through state planning.

Francisco Oliveira (1972), writing on the changing structure of Brazilian society since 1930 with attention to the theory of underdevelopment and the ideas of the Economic Commission for Latin America (ECLA), dwelt on the economic push by Vargas and the contradictions of policies under the military regime. Boris Fausto (1983 [1970]) also emphasized the 1930 revolution in identifying the consolidation of capitalism. He saw the state as representing the industrial bourgeoisie in the 1930 revolution. However, the revolution – brought about by a weak middle class – did not usher a national bourgeoisie to political power. The revolution brought an end to the hegemony of the coffee bourgeoisie but no other class emerged to offer an alternative; this led to a "state of compromise" due to the incapacity of the new class alliance to take the place of the politically collapsed coffee bourgeoisie (103).

Carlos Nelson Coutinho (1980) refers to an elitist or "Prussian path," one involving conciliation between factions of the dominant classes and with measures applied from above, yet still conserving some essential remnants of the relations of backward production, such as the *latifundio*, and ensuring the reproduction of dependency on international capitalism (32–41). Specifically, Brazil pursued a path more approximate to the Prussian road, involving an alliance of merchants and landowners so that trade with the world market did not necessarily bring capitalism because merchant capital predominated and merchant ties with landowners kept intact the precapitalist relations of production. The transition from a precapitalist slave system to capitalism, however, was shaped by the Brazilian social formation, located within an increasingly capitalist world economy.

Bresser-Pereira (1984a) argues that the transformation of Brazil from an agrarian, mercantile society into a capitalist industrial society was characterized by underdevelopment and a capitalist social formation with state and monopoly characteristics. He believes that the Brazilian industrial revolution began in the nineteenth century but decisively advanced only after 1930, although a national bourgeoisie could not consolidate due to a breach between the industrial bourgeoisie of immigrant origin and the mercantile coffee *latifundista* bourgeoisie that prevailed until 1964. He argues that, in 1930, international capital advanced in relation to mercantile capital, and the 1930 revolution undermined the power of the agrarian-export bourgeoisie and established a populist pact more favorable to industrialization. Thus, the period 1930–1960 was one of transition from the domination of the mercantile *latifundiario* and speculative capital to the rise of industrial capital, a process accompanied by the ascendency of the industrial bourgeoisie, the urban proletariat, and the new salaried middle class that became the techno-bureaucracy. The process of modernization, he argues, continued with Juscelino Kubitscheck and the developmentalism of the 1950s. The coup of 1964 opted clearly for capitalist accumulation and "a savage capitalism" driven by international finance capital. The classical European mold was avoided through a pact between the ascendant industrial bourgeoisie and the rural landed classes. In the Brazil case, any transformation of agriculture has been affected by seemingly contradictory patterns that maintain, even recreate, noncapitalist relations of labor exploitation and forms of production. This suggests that although a localized transformation of the social relations of production may be permanent in the Center-South, the distinction between a rural capitalist and a free rural proletariat remains unclear elsewhere because of regional variations and various forms of capital.

Bresser acknowledges that Paulista intellectuals erred in their assessment of the Rio experiment under the Superior Institute of Brazilian Studies (Instituto Superior de Estudos Brasileiros [ISEB]), which in retrospect focused correctly on the basic problem of relations between civil society and the state. The Paulistas, he argues, did not understand the importance of the middle classes and their nationalism conceptualized within a developmental vision. The fundamental problem is the restructuring of the state, necessitating the creation of a network of representatives under formal democracy and abandoning the mythology of direct democracy.

In sum, intellectuals who have confronted the question of how and when capitalism established itself in Brazil offer a plethora of perspectives, ranging from decisive moments around independence in the early nineteenth century, the cessation of slavery in 1888, the revolution in 1930, and consolidation under military rule after 1964. The consensus suggests that capitalism was conspicuous toward the end of the empire, with the opening of the ports and the end of slavery; decisively advanced after 1930; and was spurred on after 1964. Our discussion to this point, however, does not affirm that a bourgeois revolution along the lines of the European or North American experience occurred nor that a national bourgeoisie as envisaged by Rio and São Paulo intellectuals was able to transform the backward and underdeveloped economy. In their search for explanations, Brazilians have drawn from progressive ideas and movements.

DEVELOPMENT AND PROGRESSIVE THOUGHT

Theories of development and underdevelopment in Brazil have been constructed against the background of the various progressive currents in play since the late nineteenth century, among them anarchism, socialism, communism, and Trotskyism.

Anarchism opposes the authoritarian state and seeks some form of cooperation among free individuals. Anarchism and anarcho-syndicalism were disseminated by former European intellectuals and propagandists through short-lived newsletters, newspapers, and journals published in urban and industrial centers such as Rio and São Paulo. Theotônio dos Santos (1996b: 6–7) reports that anarchism was influential in the interior of Minas Gerais when he was a boy, and he calls it "an important part of the Brazilian and Latin American political formation." Roberto das Neves was closely connected with the anarchist and anarcho-syndicalist movements and was the director of the anarchist publishing house Editora Germinal. Ideological and leadership differences were evident among the various anarchist and anarcho-syndicalist organizations. Debates, for example, counterpoised Octávio Brandão and Astrojildo Pereira, founders of the PCB, who strongly supported the Russian Revolution, and José Oiticica, Carlos Dias, and Edgard Leuenroth, who pushed the Brazilian Workers' Confederation (Confederação Operária Brasileira [COB]) toward affiliation with the anarcho-syndicalist International Workingmen's Association or First International.

The socialist movement, overshadowed first by anarchism and later by the PCB, never achieved prominence. It suffered from divisiveness and an inability to build a broad national party base, and its following among workers and intellectuals was minimal. The Socialist Party of Brazil (Partido Socialista do Brasil [PSB]) was able to emerge from clandestinity and reconstitute itself in 1947, and it remained active until the coup of 1964; it later revived with the return of representative democracy during the 1980s, albeit with an outlook and policies that differed from its earlier days. As did its PCB competitor, it suffered from defections, but it maintained a modest presence throughout these years, receiving less than 10,000 votes for its presidential candidate in 1950, about 1 percent of the vote in 1954, and 3 percent in 1958 and 1962. It depended on electoral alliances to maintain a small representation in Congress (five seats in 1962, twenty-two seats in 2002, and thirty-four in 2010). Among its leaders was lawyer and peasant league organizer Francisco Julião, who was active in Pernambuco and the Northeast. Another was economist Paul Singer.

According to Singer (interview, São Paulo, September 26, 1983), the PSB was a mixture of social democrats and Trotskyists. His own political education, he said, "was more allied with the Trotskyist elements in the party" who had broken with the Fourth International after Trotsky's death. Among them was Mário Pedroso in Rio, who never had a leading role but was influential within the party. Among the leaders in São Paulo were Antônio Cândido, Plínio Melo, and Febus Gikovate, who, as secretary general of the party and a Trotskyist, influenced Singer. After the Second World War, Marxist thinking grew rapidly among the Brazilian intelligentsia, much of it aligned with the PCB. But by 1956, many Marxists had left the party in search of independent ideas. Singer explained that this was a time of rethinking of the Soviet experience and a rupture with sectarian Marxism. Asked about the meaning of socialism, Singer responded that it evolved out of contradictions within capitalism, led to the socialization of the means of production, and aimed toward an egalitarian society and the abolition of social classes.

Communism in Brazil owes its origins to Marx and Engels, but Lenin and Stalin also influenced it under the Third International. The PCB was founded March 25–27, 1922, by progressive intellectuals and workers involved in socialism and anarchism (see Chilcote, 1974: 15–26). From 1930 to 1937, Getúlio Vargas gained power with the help of the *tenentes*, while the PCB led a popular front, the National Liberation Alliance (Aliança Nacional Libertadora [ANL]) and an abortive uprising in November 1935. From 1937 to 1945, the party operated in clandestinity as Vargas installed his integralist Estado Novo. Thereafter, until 1972, saw a resurgence of the party, with its legality from 1945 to 1947 paving the way for electoral successes in the congress and at state and local levels; a decline followed with internal dissension following the death of Stalin in 1953, the suicide of Vargas in 1954, and serious policy differences between the Chinese and Soviet Communist Parties that resulted in 1962 in the formation of the dissident Maoist Partido Comunista do Brasil (PC do B). The sectarian and suppressive reactions of the older and dominant PCB leadership led to a massive exodus of communists – a critical blow to a party in decline. The 1964 military coup and its aftermath severely impacted the PCB and eventually led to urban guerrilla warfare organized by various offshoots of the PCB and supported in particular by the PC do B. After 1972, the party's decline continued with the political opening during the 1980s, the withdrawal of the military from power, the emergence of old and new political parties, and the new constitution. In 1992, the PCB changed its name to the Partido Popular Socialista (PPS) and removed the hammer and sickle from its flag and party emblem, although some dissidents "refounded" the PCB, which continued as a minor party.

Brazilian communism has relied on Marx and Engels, Lenin, and Mao Zedong for its understandings of delayed development and how it might be remedied. The PCB was influenced by the Third International and the Soviet Communist Party, which attributed Brazil's backwardness to feudalism and semifeudalism. This position emanated from their model of a succession of stages of development eventually arriving at capitalism, socialism, and finally communism. The basic assumption was that eventually industrial capital would devastate the noncapitalist societies and establish the conditions for the advance of capitalism outside Europe. This sequence would be led by a bourgeoisie that Marx and

Engels, in the *Communist Manifesto*, said would "nestle everywhere, settle everywhere, establish connections everywhere."

In his articles on India, published in 1853 in the *New York Daily Tribune*, Marx wrote that British capital and investment had ruined India's native industry and native fabrics in particular, reflecting "a double mission in India: one destructive, the other regenerating – the annihilation of the old Asian society, and the laying of the material foundations of Western society in Asia" (Marx, 1943: 67). Thus, capitalism had established the material conditions for a capitalist advance in India. At the same time, Marx held that capitalism would destroy the noncapitalist societies, establish itself in outlying areas, exploit peoples, and extract surplus on behalf of the advanced capitalist countries. Thus, capitalism would be regressive rather than progressive in the periphery. Writing on the Irish question, he said, "A new and international division of labor, a division suited to the requirements of its chief centers on modern industry, springs up and converts one part of the globe into a chiefly agricultural field of production, for supplying the other part which remains a chiefly industrial field" (Marx, 1967: 451).

Lenin also wrote about development and underdevelopment. In *Imperialism: The Highest Stage of Capitalism*, he said, "Not only are there two main groups of countries, those owning countries and the colonies themselves, but also the diverse forms of dependent countries which politically are independent but in fact are enmeshed in the net of financial and diplomatic dependency" (Lenin, 1967: 743–744). Elsewhere (1956), he traced the rise of capitalism in feudal Russia. Fernando Henrique Cardoso acknowledged these contributions but noted that recent changes had altered the relationship between imperialist and dependent nations: "Dependency, monopoly capitalism, and development are not contradictory terms: there occurs a kind of dependent capitalist development in the sectors of the Third World integrated in the new form of monopolistic expansion" (Cardoso, 1973: 11). David Lane (1974) pointed to Lenin's belief that the bourgeois revolution was only a brief intermediary stage in the struggle of nations to overthrow capitalism and suggested that it was this view that justified the pursuit of noncapitalist development in underdeveloped nations and inspired writers such as Paul Baran and André Gunder Frank to call for a political revolution led by the working class.

Trotskyism in Brazil has splintered into diverse perspectives, some of it stimulated by intellectuals critical of the PCB. An orthodox current, Trotskyist Revolutionary Socialist Party (Partido Socialista

Revolucionário [Trotskista] [PSR(T)]) represented students and intellectuals associated with the Fourth International. According to Michael
Löwy (personal communication, January 18, 2010), the PSR(T) disbanded
in 1953; two years later, Hermínio Sacchetta, with Paul Singer and others
including Löwy, founded the Luxemburgist Liga Socialista Independente
(Independent Socialist League) while the orthodox Trotskyists formed
the Revolutionary Workers' Party (Partido Operário Revolucionário
[POR]), which published *Frente Operária*. At the same time, inspired by
Rosa Luxemburg, Bukharin, and others and led by intellectuals from
Rio de Janeiro, São Paulo, and Minas Gerais, an independent current
appeared in the form of the Marxist Revolutionary Organization
(Organização Revolucionária Marxista [ORM]) and a periodical (initially
a newspaper and later a magazine) called *Política Operária*. This group,
generally known as Política Operária or POLOP, included the young
intellectuals Theotônio dos Santos, Vânia Bambira, Luiz Alberto Moniz
Bandeira (1978), Juárez Guimarães de Brito, Michael Löwy, Ruy Mauro
Marini, Eder Sader, and Emir Sader. Eric Sachs, a communist of German
origin living in Brazil under the pseudonym Ernesto Martins, was influential. Löwy (personal communication, January 18, 2010) describes Sachs
as a follower of Heinrich Brandler, a dissident communist of a more
"moderate" tendency than the Trotskyists who led the group known as
Arbeiter Politik. In the opinion of Emir Sader (interview, Rio de Janeiro,
July 29, 1991), POLOP's principal figure was Moniz Bandeira. Sader
was active as both a Leninist and Trotskyist and believed that the
incorporation of Trotsky and Gramsci tended to reinforce criticism of
the orthodox PCB and the Soviet Union. Ruy Mauro Marini worked to
organize a *foco militarista*, a propaganda arm aimed at mobilizing military
officers, especially in Rio de Janeiro, but he was imprisoned in 1964 and a
year later went into exile. Theotônio dos Santos left for Chile, where he
began to formulate his ideas on dependency.

Marini (interview, Rio de Janeiro, July 30, 1991) agreed that Sachs was
influential in POLOP and said that Trotskyism was not dominant, he
himself having been more Leninist at the time. The group used Trotsky's
ideas to attack the PCB, in particular the idea of combined and uneven
development. Lenin had used the idea in his works following Luxemburg
(Moniz, 1980), and later Trotsky also used it. Marini considered
POLOP important in the formation of the idea of dependency.
Theoretical interest at the time was focused more on the ideas of Baran
and Sweezy than on Trotsky's. When Frank arrived in 1963, he was much
influenced by Baran and the Rio intellectuals and drew on the ideas of

POLOP, Lenin, and others. Marini thought that it was necessary to reformulate what capitalism was in Brazil and prepare a strategy and a program, and this was what POLOP contributed to the left. He recalled that the Argentine magazine *Praxis* was important prior to the formation of POLOP and that one of its participants, Marcos Kaplan, had attended the first congress of POLOP in January 1961: "This was the beginning of our outreach internationally. The work of Silvio Frondizi was also important for us and for the theory of dependency, along with the ideas of ECLA and ISEB." Marini had begun working on his ideas on subimperialism before seeking exile in Mexico in 1965, and Theotônio dos Santos began to write in 1966 on the new dependency: "We took these ideas abroad in search of a new theory of dependency. The theory of dependency was never an academic theory. It was a political endeavor, an attempt to develop a noncommunist revolutionary theory." Marini remained in Mexico until 1969, then moved to Chile to work with Dos Santos until Salvador Allende was deposed in late 1973.

As we have seen, Florestan Fernandes referred to his early affiliation with Trotskyism in an interview with various Brazilian intellectuals (1981a: 18–23) and in his interview with me (São Paulo, September 26, 1983), and there is a reference to Trotsky in his *A revolução burguesa no Brasil* (1981b). In a discussion of his early years, he said that the PCB did not attract the radical youth of that period. After the Estado Novo, the party moved toward groups supporting Getúlio Vargas, and he "joined an extreme left Trotskyist group called Coligiação Democrática Radical [Radical Democratic Union] and remained with it until about 1940." He continued: "I always maintained contact with other groups, for example, the anarchists, the socialists, and the old militants who were not of my generation. I circulated with left people, except for the PCB ... but I was known for my Trotskyist orientation" (1981a: 18). He explained that few of his fellow activist students knew anything about Marxism in the 1950s. Once he abandoned Trotskyism, he became marginalized from politics. He had wanted to join the PCB but felt that its positions were often negative: "I discussed this dilemma frequently with Antônio Cândido when I first joined the Trotskyist group. His preference was for revolutionary socialism. After I abandoned Trotskyism, we talked again, and he encouraged me to carry on with my intellectual work and dedicate myself to my academic career" (19). Asked why intellectuals were unable to offer solutions, he responded that this was impossible for them in a class society in which the workers could not mature politically and develop as an independent class (23).

Among the elements of Trotsky's thinking that influenced Brazilian intellectuals in their theories of development and underdevelopment was, first, an apparent relationship between the theory of permanent revolution and the model of capitalist development of underdevelopment that was particularly evident in the thought of Frank and Marini. Trotsky departed from the idea of a world capitalist system as constituting a totality subject to unequal and combined development in which the advanced countries continued to develop at the expense of the colonies and backward semicolonial areas.[1] This is similar to the metropolis–satellite conception in Frank's thesis of capitalist development of underdevelopment (1967), in which the metropolis exploits the surplus of the satellites, which in turn become underdeveloped. Curiously, Francisco de Oliveira associated the dualism of center and periphery in the thought of Celso Furtado with the legacy of the Trotsky-Lenin characterization of unequal and combined development (Oliveira, 1983: 8). He believed that Furtado, with his ECLA background, did not rigorously follow a Marxist understanding of the internationalization of capital but that his contribution was innovative (11) even though his structural theory of underdevelopment was "fragile" (12).

Second, inherent in the theory of the permanent revolution is the idea that the colonial and semicolonial bourgeoisie are incapable of carrying out a bourgeois democratic revolution. Given this belief, Guido Mantega (interview, Campinas, September 12, 1984) argued that Trotsky, Frank, and Marini all emphasized the role of the proletariat in bringing about the necessary transformation through a socialist revolution. Yet Marco Aurélio Garcia (interview, September 12, 1984), an astute political observer and essential organizer of the Workers' Party (Partido dos Trabalhadores [PT]) and the Arquivo Edgard Leuenroth, insisted that Marini was trying to distinguish himself from the Trotskyists by criticizing the theory of permanent revolution as economistic, although he used the idea of antagonistic cooperation in much the same way as the theory of combined and uneven development to characterize the relations between the Brazilian bourgeoisie and capitalism. Garcia considered Trotsky's influence on dependency theory greater than that of Lenin: "Lenin dealt

---

[1] These ideas of combined and uneven development and of permanent revolution are examined by Michael Löwy (1981). Stephen Bunker's case study (1984) emphasizes modes of extraction, unequal exchange, and underdevelopment in the Brazilian Amazon from 1600 to 1980 and argues that different regional levels of development result from the interaction between changing world demand for specific commodities and the local reorganization of modes of production and extraction.

with dependency in very general terms, while Trotsky attempted to study dependency more concretely by describing its internal mechanisms."

Third, near the end of his life and just prior to the Second World War, Trotsky noted a profound crisis in that the democratic regimes of the center had to continue to exploit the periphery, whose surplus would allow for mitigation of the class struggle there. The left had to fight against fascism as well as imperialism because the bourgeoisies in some advanced countries such as Germany and Italy (which had lost their colonies) had turned from democracy to fascism in order to continue exploiting the periphery. Dos Santos (1973) argued that the bourgeoisies of peripheral countries such as Argentina and Brazil turned to fascism because it allowed for superexploitation.

Fourth, Trotsky's notion of a permanent worldwide revolution was tied to the strategic role of countries in the underdeveloped periphery that broke their ties with the metropoles and precipitated a collapse of imperialism. Marini stressed socialist revolution in the peripheral countries, arguing that this would lead to world revolution and bring about socialist revolution in backward countries (Mantega, 1982: 227). Furthermore, Trotsky's theory of permanent revolution projected an immediate transition to socialism without the bourgeois transformations suggested by Lenin, a proposition that divided the Brazilian left (136).

Instead of emphasizing capitalism in the image of the advanced countries as a means of overcoming backwardness, Dos Santos, although denying any Trotskyist influence on his thinking, stressed the Trotskyist idea of the unequal nature of development (interview, Rio de Janeiro, July 7, 1995). (Garcia agreed that Dos Santos was not influenced by Trotskyism and eventually became an anti-Trotskyist.) Garcia offered a historical overview of Trotskyism in Brazil, noting its strength in the 1930s and the 1980s. In the latter period, several currents prevailed, including the Alicerce da Juventude Socialista, linked internationally with Nahuel Moreno, Causa Operária and its journal of the same name, and Democracia Socialista, linked to the publication *Em Tempo* (interview, Campinas, September 12, 1984).

All these ideas on underdevelopment were part of an attack by independent leftist intellectuals on the intransigent positions of the PCB, particularly on the questions of semifeudalism as a basis for backwardness and the promise of the national bourgeoisie's fulfilling its historical role in the capitalist transformation. Mantega (1982) maintained that these ideas were largely inspired by Trotsky's argument that under certain conditions the proletariat of the periphery could rise to power prior to the proletariat of advanced countries, a thesis he defended in 1906 when he argued that Russian backwardness was not an obstacle to socialist revolution. He believed that under certain circumstances the low level of capitalist development in Russia could lead to a rapid rise to power of the proletariat. As did Lenin, he argued that, despite its backwardness, Russia had indeed developed some industrialization along capitalist lines, largely implanted by foreign capital aided by the state, in the last decades of the nineteenth century. Especially in Moscow and St. Petersburg, a large proletariat had developed along with a bourgeoisie that was too weak to eliminate feudal remnants. This gave the proletariat the opportunity to bring about revolutionary change. In his *Permanent Revolution*, Trotsky developed this idea, arguing that the delayed bourgeois revolution in Russia could be advanced by the proletariat, whose objectives would be agrarian reform and the democratic reconstruction of the state. Agrarian reform implied the nationalization of property and the elimination of income differences. These different patterns of progress illustrated the idea of combined and uneven capitalist development on a world scale, in which the colonies and former colonies fed the accumulation of the imperialist metropoles at their own expense; thus, peripheral capitalism remained weak, precluding the bourgeoisie from fulfilling the tasks of a democratic revolution. Mantega claimed that Trotsky interpreted capitalism in its imperialist phase as "an international system articulated by ties of domination and dependency" (143) and showed the impossibility of full democracy in the backward countries.

The progressive movements, their ideas, and influences helped shape intellectual theoretical frameworks and provide a foundation for interpreting and analyzing perplexing questions about the negative consequences of capitalism in Brazil.

THEORETICAL PERSPECTIVES

Backwardness

With regard to backwardness, the historian and social critic Caio Prado Júnior produced important work before the influential writing of economists Paul Baran (1960[1957]) and André Gunder Frank (1966, 1967).[2]

---

[2] Although I did not interview them, I knew both Baran and Frank, the former at Stanford University after taking a group of progressive Brazilian students to his home and the latter through an extensive reply to critics in the inaugural issue of *Latin American Perspectives*,

As we have seen, Prado Júnior was a member of the PCB, but his historical work challenged the traditional positions of his party. With his Argentine colleague and fellow historian Sérgio Bagú, he focused on the colonial formation. The essence of his thought appeared in several volumes on this theme, the most important being *The Colonial Background of Modern Brazil*. For him, the large rural enterprise, "a large number of individuals brought together to form *a single unit of production*, became the basic cell of the Brazilian agrarian economy ... the principal base on which the whole economic and social structure of the country was founded" (1967b[1969]: 138). The economy was based on the concentration of wealth drawn from this domestic production and the export of commodities for the international market. Its orientation to the international market reflected Portugal's efforts to enrich itself through trade while repressing independent commercial activities and manufacturing in Brazil, thus reducing the country to the status of a producer of certain commodities for international trade. The propensity of the economy to experience cycles of prosperity and decline produced stagnancy and reliance on international trade. Brazilian industry remained rudimentary as late as the early nineteenth century as a consequence of Portuguese colonial policy: "If the country's political and administrative situation, as a mere colonial appendage of a shortsighted mother country that was jealous of its privileges, was a serious handicap to its industrial development, the economic regime was even more to blame" (263). Portugal was simply an intermediary between the colonial sources of supply of tropical products and the European powers. Two-thirds of its exports consisted of colonial products, and this weakened its position: "Portugal, once a great power, passed from the middling power she had become to the mediocrity of one of Europe's most insignificant countries" (275). This allowed Brazil to break free in the nineteenth century. The prominence of commerce permitted the merchants to oppose the land-owners, and this class struggle was sharpened by nationalist loyalties, with the merchants, descendants of pioneer settlers from Portugal, supporting Brazil.

which I edit. Theotônio dos Santos has commented: "It was at UNB that I knew André Gunder Frank and where we systematically initiated a collaboration with Ruy Mauro Marini, Vânia Bambirra, and myself that lasted decades.... Frank was present when we discussed his propositions on world accumulation in CESO" [(1994: 30, 43)]. I also interviewed Caio Prado Júnior (São Paulo, August 25, 1982) who felt that the ISEB had contributed little to Brazilian thought and who confirmed that he remained a member of the PCB despite his criticisms of party policy. The ensuing discussion on theoretical perspectives draws extensively from a broader assessment in Chilcote (1984).

Prado Júnior believed that even reformist capitalism would disappear because of its own contradictions, and socialism would evolve from it: "What constitutes the essence of socialism is the replacement of the free economy characteristic of capitalism and the antagonism among individuals ... by the coordination of economic action in the interest of the collective society" (1962a: 26–27). He believed that nationalism reflected a Brazilian consciousness of the country's "dependent and subordinate situation in relation to the large financial and capitalist centers of the contemporary world" and that this situation was typical of "a peripheral country in the capitalist system ... a country situated on the margin of that system and complementary to it" (1955: 82). He saw Brazil's export economy as limited by the country's "traditional peripheral and dependent position" in the international system of capitalism (14) and argued that a nationalist policy could lead to control over the forces of production dependent on international trade.

Shortly after the military coup of 1964, Prado Júnior reassessed his position in a controversial book on the Brazilian "revolution." Although critical of the dogmatism and sectarianism that had characterized communist thinking in the past, he argued that Marxism, with its dialectical method, offered the possibility of a new historical interpretation and analysis. In particular, he criticized as irrelevant the notion that a bourgeois democratic revolution would allow for the transition from remnants of feudalism to capitalism, arguing that feudalism had never existed in Brazil (1966: 51). He attacked the PCB for its "serious errors of interpretation of Brazilian reality," suggesting that it was illusions about a progressive national bourgeoisie that were responsible for the disaster of April 1964. For him, only a revolutionary course offered a way out of economic dependence and imperialism, and he predicted that the struggle in Brazil would be similar to that of revolutionary nations in Africa and Asia, where he believed the "internal colonial formation" had been mitigated (308).

Underdevelopment

Celso Furtado refined Prado Júnior's historical interpretation, following the Argentine economist Raúl Prebisch, the Chilean economist Osvaldo Sunkel, and the Brazilian economist and sociologist Aníbal Costa Pinto, all of whom were associated with the ECLA in its formative years.[3] Born in

[3] The theory of underdevelopment that evolved within the ECLA is analyzed by Rodríguez (1981). Costa Pinto's most important work (1963) looked at issues of development such as

Pombal, Paraíba, in the Northeast, Furtado studied law in Brazil and economics in Paris, joined the ECLA in 1949, and initiated studies there on a development program for Brazil. Later, as director of the Banco Nacional de Desenvolvimento Econômico, he elaborated plans for the economic recovery of northeastern Brazil. As head of SUDENE, he influenced the regional planning process. Exiled in Chile during the 1960s, he collaborated with Sunkel, Fernando Henrique Cardoso, and others associated with the ECLA. Their structuralist approach involved a division of the world into two parts, a center of industrial countries and a periphery of underdeveloped countries. This division was the result of long-term deterioration in the terms of trade in the periphery, where imported capital goods became expensive and exchange earnings declined. The solution to this disparity, they believed, was tariff protection against high-cost imports and industrialization spurred by the building of an infrastructure of power grids, roads, raw materials, and the means whereby domestic industry could support itself. Prebisch argued that capitalism in the periphery had suffered a historical delay because of the hegemony of the center. The relations of the periphery with the center were defined by dependence so that a country could not on its own decide what to do. He felt that the state should assume a principal role in determining the pace of accumulation but without necessarily taking over the means of production to achieve this objective. What he was interested in was an autonomous capitalist solution in the periphery.

In *The Economic Growth of Brazil* (1959a, 1963b), Furtado described the rise and decline of the sugar industry and of the livestock sector that accompanied it, showing that the gradual decline of sugar had "converted a high-productivity economic system into an economy in which the majority of the population produced only what was necessary for its bare existence" (1963b: 70–71). Francisco de Oliveira considered his contribution superior to the work of Gilberto Freyre, Sêrgio Buarque de Holanda, and Caio Prado Júnior: "No other work has such ideological importance in our recent social history.... Theoretically it is a Keynesian reading of our recent social history." He argued that, in contrast to economists such as Roberto Campos and Delfim Netto, who had "sold their principles to oligarchical capital," Furtado anchored his understanding of the state "in very real bases" (Oliveira, 1983: 12–14).

direction of change, obstacles, structural marginality, and resistance and the relationship of social classes to development in Brazil. Elsewhere (1967), he criticized the mainstream literature on development and discussed nationalism, populism, and the alienation of intellectuals.

This view of Brazilian history revealed the underlying explanation of development and underdevelopment (1961, 1964b) that ran through Furtado's work. He argued that Europe had disrupted the world economy in the eighteenth century and thereafter by disrupting the precapitalist artisan system, displacing borders, and expanding into precapitalist areas. He characterized this process as the creation of "hybrid structures," some of which functioned as part of the capitalist system and others within the earlier system, with its precapitalist features. This suggested a "dualistic" economy in which underdevelopment was a "discrete historical process through which economies that have already achieved a high level of development have not necessarily passed" (1964b: 129). Underdevelopment, he suggested, was a result of the "penetration of modern capitalistic enterprise into archaic structures" (138). Elsewhere (1967b), he examined the terms "development" and "underdevelopment" and contrasted the two processes. In a brief study (1962b), he argued that Brazil, despite its underdevelopment, would advance in the industrial world of capitalism through the mechanism of the state. Although not strictly a Marxist, he considered Marxism a means for "diagnosing social reality and a guide to action" (1963a: 527–528). Oliveira (1983: 18) called this one of Furtado's "most brilliant essays" in that it transcended economics to lay out a political approach to the reform of the bases. Furtado saw Marxism as a means of liberating humankind from enslavement. He argued that Brazil was in a prerevolutionary period in which drastic change was necessary, but he was wary of state dominance, calling instead for an open society and considering foreign capital "indispensable for the development of any underdeveloped country" (Furtado, 1963a: 535). In an analysis drawing on Hegel (Furtado, 1964a), he looked at "dialectical development" as it had emerged from class struggle and capitalism and examined underdevelopment in the Northeast as a historical case study.

The social structure of the underdeveloped economy, he said, had a ruling class made up of interest groups that were unable to agree on a plan for national development: landowners connected to foreign trade who were in favor of free trade and opposed to state intervention, capitalists who supported free trade but relied on the state, and capitalists dependent on the internal market who were protectionist and used the state to ensure them the resources they needed. Below the ruling class was a mass of salaried urban workers employed in services, a class of industrial workers, and, at the bottom, a class of peasants. He argued that struggle among these classes was usually absent in underdeveloped countries because class consciousness was low and working-class ideology was not clearly formulated.

Drawing on these considerations, he characterized Brazil as being in a situation that he called "the new dependency" (Furtado, 1962a, 1971). As he saw it, the adoption of new consumption patterns through import substitution and industrialization gave rise to a peripheral capitalism that was unable to innovate and depended on outside decisions. In an early stage of this dependency and underdevelopment, an increase in exports of raw materials benefited a wealthy minority, which adapted its consumption patterns to the values of countries in the center. In a more advanced stage, import substitution might stimulate some internal development but only temporarily. Ultimately, full industrialization might solve the problem, but here, too, underdevelopment tended to perpetuate itself, especially given the imbalance in the international system brought about by multinational corporations that benefited from the increased productivity of dependent economies.

After the 1964 coup, the military regime claimed credit for an economic "miracle." Furtado (1981[1974]) exposed the myth of this miracle and called on Brazilians to acknowledge the underdevelopment of their economy. Although he pointed to the reality of contradictions and inequality, he professed optimism that Brazil would challenge the international order as forces within the country evolved in a direction favoring "those who suffer from dependence and exploitation" (89). He argued that the economy was politically unstable because of the divergent interests of the ruling classes, divided among the landed oligarchy and engaged in labor-intensive and inefficient agricultural production for export; the commercial interests that controlled international trade; and the domestic capitalists, tied to foreign capital and technology, who tended to be protectionist. Framing his discussion in terms of the dichotomy of center and periphery, he described Brazil's economy as one in perpetual crisis.

Identifying the difficulties of overcoming underdevelopment, he pointed to the hegemony of the United States (Furtado, 1966) and to structural obstacles to national development (1970), suggesting strategies for overcoming these obstacles. He laid out an understanding of underdevelopment as "a creature of the technical processes and the international division of labor commanded by the small number of societies . . . in which the dominant centers reserved for themselves the economic activities that concentrated technological progress. . . . Development and underdevelopment should be considered as two aspects of the same historical process involving the creation and the spread of modern technology" (1970: xvi). In later work, he elaborated on this idea (1978); traced the history of the Brazilian model of development (1982); reflected on the impact of development and underdevelopment on culture in periods of crisis (1984); and defended the thesis that Brazil should renegotiate its foreign debt and break with the International Monetary Fund, declare a moratorium on its debt, solve its inflation, and confront the problem of unemployment in the country (1983).

Oliveira (1983: 14) called Furtado "the theorist of underdevelopment" and described him as both the "most ideological" of Brazilian intellectuals and a nonpartisan politician who was enamored with the state and its potential autonomy and administration by technicians. Summing up, he pointed out that Furtado rebelled against the standards of Marxist thought and that all of his work was oriented toward "solving some question" and "obsessed with producing knowledge that transforms into action" (25).

Although there have been serious analyses in support of Furtado's views (for example, by Eliana Cardoso [1981]), he has not escaped criticism. As minister of planning in the Goulart administration, he shaped a controversial three-year plan that Mário Alves and Paul Singer described as a platform for federal action rather than social and economic development and "a policy of conciliation with imperialism and the *latifundio*" (1963: 6). José Lucas (1983) criticized Furtado for his inattention to class struggle and suggested that there could be no such conciliation among social classes as he advocated: "Furtado cannot understand, in his subjective view, that history is a succession of facts developed in accordance with the level of productive forces" (15). He charged him with a "selective focus on consumption" and an emphasis on import substitution that mitigated the anxieties of the national bourgeoisie (17). He identified similarities between Furtado's thought and the ideas of Theotônio dos Santos (82–95), among them their emphasis on Brazil as a model, their attention to fomenting the internal market as an alternative to exports as a way to mitigate their belief in dependent capitalism as a peculiar mode of production with its own laws, and their argument that dependent capitalism led to stagnation rather than development.

Dependency

Theotônio dos Santos elaborated his thinking on underdevelopment and dependency during the years of nationalism and political mobilization, especially during the early 1960s, when he was a professor at the

University of Brasília, and after the coup, when he was affiliated with the Center for Socioeconomic Studies (Centro de Estudios Socioeconómicos [CESO]) at the University of Chile (dos Santos, 1967). With his wife, Vânia Bambirra, he brought Chilean and Brazilian social scientists together, including Ruy Mauro Marini, to study imperialism and its impact on dependent societies (see dos Santos, 1994). He continued his research and writing at the Autonomous National University of Mexico (Universidad Nacional Autónoma de México [UNAM]) after the Chilean coup of 1973. He had been a leader of POLOP during its clandestinity in São Paulo in 1964 and 1965, and later he was a founder of the Democratic Labor Party (Partido Democrático Trabalhista [PDT]) in support of Leonel Brizzola. After an amnesty allowed his return to Brazil, he was restored to his position at the UNB in 1987 and remained there until he retired in 1994. During these years of turmoil, he was widely recognized for his work on dependency outside Brazil, but because his works had been censored, he was relatively unknown within Brazil (see dos Santos, 1996a, for a critique of the Cardoso government and further polemics on the dependency debate).

Dos Santos published a seminal piece in 1970 in the *American Economic Review* in which he offered a conceptualization of dependency. Dependency, he argued, "is conditioned by the development and expansion of another economy to which the former is subjected. The relation of interdependence between two or more economies, and between these and world trade, assumes the form of dependence when some countries (the dominant ones) can expand and can be self-sustaining, while other countries (the dependent ones) can do this only as a reflection of that expansion, which can have either a positive or negative effect on their immediate development" (1970: 231). He accepted the Marxist theory of the expansion of imperialist centers and their domination of the world economy but saw a need for a theory that addressed the laws of internal development in those countries that were the object of this expansion. In confronting the prevailing belief that underdevelopment could be overcome through capitalist modernization, he looked to alternative possibilities, first in Paul Baran's argument that unequal trade relations based on monopolistic control at the center resulted in transfers of surplus from dependent to dominant countries and second in the concepts of unequal and combined development found in the thought of Trotsky: "It is the combination of these inequalities and the transfer of resources from the most backward and dependent sectors to the most advanced and dominant ones which explains the inequality, deepens it, and transforms it into a necessary and structural element of the world economy" (231).

In this conception, dos Santos identified three historical forms of dependency: colonial dependency, in which trade monopolies were established over the land, mines, and labor of colonial societies; financial-industrial dependency, which accompanied the imperialism of the end of the nineteenth century and allowed the domination of big capital in the centers and its expansion abroad; and a new type of dependency after the Second World War, which was characterized by capital investment by multinational corporations in industry oriented to the internal markets of underdeveloped countries.

Dos Santos found that financial resources usually depended on the export sector for foreign exchange, which was conditioned by fluctuations in the balance of payments. He pointed to the export of surplus value from backward areas to the centers and from the interior of dependent colonial areas to their metropolitan centers; the reproduction within national economies of unequal and combined capitalist development on the international level; and the fact that the structure of industry and technology related to the interests of the multinational corporations rather than to the interests of national capital. The consequences were high concentrations of income and exploitation of labor power: "The alleged backwardness of these economies is not due to a lack of integration with capitalism, but ... on the contrary, the most powerful obstacles to their full development come from the way in which they are joined to this international system and its laws of development" (dos Santos, 1970: 235). Thus, the system of dependent reproduction was part of a system of world economic relations based on monopolistic control of capital. Dependent production and reproduction led to backwardness and misery and produced serious structural problems that led to more dependency and superexploitation.

The solution to this problem, he felt, was revolution. The best hope would be a confrontation between military regimes and fascism, on the one hand, and popular revolutionary governments and socialism, on the other. He offered a model of popular revolutionary war based on the experience of the early 1960s, when a popular movement of sectors of the industrial bourgeoisie and the petty bourgeoisie favored autonomous national development as an alternative to traditional approaches to underdevelopment. This movement had evolved ideologically and politically in a radical direction, sometimes embracing the establishment of a socialist society. At the same time, various political currents advocated electoral tactics and pressure on a popular government, whereas others supported popular insurrection first in the countryside and then in the city. These different groups were inspired by the Cuban Revolution, but they also depended on radicalized elements of the nationalist sector.

Dos Santos also offered a revolutionary strategy involving war on a continental scale that would progressively unify mass forces and establish political-military organizations to lead the struggle through well-organized, armed ideological fronts. He warned that the left, rather than mechanically following in the path of other revolutionaries, should build theory based on its own experience and action that took into account the level of political development within the masses.[4]

Like dos Santos, Vânia Bambirra (interview, Rio de Janeiro, July 28, 1994) was from Belo Horizonte, where a nucleus of university students, including Herbert "Betinho" de Souza, Simon Schwarzman, and Bolívar Lamounier were active in the radical Catholic Ação Popular (AP). After receiving a doctorate in economics, she was deeply involved in studies of dependency, having published a popular book on its relevance to Latin America (1973) and a critique of dependency theory (1975) that presented a typology and identified the structures and contradictions of dependent capitalism, along with a book on Marxist theory (1993). She associated dependency theory with Marxism and argued that it was viable and useful in understanding neoliberalism. Whereas Marini had contributed significantly to the theory, she said, Cardoso was putting his understanding of dependency into practice.

Asked to offer an assessment of dependency, Florestan Fernandes (interview, São Paulo, September 26, 1983) said that the term was useful but had to be examined from a broader perspective: "The most important thing is to not lose sight of imperialist domination, and if the concept of dependency is not used to diminish its importance, then it is a very useful analytical tool." He went on to suggest that dependency analysis helped us see that capitalism as it expanded in the periphery faced numerous

---

[4] Dos Santos (1994) provided an overview of dependency theory, its different directions, its strengths and weaknesses. His account of his life's work (1996b) included a detailed bibliography. An early work on dependency (1971) dealt with U.S. imperialism and the economic crisis in the underdeveloped countries of Latin America. Other works were concerned with "the dilemma" of socialism and fascism (1973), prospects for the transition to socialism in Brazil (1986a), the contradictions of liberal democracy, a theoretical understanding of the forces and modes of production (1986b), the impact of the scientific and technical revolution on the accumulation of capital (1983, 1987), and the prospects for democracy and socialism in the face of dependent capitalism (1991). For an overview of the dependency movement, see Oliven (1992).

constraints. It was useful, he said, because it helped us to characterize the domination of the major capitalist powers in the periphery. Dependency evolved when a capitalist nation of the periphery, underdeveloped and subjected to imperialism, reached a level of economic growth that allowed it to absorb the institutions and other forms of organization of the countries of the center. The center countries had an interest in incorporating the peripheral capitalist countries, and thus a dynamic relationship was established between the capitalist sectors of the periphery and the center. Therefore the idea of dependency was a tool for studying countries that, because of their level of development, did not have the same potential as the dominant countries. Dependency analysis sought to demonstrate the inequality of capitalist development. It was not simply nationalist; it demonstrated that nationalism had to become revolutionary to escape the unequal relationship with regard to development. In this sense, he said, there was a link between development and revolutionary democracy.

Associated Dependent Development

Fernando Henrique Cardoso, whose career and thought we examined earlier, began thinking and writing on underdevelopment and dependency while in exile in Chile and eventually, with Enzo Faletto, wrote *Dependency and Development in Latin America* (Cardoso and Faletto, 1969, 1979). In this work, the authors described their approach as dialectical, with emphasis "not just on the structuring conditioning of social life, but also on the historical transformation of structures by conflict, social movements, and class struggles" (1979: x). Four themes interested Cardoso in this work and in his ensuing writings: imperialism, backwardness and underdevelopment, dependency, and associated dependent development.

Cardoso argued that Lenin's theory of imperialism, although relevant to the early twentieth century, was no longer sufficient to explain the present forms of capital accumulation and external expansion (1972: 87). He cited the work on monopoly capital by Paul Baran and Paul Sweezy as explaining differences between contemporary and early capitalism; in particular, the idea that it was multinational and big corporate capital rather than bank control and finance capital that accounted for accumulation in the periphery. In his view, imperialism in its present stage permitted local participation in economic production, as big corporations reorganized the international division of labor so as to incorporate some parts of less developed economies into their productive investment. This in turn could cause internal fragmentation and shifts in power within these countries, with "modern groups" replacing the old oligarchical groups. Thus, it was possible that capitalism might bring about development in the periphery. As foreign capital was directed toward the manufacturing and selling of products to be consumed by the domestic bourgeoisie, it could stimulate development in some segments of the less developed country (1972–1973).

Cardoso argued that the 1964 coup had suppressed the national bourgeoisie and statist developmental groups and replaced them with sectors of the international bourgeoisie. The military regime had turned to these sectors, and its policies were tied to international capitalism. Thus, the bourgeoisie could not carry out its bourgeois democratic revolution. He believed that Furtado's idea that the national bourgeoisie could contain international capitalism was no longer tenable because of the new hegemony under the military regime.

Instead of developing a theory of dependency, Cardoso and Faletto focused on "situations of dependency" and identified a structural dependency that involved external and internal forces "forming a complex whole whose structural links are not based on mere external forms of exploitation and coercion, but are rooted in a coincidence of interests between local dominant classes and international ones and, on the other side, are challenged by local dominated groups and classes" (Cardoso and Faletto, 1979: xvi). Two basic situations of dependency, in their view, were enclave economies, in which foreign investment penetrated local productive processes in the form of wages and taxes, and economies controlled by the local bourgeoisie, in which the starting point for the circulation of capital was internal and accumulation was the result of "the appropriation of natural resources by local entrepreneurs and the exploitation of the labor force by the same local group" (xix). By this reasoning, the peripheral economies remained dependent even when they no longer pursued only raw materials because their capital goods production could not ensure their reproduction and expansion. This condition constituted the "new dependency," with industrialization in the periphery producing not for mass production but for consumption by the bourgeoisie (xxi–xxii).

Cardoso identified notions of dependency in the classical writings of Marx, Lenin, and Trotsky, claiming that they "often used the expression." He criticized the contemporary currents of dependency for insisting that capitalism inevitably led to stagnation and underdevelopment in the periphery. This thinking about dependency, he believed, neither represented new methodology nor contributed to intellectual history (Cardoso,

1977). He contested Frank's development-of-underdevelopment thesis, arguing that the local or national bourgeoisie was in fact capable of accumulating capital, and he took exception to Marini's assumption that penetration by multinational firms resulted in subimperialism, capitalist expansion facilitated by the local state. He criticized those who spoke of a dependency theory: "To the extent that 'dependency' has become a 'confused amalgam' of intermediate relations and articulations ... and to the extent that it is an attempt to make a 'theory' out of the haziness of an obscure 'concept' then my immediate reaction is to refuse to give the label of science to this type of ideology" (1973: 24).

Cardoso eventually associated his model of development in the periphery with dependency and illustrated it with evidence from the Brazilian experience. New forms of national politics and new international economic forces reinforced the power of the military that emerged after 1964. Along with others, he characterized the result of the coup as a "new bureaucratic-authoritarian regime" accompanied by increased interdependence in production activities at the international level. He argued that industrial firms, whether owned by foreigners or nationals, were tied to decisions made outside the country, and thus the traditional agrarian landowners had lost much of their power base and domestic merchant interests were disadvantaged.

Despite broad interest in his formulation and wide acceptance in the United States and Europe, Cardoso's work faced serious criticism. Francisco Weffort (1971) engaged him in a widely disseminated debate, and, in an unusually polemical and personal critique, John Myer (1975) exposed theoretical weaknesses and "bourgeois" underpinnings. Colin Henfrey referred to "conceptual ambiguity, particularly regarding classes" (1981: 29). Theotônio dos Santos (1996a) replied to Cardoso's criticism of his new-dependency idea and revisited the debates on dependency theory. Maria da Conceição Tavares attacked economic proposals Cardoso had set forth in connection with his candidacy for the presidency, whereas Luiz Carlos Bresser-Pereira argued that Cardoso's ideas of 1969 were the same during his government a generation later (interview, Rio de Janeiro, June 11, 2009). Pablo Rieznik (1995) pointed to the contradiction in Cardoso's early study of Argentine and Brazilian entrepreneurs in the late 1950s, which showed the absence of anti-imperialist national bourgeoisies capable of leading their nations toward autonomous development. Comparing this finding with Cardoso's later work (Cardoso and Faletto, 1969, 1979), he suggested that they failed to understand either the national problem or imperialism and noted a shift over time from a position favoring national independence and autonomous development to a position in which the national bourgeoisie and foreign capital were compatible and dependency and development no longer antagonistic. My own critique (Chilcote, 1984: 47) suggested that Cardoso may have favored socialism for Brazil, but he also opted for reformist policies in the pursuit of development; he referenced social classes but emphasized the market and trade relations rather than relations of production.

Subimperialism and Superexploitation

Ruy Mauro Marini, a product of the leftist movements that linked nationalism with Marxism during the early 1960s, participated in the formation of POLOP along with Theotônio dos Santos, Emir Sader, and Michael Löwy. After the coup of 1964, he fled into exile in Chile. His thinking on dependency evolved through association with dos Santos and research at the CESO. He moved to Mexico after the military coup in September 1973 and joined the Centro de Información, Documentación y Análisis sobre el Movimiento Obrero Latinoamericano. Calling for revolutionary action, he aligned himself with the thesis of Frank and others that capitalism created deformation and underdevelopment in the periphery; but, unlike Frank, he focused on production rather than the market and circulation. He believed that dependent capitalism was incapable of reproducing itself through the process of accumulation. Absolute surplus value could be realized in the periphery by lengthening the workday and intensifying the use of labor power, but relative surplus value, derived by lowering the cost of labor through technology and an increase in productivity, could not. Because the consumption of workers was insignificant and the economy tended to be based on the export of raw materials and other products, the prospects for industrialization were limited. Thus, a dependent capitalist economy tended to expand by pushing beyond its national borders and dominating the economies of weaker neighbors. Marini called this process "subimperialism" (1973a, 1973b).

In the framework he offered, based on passages in Marx referring to dominant and subordinate relations of development and lack of development, underdevelopment in Latin America was the outcome of dependent capitalism (Marini, 1973b: 15–16, 83). He believed that Frank's development-of-underdevelopment thesis led to "impeccable" political conclusions but criticized its assumption that a colonial situation was similar to a dependency situation (18–19). He advanced what he called a Marxist theory of dependency, using the idea of subimperialism to help explain how development could take place in a dependent economy and to highlight one of its consequences – the exploitation of labor. Inevitably, revolution rather than reform would be necessary to overcome this exploitation (1969).

As Marini described it, subimperialism could be understood in several ways. First, with the reorganization of the world economy through establishment of the World Bank and the International Monetary Fund, capitalism expanded into Latin America after the Second World War. Long a dependent country, Brazil was open to the flow of private capital as the military seized power in 1964 and reordered the economy and the structure of the class forces, repressed the working class and the opposition, and launched what Marini characterized as its "project" of subimperialism. Second, subimperialism had two components, one relating to national policy regarding productivity and the workforce and the other to an autonomous expansionism (Marini, 1978b: 34–35). Third, given its offensive against the popular forces in Brazil, the military government also had to reinforce a coalition of the ruling classes by reestablishing the compromise between the bourgeoisie and the landowner-merchant oligarchy. It facilitated investment and the introduction of new technology and promoted capitalization, especially in the countryside. Its domestic capitalism, however, was unable to effect any overall change in the national economy. Its national bourgeoisie was insignificant in Brazilian development, and autonomous national development could not occur (1969: 115). Fourth, the principal problem was the inability to create domestic markets that could absorb the increasing productivity, a contradiction that could be resolved, if only partially, through an expansion into new markets, especially its neighboring countries in South America. Thus, Brazilian government investment in projects with its neighbors was a means of shaping subimperialism.

Marini differed from others interested in dependency in his explicit emphasis on revolution. He argued that the response of workers to their plight would lead Brazil along a revolutionary course. Solidarity among the exploited classes and the emergence of a vast political movement would sharpen the contradiction between the bourgeoisie and the landowner-merchant oligarchy, impede foreign investment, and promote autonomous development. Rather than reforms and compromises, he said, the working class had to engage in revolutionary struggle against the subimperialist bourgeoisie and imperialism itself (Marini, 1969: 119–120). The revolution of the masses would be shaped by armed struggle and the vanguard of the petty bourgeoisie, and the role of this vanguard would not lead this movement but fight alongside the workers (161–162). He felt that there was little need for a "theory" of dependency, choosing instead to emphasize concepts such as subimperialism and superexploitation that would help in the struggle to overcome backwardness and the exploitation of workers in Latin America. An extensive rebuttal (1978a) to the criticism of Cardoso and Serra accentuated their differences, yet Marini's work was not well-known outside Latin America because little of it was translated into English. However, it was significant and influential, as Sader and dos Santos (2009) have shown in their reappraisal.

At the outset of this chapter, we questioned when and how capitalism reached Brazil. We surveyed an array of perspectives, concluding that although forms of mercantile capitalism had appeared early, most scholars affirm that during the late years of the empire and with the Old Republic capitalism had clearly established its presence. Throughout our study, we have shown the commitment of intellectuals to identify with the nation, overcome a legacy of inferiority stemming from the colonial period, and seek a path toward modernization and development. The ISEB initiative actively sought to implement a new ideology of developmental nationalism. It also revealed that a national bourgeoisie would not solve the Brazilian problem, whereas Paulista thinkers instead turned to historical analysis of class struggles among wealthy plantation owners, industrialists, middle classes, workers, and peasants. Inevitably, this led to new expectations but few solutions about underdevelopment. During the authoritarian period, the military encouraged foreign investment and loans for infrastructure, industrialization, and modernization of agriculture, but there was little initiative to alleviate the unemployed and underemployed masses of people in the urban shantytowns nor to implement agrarian reform that would help impoverished peasant farmers in the countryside. With the political opening, the implementation of a pluralistic political party system, the surge of social movements, and promulgation of a new constitution and formal representative democracy, many intellectuals became involved in party politics, with Fernando Henrique Cardoso leading the way. The search for a development solution soon focused on democratic outcomes involving more of the people in the political economy.

5

The Pursuit of Democracy

Class struggle among landowners, merchants, and industrialists in Brazil evolved slowly. Landowners prevailed during colonial times and into the First Republic. Under Vargas, the state intervened in an effort to bring national unity to the disparate regions of the country, natural resources were exploited, exports were expanded, foreign capital appeared, and industry began to take hold in urban centers such as São Paulo. After the Second World War, industrialization accelerated, encouraged by foreign and national capital investment, and after 1964 through the state, as the military laid down infrastructure and opened up further to capitalism. Brazilian intellectuals have weighed in on the assessment of these moments in the nation's history. Given the predominance of authoritarian rule through the imperial period of the nineteenth century, the Vargas years, and military domination after 1964, what about democracy?

All of the great revolutions of recent centuries have incorporated some element of democracy into the struggle to mitigate class distinctions and social inequalities or expand individual freedoms and rights. Brazilian intellectuals have pondered whether formal or representative democracy is a precondition for participatory democracy and whether either of these forms leads to an ideal democracy. Their perspectives and insights necessarily revolve around some conception of a better society and include some means for achieving it. Here, we look at their efforts to transform Brazilian society through popular and participatory democratic practices: through the state, urban and rural organizations, social movements, and resistance and armed struggle and sometimes direct involvement in these experiments.

INTELLECTUALS AND THE STATE

From a liberal perspective, the state is a guarantor of the common good in ensuring individual rights, placing constraints on the pursuit of material gain, and allowing the market to operate freely in civil society. Hegel distinguished three powers within the state – legislative, executive, and sovereign – and held that the state moderated and resolved conflicts in civil society. Marx characterized this conception as idealist and argued that the state perpetuated a hierarchy of classes in the interest of the ruling class, but, as the Paulista intellectual Décio Saes has argued (1984, 1985, 1987, 1994), Marx also saw the state as autonomous when the ruling class was unable to consolidate a dominant position.

Formal political practice in Brazil evolved historically through the state. According to Boris Fausto (1999: 33), under colonialism "there was a reciprocal movement of the state toward society and society toward the state, which ended up blurring the boundaries between public and private space." This view contradicted two interpretations that run through Brazilian historiography: that the state was dominant because of Portuguese centralization of power through the state bureaucracy and that colonial society, led by the large landowners, ruled over a weak state. The modern state in Brazil evolved as a hybrid of a patronage system that was a legacy of the colonial period and the empire and a stable and competent bureaucracy. According to Costa (2000: xxvii), "the export-oriented economy reflected monopoly of the means of production by a few, electoral fraud, and the system of patronage." Bresser-Pereira has traced the transformation of the absolutist state of early capitalism into the social democratic state of the twentieth century and advocated a reform of public management that might produce a social-liberal and republican state (2004b: 16–19). His model, presented but not implemented when he was a minister in the Cardoso government in 1995–1998, is founded on "a new concept of republican rights" (viii). His approach embraces the concept of participatory democracy, which, he argues, is derived from Latin American and Catholic political and social thought, gave birth to the Workers' Party (Partido dos Trabalhadores [PT]) in Brazil, is found in the 1988 constitution, and has received international attention because of Porto Alegre's experiment with "participatory budgeting" (136).

In an alternative but not particularly influential approach to the Brazilian state, Roberto Mangabeira Unger (1990), a Harvard law professor who later served in Lula's cabinet, set forth a plan for making government more efficient, removing the state from productive activities,

stabilizing markets, combating the excesses of corporations, and media-
ting social and regional inequalities. He pointed to the coexistence of two
worlds, one organized, capitalized, and favored by the state and its public
firms and the other lacking resources and prejudicial to most Brazilians.
Intertwined with economics was the problem of political cycles in which "a
reformist government, supported by a disorganized popular base,
confronts inflexible and militant elites" (15). His proposal for overcoming
this economic dualism was built on an alliance of middle- and working-
class elements through the Democratic Labor Party (Partido Democrático
Trabalhista [PDT]) and the PT.

The Brazilian state has been decisive through periods of multiparty
activity and pluralism, on the one hand, and authoritarianism, on the
other. In 1930, Vargas overcame the oligarchical forces that dominated
the republic, and for fifteen years he used his executive power to ensure
state dominance over the political parties and labor unions. His second
term ended in 1954 with his suicide in the face of economic and political
pressure. The ensuing Kubitschek government used the state apparatus to
relocate the national capital from Rio to Brasília, a visionary effort to
transcend the pervasive colonial mentality and strengthen national
identity. His vice president, João Goulart, continued in that position
with Jânio Quadros, who in 1960 was elected by a conservative alliance.
Upon Quadros's surprising resignation seven months later, the progressive
Goulart was allowed to assume a figurehead presidency.[1]

Eventually, the military relinquished power, a progressive constitution
was implemented in 1988, and Fernando Henrique Cardoso became
president from 1994 to 2002, followed by Lula in 2002 (after defeats in
1989, 1994, and 1998) and Dilma Rousseff in 2010. A brief look at the
Brazilian state under Cardoso suggests a period of transition and eventually some significant changes. Cardoso was able to resolve the problem of

---

[1] According to David Fleischer (*Brazil Focus*, February 1, 2008), a plebiscite in January 1963
restored powers to Goulart, but fifteen months later the military removed him from office
and he retired to exile in Uruguay together with his brother-in-law, Leonel Brizola. In 1976,
the military may have ordered him killed; reportedly, he died of a heart attack on his cattle
farm, but no autopsy was performed. There was suspicion that an Operation João Goulart
had been carried out by the CIA together with intelligence agencies in Brazil, Argentina, and
Uruguay. Curiously, in August 1976, former president Kubitschek was killed in a suspicious
auto crash on the highway between São Paulo and Rio. In 1985, the recently elected
president Tancredo Neves became ill and died before taking office. Moniz Bandeira
(1978[2001]) provides the best analysis of the Goulart period, while Pessoa de Morais
(1965) elaborates a sociological perspective of the Brazilian revolution before the 1964
coup.

inflation while consolidating his government around neoliberal programs. The first two years of the Lula government reflected modest growth, high unemployment, inequality, and failed agrarian reform. Initially, leftist intellectuals were skeptical and offered critical analysis of these years. For instance, Plínio Arruda Sampaio (2005), a founder of the PT, observed that the neoliberal adjustment implemented under the Cardoso government continued under Lula, conforming "rigorously to the prescription of the Washington Consensus – weak state and free market." Furthermore, the government "fully submitted to the traditional patterns of the corrupt Brazilian elite: collusion, give and take, bogus alliances, obscure financing of the electoral campaign – nothing different from the reprehensive practices of the Cardoso government." Popular movements were "weaker and confused," with the PT splintered by internal dissension and the left in retreat despite a 70 percent approval rating for Lula. Sampaio concludes, however, that the Lula government stimulated a shift from "the colonial model of yesterday to the Brazilian nation of tomorrow." Emir Sader (2003) confirms this analysis, arguing that Lula came to power because of the failure of the Cardoso regime and that the new government lacked an alternative to the neoliberalism it had claimed to oppose. Despite the rise of a New Left under the PT, a new labor central, and the mobilization of rural workers in the countryside, the left remained weak on the national question, democracy, and neoliberalism. Sader shows that the PT and Lula modified their discourse over time, emphasizing social justice in 1994, socialism in 1998, and the hegemony of finance capital in 2002. He argues that Brazil needs to reexamine its role in the international economy, renegotiating its debt and instituting participatory budgeting, fiscal reform, and the redistribution of income.

By the end of the Lula administration, significant progress had been made toward the consolidation of a social democratic welfare state. Lecio Morais and Alfredo Saad-Filho (2011) identify an important shift in Lula's second term and that the elections of October 2010 offered a choice between his moderate redistributive policies and independent foreign policy and the rigidly neoliberal policies of the Cardoso regime. The victory of Dilma Rousseff represented continuity and "the articulation between a 'national' capitalism driven by an alliance between the 'national' bourgeoisie, the popular organizations, the informal and rural sector workers, and the state" (31). Morais and Saad-Filho argue that Lula was elected by an alliance of unionized urban and rural workers that supported the PT and a nationalist redistributive and expansionist economic policy. The government then secured an alliance with domestic capital and mobilized workers and civil servants and expanded its social programs through the Bolsa Familia, which reached 11.4 million households, expansion of social security coverage, and an increase in the minimum wage. The result was a decline in poverty and an increase in real wages, especially in the Northeast. A response to the global crisis included higher state expenditures through a housing program, tax rebates, availability of credit by state-owned banks, reduction in interest rates, and expansion of social programs. These changes were popular (opinion polls showed more than 80 percent in favor of them) and ensured Lula's base of support among workers, national capital, and even some sectors of the oligarchy. The shift in state policy not only favored the popular classes but involved the nationalization of the social movement, resulting in increased "legitimacy of the state" and support for "the claim of the poor to a larger share of the products of their labor.... These changes have been called a 'democratic revolution' by some left-wing analysts" (38). Thus, the 2010 elections offered a choice between two visions of the Brazilian state, one leading to broadly based economic growth, redistribution of income, and democratization of the state and the other oriented to renewal of elite dominance over the state and economy in the direction of neoliberal dependent development.

Lula's overwhelming popularity and the changes in class and political alignment ensured Dilma Rousseff's victory in the 2010 elections. She had participated in the urban guerrilla struggle during the early 1970s and had risen through the ranks of the PDT and later the PT, eventually serving as Lula's chief of staff.[2] Morais and Saad-Filho (2011) believe that her emergence "does not signal the start of a socialist transformation in Brazil. Her government is not even committed to dismantling neoliberalism and building a democratic system of accumulation; it is also supported by an unwieldy coalition" (41). It does, however, represent an alternative to neoliberalism, and, through the social movements and pressures from below, it can augment the instruments and political will lacking in a weak

[2] An interview with Theotônio dos Santos (Rio de Janeiro, June 12, 2009) clarified that Rousseff was too young to have participated in the founding of POLOP and that her ties to Brizola and the PDT were due largely, after her release from prison in 1973, to her moving to Rio Grande do Sul where she completed a degree in economics. Dos Santos considered her intelligent, loyal to Lula, and one of the competent people around him who had learned from Brizola how to be a nationalist and defend the interests of the nation rather than selling out to foreign capital. Carvalho (2009) provides biographical details of Rousseff's early life, affirming that she joined the POLOP in about 1967 and helped organize the National Liberation Command (Comando de Libertação Nacional [COLINA]) and its later integration into the Vanguarda Armada Revolucionária-Palmares (VAR-Palmares).

state. The assumption here is that the government may represent a continuing opening to the mass population in the direction of implementing policies that would improve their standard of living and participation through the parties, as well as in social movements.

Formal democracy in Brazil involves a plurality of political parties. The people are represented in a chamber of deputies and a senate through which proposals, ideas, and laws filter. Many parties coalesce into coalitions. For example, during the municipal elections of October 2004, the vote totals clustered around the "faithful" Lula coalition (PT, Partido Liberal [PL], Partido Trabalhista Brasileira [PTB], Partido Socialista do Brasil [PSB], Partido Comunista do Brasil [PC do B]), which received a plurality of votes in fifteen of the twenty-six states and 33.6 percent nationwide (with 31,965,253 votes) but an absolute majority in only two states, Acre and Amapá. In densely populated states such as São Paulo, the "Lula group" polled 37.63 percent of the vote, a near tie with the second-largest coalition, the Partido da Social Democracia Brasileiro (PSDB)-Partido da Frente Liberal (PFL) "opposition" (37.54 percent); and in the state of Rio de Janeiro, the Lula group beat the PSDB-PFL by 31.21 percent to 28.91 percent. Nationwide, the PSDB-PFL polled 26,980,313 votes (28.4 percent).

Emerging with the democratic opening, the PT was made up of many leftist factions, including both Trotskyist and communist, an amalgam that slowly gained influence and eventually power (Meneguella, 1989).[3] It filled the political space left by the Brazilian Communist Party (Partido Comunista Brasileiro [PCB])'s loss of influence within organized labor, and, in its infancy, intellectuals like Michael Löwy, Marco Aurélio Garcia, Leondor Kondor, and Carlos Nelson Coutinho did not hesitate to offer perspectives on Marxism and its relevance to theory and practice within

---

[3] Divisions within the PT were evident in its third congress, as reported by David Fleischer (*Brazil Focus*, September 1–7, 2007), who identifies six factions: Construindo um Novo Brasil, a center majority faction made up of the former Campo Majoritário and former Articulação and led by José Dirceu and Lula; Mensagem ao Partido, a center-left faction of ex-Democracia Socialista members and dissidents from Campo Majoritário, a leftist dissident group with ties to the Trotskyist Fourth International; Por Todos os Sonhos, a center-left faction formerly known as the Movimento PT; Novo Rumo, a center-left faction; A Esperança é Vermelha, a left faction formerly known as Articulação de Esquerda; and PT de Lutas e de Massas, a center faction. By late 2013, six factions or "tendencies" comprised the PT: Construindo um Novo Brasil (69.81 percent of membership); Mensagem ao Partido (18.3 percent); Articulação de Esquerda (6.62 percent); O Trabalho (1.48 percent); Resistência Petista (3.13 percent); and Esquerda Marxista (0.65 percent) as reported in *Brazil Focus*, November 9–15, 2013.

the party (Franco et al., 1991). Florestan Fernandes, one of its founders, had warned that the PT needed to emphasize raising people's awareness rather than winning congressional seats. Francisco Weffort, another founder, warned the party against abandoning its objective of having a social and cultural life outside the party. Just before joining the Cardoso government, he said, "The PT trajectory has not been one of defeat.... Only the PT can defeat the PT" (Bradford and Kucinski, 1995: 97). Despite its inconsistencies and infighting, the PT grew rapidly to become, by 2012, Brazil's leading political party.

Florestan Fernandes's admonition to the national PT to focus on its base rather than on congressional politics may help to explain the party's reluctance to institutionalize and extend participatory democracy at the local level. He was implying that development from below, at the municipal level, for example, could involve more people in the resolution of problems and lead to changes that affect everyday life rather than depending on elected representatives at the state and national levels. During the 1990s, I observed such success in Icapuí, a small municipality in the northeastern state of Ceará where a younger generation of PT militants had used an electoral victory to extend social services by building schools and health clinics in an effort to resolve needs never before satisfied. Gianpaolo Baiocchi (2005) has given us a case study of an experiment with participatory democracy in the southern city of Porto Alegre through a participatory budgeting process that represented an example of the PT vision of involvement from below. Although the PT lost in local elections in 2004, the budgetary process it had implemented promised to remain intact, carefully monitored by workers and poor people no matter which political party was in power. According to Baiocchi (160–161), although the PT had not formally institutionalized the budgetary process, there was "good reason to count on organized civil society to monitor the institution and press for continued openness.... This organized civil society has an immense capacity for monitoring the government and putting pressure on it. It will be practically impossible to run an institution of participatory budgeting that does not conform to high standards or that tries to manipulate participants." What appears to have occurred in Porto Alegre is that, by emphasizing electoral politics and not exercising its hegemony over civil society, the PT permitted participatory democracy from below, but it was unable to consolidate its power as a political party and prevent its opposition from gaining control of local politics (161). Löwy (2000) confirms how unionists, leftist Christians, and Marxist militants successfully came together in Porto Alegre to manage municipal government in ways different from bourgeois politicians by insisting on no corruption, no nepotism, and emphasizing the needs of poor and working-class neighborhoods through the participatory budget: "it is the population itself which determines, in an original demonstration of direct democracy, if the budget's funds should be used to build a road, a school, or a medical center" (16).

This is but an example, whatever its prospects, of an innovative approach that led to participatory decision making. Established political institutions such as state apparatuses, political parties, or even labor unions and social movements may co-opt or undermine such experiments, those involved may be discouraged or lose interest, and the process involved may reveal serious deficiencies. Yet such initiatives also inspire and motivate people to become involved.

INTELLECTUALS AND LABOR

The labor movement evolved out of the early socialist and anarcho-syndicalist tendencies dating to the late nineteenth century and involved major protests and strikes in Rio, São Paulo, Santos, Porto Alegre, and other large cities. The PCB drew much of its leadership and membership from organized labor and prominent intellectuals such as its early secretary general, Astrogildo Pereira. The party supported important strikes, the establishment of several labor confederations, and, during the late 1930s, an electoral front with workers and peasants. Under Vargas and the influence of integralism, the government served as arbiter between capital and labor and manipulated labor through a paternalistic labor code and a vast program of social welfare. This corporatist system continued after the fall of the Vargas dictatorship in 1945 as the labor ministry controlled workers through the union tax and the threat of intervention, whereas the communists opted for working within the official unions rather than forming rival organizations.

With the establishment of the PT, the traditional labor movement, largely under communist control (Telles, 1962), was challenged by the Unified Workers' Central (Central Única dos Trabalhadores [CUT]) and labor unions seeking autonomy. The CUT emerged strong but did not oppose the union tax that, since Vargas times, has been the essential mechanism that links labor to the state. The heart of their concern was the industrial center of São Paulo and surrounding urban centers. Scholarly study (French, 1992; Keck, 1992) of the formative years of the PT from the early 1970s into the early 1980s showed how a political party originally inspired by labor leadership evolved through the constraints imposed by the democratic transition from dictatorship. Indeed, middle-class intellectuals comprised the PT, whereas its leaders came from state-sponsored union structures (Rodrigues, 1990a, 1990b). Especially important were the strikes from 1978 to 1980 that contributed to the end of the dictatorship and the opening to democracy (Antunes, 1988b). This history is delineated by Antunes (1991) in a comparison of the old and new unionism and the founding of central labor organizations in Brazil, whereas Armando Boito (1991) draws out the ties between union-ism and the state.[4]

---

[4] Important (especially Paulista) intellectual contributions to the study of Brazilian labor in Brazil include Edgar Carone's (1979/1981/1984) compilation of documents on the Brazilian labor movement, systematically organized chronologically and by leftist move-ment. The initial volume contained documents from 1877 to 1944 on reformist socialism, anarchism, the early PCB, and Trotskyism, including a 1935 political split reported by the Brazilian section of the Liga Comunista Internacionalista. The second volume (1945–1964) included documents of the PSB, Trotskyism, the POLOP, and the AP. The third volume consisted of documents of the urban revolutionary groups such as the National Liberation Action (Ação Libertadora Nacional [ALN]), the PC do B, the Eighth of October Revolutionary Movement (Movimento Revolucionário 8 de Outubro [MR-8]), the Brazilian Revolutionary Communist Party (Partido Comunista Brasileiro Revolucionário [PCBR]), the Revolutionary Popular Vanguard (Vanguarda Popular Revolucionário [VPR]), and the POLOP. With a preface by Astrogildo Pereira, a book by Telles (1962) offered a history of the Brazilian labor movement from 1946 to 1962, including an analysis of the role of parties in labor unity and activity, in particular, the PCB and the PTB. Hercules Corrêa (1980) contributed writings in exile by a labor leader and member of the Central Committee of the PCB. Finally, Boris Fausto (1983) produced a serious historical study of urban work and social conflict from 1890 to 1920, the formative period of the labor movement in Rio and São Paulo, with emphasis on the role of the anarchist movement. Together with Fausto, Antônio Cândido, Paula Beiguelman, and others, Antônio Arnoli Prado (1986) examined anarchism. Ricardo Antunes looked at labor struggles in the period 1879–1980 (1988a) and in the early 1930s (1988b) and produced an overview of the old and new unionism (1991). Complementing these works was António Arnoli Prado's (1986) anthology of essays on anarchism by Antônio Cândido, Boris Fausto, Paula Beiguelman, and others. Emir Sader (1988) profiled new workers and their struggles around São Paulo from 1970 to 1980.
  Beyond this historical documentation, São Paulo intellectuals contributed signifi-cantly to a deep understanding of issues related to the working class and the labor movement. Leôncio Martins Rodrigues was the author of important works on labor in Brazil, including an interpretive history of strife within the Brazilian labor movement from the late nineteenth century to 1964 (1966). Drawing on a survey of workers, Rodrigues (1970) also examined questions of migration and workers' relations with the firm, the union, and the political system. His study of parties and unions (1990b) included an insightful essay on the PT showing that the party base included intellectuals and middle-class people as well as labor leaders who originated in the state-sponsored unions. His work on the CUT (1990a) was an effort to identify militants and their ideology. Luiz Pereira (1965) looked at the nature of work in capitalist society, labor

The 1930s under Vargas were accompanied by changes that affected relations between traditional small farmers, tenants, sharecroppers, and rural workers, on the one hand, and large landowners, on the other. The impact of drought, especially in the Northeast, resulted in large numbers of farmers leaving their land for urban life, thereby increasing demand for migrant labor. Regional agricultural monopolies evolved, and prices increased due to limitations on distribution and control of markets. At the same time, inflation isolated rural workers from the national market, and they were prohibited from organizing and seeking social security and other benefits. Nevertheless, various kinds of rural organizations emerged. The communists, for instance, organized dissident peasants early on, forming a peasant league in about 1928 on the large coffee plantations of Sertãozinho and Ribeirão Prêto. From 1946 to 1948, the Pernambucan branch of the party organized peasants into leagues. About 1954, the PCB brought sharecroppers together on the coffee and sugar farms to form the Brazilian Laborers' and Agricultural Workers' Union (União dos Lavradores e Trabalhadores Agrícolas do Brasil [ULTAB]), which pursued legislation protecting workers in the countryside. Five years later, Francisco Julião, a lawyer and state deputy in Pernambuco, successfully defended peasants of the Galiléia plantation in the *agreste* zone between the wet coastal sugar lands and the dry cattle interior backlands, and the state then expropriated the property to become a cooperative, with the peasants forming a league; thereafter, a movement evolved with more than two hundred leagues scattered among states stretching from Pernambuco to Paraíba and south to São Paulo. Progressive Catholic priests also attempted to organize the rural proletariat into unions, first in the state of Rio Grande do Norte. By 1963, hundreds of Church-sponsored unions had been organized throughout the Northeast and south as far as Rio Grande do Sul. Finally, in October 1963, the leftist politician Leonel Brizola launched the Groups of Eleven as a means of mobilizing rural protest through guerrilla warfare (Chilcote, 1972: 268–273).

in situations of development and underdevelopment, and the impact on workers of urbanization and industrialization. Celso Frederico (1978) presented an extremely interesting case study of workers in the industrial suburbs of São Paulo and the dialectical process provoked by populism and "false consciousness." He was particularly interested in the "transitional character of an agrarian society that is modernizing" (13) and the mix of rural and urban values that affected behavior. In a three-volume work (1990–1991), he brought together essays by others on the working class in the context of the so-called Brazilian miracle.

A transition from traditional *latifundios* to capitalist agriculture accompanied the emergence of a rural labor movement in the countryside and the decline of the peasantry and its subsistence farming, tenant farming, and other backward practices (Anthony Pereira, 1997). Illustrating this transition, the demand for ethanol from sugarcane in Ceará transformed the relations of production as peasants gave up their lands and subsistence farming to become wage earners (Martins, 2000). João Pedro Stedile (2007), the head of the Movement of Landless Rural Workers (Movimento dos Trabalhadores Rurais Sem-Terra [MST]), explains the implications of these changes, asserting that the neoliberal agrarian model developed since about 1990 culminated in an unequal alliance between the country's dominant classes and international capital, denationalization, and an even more dependent Brazilian economy: "The role of government in the economy has been cut back. Policies have been enacted that privilege the transfer of wealth to the financial system through the state sector." He argues that under Lula the neoliberal model in agriculture emanated from an alliance between the major capitalist farmers and ranchers and the multinationals that controlled the international commodity trade and agro-industry. Workers in the countryside lost their jobs and migrated to cities. Land holdings grew as smaller properties were absorbed. Ultimately, ten transnational companies controlled virtually all agrarian production, pesticides, transgenic seeds, and foreign commodities trading.

As an alternative to this model, Stedile (2007) advocates family-run and *campesino* agriculture supported by rural social movements, church groups, environmentalists, and rural people. This model calls for the organization and occupation of small and medium-sized farms, aid for five million agricultural families on smallholdings, and an agrarian reform that would guarantee land to four million landless families. He sees a struggle between the capitalist farmers and ranchers aligned with multinationals, on the one hand, and family farmers, *campesinos*, and their movements, united with urban workers, on the other. Although critical of the Lula government, he acknowledges measures that have helped the *campesino* movement: expansion of employment and income insurance for farmers to protect them against natural disasters, an increase in loans to small rural producers, and rural education programs. At the same time, he says, the government has also "served the interests of the rural elite by its inactions. It has failed to fulfill its promises to settle the landless families occupying large estates and implement an encompassing agrarian reform program." Overall, it has favored the export-oriented agribusiness sector over family-owned agriculture.

INTELLECTUALS AND SOCIAL MOVEMENTS

The democratic opening brought the early stirrings of social movements and interest among scholars in studying them (Alvarez, Dagnino, and Escobar, 2000). Movements evolved around peasant farmers, women's rights, equality for Afro-Brazilians, and other causes. Maria Célia Pinheiro Machado Paoli (interview, São Paulo, August 21, 1992), originally from Curitiba, was an early student of these social movements. At the University of São Paulo (USP), she initially studied with Florestan Fernandes. Of her fellow graduate students at USP she said, "We abandoned politics in favor of carrying on with the university tradition of preparing future intellectuals. We were dedicated to teaching, but many of our colleagues turned to the armed struggle as our generation entered into the resistance." She completed a master's thesis (1974) under José de Sousa Martins on the role of marginalized workers in the surplus of labor available to the market and its contribution to the development process in São Paulo: "My thesis on marginality and underemployment in the countryside drew from my living and working in a *favela* and also teaching in the university. Gramsci was of interest at that time with his theme of hegemony, and we also looked at structural Marxism and Althusser." Later, she turned to class and the state, examining the Brazilian working class through history and the formation of the Brazilian state; under the direction of British Marxist Eric Hobsbawm, she wrote a doctoral dissertation on labor, law, and the state in Brazil from 1930 to 1950: "Here I looked not only at the Vargas state but at the working class during this period. An important turning point was in 1978 with the strikes in São Bernardo. From that time, we turned to social movements during the early 1980s." On her return from study in England, she joined the PT, became interested in feminism through Bete Lobo (the wife of Marco Aurélio Garcia), and worked with Eder Sader at the USP: "Eder was an activist, very Leninist in his thinking. . . . My Marx was a pluralist Marx that focused on the citizenry all the way to hegemony, a Marx with a political theory. His Marx did not have a political theory; it was based on economic determinism and more traditional than mine." Paoli wrote a useful historiography of the Brazilian worker (1987), and with Eder studied the Brazilian worker in São Paulo. Together, they were especially critical of previous academic scholarship on the working class (Paoli, Sader, and Telles, 1983) and on the popular classes in Brazilian sociological thought (Sader and Paoli, 1986). Paoli then examined gender and social movements in the contemporary social sciences (1991) and the impact of the new social movements in Brazil on the struggle for political space and the control and distribution of national resources and their challenge to the legitimacy of the dominant system (1992).[5]

As an intellectual whose ideas brought adult literacy to impoverished masses, Paulo Freire inspired the Movimento Popular de Cultura led by progressive Catholics in Northeast Brazil during the early 1960s, and later his approach was carried to other poor areas of the world. His method involved dialectically relating words that had meaning for people in a particular locality (such as hunger-food, poor-rich, slum-house) and linking them with simple images. It focused on improving the standard of living for the common people and was adopted by the United Nations Educational, Scientific, and Cultural Organization (UNESCO). In a lengthy interview, Freire (1985) offered glimpses of a life and career of many interests. The youngest of four children born in João Pessoa, he studied in public schools, eventually in Recife, and finished with a degree in law. He was impressed by Gilberto Freyre and Oliveira Vianna, Caio Prado Júnior, and Antônio Cândido and by the early Marx and the ideology of liberation. His writing was devoted to culture (Freire, 1971) and the pedagogy of the oppressed (1970, 2005). Explorations of his life and pedagogy have been produced by Moacir Gadotti (1994), Peter McLaren (2000), and Henry A. Giroux (1910). In the latter's opinion, Freire's "critical pedagogy currently offers the very best, perhaps the only, chance for young people to develop and assert a sense of their rights and responsibilities to participate in governing, and not simply being governed by prevailing ideological and material forces."

The economist and activist Ladislau Dowbor collaborated on the literacy projects of Freire, his father-in-law, in Northeast Brazil and in Guinea Bissau after independence in 1975. Dowbor, an economist, was born in France of Polish parents in 1941 and raised in Brazil after 1951. As a reporter in Pernambuco, he came to know Paulo Freire, Celso Furtado, Gilberto Freyre, and others (Dowbor, 2011). He describes his autobiography (2005) as "a mosaic of experiences," including problems and solutions and efforts to assess theory through practice. His early studies

---

[5] These issues were reflected in an earlier collection of essays (Paoli et al., 1982) on violence in Brazil and how people resolved conflict outside a system that restricted citizenship rights, including a fascinating study by Maria Victória Benevides on neighborhood lynchings as one recourse to that predicament. Later, Benevides (1991) expressed dissatisfaction with both direct and indirect forms of participation and opted for a "semidirect democracy." Evelina Dagnino (1994) edited a useful collection of essays on populism and social movements. Irlys Alencar Barreira (2011) updates and reassesses the work on these themes.

with Jean Piaget and the reading of Marx were for him "a defining moment, which drew together my studies of economics with the broader universe of knowledge" (14). He accompanied the armed struggles in Vietnam and in the Portuguese colonies in Africa and then, during the late 1960s in Brazil, joined the revolutionary movement, was arrested, imprisoned, and interrogated, and eventually found exile through exchange for the kidnapped German ambassador. He taught development economics at the University of Coimbra after the revolutionary coup of 1974, and this led to involvement in the newly independent governments of Guinea Bissau and elsewhere in Lusophone Africa. His early writing (1982) argued that development and underdevelopment are two poles of the same process. In 1986, he moved to Nicaragua with a similar project. His return to Brazil and teaching at Pontifícia Universidade Católica (PUC) in São Paulo brought him in contact with Paul Singer. He later served as secretary in the São Paulo municipal government under Luiza Erundina. He sees as a central problem "recovering the regulatory function of the state, and ... strengthening the organization of civil society" (119). His progressive vision for a renewal of society is as follows: "The idea of a participatory democracy, anchored in decentralized systems of social management, and based on the free access to information and culture, clears the way for a politically coherent system because it is based on a balanced coordination of the actually existing social forces" (12).

On the black movement, we have noted the efforts of sociologist Alberto Guerreiro Ramos to draw attention to race in Brazil and achieve recognition for Afro-Brazilian intellectuals. Sales Augusto Santos (2011) points out that distinguished black intellectuals such as Guerreiro Ramos and Abdias do Nascimento never achieved professorships in Brazilian universities although both held university posts in the United States. He traces the history of the Unified Black Movement (Movimento Negro Unificado [MNU]), founded in 1978 in protest against racial discrimination in Brazil, and he examines the activities of black institutions such as the research-oriented Brazilian Association of Black Researchers (Associação Brasileira de Pesquisadores Negros [ABPN]). He points to the small numbers of blacks teaching in universities (e.g., representing less than 1 percent of the faculty at the University of Brasília) and reports a significant increase in the numbers and militancy of black intellectuals since the 1980s. Whereas Santos minimizes the impact of class and labor markets on racial discrimination, Florestan Fernandes argued (1964, 1969) that discrimination in Brazil was largely a product of class distinctions under capitalist development.

Brazil's most important social movement, the MST, began in the state of Rio Grande do Sul, where landless people learned to come together, take action, occupy land, and carve out their own farms in the face of an intransigent bureaucracy and ineffective agrarian reform (for background, see Bernardo Mançano Fernandes, 1996, 2000). The MST also created settlements in the Northeast and in the Amazon: "In many ways – including political organization, the basic freedoms of independence and autonomy, and access to a steady diet – the settlers' lives have improved. They continue to plan and organize themselves to fight for a better life" (Wright and Wolford, 2003: 179). Initially, the success of the MST was spurred on by enthusiasm for the Lula government. Its strategy is to pressure the government to turn over land owned by large landholders who were making poor use of their holdings and to carry out serious agrarian reform. The MST collaborates with other social movements concerned with inequality in the countryside, such as the Movimento dos Pequenos Agricultores, the Movimento dos Atingidos por Barragens, the Movimento das Mulheres Camponesas, the Comissão Pastoral da Terra, and the Associação Brasileira de Reforma Agrária.

The *comunidades eclesiais de base* or ecclesiastical base communities that emerged during the dictatorship flourished in the political opening and the transition to democracy but declined with Vatican intervention. There may have been as many as 100,000 of them, made up of millions of Catholics involved in the search for solutions to poverty. Advocates of liberation theology considered them the vanguard of a renovated religious and social structure (Betto, 1981). Hewitt (1991), who studied twenty-two base communities in the São Paulo area, concluded that they influenced social change, became engaged in concrete struggles to improve local conditions, and assimilated the ideals of good citizenship (107). According to Father Dominique Barbé (1982: 105–106), base communities searched for answers to everyday problems, participated in broader popular movements to improve living conditions, mobilized workers to join together and gain control of their unions, and joined with political parties, the PT in particular, to influence decisions at all levels of politics.

During the 1980s, a plethora of studies on women and feminism in Brazil appeared. Heleieth Saffioti (1978), for example, looked at the role of women in slave-owning society and capitalism, examined education for women from colonial to contemporary times, and identified manifestations of feminism. Studies like this prompted Emilia Viotta da Costa (2000) to revise her study of empire in nineteenth-century Brazil by including a chapter on women. She argued that "the picture of the helpless woman, a prisoner in the web of patriarchalism, characteristic of traditional historiography gave way to a more diversified and complex image raising important questions" (xiii–xiv). Sonia Alvarez (1990) studied women in São Paulo during the decline of authoritarianism and the transition to civilian rule, focusing on social movements that included women from the popular classes, "who were excluded from the pact of domination under authoritarian rule" but "provided the elite opposition with an organizational base that could be mobilized in favor of democracy" (15). Specifically, she argued that the regressive policies of the military regime disrupted working-class families and pushed millions of women into the workforce, community struggles, opposition to the regime, and male-dominated professions as higher education expanded.

In the cultural sphere, the ascendancy of the bossa nova coincided with the rise of nationalism and continued into the sixties and seventies. Criticism in song was evident as early as 1960 and was conspicuous among the radical students associated with the National Union of Students (União Nacional dos Estudantes [UNE]), whose nationalist songs decried foreign cultural influences and called on Brazil to abandon the colonial mentality of the past. One song described Brazil as "a sleeping giant that awakened to find itself an underdeveloped country" and that the people "live less and suffer more" as they "think, dance, and sing as North Americans" and "underdevelopment, underdevelopment is what national life is." Another song identified João da Silva as a false nationalist and "citizen without compromise" who "washes with Palmolive, uses Colgate, shaves with Gillette, puts on Aqua Velva." About this time, students and young intellectuals founded the Centro Popular de Cultura, which disseminated dissident music, popular revolutionary art, and anthologies of social poetry edited by Moacir Félix (1962–1963).

After 1964, cultural movements were associated with resistance to the military regime. Many composers, performers, and poet-musicians contributed to a movement known as Brazilian Popular Music (Música Popular Brasileira [MPB]). Chico Buarque, Caetano Veloso, Gilberto Gil, and Milton Nascimento joined forces in this movement at a time of repression. Until he was arrested (along with Gil) and forced into exile in 1969, Veloso led what became known as the Tropicália movement. Roberto Schwarz criticized the movement for touching on social issues without denouncing injustice or poverty: "Tropicalismo fixed an atemporal view of Brazil.... The songs took inventory of a contradictory socioeconomic and cultural reality without indicating historical causes or ways to overcome the situation" (quoted in Perrone, 1989: 63).

Roberto Schwarz (1992) pointed to the continuing cultural productivity of the left under the military dictatorship in the early years after the 1964 coup: "The cultural presence of the left was not suppressed during this period; rather, it continued to flourish" (127). He argued that, in general, "socialist intellectuals were spared imprisonment, unemployment, and exile they had been expecting" because the only radical material they produced was for their own consumption. Only those who organized workers, peasants, and soldiers suffered torture and imprisonment. Yet, without realizing it, leftist intellectuals through their teaching, writing, and discussions contributed to "the creation, within the petit-bourgeoisie, of a massively anticapitalist generation" with a "readiness to become involved in the class struggle" (128) and thereby contribute to the urban armed struggle and resistance to the regime. Ladislau Dowbor (2005: 21), who participated in this struggle, saw these years as a time "for indignation to translate into popular action with some degree of organization."

INTELLECTUALS AND REVOLUTIONARY STRUGGLE, RESISTANCE, AND REVOLT

Brazil has a lengthy history of resistance and protest (Chilcote, 1972: 243–280). Few Brazilian intellectuals participated in these interventions, but they have written about them. The most important of these studies was Euclydes da Cunha's classic *Rebellion in the Backlands* (1944), based on the 1893–1897 rebellion at Canudos in opposition to the First Republic. Four federal expeditions were sent to restore order, and the people of Canudos fought fiercely to the last person. Cunha's study looks at Antônio Conselheiro, who led the rebellion, as a charismatic religious figure who unified a community to reject materialistic life and resist the authority of the Republic. There also have been studies of social bandits such as Antônio Silvina, who attacked convoys and distributed the goods among rural people, and Lampião, whose movement was broken into small disciplined groups that operated like guerrillas in the countryside, confronting not only established authority but societal injustice. Catholic resistance was represented by the movement of Padre Cícero, who mobilized local forces to defeat the militia of the state of Ceará and establish himself as the patriarch of all the Northeast.

The long march of Luiz Carlos Prestes in the backlands threatened the patriarchal order and raised rural people's political consciousness and awareness of social problems. Eventually, Prestes emerged as head of the PCB. Unable to consolidate his power early, Vargas was challenged by an abortive revolt in São Paulo during 1932. Eventually, he was able to formulate plans for economic and social change in the form of a new constitution, a popular front, and the rise of a fascist movement. On November 23, 1935, an uprising led by the PCB began with a barracks revolt in Natal, where rebel soldiers, joined later by peasants and workers, occupied the city, seized the police headquarters, and formed a revolutionary committee. A day later, a suburban military barracks in Recife was taken, and on November 27 rebels in Rio seized the Praia Vermelho garrison. Government troops quickly repressed the revolts, which then served as a pretext not only for suppressing the PCB but for assuming extraordinary emergency powers. Thereafter, the PCB turned to its traditional policy of alignment with noncommunist popular forces. During the early 1960s, however, communist intellectuals left the party to form their own groups, which turned to guerrilla warfare (Cannabrava, 1970; Carone, 1984).

In December 1966, Carlos Marighella denounced the PCB for its bourgeois and conciliatory stance and declared that he was ready to join the revolutionary armed struggle. In August, he had attended a conference of the Organization of Latin American Solidarity in Havana, Cuba, and this led to his ouster from the party, along with Jacob Gorender and others. They retained their influence in the São Paulo state party committee, which proclaimed Marighella its secretary and called for mass armed struggle. Gorender and another dissident communist, Mário Alves, later formed the Brazilian Revolutionary Communist Party (Partido Comunista Brasileiro Revolucionário [PCBR]), while Marighella founded Ação Libertadora Nacional (ALN), and other revolutionaries established the Eighth of October Revolutionary Movement (Movimento Revolucionário do 8 de Outubro [MR-8]), named for the date of Che Guevara's death. The ALN and MR-8 were responsible for kidnapping U.S. ambassador C. Burke Elbrick, whom they later exchanged for fifteen political prisoners, including the PCB leader Gregório Bezerra. They also organized bank robberies in São Paulo and Rio de Janeiro. In January 1970, the VAR-Palmares hijacked a Brazilian plane to Cuba. In December, the Comando Juárez Guimarães de Brito affiliated with the Popular Revolutionary Vanguard (Vanguarda Popular Revolucionária [VPR]), named for a guerrilla leader who had died earlier. Led by Captain Carlos Lamarca who had deserted the Brazilian army and joined the VPR, they abducted the Swiss ambassador. In June 1969, Marighella produced a manual of urban guerrilla warfare that was widely circulated. The regime launched a counterrevolutionary campaign that ended in the death of Marighella on November 4,

1969, and Carlos Lamarca on September 17, 1971. Frei Betto (1982) tells us that the ALN included Dominican priests, among them Frei Tito de Alencar Lima, whose example symbolized the plight of torture victims in Brazil.

Other militant groups turned toward rebellion. The Stalinist, pro-Chinese PC do B criticized the conciliatory position of its counterpart the PCB and became active in dissident student revolutionary movements in Guanabara and São Paulo. POLOP, hoping to create a coalition of leftist forces in Brazil, called for guerrilla struggle in the countryside and proletarian uprisings in the cities. Before 1964, Popular Action (Ação Popular [AP]) had aligned itself with the PCB to dominate the UNE, but after the coup it declared itself Marxist and became affiliated with revolutionary groups.

With their emphasis on the kidnapping of prominent persons and bank robberies, the urban guerrillas were a new phenomenon in the left's attempt to transform Brazilian society, and they captured national and even international attention. The Paulista intellectual João Quartim de Moraes (1971: 189–191) pointed out that whereas the rural guerrillas took advantage of their mobility to fight a war of attrition and choose the terrain on which to operate, the urban guerrillas had to operate in clandestinity and isolation from the masses. Again, whereas rural guerrillas could shift their forces and recruit from the peasantry in building up a people's army, the urban movement could only recruit cadres: "Revolutionary war in the city is a form of struggle on the border between war and politics" (190). Quartim argued that no organization should do battle with limited resources as the PCBR had tried to do in early 1970.

Many of these movements involved intellectuals directly. Ladislau Dowbor, who, as we have seen, later became a reputable economist, participated in the urban guerrilla offensive through the VPR. Artists whose resistance to cultural suppression had developed through the UNE's popular culture centers and the Freire-inspired Movimento Popular de Cultura joined the leftist movements, and eighteen of them were imprisoned for having done so (Ridenti, 1993: 73). Although he questioned Roberto Schwarz's view that, "in spite of the rightist dictatorship, there [was] a relative cultural hegemony of the left in the country," arguing instead that a technocratic military hegemony under governmental authority took the place of the populism of the left to preserve the hegemony of the bourgeoisie (90), Ridenti acknowledged the influence of intellectuals not only in the PCB but in the armed urban movements, especially the MR-8 (161). Michael Löwy (1979) suggested, however, that although the intellectuals in the universities, churches, and even various apparatuses of the state were in a position to oppose the capitalist order and join leftist organizations, they rarely took prominent roles in those organizations.

The most developed guerrilla experience in a rural area was led by the PC do B in the region of Araguaia, in southern Pará. Early in 1972, militants of the party, most of them Paulistas, organized three groups of twenty-one persons each subdivided into subgroups of seven. It took the army three major offensives over nearly two years to subdue the movement, with the actions vividly described by the journalist Fernando Portela in the *Jornal da Tarde* and sensationally reproduced in a book with interviews, images, and documents (Portela, 1979). Among the prominent participants was José Genoíno Neto, who later became a PT federal deputy. Pedro Pomar acknowledged that the defeat of his PC do B was due partly to its emphasis on the idea of the *foco*, which had been discredited after the death of Che Guevara. Its emphasis on a military rather than a political strategy was elaborated on by Pomar's son, Wladimir Pomar (1980, 1982), Jacob Gorender (1987), and Daniel Reis Filho (1990, Reis Filho et al., 1991). Ridenti (1993: 236) wrote of the difficulty that the São Paulo guerrillas, many of them intellectuals, had in relating to the workers of the region and quotes Genoíno as saying that the people of the region were unaware that the Paulistas were there to carry out a guerrilla struggle: "There was a contradiction between political work and military work that was never apparent in the conception of the PC do B. . . . Lacking experience in political and union struggle, the peasant movement was unable to assimilate to the armed struggle." Ridenti's analysis showed, however, that the defeat of the urban guerrillas did not obscure the "fantasy of the Brazilian revolution" that lived on in the aspirations of the left.

Our discussion has focused on the influence of intellectuals not only because of the ideas, strategies, and tactics they advocated but because of their participation in real-life events that brought about economic, political, and social change. Brazilian economic progress and capitalism have been both advanced and limited by the state under authoritarian and formal representative rule. The national bourgeoisie has evolved all too slowly and has largely failed to fulfill the role envisaged for it by intellectuals influenced by the European and North American experiences. Especially in recent decades, the state has conditioned and moderated a proliferation of political parties that evolved from the multiparty system that had preceded the two-party system imposed by the military regime.

Opposition to the dictatorship had been accompanied by intellectual involvement in political life through the emerging political parties, the revitalized labor unions, resistance through the widely mobilized social movements, and even participation in revolutionary armed struggle in the cities. With the democratic opening, intellectuals joined in shaping two blocs of political parties, first under Cardoso, who brought stability through the control of inflation and the introduction of a neoliberal economy through which foreign and national capital could operate jointly, and later under Lula and progressive intellectuals who began to shift attention to the nation and to the resolution of the economic and social problems of its people. Throughout the transition from authoritarian to democratic representative government, the PT coalesced progressive ideological currents while assimilating movements from below, including urban and rural labor, the new social movements, and intellectual remnants of the urban guerrilla movements that had once challenged the dictatorship.

Caio Navarro Toledo has emphasized (interview, São Paulo, July 12, 1995) that, apart from Weffort's *Por que democracia?* (1984) and Carlos Nelson Coutinho's *A democracia como valor universal* (1980), the left never attributed much importance to democracy, which was seen as a tactical instrument. The focus on democracy in the thought of Weffort and others led to "the illusion that radical social transformation would take place and that class relations would fade away within a capitalist society. The outcome of this thinking is a tendency toward liberalism, realization of neoliberal reforms, and opening of alliances with conservative sectors." As for what kind of democracy would most effectively serve Brazil, certainly representative forms of democracy will remain in place, but it may be that interesting attempts to broaden participation over the past century will also appear in the future. Brazil's problems are immense and its capitalism strong, yet there is hope that it will commit itself to improving the conditions of all its people.

Conclusion

At the outset, I examined various understandings of the intellectual, turning attention to the organic intellectual and his or her cultural production while engaging with society and its problems and influencing public life. I suggest that study of Brazilian intellectuals is relevant to comparative study elsewhere, whether the focus be on the New York intellectuals of the 1930s and 1940s or the New Left of the 1960s. The initial chapter provides a historical context for understanding Brazilian intellectual life. It chronologically reviews and analyzes major periods of intellectual activity during the twentieth century, from ruling class and regional oligarchical perspectives, to the search for a national vision under Vargas, to a radical vision in the two decades leading up to authoritarian rule in 1964, the armed resistance to the military, the opening to a pluralist alternative under political parties and social movements, and the gradual cultural decline thereafter. It also draws on various interpretations and syntheses of intellectual life to show different overviews of how intellectual activity has shaped major perspectives over the past century.

We learned that intellectuals experienced a lengthy obsession with building a national culture, transcending foreign influence, and overcoming a colonial legacy in search of a unique influential identity to overcome a feeling of inferiority. We also noted a tradition of public intellectuals as participants in politics and society, either to solve problems and better society or to seek power for personal benefit and enhancement.

We examined intellectual thought with ideas, theories, and strategies for change emanating from progressive ideologies and movements such as anarchism, anarcho-syndicalism, socialism, communism, and Trotskyism, which we introduce early in our story to provide a historical framework for looking at how ideas evolve and adapt to changing conditions, stimulated in large measure by the elusive search for development and nation building.

We probed how intellectual productivity is manifested through books and periodicals, including newspapers and academic journals, showing how the Brazilian intellectual traditionally has functioned both at a popular level through newspaper and television and in scholarly ways through academic journals. At the same time, political democracy represented by a plurality of political parties and usually single-issue social movements may be conditioned by demands of the university to publish in academic journals rather than engage with society at large, thereby diminishing the role of the activist intellectual in mobilizing power, encouraging class struggle, and promoting popular societal changes.

Our discussion focused on intellectuals such as Ellis, Azevedo, and Simonson who, over the course of a half century, influenced thought, shaped scientific education, and mobilized academic institutions in defense of the industrial, technocratic, and other bourgeois fractions. Thus, social class affiliation, preference, and loyalty become important to institution building in a changing environment. It is particularly interesting to observe how foreign scholars, primarily French but also North American, were mobilized in the building of social science in Brazil – furthermore, that some of them were able to build their own academic reputations based on their research and writings about Brazil. It is also significant that although scholarly methods tended to follow practices outside Brazil such as Florestan Fernandes's insistence on structural functionalism, there also was recognition that social class could serve as an important variable in analysis of class origins, class preference, and class struggle. Thus, attention to class emerges as an essential variable in the academic studies of many of his students.

My intent is to reveal useful understanding about changing political thought in Brazil over time. My discussion also draws out a central thesis that although Rio intellectuals emphasized the state and envisaged the national bourgeoisie as the means to overcome the legacy of colonial backwardness and dependency on foreign ideas and culture, the São Paulo intellectuals looked to civil society and the establishment of new academic institutions in the search for national identity and Brazilian development. In this process, they drew on emerging empirical models of investigation outside Brazil while formulating their own innovative approaches and theories to understand Brazilian reality and uniqueness.

This leads to the need to identify intellectual roots and initiatives, especially during the Vargas period of the New State, that link closely to the rapid and expansive intellectual activities that take place after 1945, along with the establishment of institutions of higher education. These result in important advances at the University of São Paulo (USP) and the short-lived experiment of the Higher Institute of Brazilian Studies (Instituto Superior de Estudos Brasileiros [ISEB]) as a government-sponsored entity, thereby setting up the backdrop for the detailed analysis in the second chapter on Rio de Janeiro as the political center of intellectual activities and in the third chapter on São Paulo, where intellectuals evolved within the flourishing economic center of the country.

Attention to Rio necessarily focuses on the origins and rise and fall of a group of intellectuals in search of a national ideology of development (developmental nationalism) and determined to break with a colonial legacy of backwardness and foreign dependence in pursuit of a path toward modernization and national unity. Unlike their Paulista rivals, whose careers generally depended on the university, they envisaged their mission as an appendage of the state, dependent on it for financial and material resources and anticipating that the nation would embrace their ideas. Their bold experiment began in 1953 and abruptly ended with the military coup of 1964. I examined this unique case through analysis of its three historical phases. We learned that intellectuals of differing political views and experiences both in the private and public sectors were able to collaborate and find common purpose in the face of infighting and even a major confrontation that received national attention. I also have presented their stories through their own words and personal reflections by drawing from lengthy recorded interviews I was able to secure shortly after the demise of the ISEB and from reading their published writings. The interviews are especially interesting and reveal their concerns, preferences, analysis of issues and controversies, and collegial observations of accomplishments and failings within the institute. They achieved recognition as intellectuals publically engaged in influencing society to embrace a new national consensus while simultaneously speaking and writing for publication in ISEB publications, respected journals, and the popular press. Many of them carried their message and ideas through institutional networks outside the ISEB. Thus, we briefly examined their influence through the military and the student movements, as well as in parliament itself, which had adopted the slogans and demands of a popular national movement mobilized around nationalism and resistance to foreign influence. Ultimately, so many of their ideas were also conveyed through small pamphlets succinctly and purposely organized around controversial issues such as nationalism and imperialism and circulated in tens of thousands of copies, itself an amazing feat given that, traditionally, most published writing in Brazil at that time was limited to press runs of 500–1,000 copies.

It was not my purpose to distinguish an ideological framework to differentiate among the three periods of ISEB history, but I am very clear that the early period is less ideological. The ISEB's founders described formulating through the state a national ideology (despite diverse perspectives they came together over this objective) during this period, whereas in the transitional period they confronted a major issue in Helio Jaguaribe's advocacy of foreign capital as a means to develop the petroleum industry, and it was around this position that they split. Furthermore, in the third period, under Álvaro Vieira Pinto and his acceptance of more progressive views, including Marxism, ISEB intellectuals assumed more activist roles inside and outside the ISEB. This is a period in which state support, certainly under Jânio Quadros, lessened, and although there was affinity between many ISEB intellectuals and the nationalism promoted by João Goulart, resources for the ISEB remained scarce.

One of my reviewers very interestingly identified two implicit lines of analysis and asked me to explain the shift in outlook among the early ISEB founders and the new generation of activist intellectuals who assumed a more political role later on. The first suggests that, during the 1950s, industrial expansion in Brazil did not evolve into the national capitalism anticipated by the ISEB's founders and indeed stimulated the presence of foreign capital, thus affirming that, in fact, the large industrial bourgeoisie could not emulate the role of a national bourgeoisie as in the historical experiences of Western Europe and the United States. This in turn led to a newer generation of ISEB intellectuals who looked to internal Brazilian market and to small and medium industrialists embedded in the national economy and often reliant on the state. Thus, the state rather than the industrial bourgeoisie would assume leadership of the developmental mission. The second line assumes that the ISEB, itself dependent on the state for financing, had to pay attention to the policies and objectives of various governments in power. Thus, in the first period, it was caught up in the industrial policies of Kubitscheck, but under Goulart it followed more closely a radical program. In the early period, Jaguaribe was deeply involved and desirous of managing a steel industry in Guanabara state, and although he was not opposed to state coordination of the national economy, his controversial views favorable to the participation of foreign capital in the petroleum industry may have been motivated by policies of the Kubitschek government that encouraged foreign investment in the emerging industrial development of the mid- and late 1950s. This pragmatic outlook, of course, brought dissension and ultimately his withdrawal from the ISEB, and it undermined the mission that originally brought the founders together. It is evidence of the confusion and controversy that developmental policy can provoke in the political arena. It is also clear by later events and the nationalist sentiment of the early 1960s that Brazil lacked a dynamic national bourgeoisie. Even the Brazilian Communist Party (Partido Comunista Brasileiro [PCB]) that had for many years attracted progressive intellectuals and favored a national bourgeoisie as a means for mobilizing the working class and the peasantry found itself somewhat marginalized and its own ranks divided over this question. Indeed, after 1964, one of its most distinguished members, Caio Prado Júnior (1966), offered a devastating critique of this proposition.

My attention to Paulista intellectuals identifies two currents, one that led progressive writers to publish views and analyses outside the academy in the prestigious journals *Anhembi* and *Revista Brasiliense*, and the other to build a strong research and graduate program in the university by mixing mainstream European and North American theory and methodology with serious field studies of relevant Brazilian issues and problems. Two distinguished scholars, Caio Prado Júnior and Florestan Fernandes, led those currents, with Prado drawing on a Marxist approach to question and challenge traditional assumptions about Brazilian backwardness and the path to capitalism and Fernandes relying on Weber and Durkheim for systematic investigation about race, labor, education, industrialization, and other themes relevant to understanding specific Brazilian problems. Their family backgrounds differed distinctly, with Prado born to wealth and Fernandes evolving from modest middle-class origins. Both of them were active in the political left, Prado within communist circles and Fernandes early on as a Trotskyist and later socialist. Both were elected deputies to the national congress. Yet their scholarly paths differed as Prado assumed a role as public and organic intellectual outside the university, stimulating debates through his journal and disseminating monographs through his own publishing house, whereas Fernandes chose to influence through teaching, administering, and ushering bright graduate students through the university and publishing the results of academic investigation – some of it (perhaps to gain broader public attention) even appearing in Prado's journal. Both influenced a new generation of serious scholars whose publications represented a break-through in Brazilian studies and influenced academics outside Brazil to rethink their own approaches. For instance, both influenced a paradig-matic shift in thinking about development that criticized mainstream theory emanating from Europe and North America and offered new approaches and frameworks for explaining backwardness and under-development, and both participated in and sought ways to construct democracy in Brazil.

Interestingly, Antônio Cândido bridges these two currents in several ways. Like Prado and Fernandes, he also was politically active in public life as a socialist and affiliated with the Workers' Party (Partido dos Trabalhadores [PT]), but he also taught both literature and sociology within the university. Unlike them, he was less interested in foreign theory and methodologies and drew inspiration and ideas from prominent Brazilian intellectuals, including historians Prado and Sêrgio Buarque de Holanda and economists Celso Furtado and Roberto Simonsen. His interdisciplinary search for a national consciousness and Brazilian identity involved a critical assessment of the influence of a colonial mentality on literature. He not only wrote on important historical and political questions, but his thinking also inspired others like Roberto Schwarz to critically examine literature in relation to contemporary issues.

Like their contemporaries elsewhere, the younger generation of Paulista intellectuals looked to alternative ways of analyzing Brazilian problems. It may not be surprising that they turned to Marx and his work and met frequently through the *Capital* Group. I have drawn from my interviews with two generations of these intellectuals to capture how they came together, what they focused on, and their differing perspectives. We see their thinking through a series of profiles that reflect their relation-ship to others in the group. Overall, I portray them as a relatively cohesive group of individuals able to dialogue with each other, discover both common and unique perspectives, and engage in creative approaches, constructive criticism, and innovative ways of interpreting and under-standing serious problems. Undoubtedly, this experience influenced them and shaped their own interpretation and analysis in the investigation that accompanied their graduate studies. Their informal seminar comple-mented their course work in refreshing and challenging ways, thereby laying the foundation for innovative study of Brazil.

The 1960s brought a plethora of scholarly publications by a younger generation of scholars influenced by their mentors and the changing cultural milieu of a society looking for new direction. Their quest was interrupted by the 1964 coup that abruptly ended the hopes and prospects intellectuals had envisaged in Rio through the ISEB as a state-sponsored center designed to overcome past disillusionment and rally the nation to mobilize resources internally, manage foreign influence, and mitigate imperialism. Their fundamental premise assumed that capitalist development would pave the way, build the forces and means of production to a point at which all Brazilians could share in material gain. Military rule and the imposition of a national security state accompanied by censorship and controls forced prominent intellectuals out of the universities, imprisoning many of them, leading to clandestinity and exile, and, for many of them, years of obscurity within Brazil. Cardoso and Furtado reached exile in Chile, along with Theotônio dos Santos, Ruy Mauro Marini, and others; there, they elaborated their theories of underdevelopment, dependency, and imperialism and refined their understanding of backwardness and prospects for national development. Eventually, most of the exiles returned to join the opposition and resistance to the authoritarian regime, some of them even participating in the urban revolutionary movements that appeared at the end of the decade.

Once back in Brazil, Cardoso and many of his colleagues chose a moderate response to the dictatorship, and a year following a brutal crackdown in 1968 of the opposition, they mobilized around the Brazilian Center for Analysis and Planning (Centro Brasileiro de Análise e Planejamento [CEBRAP]) as a means not only to continue their scholarly activity but also to provide serious assessments of an authoritarian Brazil in which the military leadership was controlling national planning while permitting foreign capital to invest in its development projects. Shielded by their research institute as a private entity, they also became politically involved in the opposition Brazilian Democratic Movement (Movimento Democrático Brasileiro [MDB]) party and eventually in a social democratic offshoot, the Brazilian Social Democratic Party (Partido da Social Democracia Brasileiro [PSDB]). Not to be overshadowed by this initiative, seven years later, Weffort and other dissident intellectuals established the Center for Studies of Contemporary Culture (Centro de Cultura Contemporânea [CEDEC]) as a rival research institution and PT think tank. Both institutions were supportive of investigation that might expose the regime's weaknesses. They differed, however, in their political preferences, with the CEBRAP devoting study to societal problems, appearing moderate and apolitical, but also involving progressive intellectuals, and with the CEDEC appearing progressive, interested in mass politics and oriented to the workers' party and its dissident left groups, to the reorganization of urban labor unions, and involved in studying social movements in general, including ties with the landless rural movement.

I have long been interested in development on a theoretical level but feel it also important to relate developmental theory to experience. Here, we draw on major theories influenced by Brazilian historical patterns as intellectuals have investigated and written about them. Their research led to questioning about the relevance to Brazil of the capitalist path to development that has occurred elsewhere. I also have grappled with the direction of democratic practice, myself generally disillusioned with formal representative systems of politics such as that practiced in the United States, where corporations and big capitalists exercise much influence, and I have been interested in experiments in participatory democracy, which, under capitalism, may be undermined by influential capital but which sometimes lead to broad involvement in solving societal problems. Brazilian scholars also are interested in these aspects of democracy, their nation having experienced periods of colonial rule under Portugal, oligarchy under the Old Republic, authoritarianism under Vargas, and firm rule under the military after 1964, but also openings after the Second World War and since the early 1980s.

I address two major themes in Chapters 4 and 5. The first relates to development through history, with attention paid to early economic systems, including feudalism and other precapitalist modes of production. This ultimately leads to capitalism as we are familiar with it in the modern world. Our attention necessarily runs to the European and North American experiences, how and when capitalism emerged, and, given its contradictions, the prospects for a better, more egalitarian society. Thus, I turn to various perspectives about when capitalism appeared in Brazil because intellectuals have looked deeply into this question, and it was very important in challenging traditional interpretations that attributed backwardness to feudalism and semifeudalism. A key moment may have been the 1964 coup and the abrupt cessation of intense political discourse and popular demand for change. Brazilian academics sought freedom and refuge in exile, and this undoubtedly contributed to new thinking. In their search for a developmental path, intellectuals debated theories about dependency and underdevelopment and related their new ideas to revision of historical interpretations about the past while they resisted dictatorship. The rhetoric shifted from denunciations of foreign capital and imperialism to serious analysis on why capitalism had blocked development and what to do with it. Thus, we were presented with a remarkable set of alternative theories about the prospects for development, given Brazil's backwardness and underdevelopment.

The second theme evolves out of the democratic openings occurring during the last half of the twentieth century, initially evolving from the ouster of Vargas in 1945, continuing to the 1964 coup, and later involving the transition from military authoritarianism to representative democracy in the early 1980s. Both moments spurred studies of labor, both involved activism in politics, and both were accompanied by cultural shifts. São Paulo intellectuals were especially involved in these advances. Their collective response to the dominant authoritarian ideology assumed many forms: early on through movements of armed struggle; later, in the resurgent labor unions, the rise of the new social movements, and emerging political parties. Eventually, under the state and a new 1988 constitution, the formal representative system takes hold, and the political parties assimilate popular elements that agitate for a new democracy. Intellectuals not only refocused historical writing around struggles against repression, they also searched for ways to transform their nation into a participatory society and experimented with new forms of popular democratic involvement through a New Left agenda around electoral campaigns that allowed the PT under Lula to emerge as a leading political force.

Many of the research institutes that accompanied the political opening carry on today. Still attracted to public life, intellectuals joined the Cardoso, Lula, and Rousseff governments, recruited out of the universities where they have served as professors and scholars. Transformed from opponents and resisters to authoritarian rule, they turned from pondering questions about Brazil's future to finding ways that would improve the quality of life for all Brazilians while establishing the nation's place on the global scene.

At the outset of this study, I identified as organic intellectuals those scholars, teachers, writers, and others who are involved in culture and engaged with society. I acknowledged that I did not think of intellectuals as comprising a class, but I was interested in their relations to other classes. It is also clear after 1930 and particularly after 1964 that their cultural production and their political participation influenced Brazil to awaken from its obsession with an inferior colonial past and to bring Brazilians together in common purpose to transcend past difficulties and unite the country in common purpose. Thus, my principal concern has been a critical assessment of the production of ideas and knowledge by intellectuals and their impact on economic and political life. To the question of whether they empathize with the bourgeoisie or proletariat, there are those who, like Prado Júnior, a wealthy member of the bourgeoisie, or Florestan Fernandes, an academic of modest origins, were committed to scholarly studies that transcended traditional perspectives and were also involved in building a popular movement around national autonomy, socialism, and a better Brazil. This study shows that intellectual opposition to authoritarian rule remained strong, even under repressive conditions, while their thinking about development and democracy matured and eventually contributed to new interpretations and theory about backwardness and underdevelopment in the developing world. In this process, some intellectuals attempted to put their ideas and perspectives into practice, resorting even to armed revolutionary alternatives. I also asked if their production appeared in abstract or concrete forms, and we learned that it tended to be less abstract in times of crisis or need for action, but it also was more critical and creative when intellectuals operated outside Brazil, as occurred after 1964, when many of them sought exile. We noted that the content of their ideas and knowledge was not necessarily shaped by bourgeois ideals associated with the emerging capitalist society, as was probably the situation for Jaguaribe and some of the founders of the ISEB who favored a national capitalism or Cardoso in his advocacy of an associated dependent development. We also looked at whether intellectuals were inspired by positivist and liberal views or by Marxist perspectives and found that whereas most of the ISEB founders in Rio leaned toward liberal perspectives, a younger generation adopted socialism alongside their advocacy of a developmental nationalism, whereas the Paulista intellectuals, influenced by their readings into Marx, assumed more radical views. Their beliefs did not diminish in the face of the dictatorship but, in the political opening, as many of them joined the ensuing governments, they became involved in policy questions and reforms rather than radical solutions. Their scholarly production declined, accompanied by a general retreat from Marxism, a trend visible elsewhere in Europe and the United States. As the ensuing governments confronted problems (inflation and ensuring stability under Cardoso; and poverty, stimulating the economy, and raising the standard of living under Lula and Rousseff), intellectuals may have retained their ideals and aspirations, but now it was time for them to concentrate on their professional careers within the university or state. Their withdrawal from being active and engaged scholars may have been due not only to the retreat from Marxism and decline of the left within Brazil, but also to reforms within the universities that raised standards for advancement, necessitating increased intellectual production while stimulating competition for jobs and recognition.

Brazil faces many problems, many of them associated with global economic and political instability. The country continues on a capitalist path that is drawing more and more of its marginal population into a mainstream that shows modest progress in transcending extreme poverty, unemployment, and hunger, and in resolving the basic needs its people must attain. Whither the intellectuals in this process? It is likely that their contribution will be more an assessment of accomplishments and failures rather than advocacy of new perspectives that may lead to a radical transformation.

Interviews with Brazilian Intellectuals

I list my interviews here and identify the format in which they are available. Most are tape recorded and digitized. Many of them have been transcribed and some of them translated to English; I prepared summaries of principal interviews so as to digest content and be able to integrate them into my text. All this material is deposited into my archive in Special Collections and Archives at the University of California, Riverside (see http://library .ucr.edu/content/collections/spcol/universityarchives/uo12.pdf).

Key: *d*, digitized; *s*, summarized; *t*, transcribed; *x*, tape recorded

Almeida, Angela Mendes de. Interview. *s* Rio de Janeiro. July 5, 1995
Almeida, Cândido Mendes de. *stx* Rio de Janeiro, May 17, 1967
Almeida, Rômulo. *stx* Rio de Janeiro, October 8, 1967
Alves, Márcio Morreira. *stx* Rio de Janeiro, July 20, 1983
Alves, Maria Helena. *x* Riverside, California, March 7, 1983 (2 tapes); Rio de Janeiro, July 20, 1982
Andrade, Marília de. *s* São Paulo, July 12, 1995
Antunes, Ricardo. *tx* São Paulo, September 28, 1995
Arraes, Miguel. *s* Recife, July 30, 1983
Arruda, Marcos. *tx* Rio de Janeiro, July 20, 1983 ?; *stx* de Janeiro, August 2, 1983
Bambira, Vânia. *tx* Rio de Janeiro, July 28, 1994
Barbosa, Júlio. *sx* Belo Horizonte, June 12, 1967
Boito, Armando. *tx* São Paulo, July 11, 1995
Bresser-Perreira, Luiz Carlos. *sx* Fortaleza, May 29, 1984; *sx* Fortaleza, August 24, 1984; and *x* Washington DC, September 29, 1995; *s* Montreal, June 6, 2007; *sx* Rio de Janeiro, June 11, 2009

Campos, Demar. *stx* Rio de Janeiro, June 8, 1967

Cardoso, Fernando Henrique. *x* São Paulo, July 23,?; *tx* São Paulo, September 26, 1983

Castro, Paulo de. *s* Rio de Janeiro, July 1964

Chaves Neto, Elias. *stx* São Paulo October, 30, 1969

Chiauí, Marilena. *tx* São Paulo; *x* May 24, 1985; *x* August 21, 1992

Corbisier, Roland. *stx* Rio de Janeiro, May 29, 1967

Coutinho, Carlos Nelson. *tx* Rio de Janeiro, July 27, 1994

Debrun, Michel. *stx* Rio de Janeiro, 1967; Campinas, July 1984

Dinis, Eli. *tx* Botafogo, July 6, 199

Domingos, Manuel. *tx* Fortaleza, June 12, 1997

Dowbar, Ladislaw. *stx* São Paulo, September l, 1983; *x* July 12, 1994

Dreifuss, René. *s* Rio de Janeiro, July 6, 1995 (Notes)

Fernandes, Florestan. *stx* São Paulo, September 26, 1983

Furtado, Celso. *s* Santiago, Chile, July 1964

Garcia, Marco Aurélio. *stx* Campinas, September 12, 1983; *tx* São Paulo, July 12, 1995

Giannotti. José Artur. *tx* São Paulo, October 26, 1984

Gorender, Jacobo. *stx* São Paulo, August 28, 1982

Ianni, Octávio. *s* São Paulo, 1983 or 1984?

Jaguaribe, Helio. *x* Riverside, California, *stx* October 17, 1966; *stx* Rio de Janeiro, October 27, 1967; *sx* Rio de Janeiro, July 23, 1994

Konder, Leondro. *stx* Rio de Janeiro, July 29, 1991

Lôwy, Michael. *s* Paris, October 18, 1985

Manteiga, Guido. *dstx* Campinas, September 12, 1984

Marini, Ruy Mauro. *tx* Rio de Janeiro, July 30, 1991

Martins, Carlos Eduardo. *x* Rio de Janeiro, June 8, 2009

Martins, Carlos Estevam. *stx* São Paulo. September 19, 1983

Martins Filho, João Roberto. *tx* São Paulo, July 11, 1995

Moiss, José Álvaro. *tx* São Paulo, May 31, 1994; *x* São Paulo, May 31, 1994

Oliverra, Francisco de. *tx* Aguas de São Pedro, October 24, 1984; *st* São Paulo, October 26, 1984

Paim, Gilberto. *stx* Rio de Janeiro, May 22, 25, 1967

Paoli, Maria Celia. *tx* São Paulo, August 21, 1992

Pelegrini, Tanya. *tx* São Paulo, July 11, 1995

Pereira, Osny Duartes. *stx* Rio de Janeiro, May 31, 1967

Prado Júnior, Caio. *stx* São Paulo August 25, 1982

Quartim, João. *s* Campinas, October 25, 1984 (see Sader)

Ramos, Alberto Guerreiro. *stx* Riverside, California, November 18, 1966

Rangel, Inácio. *stx* Rio de Janeiro, May 25, 1967
Ridente, Marcelo. *tx* Washington DC, September 29, 1995
Rodrigues, Leôncio Martins. *x* São Paulo, October 25, 1984; *tx* São Paulo, July 11, 1992
Sader, Emir. *x* Rio de Janeiro, July 29, 1991; *tx* Rio de Janeiro, July 7, 1995; *x* Rio de Janeiro, June 9, 2004
Sader, Emir, and João Quartim. *s* October 25, 1984
Saes, Dêcio. *tx* Campinas, July 10, 1995
Saes, Dêcio, and José Arico. *s* Campinas, August 21, 1983
Santos, Theotônio dos. *tx* Rio de Janeiro, July 7, 1995; *sx* Rio de Janeiro, June 12, 2009
Santos, Wanderlay Guillherme dos. *stx* Rio de Janeiro, May 5, 9, 19, 1967
Schwarz, Roberto. *tx* São Paulo, September 20, 1983
Singer, Paul. *tx* São Paulo, September 26, 1983; *x* São Paulo. July 10, 1984; *tx* São Paulo, June 10, 1005
Sodré, Nelson Werneck. *sx* Rio de Janeiro, May 29, 1967
Souza, Amaury de. *tx* Rio de Janeiro, July 6, 1995
Toleto, Caio Navarro. *tx* São Paulo, July 12, 1995
Weffort, Francisco. *tx* São Paulo, September 26, 1983

GROUP TAPES AND OTHER RELEVANT EVENTS

Birambara, Flávio et al. *s* São Paulo, July 1984
Carvalho, Iván de Fortaleza. *x* June 11, 1997 (presentation)
Colóquio Sobre Marx. *x* Campinas. August 21, 1983
Debate. Casa de Cadernos Brasileiros. "Rumos de Esquerda." *x* Rio de Janeiro, May 13, 1967; participants include Jean Marie Domenech, Cândido Mendes de Almeida, Vicente Barreto, Leondor Kondor, Wanderley Guilherme, Nelson Melo e Souza, Márcio Moreira Alves Lauro Camargo, Cleanto Paiva Leite
Debate. PT vs. PMDB (PCB). *x* São Paulo. August 27, 1982; participants include Fernando do Veloso, Anísio Batista de Oliveira (PT), José Zico Prado de Andrade (PT), and Luís Tenório de Lima (PMDB/ PCB)
Dutra, Eliana Regina de Freitas, Eder Sader, Luís Werneck Viana. "Os intelectuais: o novo atos no sindalismo de transição." Ampocs. *x* October 25, 1984
Freire, Paulo 1985. "Caminhos de Paulo Freire," *Ensaio* No. 14 (May), 1–27. Interview with J. Chasin, Rui Gomes Dantas, and Vicente Madeira
Saes, Dêcio. "Marx e teorias do estado" José Aricó. "Pensamiento marxista en la América Latina." Campinas, August 21, 1983

Semanários Sobre Capital (Paul Singer, Fernando Novais, José Arthur Giannotti, Roberto Schwarz). *stx* August 23, 1983; three tapes

Silva, Luís Inácio da. Campaign speeches in Caraguatuba and Ubatuba, *x* August 28, 1982

Visit to a Comunidade de Base, with Wanda in Vila Remo in Santo Amaro, *s* August 28, 1982

Vilela, Theotônio. *x* São Paulo, July 21, 1983 (speech to Assembleia Legislativa)

References

This list identifies all references cited in the text and is drawn from roughly 5,000 books and pamphlets, as well as more than 2,000 journal and newspapers articles (index cards and most of these publications are in my archive in Special Collections and Archives in the Tomás Rivera Library of the University of California, Riverside). I have identified significant but not all publications of the principal intellectuals discussed in my study, relating them to my extensive interviews about their ideas and thinking. My study intends to be comprehensive and to transcend other studies of Brazilian intellectuals, including the overviews by French sociologist Daniel Pécaut (1990), Brazilian economist Guido Mantega (1984), and the recent anthology edited by Abu-El-Haj and Chilcote (2011). Wilson Martins (1976) lays out extensive biographical details in his multivolume history of the Brazilian intelligentsia. The Higher Institute of Brazilian Studies (Instituto Superior de Estudos Brasileiros [ISEB]) experiment has received the most attention, led by Caio Navarro de Toledo (1978, 2005) and including studies by Abreu (1975) and Bariani (2005), critiques by Ianni (1985), Moreira (1959), Motta (2000), Pereira (1998a), a retrospective by a participant (Sodré, 1978), four doctoral dissertations (Debert, 1986; Gaylord, 1991; Pereira, 2003; Vale 2001), and four masters theses (Abranches, 1997; Cortez, 1993; Marinho, 1986; Pereira, 1998b; Pires 1987).

Abranches, Aparecida Maria. 1997. "Os percalços da crítica; o ISEB e a conjuntura pre-64." MA Thesis. Rio de Janeiro. Instituto Universitário de Pesquisas do Rio de Janeiro (IUPERJ).
_____ 1999. "Ciências sociais e vocação política: o caso do ISEB," in Marcos Chor Maio and Gláucio Villas Bôas (eds.), *Ideias de modernidade e sociologia no Brasil: ensaios sobre Luiz Aguiar Costa Pinto*. Porto Alegre: Editora Universidade/UFRGS. Pp. 329–343.
Abrantes, Paulo Eduardo. 1992. *Sentimento da dialética na experiência intelectual brasileira. Dialética e dualidade segundo Antônio Cândido e Roberto Schwarz*. São Paulo: Editora Paz e Terra. Pp. 107.
Abreu, Alzira Alves de. 1975. "Nacionalisme et action politique au Brésil: une étude sur l'ISEB." PhD Dissertation. Paris: Université René Descartes Sorbonne.

Abreu, Alzira Alves de et al. 2001. "Verbete: Instituto Superior de Estudos Brasileiros (ISEB)," in *Dicionário histórico-bibliográfico brasileira (1930–1983)*. Rio de Janeiro: Editora FGV. Pp. 2801–2803.

Abu-El-Haj, Jawdat. 2005. "Da era Vargas à FHC: transições políticas e reformas administrativas," *Revista de Ciências Sociais*, 36(1–2): 33–51.

Abu-El-Haj. Jawdat, and Ronald H. Chilcote. 2011. "Intellectuals, Social Theory, and Political Practice in Brazil," *Latin American Perspectives*, 38(3/May): 5–39.

Almeida, Cândido Antônio Mendes de. 1957. "Nacionalismo e desenvolvimento," *Revista do Clube Militar*, 148: 19–24.

1958. "O intellectual frente no processo histórico." Lecture April 18, 1958. Curso Regular de História, Instituto Superior de Estudos Brasileiros, Ministério da Educação e Cultura. Pp. 8 (mimeographed).

1960. *Perspectiva atual da América Latina*. Rio de Janeiro: Instituto Superior de Estudos Brasileiros, Ministério da Educação e Cultura. Pp. 50.

1962. "Desenvolvimento e problemática do poder." *Síntese Política, Ecônomica e Social (Rio de Janeiro)*, 4(14, April/June): 60–91.

1963. *Nacionalismo e desenvolvimento*. Rio de Janeiro: Instituto Brasileiro de Estudos Afro-Asiáticos. Pp. 398.

1968. "Nationalism and Development: The Emergence of the Brazilian Intelligentzia and Its Responsibilities towards Portuguese Africa." Paper presented to the University of California Project, "Brazil-Portuguese Africa," Riverside and Los Angeles, 77 (mimeographed).

1980. "The Post-1964 Brazilian Regime: Outward Redemocratization and Inner Instituionalization," *Government and Opposition*, Winter: 48–74.

2005. "ISEB: fundação e ruptura," in Caio Navarro de Toledo (ed.), *Intelectuais e política no Brasil: a experiência do ISEB*. Rio de Janeiro: Editora Revan. Pp. 13–30.

Almeida, Lúcio Flávio de. 1995. *Ideologia nacional e nacionalismo*. São Paulo: Eduç.

Almeida, Martins de. 1932. *Brasil errado: ensaio político sobre os erros do Brasil como paiz*. Rio de Janeiro: Schmidt-Editor, Civilização Brasileira. Pp. 202.

Almeida, Rômulo de. 1939. "Educação para a democracia brasileira," *Cadernos da Nossa Hora*, 1(May): 32–56.

1943. "A mobilização econômica e o planejamento da expansão do pais," *Cultura Política*, 3(27/May): 55–65.

Alvarez, Sonia. 1990. *Engendering Democracy in Brazil: Women's Movements in Transition Politics*. Princeton, NJ: Princeton University Press. Pp. 304.

Alvarez, Sonia, Evelina Dagnino, and Arturo Escobar (eds.). 2000. *Cultura de política nos movimentos sociais latino americanos*. Belo Horizonte: Editora UFMG.

Alves, Márcio Moreira. 1964. *A velha classe*. Introduction by Antônio Callado. Rio de Janeiro: Companhia de Artes Gráficas. Pp. 148.

1966. *Torturas e torurados*. Preface by Alceu Amoroso Lima. Rio de Janeiro: Idade Nova. Pp. 235.

1973. *A Grain of Mustard Seed: The Awakening of the Brazilian Revolution*. Garden City, NY: Doubleday Anchor Press. Pp. 194.

1975. *Os soldados socialistas de Portugal*. Lisbon: Iniciativas Editoriais. Pp. 217.

1978. *A igreja e a política no Brasil*. Lisbon: Livraria Sá da Costa. Pp. 313.

Alves, Maria Helena. 1985. *State and Opposition in Military Brazil*. Austin: University of Texas Press.

Alves, Mário. 1958. "3 de outubro e o movmento nacionalista," *Estudos Sociais*, 3–4(September–December): 259–265.

1962. "A burguesia nacional e a crise brasileira," *Estudos Sociais*, 15 (December): 231–247.

Alves, Mário, and Paul Singer. 1963. *Análise do Plano Trienal*. São Paulo: Editora Universitária da União Nacional dos Estudantes. Pp. 90.

Alves, Mário, and Philip Evanson. 2011. *Living in the Crossfire: Favela Residents, Drug Dealers, and Police Violence in Rio de Janeiro*. Philadelphia: Temple University Press.

Anderson, Terry H. 1995. *The Movement and the Sixties*. New York: Oxford University Press. Pp. 500.

Andrade, Almir de. 1941. "A evolução política e social do Brasil," *Cultura Política*, 1(1/March): 5–8.

Andrade, Manuel Correia de. 1964. *A terra e o homen no Nordeste*. São Paulo: Editora Brasiliense. Translated and published as *The Land and People of Northeast Brazil*. Albuquerque: University of New Mexico Press, 1980. Pp. 265.

1968. *Paisagens e problemas do Brasil*. São Paulo: Editora Brasiliense. Pp. 273.

1970. *Espaço, polarização e desenvolvimento (a teoria dos pólos de desenvolvimento*. São Paulo: Editora Brasiliense.

Andrade, Régis de Castro. 1979. "Perspectivas no estudo do populismo brasileiro," *Encontros Com a Civilização Brasileiro*, 7(January): 41–86.

Antunes, Ricardo. 1988a. *Classe operária, sindicatos e partido no Brasil: um estudo sobre a consciência de classe, da revolução de 30 até a Aliança Nacional Libertadora*, 2nd ed. São Paulo: Cortez e Editora Ensaio. Pp. 187.

1988b. *A rebeldiado trabalho: o confront operário no ABC Paulista: as greves de 1978/80*. Campinas: Editora Ensaio.

1991. *O novo sindicalismo*. São Paulo: Editora Brasil Urgente. Pp. 150.

Antunes, Ricardo ed. 1992. *Hermínio Sacchetta: O caldeirão das brusas e outros escritos políticos*. Campinas: Editora da Universidade Estadual de Campinas and Pontes Editores. Pp. 161.

Araújo, Braz José. 1977. "Caio Prado Júnior e a questão agrária no Brasil," *Temas de Ciências Humanas*, 1: 17–89.

Arrabal, José, and Mariângela Alves de Lima. 1983. *Teatro: o seu demónio é beato*. São Paulo: O Nacional e o Popular na Cultura Brasileira, Editora Brasiliense. Pp. 220.

Arraes, Miguel. 1971. *Brasil: pueblo y poder*. Preface by Ruy Mauro Marini. Mexico City: Colección Ancho Munco (32), Ediciones Era. Pp. 180.

1974. *A nova face da ditadura brasileira*. Lisbon: Seara Nova. Pp. 142.

1982. "Crise da democracia e a abertura no Brasil," *Encontros com a Civilização Brasileira*, 29(November): 163–174.

Arruda, Maria Arminda do Nascimento. 1989. *Modernidade possível: Cientistas sociais em Minas Gerais*. São Paulo: Instituto de Estudos Econômicos e Políticos de São Paulo.

1990. *Mitologia de mineiridade*. São Paulo: Editora Brasiliense.

2001. *Metrópole e cultura: São Paulo no meio século XX*. São Paulo: EDUSC.

2011. "Modern Society and Culture in Brazil: The Sociology of Florestan Fernandes," *Latin American Perspectives*, 178, 38(3/May): 99–111.

Arruda, Marcos. 2003. *Humanizar o infra-humano: A formação de ser humano integral: Homo evolutivo, práxis e economia solidária*. Rio de Janeiro: PACS and Editora Vozes.

Avritzer, Leonardo and Boaventura de Sousa Santos. 2002. "Para ampliar o cânone democrático," in Boaventura de Sousa Santos (ed.), *Democratizando e democracia*. Rio de Janeiro: Editora Civilização Brasileira. Also in Boaventura de Sousa Santos and Leonardo Avritzer, "Introduction: Opening up the Canon of Democracy" in Boaventura de Sousa Santos (ed.), 2005, *Democratizing Democracy: Beyond the Liberal Democratic Canon*. London: Verso. Pp. xxxiv–lxxiv.

Azevedo, Fernando de. 1937[1926]. *A educação pública em São Paulo: O inquérito para "O Estado de São Paulo,"* 2nd ed. São Paulo: Companhia Editora Nacional.

1939. *Princípios de sociologia: Pequena introdução ao estudo de sociologia*, 3rd ed. São Paulo: Companhia Editora Nacional.

1943/1944[1940]. *A cultura brasileira; introdução ao estudo da cultura no Brasil*, 1st ed., São Paulo: IBGE; 2nd ed., São Paulo: Editora Nacional, 1944; 3rd ed., Brasília: Editora Universidade de Brasília, 1963. Pp. 803.

1953. *A educação e seus problemas*. São Paulo: Companhia Editora Nacional Melhoramentos.

Baiocchi, Gianpaolo. 2005. *Militants and Citizens. The Politics of Participatory Democracy*. Stanford, CA: Stanford University Press. Pp. 224.

Bambirra, Vânia. 1973. *El capitalismo dependiente latinoamericano*. Santiago, Chile: Centro de Estudios Socio-economómics de Chile, Editorial Prensa Latinoamericana. 3rd ed., Mexico City: Siglo Veintiuno, 1983. Pp. 180.

1975. *Teoria de la dependencia: una anticrítica*. Mexico City: Ediciones Era. Pp. 114.

1993. *A teoria marxista da transição e a prática socialista*. Brasília: Editora da Universidade de Brasília.

Baran, Paul. 1960[1957]. *The Political Economy of Growth*. New York: Prometheus. Originally published by Monthly Review Press.

1988. "The Commitment of the Intellectual," *Monthly Review*, 39(March): 51–62.

Barbé, Dominique. 1982. *Grace and Power: Base Communities and Nonviolence in Brazil*. Maryknoll, NY: Orbis Books. Pp. 150.

Barcellos, Jalusa. 1994. *CPC da UNE; uma história de paixão e consciência*. Botafogo: Editora Nova Fronteira. Pp. 459.

Bariani, Edison. 2005. "ISEB: fábrica de controvérsias," *Espaço Acadêmico*, 45(February). Available at http://www.espacoacademico.com.br/045/45cbar iani.htm.

Barreira, Irlys Alencar F. 2011. "Social Movements, Culture, and Politics in the Work of Brazilian Sociologists," *Latin American Perspectives*, 38(3/May): 150–168.

Bastide, Roger. 1964. *Brasil Terra de contrastes*, 2nd ed. São Paulo: Difusão Européia do Livro. Pp. 261.

Bastide, Roger, and Florestan Fernandes. 1955. *Brancos e negros em São Paulo*. São Paulo: Companhia Editora Nacional. Pp. 371.

Bastos, Elide Rugai. 2006. *Conversas com sociólogos brasileiros*. São Paulo: Editora 34.

Bastos Filho. 1960. "Review of Guerreiro Ramos' '*O problema nacional do Brasil*.'" *Revista Brasiliense*, 32(November–December): 165–174.

Beiguelman, Paula. 1967. *Formação política do Brasil*. São Paulo: Livraria Pioneira Editora, 2 vols.

Benevides, Maria Victória de Messquita. 1991. *A cidandania ativa: referendo, plebiscito e iniciativa popular*. São Paulo: Editor Atica. Pp. 208.

Berlinck, Cyro. 1964. "Liderança e liberdade," *Sociologia*, 26(3): 281–305.

Berman, Paul. 1996. *A Tale of Two Utopias: The Political Journey of the Generation of 1968*. New York: W.W. Norton. Pp. 351.

Betto, Frei. 1981. *O que é comunidade ecclesial de base*. São Paulo: Coleção Primeiros Passos (19), Editora Brasiliense. Pp. 116.

1982. *Batismo de sangue: os dominicanos e a morte de Carlos Marighella*, 2nd ed. Rio de Janeiro: Editora Civilização Brasileira. Pp. 283.

Biderman, Ciro, Luís Felipe Coza, and José Márcio Rego. 1996. *Conversas com economistas brasileiros*. Vol. 1. São Paulo: Editora. Pp. 34.

Bielschowsky, Ricardo. 1988. *Pensamento econômico brasileiro: o ciclo ideológico do desenvolvimentismo*. Rio de Janeiro: IPWA/INPES.

Bittencourt, Paulo Taques, Michel Rabinovitch and José Goldenberg. 1961. "Reunião da 'Revista Brasiliense,'" *Revista Brasiliense*, 33(January–February): 101–113.

Bloom. Allan. 1987. *The Closing of the American Mind*. New York: Simon and Schuster. Pp. 392.

Bloom, Alexander. 1986. *Prodigal Sons: The New York Intellectuals and Their World*. New York: Oxford University Press. Pp. 461.

Boggs, Carl. 1993. *Intellectuals and the Crisis of Modernity*. Albany: State University of New York Press. Pp. 222.

Boito, Armando. 1991. *O sindicalismo de estado no Brasil: uma análise crítica da estrutural sindical*. Campinas: Editora da UNICAMP; São Paulo: HUCITEC. Pp. 312.

Bonilla, Frank. 1963. "A National Ideology of Development: Brazil," in Kalman H. Silvert (ed.), *Expectant Peoples: Nationalism and Development*. American Universities Field Staff. New York: Random House. Pp. 232–264.

Boshi, Renato Raul. 1979. *Elites industriais de democracia: hegemonia burguesa e mudança política no Brasil*. Rio de Janeiro: Edições Graal. Pp. 249.

Bradford, Sue and Bernardo Kucinski. 1995. *Brazil: Carnival of the Oppressed: Lula and the Brazilian Workers' Party*. London: Latin American Bureau. Pp. 120.

Bresser-Pereira, Luiz Carlos. 1968. *Desenvolvimento e crise no Brasil*. Rio de Janeiro: Zahar Editores.

1973. "O novo modelo brasileiro de desenvolvimento," *Dados*, 11: 122–145.

1977. *Estado e subdesenvolvimento industrializado*. São Paulo: Editora Brasiliense. Pp. 358.

1981. *A sociedade estatal e a tecnoburocracia*. São Paulo: Brasiliense.
1982a. *Economia brasileira: uma introdução crítica*. São Paulo: Editora Brasliense. Pp. 169.
1982b. "Seis interpretações sobre o Brasil," *Revista de Ciências Sociais*, 25(3): 269–306.
1984a. *Development and Crisis in Brazil, 1930–1983*. Boulder, CO: Westview Press.
1984b. "Six Interpretations of the Brazilian Social Formation," *Latin American Perspectives*, 11(1/Winter): 73–102.
1985. *Pactos politicos do populismo a redemocratizção*. São Paulo: Editora Brasiliense. Pp. 222.
1986. *Lucro, acumulação e crise: A detendência declinante da taxa de lucro reexaminada*. São Paulo: Editora Brasiliense. Pp. 278.
1991. *Os tempos heróicos de Collor e Zélia: Aventuras da modernidade de desventuras da optodoxial*. São Paulo: Livraria Nobel. Pp. 98.
1993. "Economic Reforms and Cycles of State Inervention," *World Development*, 23(8): 1337–1353.
1997. "Managerial Public Administration: Strategy and Structure for a New State," *Journal of Post-Keynesian Economics*, 20, 1(Fall): 7–23.
2004a. "O conceito de desenvolvimento do ISEB rediscutido," *Dados (Rio de Janeiro)*, 47(1): 49–84.
2004b. *Democracy and Public Management Reform: Building the Republican State*. New York: Oxford University Press. Pp. 317.
2005. "Do ISEB e do CEPAL a teoria da dependência," in Caio Navarro de Toledo (ed.), *Intelectuais e política no Brasil: a experiência do ISEB*. Rio de Janeiro: Editora Revan. Pp. 201–232.
2007. *Macroeconomia da estagnação: crítica da ortodoxia convencional no Brasil pós-1994*. São Paulo: Editora. Pp. 34.
2011. "From the National-Bourgeoisie to the Dependency Interpretation of Latin America," *Latin American Perspectives*, 38(3/May): 49–58.
Brick, Howard. 1986. *Daniel Bell and the Decline of Intellectual Radicalism: Social Theory and Political Reconciliation in the 1940s*. Madison: University of Wisconsin Press.
Bunker, Stephen G. 1984. "Modes of Extraction, Unequal Exchange, and the Progressive Underdevelopment of an Extreme Periphery: The Brazilian Amazon 1600–1980," *American Journal of Sociology*, 80(5): 1017–1064.
Burgess, Mike and Daniel Wolf. 1979. "The Concept of Power in the Brasilian Higher War College." Toronto: LARU Working Paper (27). Pp. 21.
Calvert, Gregory Nevala. 1991. *Democracy from the Heart: Spiritual Values, Decentralism, and Democratic Idealism in the Movement of the 1960s*. Eugene, OR: Communitas Press. Pp. 301.
Calvino Filho. 1957. "O Sr. Caio Pardo Júnior e a falsa tese dos 'capitalistas sóbrios,'" *Novos Tempos*, 21(October–November): 11–16.
Campos, Roberto de Oliveira. 1964. *Economia, planejamento e nacionalismo*. Rio de Janeiro: APEC Editora. Pp. 324.
Cândido, Antônio. See Antônio Cândido de Mello Souza.

Cannabrava Filho, Paulo. 1970. *Militarismo e imperialismo en Brasil.* Buenos Aires: Editorial Tempo Contemporaneo. Pp. 221.

Cano, Wilson. 1977. *Raizes da concentração industrial em São Paulo.* Rio de Janeiro: Editorial DIFEL.

Capital Retrospective. 1983. "Summary of Panel Discussion 'Seminários sobre O Capital,'" Campinas, August 2. Pp. 5 (typescript).

Cardoso, Eliana. A. 1981. "Celso Furtado Revisited: The Postwar Years," *Economic Development and Cultural Change,* 30(1/October): 117–128.

Cardoso, Fernando Henrique. 1958. "Educação e desenvolvimento econômico," *Revista Brasiliense,* 17(May–June): 70–81.

1962a. *Capitalismo e escravidão no Brasil meridional: o negro na sociedade do Rio Grande do Sul.* São Paulo: Difusão Européia de Livre. Pp. 339.

1962b. "Proletariado no Brasil: situação e comportamento social," *Revista Brasiliense,* 41(May–June): 98–122.

1964. *Empresário industrial e desenvolvimento econômico.* São Paulo: Difusão Européia do Livro. Pp. 196.

1968. *Cuestiones de sociologia del desarrollo da América Latina.* Santiago: Editorial Universitaria. Pp. 180.

1970. *Dependência e desenvolvimento na América Latina.* Rio de Janeiro: Zahar.

1971. *Política e desenvolvimento em sociedades dependentes: ideologias do empresariado industrial argentino e brasileiro.* Rio de Janeiro: Zahar.

1972. "Dependency and Development in Latin America," *New Left Review,* 74(July–October): 83–95.

1972–1973. "Industrialization, Dependency and Power in Latin America," *Berkeley Journal of Sociology,* 17: 79–95.

1973. "Dependency Revisited," Lecture, East Campus Lecture Hall, University of Texas at Austin, April 19, 1973. Unidentifiable publication. Pp. 11–38.

1977. "The Consumption of Dependency Theory in the United States," *Latin American Research Review,* 12(3): 7–24.

1979. *O modelo politico brasileiro e outros ensaios.* São Paulo: DIFEL Editorial. Pp. 213.

1980. *As idéias e seu lugar: ensaios sobre as teorias do desenvolvimento.* Petrópolis: Editora Vozes. Pp. 163.

1980–1981. "Regime político e mudança social (algumas reflexões a propósito do caso brasileiro," *Revista de Cultura e Política,* 3(November–January): 7–25. With commentary by Carlos Estevam Martins, José Álvaro Moisés, and others. Pp. 27–46.

2006. *The Accidental President. A Memoir.* New York: Public Affairs. Pp. 291.

Cardoso, Fernando Henrique, and Enzo Faletto. 1969. *Dependencia y desarrollo en América Latina: ensayo de interprétación sociológica.* Mexico City: Siglo Veintiuno.

1970. *Dependência e desenvolvimento na América Latina: ensaio de interpretação sociológica.* Rio de Janeiro: Zahar.

1979. *Dependency and Development in Latin America.* Trans. Marjory Mattingly Urquidi. Berkeley: University of California Press.

Cardoso, Iliane. 1982. *A universidade do comunhão paulista.* São Paulo: Cortez.

Cardoso, Ruth (ed.). 1986. *A aventura antropológica*. Rio de Janeiro: Paz e Terra.
Cardoso de Mello, João Manoel. 1982. *O capitalism tardio*. São Paulo: Editora Brasiliense.
Carey, John. 1993. *The Intellectuals and the Masses: Pride and Prejudice among the Literary Intelligentsia 1880–1939*. New York: St. Martin's Press. Pp. 246.
Carone, Edgard. 1979/1981/1984. *Movimento operário no Brasil. 1877–1944; 1945–1964; 1964–1984*. São Paulo: Difel Editorial. 3 vols.
Carvalho, Luiz Marklouf. 2009. "As armas e os varões," *Revista Piauí: pra quem tem um clique a maise*, 31: 1–9. http://revistapiaui.estadao.com.br/edicao-31/vultos-da-republica/as-armas-e-os-varoes.
Castro, Josué de. 1961. *Geopolítica da fome: ensaio sobre os problemas de alimentação e de população do mundo*. São Paulo: Editora Brasiliense. 2 vols.
  1956. "Nacionalismo e pauperismo," *O Semanário*, 76(September 19–26): 15.
Cerqueira Filho, Gisálio. 1980 "O intelectual e os setores populares," *Encontros com a Civilização Brasileira*, 24(June): 15–20.
Chauí, Marilena. 1978. "A ideologia acrima de qualquer suspeita," *Almanaque* (São Paulo), 7: 113–116.
  1980a. "Ideologia e educação," *Educação e Sociedade, II*, 5(January): 24–40.
  1980b. *O que é ideologia*. São Paulo: Editora Brasiliense. Pp. 125.
  1982. *Cultura e democracia*, 3rd ed. São Paulo: Editora Moderna. Pp. 220.
  1983. *Seminários*. São Paulo: Editora Brasiliense. Pp. 106.
Chauí, Marilena, Sylvia Maria, and Franco Carvalho. 1978. *Ideologia e mobilização popular*. Rio de Janeiro: Série CEDEC/ Paz e Terra (No. 3). Pp. 209.
Chaves Neto, Elias. 1955. "Política de união nacional," *Revista Brasiliense*, 1(September–October): 48–65.
  1956. "Cultura marxista," *Revista Brasiliense*, 6(July–August): 59–68.
  1960. "Cinco anos de existência," *Revista Brasiliense*, 31(September–October): 1–3.
Chilcote, Ronald H. 1972. *Protest and Resistance in Angola and Brazil: Comparative Studies*. Berkeley and Los Angeles: University of California Press. Pp. 317.
  1974. *The Brazilian Communist Party: Conflict and Integration, 1922–1972*, New York: Oxford University Press. Pp. 361. Translated to Portuguese as *Partido Comunista Brasileiro: conflito e integração*. Rio de Janeiro: GRAAL, 1982.
  1984. *Theories of Development and Underdevelopment*. Boulder, CO: Westview Press.
  1985a. "A crise dos intelectuais," *Lua Nova 2*, 3(July–September): 82–86.
  1985b. "Reflections on Brazilian Political Thought and the Crisis of the Intellectual," *Luso-Brazilian Review*, 22(Winter 1985):111–121.
  1990. *Power and the Ruling Classes in Northeast Brazil: Juazeiro and Petrolina in Transition*. Cambridge and New York: Cambridge University Press. Pp. 383. Translated and published in Portuguese as *Transição capitalista e a classe dominante no Nordeste*, São Paulo: Editora da Universidade de São Paulo (T. A. Queiroz, ed.), 1991. Pp. 368.
  2007. "Memoirs of Brazilian Intellectuals," *Latin American Perspectives*, 34(5/September): 160–164.

Ciacchi, Andréa. 2007. "Gioconda Mussolini: uma travessia bibliográfica," *Revista de Antropologia*, 50: 181–223.

Cohen, Amélia (ed.). 2001. "CEDEC 25 anos: pensar o Brasil," *Lua Nova*, 54: 1–133.

Cohn, Gabriel. 1968. *Petróleo e nacionalismo*. São Paulo: Difusão do Libro.

Colóquio Sobre Marx. 1983. Written Summary Drawn from Chilcote Recording of Panel Discussion on the Capital Group by Its Participants. Campinas, UNICAMP, August 21.

Commentary. 1958a. "Nacionalismo e luta de classes,"*Anhembi*, 31(91/July), 1–5.

1958b. "O livro 'O nacionalismo na atualidade brasileira,' de Helio Jaguaribe...provoca confusão nas fileiras nacionalistas," *O Semanário*, 139(11–18 December): 10–11.

1958c. "Vitória contra o entreguismo de Helio Jaguaribe," *O Semanário*, 139(December 11–18: 3.

1958d. "Um novo Jaguaribe," *O Semanário*, 141(December 25–31): 4.

1959. "Crise provocada pela UNE..." *O Semanário*, 142(January 8–14): 4.

Cooney, Terry A. 1986. *The Rise of the New York Intellectuals: Partisan Review and Its Circle, 1934–1945*. Madison: University of Wisconsin Press. Pp. 350.

Corbisier, Roland. 1950. *Consciência e nação*. São Paulo: Edição da Revista Colégio. Pp. 197.

1952. *Situação e problemas da pedagogia*. São Paulo: Revista dos Tribunais. Pp. 39.

1956a. *Responsabilidade das elites*. São Paulo: Livraria Martins Editora. Pp. 243.

1956b. "Situação e alternatives da cultura brasileira," *Digesto Econômico (Rio de Janeiro)*, 7(130 July/August): 37–57.

1957. "Nacionalismo," *Digesto Econômico (Rio de Janeiro)*, 14(138 November/December): 59–69.

1958. *Formação e problema da cultura brasileira*. Rio de Janeiro: ISEB.

1959. "Conspiração contra o nacionalismo brasileiro," *O Seminário*, 185(November 13–20): 4.

1960a. *Brasília e o desenvolvimento nacional*. Rio de Janeiro: Instituto Superior de Estudos Brasileiros, Ministério da Educação e Cultura. Pp. 74.

1960b. *Formação e problema da cultura brasileira*. Rio de Janeiro: Instituto Superior de Estudos Brasileiros, Ministério da Educação e Cultura. Pp. 112.

1961. "Aliança dos socialistas e trabalhistas." *O Seminário*, 273(August 26–September 2).

1966a. "Notas para uma definição da cultura," *Revista Civilização Brasileira*, 5–6(March): 231–248.

1966b. "O problema nacional brasileiro," *Revista Civilização Brasileira*, 7(May): 348–363.

1968. *Reforma ou revolução?* Rio de Janeiro: Civilização Brasileira. Pp. 274.

1976a. *Filosofia e crítica radical*. São Paulo: Livraria Duas Cidades. Pp. 258.

1976b. "O nacionalismo segundo o ISEB," in his 1976a. São Paulo: Duas Cidades. Pp. 17–23.

1978. *Autobiografia filosófica: das ideologias à teoria da práxis*. Rio de Janeiro: Editora Civilização Brasileira. Pp. 330. Preface by Nelson Werneck Sodré.

1980. *Os intelectuais e a revolução*. Rio de Janeiro: Avenir Editora. Pp. 80.

Corrêa, Hercules. 1980. *A classe operária e seu partido: textos politicos do exílio.* Rio de Janeiro: Retratos do Brasil (137), Editôra Civilização Brasileira. Pp. 247.

Corrêa, Mariza. 1987. *História da antropologia no Brasil (1930–1960).* São Paulo: Vértice/Editora da UNICAMP.

2003. "*Revista de Antropologia*: 1952–2003." *Revista de Antropologia,* 46: 370–381.

Cortez, Grangeiro. 1993. "O pensamento político dos intelectuais marxistas no Brasil 1954 a 1964." MA Thesis. Universidade Federal de Ceará. Pp. 249.

Costa, Emília Viotti da. et al. 1978. "A revolução burguesa no Brasil," *Encontros com a Civilização Brasileiral,* 4 (October 1978): 176–207.

Costa, Emília Viotti da. 2000[1985]. *The Brazilian Empire: Myths and Histories.* Chapel Hill: University of North Carolina Press. Pp. 320.

Costa, Oswaldo. 1956. "O nacionalismo não é uma data; é um processo histórico," *O Semanário,* 27(October 4–11): 2.

Costa Pinto, L A. 1963. Sociologia e desenvolvimento. Temas e problemas de nosso tempo. Rio de Janeiro: Editora Civilização Brasileira. Pp. 314.

1967. *Desenvolvimento econômico e transição social.* Rio de Janeiro: Instituto de Ciências Sociais da Universidade Federal. Pp. 150.

Couri, Norma. 1984. "A atração dos políticos pelas letras vem dos tempos dos mandarins e chega aos de Badaró," *Folha de São Paulo* (October 4).

Coutinho, Carlos Nelson. 1979. "Cultura e democracia no Brasil," *Encontros com a Civilização Brasileira,* 17(November 1979): 19–48.

1980. *A democracia como valor universal.* São Paulo: Livraria Editora Ciências Humanas. Pp. 118.

1981. "Os intelectuais e a organização da cultura no Brasil," *Temas de Ciências Humanas,* 10: 93–128.

1986. *Literatura e ideologia em Brasil. Tres ensayos de crítica marxista.* Havana: Cadernos Casa (No. 32), Casa de las Américas. Pp. 117.

1989. *Gramsci: um estudo sobre seu pensamento político.* Rio de Janeiro: Editora Campus. Pp. 142.

1990. *Cultura e sociedade no Brasil: ensaios sobre idéias e formas.* Belo Horizonte : Coleção Nossa Terra, Oficina de Livros. Pp. 215.

1992. *Democracia e socialismo: as questões de princípio e contexto brasileiro.* São Paulo: Cortez and Autores Associados (Polêmicas do Nosso Tempo 51). Pp. 88.

2006. *Intervenções: Marxismo na batalha das ideias.* São Paulo: Cortez.

Coutinho, Carlos Nelson and Marco Aurélio Nogueira (eds.). 1985. *Gramsci e a América Latina.* Rio de Janeiro: Editora Paz e Terra. Pp. 159.

Cruz Costa, João. 1956 [1945]. *Contribuição a história das idéias no Brasil: O desenvolvimento da filosofia no Brasil e a evolução histórica nacional.* Rio de Janeiro: Livraria José Olympio. Pp. 483.

1962. "As transformações do pensamento brasileiro no século XX e o nacionalismo," *Revista Brasiliense,* 40(March–April): 51–64.

1964. *A History of Ideas in Brazil.* Berkeley: University of California Press. Pp. 450.

Cunha, Euclydes da. 1944. *Os Sertões: Rebellion in the Backlands.* Chicago: University of Chicago Press.

Cunha, Luiz Antônio. 1983. *A universidade crítica. O ensino superior na república populista.* Rio de Janeiro: Livraria Francisco Alves Editora. Pp. 260.

Dagnino, Evelina (ed.). 1994. *Anos 90. Política e sociedade no Brasil.* São Paulo: Editora Brasiliense.

Dagnino, Evelina, Alberto Olivera, and Aldo Panfichi (eds.). 2006. *A disputa pela construção democrática na América Latina.* Rio de Janeiro: Paz e Terra.

Debert, Guita Grin. 1986. "A política do significado no início dos anos 60: o nacionalismo no Instituto Superior de Estudos Brasileiros (ISEB) e na Escola Superior de Guerra (ESG)." PhD Dissertation. São Paulo: Universidade de São Paulo.

Debray, Régis. 1981. *Teachers, Writers, Celebrities: The Intellectuals of Modern France.* Trans. David Macey. London: Verso. Pp. 251.

Debrun, Michel. 1957. *Ideologia e realidade.* Rio de Janeiro: Instituto Superior de Estudos Brasileiros, Ministério da Educação e Cultura. Pp. 286.

1962. *O fato polítco.* Rio de Janeiro: Fundação Getúlio Vargas. Pp. 142.

1963. "A compreensão ideológica de história," *Revista Brasiliense,* 46(March–April): 82–100.

1964. Nacionalisme et politiques du développement au Brésil, *Sociologie du Travail,* 6(July–September): 235–257.

1983. *A "conciliação" e outras estratégias.* São Paulo: Editora Brasiliense. Pp. 173.

D'Incao, Maria Ángela (ed.). 1987a. *História e ideal: Ensaios sobre Caio Prado Júnior.* São Paulo: Editoira Brasiliense. Pp. 506.

1987b. *O saber militante: Ensaios sobre Florestan Fernandes.* São Paulo: Editora da UNESP.

Diniz, Eli. 1978. *Empresário, estado, e capitalismo no Brasil.* Rio de Janeiro: Paz E Terra.

2011. "Democracy, State, and Industry: Continuity and Change between the Cardoso and Lula Administrations," *Latin American Perspectives,* 38(3/May): 59–77.

Dorin, Lannoy. 1963. "A 'Revista de Brasil,'" *Revista Brasiliense,* 45(January–February): 52–67.

Dowbor, Ladislau. 1982. *A formação do capitalism dependente no Brasil.* São Paulo: Editora Brasiliense. Pp. 213.

2005. *The Broken Mosaic: For an Economics beyond Equations.* London and New York: Zed Books. Pp. 163. Translated from *O mosaic partido: a economia além das equações,* Petrópolis: Editora Vozes, 2000. Pp. 148.

2011. "Intellectuals in a Network: A New Generation Faces the Challenges of Development," *Latin American Perspectives,* 38(3/May): 78–98.

Dreifuss, René. 1981. *A conquista do estado (Ação política, poder e golpe de classe.* Petrópolis: Editora Vozes.

Duarte, Paulo. 1950. "Justiça social por que preço?," *Anhembi,* 1 (1/December): 3–27.

Dulles, John. 1984. *A Facultade de Direito de São Paulo e a resistência anti-Vargas.* São Paulo: EDUSP.

Editors O Globo. 1960. "Não é dar melhor, mas o ISEB tem sua história," *O Globo*, March 25 (Supplement): 3.

Ellis Júnior, Alfredo. 1934[1924]. *Bandeirismo paulista e o recuo do meridiano*, 2nd ed. São Paulo: Companhia Editora Nacional.

1936[1926]. *Os primeiros troncos paulistas e o cruzamento euroamericano*, 2nd ed. São Paulo: Companhia Editora Nacional.

1937. *Evolução da economia paulista e o cruzamento euroamericano*. São Paulo: Companhia Editora Nacional.

1944. *Raposo Tavares e sua época*. Rio de Janeiro: José Olympio.

Faoro, Raymundo. 1975[1957]. *Os donos de poder: formação do patronato politico brasileiro*, 2nd ed. 2 vols. (1st ed., 1957). Porto Alegre: Editora Globo. Pp. 270.

Farber, David (ed.). 1994. *The Sixties: From Memory to History*. Chapel Hill: University of North Carolina Press. Pp. 333.

Faucher, Philippe. 1981. *Le Bresil des militaries*. Montreal: Les Presses de l'Université de Montréal. Pp. 367.

Fausto, Boris. 1976. *Trabalho urbano e conflito social*. São Paulo: DIFEL. Pp. 283.

1983[1970]. *A revolução de 1930*. São Paulo: Editora Brasiliense. Pp. 118.

1988 "Estado, classe trabalhadora e burguesia industrial (1920–1945): uma revisão," *Estudos CEBRAP*, 20: 6–37.

1999. *A Concise History of Brazil*. Cambridge: Cambridge University Press. Pp. 262.

Félix, Moacir (ed.). 1962–1963. *Violão de rua*. 3 vols. Rio de Janeiro: Editora Civilização Brasileira.

Fernandes, Bernardo Mançano. 1996. MST. Movimento dos Trabalhadores Rurais Sem-terra. Formação e territorialização em São Paulo. São Paulo: Editora Hucitec. Pp. 285.

2000. *A formação do MST no Brasil*. Petrópolis: Editora Vozes. Pp. 319.

Fernandes, Florestan. 1948. "A análise sociológica de classes sociais." *Sociologia*, 10: 91–113.

1953 *Ensaio sobre o método de interpretação funcionalista na sociologia*. São Paulo: EDUSP.

1956. "Ciência e sociedade na evolução social do Brasil," *Revista Brasiliense*, 6(July–August): 46–58.

1958a. *A etnologia e a sociologia no Brasil*. São Paulo: Editora Anhembi. Pp. 327.

1958b. "O padrão de trabalho científico dos sociólogos brasileiros," in his 1958a work.

1959a. "O folclore de uma cidade em mudança," *Anhembi*, 36(106/September): 16–30. Continued in 37(107/October 1959): 260–282; 37(110/January 1960): 280–307; 37(111/February 1960): 517–532; 38(112/March 1960): 71–86; and 38(113/April 1960): 290–306.

1959b. *Fundamentos empíricos da explicação sociológica*. São Paulo: Companhia Editora Nacional.

1960 "O cientista brasileiro e o desenvolvimento da ciência," *Revista Brasiliense*, 31(September–October): 85–121.

1961. "Unidade das ciências sociais e a antropologia," *Anhembi*, 44(132/November): 453–470.

1962. "A educação popular no Brasil," *Revista Brasiliense*, 39(January–February): 128–138.

1964. *A integração do negro na sociedade de classe*. 2 vols. São Paulo: Companhia Editora Nacional.

1965a. *A integração do negro na sociedade de classes*. São Paulo: Dominus Ed., USP.

1965b. "A 'Revolução Brasileira' e os intelectuais" *Revista Civilização Brasileira*, 1(March): 325–337.

1966. *Educação e sociedade no Brasil* São Paulo: Editora da Universidade de São Paulo. Pp. 620.

1968. *Sociedade de classes e subdesenvolvimento*, 3rd ed. Rio de Janeiro: Zahar Editores. Pp. 267.

1969. *The Negro in Brazilian Society*. New York: Colombia University Press.

1970[1951]. *Função social da guerra na sociedade dos Tupinambás*, 2nd ed. São Paulo: Pioneira.

1974. *A revolução burguesa no Brasil: Ensaio de interpretação sociológica*. Rio de Janeiro: Zahar Editores (2nd ed., 1975; 3rd ed., 1981). Pp. 413.

1975. *Capitalismo dependente e classes sociais na América Latina*, 2nd ed. Rio de Janeiro: Zahar Editores (3rd ed., 1981). Pp. 157.

1977[1980]. *A sociologia no Brasil: Contribuição para o estudo da sua formação e desenvolvimento*. Petrópolis: Editora Vozes. Pp. 270.

1978. *O folklore em questão*. São Paulo: Editora Hucitec. Pp. 227.

1979. "Tarefas dos intelectuais na revolução democrática." *Encontros com a Civilização Brasileira*, 14(August): 25–33.

1981a. "Entrevista: Florestán Fernandes, a pessoa e o político," *Nova Escrita Ensaio*, 4(December): 9–39.

1981b. *O que é revolução*. São Paulo: Coleção Primeiros Passos (No. 25), Editora Brasiliense. Pp. 121.

1981c. *Reflections on the Brazilian Counter-Revolution: Essays by Florestan Fernandes*. Edited and introduction by Warren Dean. Armock, NY: M. E. Sharpe. Pp. 187.

(ed.). 1983. *Marx/Engels*. São Paulo: Grandes Cientistas Sociais (No. 36), Editora Atica. Pp. 496. Anthology of writings reviewed by José Paulo Netto, "Marx (e Engels) Segundo Florestan," *Voz da Unidade*, 167(August 26, 1953): 14.

1989. *Pensamento e acão: o PT e os remos do socialismo*. São Paulo: Editora Brasiliense. Pp. 226.

Flacks, Richard. 1988. *Making History: The American Left and the American Mind*. New York: Columbia University Press. Pp. 313.

Font, Mauricio. 1992. "City and Countryside in the Onset of Brazilian Industrialization," *Studies in Comparative International Development*, 27(Fall): 26–56.

Font, Mauricio (ed.). 2001. *Charting a New Course. The Politics of Globalization and Social Transformation. Fernando Henrique Cardoso*. Lanham, MD: Rowman and Littlefield. Pp. 354.

Forjaz, Maria Cecília Spina. 1989. *Tenentismo e as forças armadas na revolução de 1930*. São Paulo: Forense Universitária.

Franco, Augusto de, et al. 1991. *O PT e o Marxismo*. São Paulo: Cadernos de Teoria e Debate. Pp. 108.

Franco, Maria Sylvia Carvalho. 1963. "O estudo sociológico de comunidades," *Revista de Antropologia*, 11: 29–39.

1977. "Apresentação," in *Caio Navaro de Toledo, ISEB: fábrica de ideologies*. São Paulo: Ática [Ensaios, No. 28]. Pp. 11–15.

Frank, André Gunder. 1963. "Integração econômico na América Latina," *Revista Brasiliense*, 48(July–August): 6–11.

1964. "A agricultura brasileira: capitalismo e o mito do feudalismo," *Revista Brasiliense*, 51(January–February): 45–70.

1966. Frank, André Gunder. "The Development of Underdevelopment," *Monthly Review*, 18(September): 17–31.

1967. *Capitalism and Underdevelopment in Latin America: Historical Studies of Chile and Brazil*. New York: Monthly Review Press.

Frederico, Celso. 1978. *Consciência operário no Brasil: estudo com um grupo de trabalhadroes*. São Paulo: Editora Atica. Pp. 140.

1990–1991. *A esquerda e o movimento operário 1964–1984*. Belo Horizonte: Nossa Terra. 3 vols.

Freire, A. de Abreu. 1966. "Marxismo e história," *Síntese Política Econônica Social (SPES)*, 8(32/October–December): 20–50.

Freire, Dorian Jorge. 1960. "Campanha contra o ISEB," *Revista Brasiliense*, 28(March–April): 120–121.

Freire, Paulo. 1970. *Pedagogy of the Oppressed*. New York: Herder and Herder. Pp. 186.

1971. *Sobre la acción cultural*. Santiago, Chile: ICIRA. Pp. 117.

1985. "Caminhos de Paulo Freire," *Ensaio*, 14(May): 1–27.

2005. *Pedagogia do oprimido*. São Paulo: Paz e Terra.

French, John D. 1992. *The Brazilian Workers' ABC: Class Conflict and Alliances in Modern São Paulo*. Chapel Hill: University of North Carolina. Pp. 378.

Freyre, Gilberto. 1964 [1933]. *The Masters and the Slaves: A Study in the Development of Brazilian Civilization*. Trans. Samuel Putman. New York: Alfred A. Knopf. Pp. 432. Originally 1946, *Casa grande e senzala*, Rio de Janeiro: Editora José Olympio.

Furtado, Celso. 1944. "A feição functional da democracia moderna," *Cultura Política*, 4(36/January): 55–58.

1958. *Perspectivas da economia brasileira*. Rio de Janeiro: Instituto Superior de Estudos Brasileiros, Ministério da Educação e Cultura. Pp. 81.

1959a. *Formação económica do Brasil*. Rio de Janeiro: Editora Fundo de Cultura. Pp. 284.

1959b. *A operação nordeste*. Rio de Janeiro: Instituto Superior de Estudos Brasileiros, Ministério da Educação e Cultura. Pp. 78.

1961. *Desenvolvimento e subdesenvolvimento*. Rio de Janeiro: Editora Fundo de Cultura. Pp. 268.

1962a. *A nova dependência*. Rio de Janeiro: Editora Paz e Terra. Pp. 150.

1962b. *A pré-revolução brasileira*. Rio de Janeiro: Editora Fundo de Cultura. Pp. 117.

1963a. "Brazil: What Kind of Revolution?," *Foreign Affairs*, 41(April): 526–535.

1963b. *The Economic Growth of Brazil: A Survey from Colonial to Modern Times*. Trans. Ricardo W. de Aguiar and Eric Charles Drysdale. Berkeley: University of California Press. Pp. 285.

1964a. *Dialéctica do desenvolvimento*. Rio de Janeiro: Editora Fundo de Cultura. Pp. 170.

1964b. *Development and Underdevelopment*. Trans. Richardo W. de Aguiar and Eric Charles Drysdale. Berkeley and Los Angeles: University of California Press. Pp. 181.

1965. *Diagnosis of the Brazilian Crisis*. Trans. Suzette Macedo. Berkeley and Los Angeles: University of California Press. Pp. 168.

1966. *A hegemonia dos Estados Unidos e o futuro da América Latina*. Rio de Janeiro: Associação Brasileira Independência e Desenvolvimento (ABID). Pp. 22.

1967a. "O Brasil ou os entraves ao desenvolvimento," *Paz e Terra I*, 4(August): 165–182.

1967b. *Teoria e política do desenvolvimento econômico* (2nd ed., 1977). São Paulo: Biblioteca Universitária – ciências sociais (No. 2), Companhia Editora Nacional. Pp. 262.

1970. *Obstacles to Development in Latin America*. Garden City, NY: Anchor Books. Pp. 204.

1971. "Dependencia externa e teoria económica," *El Trimestre Económico*, 38(2/April–June): 335–349.

1978. *Criatividade e dependência na civilização industsrial*. Rio de Janeiro: Paz e Terra. Pp. 181.

1981[1974]. *O mito do desenvolvimento econômico*. Rio de Janeiro: Paz e Terra. Pp. 117.

1982. *Análise do "modelo" brasileiro*, 7th ed. Rio de Janeiro: Editora Civilização Brasileira. Pp. 122.

1983. *Não a recessão e ao desemprego*. Rio de Janeiro: Editora Paz e Terra. Pp. 107.

1984. *Cultura e desenvolvimento em época de crise*, 2nd ed. Rio de Janeiro: Editora Paz e Terra. Pp. 128.

2000. "Reflexões sobre a crise brasileira," *Novos Estudos CEBRAP* 57(July) : 3–8.

Gadotti, Moacir. 1994. *Reading Paulo Freire: His Life and Work*. Albany: State University of New York Press. Pp. 204.

Galvão, Maria Rita, and Jean-Claude Bernardet. 1983. *Cinema: repercussões em caixa de ecoideológica (As ideias de 'nacional' e 'popular' cinematográfico brasileiro*. São Paulo: Editora Brasiliense. Pp. 266.

Garcia, Marco Aurélio. 1992. "O PT e a 'nova ordem,'" *Teoria e Debate*, 18(2): 38–47.

Gaylord, Donald Roderick. 1991. "Instituto Superior de Estudos Brasileiros (ISEB) and Developmental Nationalism in Brazil, 1955–64." PhD Dissertation. Tulane University.

Giannotti, José Arthur. 1960. "Notas para uma análise metodológica de 'O Capital,'" *Revista Brasiliense*, 29(May–June): 60–72.

1983. *Trabalho e reflexao: ensaios para uma dialética do sociabilidade*. São Paulo: Editora Brasiliense. Pp. 374.

1984. "Acabou o capitalismo, é a barbarie?," *Presença*, 3(May): 37–52.

1985. *Origens da dialética do trabalho: estudo sobre a lógica do joven Marx.* Porto Alegre: L & PM Editores.

1989. "CEBRAP, vinte anos depois," *Novos Estudos CEBRAP*, 25(October): 3–7.

1998. "Recepções de Marx," *Novos Estudos CEBRAP*, 50: 115–124.

1999. "CEBRAP 30 anos," *Novos Estudos CEBRAP*, 55(November): 3.

Giroux. Henry A. 1910. "Lessons to Be Learned from Paulo Freire as Education Is Being Taken Over by the Mega Rich." November 23. http://www.truth-out .org/lessons-be-learned-from-paulo-freire-education-is-being-taken-over-mega-rich65363.

Gitlin, Todd. 1987. *The Sixties: Years of Hope. Days of Rage.* New York: Bantam.

Goertzel, Ted. C. 1999. *Fernando Henrique Cardoso: Reinventing Democracy in Brazil.* Boulder: Lynne Rienner Publishers. Pp. 219.

Gohn, Maria da Gloria. 1997. *Teorias dos movimentos sociais.* São Paulo: Edições Loyola.

Gorman, Paul R. 1996. *Intellectuals and Popular Culture in Twentieth Century America.* Chapel Hill: University of North Carolina Press. Pp. 242.

Gorender, Jacob. 1958. "Correntes sociológicas no brasil," *Estudos Sociais*, 3–4(September–December): 335–352.

1978. *O escravismo colonial.* 2nd ed. São Paulo: Ensaios (29), Editora Ática. Pp. 592.

1982[1974]. *A burguesia brasileira,* 2nd ed. São Paulo: Tudo é História (29), Editora Brasiliense. Pp. 116.

1984[1974]. *A revolução burguesa no Brasil,* 3rd ed. Rio de Janeiro: Zahar Editores.

1987. *Combates nas trevas: a esquerda do brasileira da ilusões perdidas a lutas armada,* 3rd ed. São Paulo: Serie Temas Brasil Contemporâneo, Editora Ática. Pp. 255.

Gouldner, Alvin W. 1979. *The Future of Intellectuals and the Rise of the New Class: A Frame of Reference, Theses, Conjectures, Arguments, and an Historical Perspective on the Role of Intellectuals and Intelligentsia in the International Class Context of the Modern Era.* New York: Seabury Press. Pp. 121.

Gramsci, Antonio. 1971 *The Prison Notebooks: Selections.* New York: International Publishers.

Guimarães, Alberto Passos. 1963. *Inflação e monopólio no Brasil.* Rio de Janeiro: Civilização Brasileira.

1964. *Quatro séculos de latifúndio.* Rio de Janeiro: Editora Paz e Terra.

Guimarães, Renato. 1962. "Desenvolvimento e marxismo," *Estudos Sociais*, 14(September): 109–134. Continued in 15(December 1962): 273–284.

Gullar, Ferreira. (pseud. for José Ribamar Ferreira). 1965. *Cultura posta em questão.* Rio de Janeiro: Editora Civilização Braileira. Pp. 126.

1969. *Vanguarda e subdesenvolvimento: ensaios sobe arte* (2nd ed., 1978). Rio de Janeiro: Editora Civilização Brasileira. Pp. 143.

1979. "Vanguardismo e cultura popular no Brasil," in Marco Aurélio Nogueira et al. (eds.), *Temas de ciências humanas.* Vol. 5. São Paulo: Livraria Editora Ciências Humanas. Pp. 75–92.

Hamburger, Amélia Império, Maria Amélia Dantas, Paty Michel, and Patrick Petitjean (eds.). 1996. *A ciência nas relações Brasil-França, 1850–1950.* São Paulo: EDUSP/FAPESP.

Hayden, Tom. 1988. *Reunion. A Memoir.* New York: Random House. Pp. 539.

Henfrey, Colin. 1981. "Dependency, Modes of Production, and the Class Analysis of Latin America," *Latin American Perspectives,* 8(3–4/Summer and Fall): 17–54.

Hewitt, W. E. 1991. *Base Christian Communities and Social Change in Brazil.* Lincoln: University of Nebraska Press. Pp. 150.

História da UNE. [1961]. Vol. 1 Butanta, São Paulo: Coleção História Presente (4), Editora Livramento. Pp. 127.

Hoge, James. 1995. "Fulfilling Brazil's Promise: A Conversation with President Cardoso," *Foreign Affairs,* 74(July–August): 62–75.

Holanda, Sêrgio Buarque de. 1956[1935]. *Raízes do Brasil,* 3rd ed. Rio de Janeiro: Livraria José Olympio Editora. Pp. 329. (4th ed., Brasilia: Editora Universidade de Brasilia.)

Ianni, Octávio. 1957. "Aspectos do nacionalismo brasileiro," *Revista Brasiliense,* 14(November–December): 121–133.

1961 "Condições constitucionais do comportamento polítco operário," *Revista Brasiliense,* 36(July–August 1961): 16–39.

1962. *As metamorfoses do escravo.* São Paulo: Difusão Europeia do Livro.

1963. *Industrialização e desenvolvimento social no Brasil.* Rio de Janeiro: Editora Civilização Brasileira. Pp. 269.

1964 "Political Process and Economic Development in Brazil." *New Left Review,* Part 1, 25(May–June): 39–52; Part 2, 26(Summer): 50–68.

1965. *Estado e capitalism: Estrutura social e industrialização no Brasil.* Rio de Janeiro: Editora Civilização Brasileira. Pp. 270.

1968. *O colapso do populismo no Brasil.* Rio de Janeiro: Editora Civilização Brasileira.

1971. *Estado e planejamento econômico no Brasil (1930–1970).* Rio de Janeiro: Civilização Brasileira.

1975. *Sociologia e sociedade no Brasil.* São Paulo: Editora Alfa-Omega. Pp. 137.

1978. "O estado e a organização da cultura," *Encontros com a Civilização Brasileira,* 1(July): 216–241.

1981. "O ciclo da revolução burguesa no Brasil," *Temas de Ciências Humanas,* 10: 1–34.

1983. *Revolução e cultura.* Rio de Janeiro: Civilização Brasileira. Pp. 134.

1984. *O ciclo da revolução burguesa.* Petrópolis: Editora Vozes. Pp. 112.

1985. "Neobismarkismo (ISEB)," in Octávio Ianni (ed.), *O ciclo da revolução burguesa,* 2nd ed. Petrópolis: Vozes. Pp. 55–62.

1986. "A crise do estado-nação," *Revista Novos Rumos,* 1(January–March): 35–45.

1989. *Sociologia da sociolgia: o pensmento sociológico brasileiro,* 3rd ed. São Paulo: Editora Ática. Pp. 239.

1995. "Imperialismo e globalização," *Crítica Marxista,* 2: 130–131.

Ianni, Octávio, Paul Singer, Gabriel Cohn, and Francisco C. Weffort. 1965. *Política e revolução social no Brasil.* Rio de Janeiro: Editora Civilização Brasileira. Pp. 198.

IBESP Plan. 1956. "Para uma política nacional de desenvolvimento," *Cadernos do Nosso Tempo*, 5(January–March): 47–188.

Iglésias, Francisco (ed.). 1982. *Caio Prado Júnior: História*. São Paulo: Editora Ática. Pp. 207.

ISEB. 1956. *Introdução aos problemas do Brasil*. Rio de Janeiro: MEC/ Departamento de Imprensa Nacional. Pp. 233.

Isserman, Maurice. 1987. *If I had a Hammer...The Death of the Old Left and the Birth of the New Left*. New York: Basic Books. Pp. 259.

Jacoby, Russell. 1987. *The Last Intellectuals. American Culture in the Age of Academe*. New York: Noonday Press. Pp. 290.

Jaguaribe, Helio. 1953. "A crise brasileira," *Cadernos do Nosso Tempo*, 1(October–December): 120–160.

1954. "A crisis de nosso tempo no Brasil," *Cadernos do Nosso Tempo*, 2(January–June): 1–17.

1957a. *A filosofia no Brasil*. Rio de Janeiro: Instituto Superior de Estudos Brasileiros, Ministério da Educação e Cultura. Pp. 54.

1957b. "Sucinta análise do nacionalismo brasileira." *Revista do Clube Militar*, 141: 11–14.

1958a. *Condições institucionais do desenvolvimento*. Rio de Janeiro: Instituto Superior de Estudos Brasileiros, Ministério da Educação e Cultura. Pp. 53.

1958b. *O nacionalismo na atualidade brasileira*. Rio de Janeiro: Instituto Superior de Estudos Brasileiros, Ministério da Educação e Cultura. Pp. 305.

1961. *Burguesia y proletariado en el nacionalismo brasilero*. Buenos Aires: Ediciones Coyoacán. Pp. 77.

1962. *Desenvolvimento econômico e desenvolvimento político*. Rio de Janeiro: Editora Fundo de Cultura. Pp. 221.

1966a. *The Brazilian Structural Crisis*. Riverside: Seminar Series Report No. 1, Latin American Research Program, University of California, Riverside. Pp. 16.

1966b. "Brazilian Nationalism and the Dynamics of Its Political Development," *Studies in Comparative International Development*, 2(4): 55–69.

1967. *Problemas do desenvolvimento Latino-americano*. Rio de Janeiro: Civilização Brasileira. Pp. 202.

1967–1968. "Political Strategies of National Development in Brazil," *Studies in Comparative International Development*, 3(2): 27–48.

1968. *Economic & Political Development: A Theoretical Approach: A Brazilian Case Study*. Cambridge, MA: Harvard University Press. Pp. 202.

1970a. "Causes of Latin American Underdevelopment." Rio de Janeiro: Instituto Universitário de Pesquisas do Rio de Janeiro. Pp. 27 (mimeographed).

1970b. "O modelo polítco e a estrutura econômico-social brasileira," *Encontros com a Civilização Brasileira*, 4(October): 129–166.

1977a. "A condição imperial," *Dados*, 15: 3–24.

1978. "Modernização, desenvolvimento nacional e desenvolvimento social," *Encontros com Civilização Brasileira*, 2(August): 41–55.

1979. "ISEB. Um breve depoimento e uma reapreciação crítica." *Cadernos de Opinão* (Rio de Janeiro), 14(October–November): 94–110.

1981. "A crise brasileira," in Simon Schwartzman (ed.), *O pensamento nacionalista e os 'Cadernos de Nosso Tempo.'* Brasília: Câmera dos Deputados/ Editora da UNB.

1982. "Populismo, autoritarismo e democracia, nas presentes condições brasileiras," *Encontros com a Civilização Brasileira*, 29(November): 175–195.

1983 "Terceiro Painel: Guerreiro Ramos e o desenvolvimento brasileiro," *Revista da Aministração Pública* (Rio de Janeiro), 17(2/April–June): 63–92.

1990. *Alternativas do Brasil*, 3rd. ed. Rio de Janeiro: Editora José Olympio. Pp. 145.

2005. "O ISEB e o desenvolvimento nacional." Pp. 31–42 in Toledo (2005).

Jaguaribe, Helio et al. 2000[1986]. *Brasil, 2000. Para um novo pacto social*, 3rd ed. Rio de Janeiro: Paz e Terra. Pp. 196.

Johnson, Dale (ed.). 1982. *Class and Social Development: A New Theory of the Middle Class*. Beverly Hills: Sage Publications.

Katsiaficas, George. 1987. *The Imagination of the New Left: A Global Analysis of 1968*. Boston: South End Press. Pp. 323.

Kahl, Joseph A, 1976. *Modernization, Exploitation and Dependency in Latin America: Germani, González Casanova, and Cardoso*. New Brunswick: Transaction Books. Pp. 215.

Keck, Margaret E. 1992. *The Workers' Party and Democratization in Brazil*. New Haven, CT: Yale University Press. Pp. 315.

Kondor, Leondro. 1967. "A rebeldia, os intelectuais e a juventude," *Revista Civilização Brasileira*, 15(September).

1991. *Intelectuais brasileiros & marxismo*. Belo Horizonte: Oficina de Livros. Pp. 132.

Kondor, Leondro, Gisálio Cerqueira Filho, and Eurico de Lima Figueiredo (eds.). 1983. *Por que Marx?* Rio de Janeiro: Edições Graal. Pp. 357.

Korda, Michael. 1999. *Another Life: A Memoir of Other People*. New York: Random House. Pp. 530.

Kubitschek, Juscelino, Clovis Salgado, Adyr May, and Roland Corbisier. 1957. *Discursos Rio de Janeiro*: Instituto Superior de Estudos Brasileiros, Ministério da Educação e Cultura. Pp. 63.

Kuhn, Thomas. 1970. *The Structure of Scientific Revolutions*, 2nd ed. Chicago: University of Chicago Press.

Lafetá, João Luiz, and Lígia Chiappini M. Leite. 1983. See Zilio (1983).

Lagôa, Ana. 1983. SNI: *Como nasceu. Como funciona*. São Paulo: Editora Brasiliense. Pp. 133.

Lambert, Jacques. 1967. *Os dois Brasis*, 2nd ed. São Paulo: Companhia Editora Nacional. Pp. 277.

Lane, David. 1974. "Leninism as an Ideology of Soviet Development," in Emmanuel De Kadt and Gavin Williams (eds.), *Sociology and Development*. London: Tavistock Publications. Pp. 23–37.

Laskin, David. 2000. *Partisans: Marriage, Politics, and Betrayal among the New York Intellectuals*. New York: Simon and Schuster. Pp. 319.

Leal, Vítor Nunes. 1975[1948]. *Coronelismo, enxada e voto: o municipio e o regime representativo, no Brasil*. São Paulo: Alfa-Omega. Pp. 276.

Leite, Dante Moreira. 1954. *O caráter nacional brasileiro: Descriçaõ das características psicológlicas do brasileiro através de ideologias e esteriótipos.* São Paulo: Boletim da FFCL (230), USP.

1969[1954]. *O caráter nacional brasileiro, história de uma ideologia,* 3rd ed. São Paulo: Livraria Pioneira Editora. Pp. 339.

Leite, Júlio César P. 1983. "Guerreiro Ramos e a importância do conceito da redução sociológicano desenvolvimento brasileiro," *Revista de Administracão Pública,* 17(1/January–February): 77–83.

Lenin, V.I. 1956. *The Development of Capitalism in Russia: The Process of the Formation of a Home Market for Large-Scale Industry.* Moscow: Foreign Languages Publishing House.

1967. *Selected Works.* Moscow: Progress Books.

Leoni, Briglitte Hersant. 1997. *Fernando Henrique Cardoso: O Brasil do possível.* Rio de Janeiro: Editora Nova Fronteira. Pp. 360.

Levine, Lawrence W. 1996. *The Opening of the American Mind.* Boston: Beacon Press. Pp. 212.

Lima, Heitor Ferreira 1976 *História do pensamento econômico brasileiro.* São Paulo: Companhia Editora Nacional.

Lima, Hermes. 1945. *Notas a vida brasileira.* São Paulo: Editora Brasiliense. Pp. 177.

1954. *Lições da crise.* Rio de Janeiro: Livraria José Olympio Editora. Pp. 86.

1955. Significação do nacionalismo," *Cadernos do Nosso Tempo,* 4(April–August): 85–100.

1958. "Variações críticas sobre o nacionalismo," *Revista Brasiliense,* 18(July–August): 8–24.

Lima, Alceo Amoroso. 1958. "O estado e a educação," *Síntese Política Econônica Social (SPES),* 1 (1/May–June): 4–21.

Lima Filho, Oswaldo. 1956. "Polítca nacionalista definida em 11 pontos," *O Semanário,* 34(November 22–29).

Lima Sobrinho, Barbosa. 1966. "Alberto Torres, sua vida e sua obra," *Revista Civilização Brasileira,* 5–6(March): 325–342.

Lopes, Juárez Rubens Brandão. 1964. *Sociedade industrial no Brasil.* São Paulo: DIFEL.

1967. *Crise do Brasil arcaico.* São Paulo: DIFEL. Pp. 193.

Lott, Eric. 2006. *The Disappearing Liberal Intellectual.* New York: Basic Books. Pp. 260.

Lovato, Angélica. 2009. "Enio Silveira e os Cadernos do Povo Brasileira," *Lutas Sociais,* 23(Second Semester): 93–103.

Love, Joseph. 1982. *A locomotiva: São Paulo na federação brasileira.* Rio de Janeiro: Paz e Terra.

Löwy, Michael. 1960. "Notas sobre a questão agrária no Brasil," *Revista Brasiliense,* 31(September–October): 55–71.

1962a. "Consciência de classe e partido revolucionário," *Revista Brasiliense,* 41(May–June): 138–160.

1962b. "Homem e sociedade na obra do jovem Marx," *Revista Brasiliense,* 42(July–August): 90–105.

1973. *The Marxism of Che Guevara*, 2nd ed. New York: Monthly Review Press (Reprinted Rowman and Littlefield, 2008).

1975. "Is There a Law of Arrested and Un-combined Development?," *Latin American Perspectives*, 2(4): 118–120.

1979. *Para uma sociologia dos intelectuais revolucionários*. São Paulo: Ciências Humanas.

1981. *The Politics of Combined and Uneven Development: The Theory of Permanent Revolution*. London: New Left Books.

2000. "A 'Red' Government in the South of Brazil," *Monthly Review*, 52(November 2000): 16–20.

Lucas, Fábio. 1958. "A margem da revolução brasileira," *Estudos Sociais*, 3–4(September–December): 362–371.

Lucas, José. 1983. *Não a teoria do subdesenvolvimento*. São Paulo: Kairós Livraria e Editora. Pp. 148.

Maio, Marcus Chor. 1999. "O Projeto UNESCO e a agenda das ciências sociais no Brasil nos anos 40 e 50," *Revista Brasileira de Ciências Sociais*, 14(41): 141–158.

2011. "Florestan Fernandes, Oracy Nogueira, and the UNESCO Project on Race Relations in São Paulo," *Latin American Perspectives*, 38(3/May): 136–149.

Mantega, Guido. 1982. "Raizes e formação da economia política brasileira." PhD dissertation. São Paulo: Universidade de São Paulo.

1984. *A economia política brasileira*. São Paulo and Petrópolis: Polis/Vozes. Pp. 288.

1997. "O pensamento econômico brasileiro de 60 a 80: os anos rebeldes," chapter 3. Pp. 107–157 in Maria Rita Garcia Loureiro, *Os economistas no governo: gentão econômica e democracia*. Rio de Janeiro: Fundação Getúlio Vargas Editora.

Mantega, Guido, and José Márcio Rego. 1999. *Conversas com economistas brasileiros*, Vol. 1. São Paulo: Editora 34.

Marini, Ruy Mauro. 1969. *Subdesarrollo y revolución*. Mexico City: Siglo Veintiuno Editores.

1973a. "Dependencia y subimperialismo en América Latina," *Cultura en México (Suplemento de Siempre)*, 1030(March 31):5–8.

1973b. *Dialéctica de la dependencia*. Mexico City: Ediciones Era.

1978a. "Las razones del neodessarrollismo (respuesta a F. H. Cardoso y J. Serra),: *Revista Mexicana de Sociología*, 40(E): 57–106. Response to criticism of José Serra and Fernando H. Cardcoso, "Las desventuras de la dialéctica de la dependencia," *Revista Mexicana de Sociología*, 40(1978): 9–55. Also in Estudos CEBRAP, 23(January–February 1979): 35–80.

1978b "World Capitalist Accumulation and Sub-imperialism," *Two Thirds*, 1(Fall): 29–39.

1990. *Memória*. Rio de Janeiro. Pp. 109.

Marinho, Luís Carlos de Oliveira. 1986. "O ISEB em seu momento histórico." MA Thesis. Universidade Federal do Rio de Janeiro.

Martins, Carlos Estevam. 1963. *A questão da cultura popular*. Rio de Janeiro: Tempo Brasileiro. Pp. 115.

1977. *Capitalismo de estado e modelo político no Brasil*. Rio de Janeiro: Graal. Pp. 425.

N.d. "Brazil and the United States from the 1960s to the 1970s." [São Paulo]. Pp. 63. Followed by a response from Maria Conceição Tavares, manuscript. Pp. 24.

Martins Filho, João Roberto. 1987. *Movimento estudantil e ditadura military: 1964–1968*. Campinas: Papirus Livraria Editora. Pp. 215.

1995. *O palácio e a caserna: a dinámica militar das crises políticas na ditadura (1964–1969)*. São Carlos: Editora da UFSF. Pp. 204.

Martins, José de Souza. 1963. "O Plano Trienal e a marcha da revolução burguesa," *Revista Brasiliense*, 149(September–October): 41–52.

1978. *Sobre o modo capitalist de pensar*. São Paulo: Editora HUCITEC.

1998. *Florestan: Sociologia e consciência social no Brasil*. São Paulo: EDUSP/ FAPESP.

Martins, Mônica Dias. 2000. "Açucar no sertão: a ofensiva capitalista no Vale do Curo." PhD Dissertation. Fortaleza: Universidade Federal do Ceará.

Martins. Wilson. 1976. *História da inteligência brasileira* (7 vols.). São Paulo: Editora Cultrix.

Marx, Karl. 1943. *Articles on India*. Bombay: People's Publishing House.

1967. *Capital: A Critique of Political Economy*. New York: International Publishers.

McLaren, Peter. 2000. *Che Guevara, Paulo Freire, and the Pedagogy of Revolution*. Foreword by Ana Maria Araújo Freire. Lanham, MD: Rowman & Littlefield. Pp. 221.

Meirelles, Bolivar Marinho Soares de. 1990. "Conflitos políticos e ideológicos nas forças armadas brasileiras (1945–1964)." MA Thesis. Rio de Janeiro: Escola Brasileira de Administração Pública, Fundação Getúlio Vargas. Pp. 172.

Melo Franco, Afonso Arinos de. 1933. *Introdução a realidade brasileira*. Rio de Janeiro: Schmidt-Editor, Civilização Brasileira. Pp. 259.

1936. *Conceito de civilização brasileiro*. São Paulo: Companhia Editora Nacional. Pp. 238.

Meneguella, Rachel. 1989. *PT e formação de um partido, 1979–1982*. Rio de Janeiro: Editora Paz e Terra. Pp. 228.

Menezes, Djacir. 1972. *O Brasil no pensamento brasileiro*. Rio de Janeiro: Conselho Federal de Cultura, Ministério da Educação e Cultura. Pp. 607.

Miceli, Sêrgio. 1984. *Estado e cultura no Brasil*. São Paulo: Difel Editorial.

1999. *O que ler nas ciências sociais no Brasil: 1970–1995*. São Paulo: Sumaré.

Miceli, Sêrgio (ed.). 1979. *Intelectuais e classe dirigente no Brasil (1920–1945)*. São Paulo: DIFEL. Pp. 210.

(ed.). 1989. *História das ciências sociais no Brasil*, Vol. 1. São Paulo: Vértice-IDESP.

Miglioli, Jorge. 2005. "O ISEB e a encruzilhada nacional," in Caio Navarro Toledo (ed.), *Intelectuais e política no Brasil*. Rio de Janeiro: Revan. Pp. 59–76.

Mills, C. Wright. 1963. *Power, Politics, and People: The Collected Essays of C. Wright Mills*, edited by Irving Louis Horowitz. New York: Oxford University Press.

Miller, James. 1987. *"Democracy Is in the Streets": From Port Huron to the Siege of Chicago*. New York: Simon and Schuster. Pp. 431.

Moisés, José Álvaro. 1995. *Os brasileiros e a democracia: bases sócio-políticas da legitimidade democrática*. São Paulo: Editora Ática. Pp. 301.

Moisés, José Álvaro, and J. A. Guilhon Albuquerque (eds.). 1989. *Dilemas da consolidação da democracia*. Rio de Janeiro: Editora Paz e Terra. Pp. 269.

Moniz, Edmundo. 1980. "A crisis mundial do imperialismo e Rosa Luxemburgo," *Encontros com a Civilização Brasileira*, 25(July): 195–202.

Moniz Bandeira, Luiz Alberto. 1978[2001]. *O governo João Goulart: as lutas sociais no Brasil, 1963–1964*, 3rd ed. Rio de Janeiro: Editora Civilização Brasileira. Pp. 317.

Moraes, Reginaldo, Ricardo Antunes, and Vera B. Ferrante (eds.). 1986. *Inteligência brasileira*. São Paulo: Editora Brasiliense. Pp. 305.

Morais, Pessoa de. 1965. *Sociologia da revolução brasileira. Análise e interpretação do Brasil de hoje*. Preface by Gilberto Freyre. Rio de Janeiro: Editora Leitura. Pp. 317.

Morais, Lecio, and Alfredo Saad-Filho. 2011. "Brazil Beyond Lula: Forging Ahead or Pausing for Breath?," *Latin American Perspectives*, 38(2/March): 31–44.

Moreira, João Roberto. 1959. "O ISEB e os católicos," *A Ordem (Rio de Janeiro)*, 5(15/August–December): 729–723.

Mota, Carlos Guilherme. 1980[1974]. *Ideologia da cultura brasileira (1933–1974)*. São Paulo: Editora Ática. Pp. 303.

Motoyama, Shozo (ed.). 2005. *USP, 70 anos*. São Paulo: EDUSP.

Motta, Luiz Eduardo P. 2000. "O ISEB no banco dos réus," *Comun (Rio de Janeiro)*, 5(15/August–December): 119–145.

Myer, John. 1975. "A Crown of Thorns: Cardoso and Counter-Revolution," *Latin American Perspectives*, 2(1/Spring 1975): 33–48.

Nakano, Yoshiaki, José Marcio Rego, and Lilian Furquim (eds.). 2004. *Em busca do novo. O Brasil e o desenvolvimento na obra de Bresser-Pereira*. Rio de Janeiro: Editora FGV. Pp. 640.

Noguera, Marco Aurélio. 1978. "Temas, 3 anos depois," *Temas de Ciências Humanas*, 8: viii.

Nogueira, Oracy. 1968. *Pesquisa social: Introdução às suas técnicas*. São Paulo: Companhia Editora Nacional.

Novais, Fernando. 1983a. "Caio Prado Jr historiador," *Novos Esudos CEBRAP*, 1(2/July): 66–70.

1983b. *Portugal e Brasil na crise do antigo sistema colonial*, 2nd ed. São Paulo: Editora Hucitec. Pp. 420.

Oliveira, Francisco de. 1972. "Economia brasileira: Crítica e razão dualista," *Estudos CEBRAP*, 2: 5–82.

1976. *A economia brasileira: crítica a razão dualista*. São Paulo: Editora Brasiliense.

1977a. *A economia da dependência imperfeita*. Rio de Janeiro: Graal. Pp. 159.

1977b. *Elegia para uma Re(li)gião: SUDENE, Nordeste. Planejamento e conflitos de classes*. Rio de Janeiro: Editora Paz e Terra. Pp. 132.

Oliveira, Francisco de (ed.). 1983. *Furtado: economia*. São Paulo: Editora Ática. Pp. 224.

Oliveira, Lucia Lippi. 1995. *A sociologia de Guerreiro*. Rio de Janeiro: Editora UFRJ.

Oliveira Vianna, F. J. 1933. *Evolução do povo brasileiro: I – evolução da sociedade; II – evolução da raça; III evolução da raça; III – evolução das instituições política.* São Paulo: Companhia Editora Nacional. Pp. 275.

1949. *Instituições políticas do Brasil.* 2 vols. Rio de Janeiro: José Olympio Editora.

1958. *Introdução à história social da economia pré-capitalista no Brasil.* Rio de Janeiro: José Olympio.

Oliven, Ruben George. 1982. *Violência e cultura no Brasil.* Petrópolis: Editora Vozes. Pp. 86.

1984. "The Production and Consumption of Culture in Brazil," *Latin American Perspectives,* 11(1/Winter): 103–115.

1992. *The Dependency Movement: Scholarship and Politics in Development Studies.* Cambridge: Harvard University Press. Pp. 362.

Page, Joseph. A. 1972. *The Revolution That Never Was: Northeast Brazil 1955–1964.* New York: Grossman Publishers.

Paim, Gilberto. 1957. *Industrialização e economia natural.* Preface by Inácio Rangel. Rio de Janeiro: Instituto Superior de Estudos Brasileiros, Ministério da Educação e Cultura. Pp. 122.

1960 "Uma pesquisa sobre as empresas de capital estrangeiro," *Estudos Sociais,* 7(March): 280–290.

Paiva, Vanilda Pereira. 1980. *Paulo Freire e o nacionalismo-desenvolvimentismo.* Rio de Janeiro: Editora Civilização Brasileira.

1986. *Paulo Freire e o nacionalismo-desenvolvimentista,* 2nd ed. Rio de Janeiro: Editora da Civilização Brasileira.

Paoli, Maria Célia Pinheiro Machado. 1974. *Desenvolvimento e marginalidade: Um estudo de caso.* São Paulo: Livraria Pioneira Editora. Pp. 158.

1987. "Os trabalhadores urbanos na fala dos outros: tempo, espaço e classe na história operária brasileira." Pp. 53–101 in José Sêrgio Leite Lopes (ed.), *Cultura e identidade operária.* São Paulo and Rio de Janeiro: Marco Zero/ Editora da UFRJ.

1991. "As ciências sociais, os movimentos sociais e a questão do género," *Novos Estudos CEBRAP,* 31(October): 107–120.

1992. "Citizenship, Inequalities, Democracy and Rights: The Making of a Public Space in Brazil," *Social and Legal Studies,* 1(1992): 143–159.

Paoli, Maria Célia Pinheiro Machado. et al. 1982. *A violência brasileira.* São Paulo: Editora Brasiliense. Pp. 117.

Paoli, Maria Célia, Eder Sader, and Vera da Silva Telles. 1983. "Pensando a classe operária: os trabalhadores sujeitos ao imaginário acadêmico," *Revista Brasileira de História,* 6(September): 129–149.

Pécaut, Daniel. 1990. *Os intelectuais e a política no Brasil. Entre o povo e a nação.* São Paulo: Editora Atica.

Pelligrini, Tânia. 1995. "Aspectos da produção cultural brasileira contemporânea," *Crítica Marxista,* 2: 69–91.

Penha, João da. 1982. "Itinerário filosófico de Roland Corbisier," *Encontros com a Civilização Brasileira,* 28(October): 169–183.

Peralva, Osvaldo. 1957a. "O carácter popular do nacionalismo brasileiro," *Novos Tempos,* 3(December): 42–47.

Peralva, Osvaldo et al. 1957b. "A crise no seio do PCP," *Novos Tempos*, 1(September): 56–61.

Peregrino, Umberto. 1966. "Da Escola Superior de Guerra," *Cadernos Brasileiros*, 33(November–December): 29–38.

Pereira, Alexsandro Eugenio. 1998a. "A crítica e a polémica em torno do ISEB," *Revista de Sociologia e Política (Curitiba)*, 10(11): 259–265.

 1998b. "Estado, capital estrangeiro e desenvolvimento econômico na produção intelectual do ISEB (1955–1964)." MA Thesis. São Paulo: Universidade de São Paulo.

 2003. "O ISEB na perspectiva de seu tempo: intelectuais, política e cultura no Brasil (1952–1964)." PhD Dissertation. São Paulo: FFLCH/USP.

Pereira, Anthony W. 1997. *The End of the Peasantry: The Rural Labor Movement in Northeast Brazil, 1961–1988*. Pittsburgh, PA: University of Pittsburgh Press. Pp. 232.

Pereira, João Batista Borges. 1994. "Emílio Willems e Egon Schaden na história de antropologia," *Estudos Avançadas*, 8(22): 249–253.

Pereira, Luiz. 1965. *Trabalho e desenvolvimento no Brasil*. São Paulo: Difusão Européia do Livro. Pp. 302.

Pereira, Osny Duarte. 1956. "Outras sabotagens a Petrobrás," *O Semanário*, 70(August 8–15): 3. See also 1956: 71(August 15–28): 3.

 1959a. "Como surgiu o nacionalsmo econômico," *O Seminário*, 155(April 16–22): 3.

 1959b. "A magistratura e o nacionalismo," *O Semanário*, July 4–10: 3.

 1960. *Estudos nacionalistas: considerações a margem do Brasil contemporâneo*, 2 vols. São Paulo: Editor Fulgor.

 1962. *Quem faz as leis no Brasil?* Rio de Janeiro: Civilização Brasileira.

 1963. "O ISEB." O desenvolvimento e as reformas de base," *Revista Brasiliense*, 47(May–June): 23–41.

 1967. *Ferro e independência: um desafio a dignidade nacional*. Rio de Janeiro: Editora Civilização Brasileira. Pp. 591.

 1975. *Multinacionais no Brasil (aspectos sociais e politicos*. Rio de Janeiro: Editora Civilização Brasileira. Pp. 227.

 1995. *Minha passagem pelo ISEB*. Rio de Janeiro: Depoimento em seminariesna Associação Brasileira de Imprensa e na Bibllioteca Nacional.

Perrone, Charles A. 1989. *Masters of Contemporary Brazilian Song: MPB 1965–1985*. Austin: University of Texas Press. Pp. 253.

Pires, Cecília Maria Pinto. 1987. "O ISEB e a questão do nacionalismo." MA Thesis. Universidade Federal do Rio de Janeiro.

Pomar, Wladimir. 1980. *Araguaia: o partido e a guerrilha*. São Paulo: Brasil Debates.

 1982. "Questões de táctica na luta contra a ditadura," *Teoria Política*, 4: 9–41. See also response from Duarte, Ozeas. 1982. "A questão da democracia e o programa da classe operária 'replica a Wladimir Pomar,'" *Teoria Política*, 4: 42–72. See also rejoinder by Pomar. 1984. "Voltanto a questão da democracia para o proletariado," *Teoria Política*, 5–6:130–160.

Portela, Fernando. 1979. *Guerra de guerrilhas no Brasil*. São Paulo: Global Editora. Pp. 263.

Poulantzas, Nicos. 1975. *Classes in Contemporary Capitalism*. London: NLB.

Prado, Antônio Arnoni (ed.). 1986. *Libertários no Brasil. Memória, lutas, cultura.* São Paulo: Editora Brasiliense. Pp. 308.

Prado Júnior, Caio. 1933. *Evolução política do Brasil e outros estudos* (2nd ed., 1957; 4th ed., 1963). São Paulo: Brasilliense. Pp. 264.

1942. *Formação do Brasil contemporâneo* (2nd ed., 1963). São Paulo: Brasiliense. Pp. 391.

1955. "Nacionalismo brasileiro e capitais estrangeiros," *Revista Brasiliense,* 2(November–December): 80–93.

1959. "Nacionalismo e desenvolvimento," *Revista Brasiliense,* 24(July–August): 9–15.

1960a. "Contribuição para a análise de questão agrária no Brasil," *Revista Brasiliense,* 28(March–April): 165–238.

1960b. "As eleições de 3 de Outubro," *Revista Brasiliense,* 32(November–December): 1–18.

1960c. "A reforma agrária e o momento nacional," *Revista Brasiliense,* 29(May–June): 1–16.

1961a. "O desenvolvimento econômico e o problema da capitalização," *Revista Brasiliense,* 34(March–April): 46–56.

1961b. "Panorama da política brasileira," *Revista Brasiliense,* 38(November–December): 1–15.

1962a. "Nova contribuição para a análise da questão agrária no Brasil," *Revista Brasiliense,* 43(September–October): 11–52.

1962b. "Perspectivas da política progressista e popular brasileira," *Revista Brasiliense,* 44(November–December): 1–8.

1963[1945]. *História econômica do Brasil,* São Paulo: Editora Brasiliense, 8th ed. Pp. 354.

1964. "Marcha da questão agrária no Brasil," *Revista Brasiliense,* 51(January–February): 1–9.

1966. *A revolução brasileira.* São Paulo: Editora Brasiliense. Pp. 332.

1967a. "Adentro a revolução brasileira," *Revista Civilização Brasileira,* 14(July): 43–74.

1967b[1969]. *The Colonial Background of Modern Brazil.* Trans. Suzette Macedo. Berkeley: University of California Press. Pp. 530.

Purcell, Susan Kaufman, and Riordan Roett (eds.). 1997. *Brazil under Cardoso.* Boulder, CO: Lynne Rienner. Pp. 119.

Quartim de Moraes, João. 1970. "Régis Debray and the Brazilian Revolution," *New Left Review,* 59(January–February 1970): 61–82.

1971. *Dictatorship and Armed Struggle in Brazil.* Trans. David Fernbach. New York: New Left Books and Monthly Review Press. Pp. 250.

(ed.). 1995. *História do marxismo no Brasil. Vol. 2 Os influxos teóricos.* Campinas: Editora da UNICAMP. Pp. 246.

Queiroz, Maria Isaura Pereira de. 1965. *O messianismo no Brasil e no mundo. São Paulo: Ciências Sociais* (5). São Paulo: Editora da Universidade de São Paulo. Pp. 373.

Ramos, Alberto Guerreiro. 1939. "Sentido da poesia contemporânea," *Cadernos da Nossa Hora,* 1(May): 86–103.

1940 "Nota sobre Jacinto Passos," *Cadernos da Nossa Hora,* 6(January): 149.

References   267

1950. *Uma introdução ao histórico da organização racional do trabalho.* Rio de Janeiro: Departamento de Imprensa Nacional.

1952. *A sociologia industrial: formação, tendências, atuais.* Rio de Janeiro. Pp. 176.

1954. *Cartilha brasileira do aprendiz de sociólogo (Prefacio a uma sociologia nacional).* Rio de Janeiro: Editora Andes. Pp. 173.

1955. "A ideologia da 'Juenesse Dorée,'" *Cadernos do Nosso Tempo,* 4(April–August): 101–112.

1956a. "A dinâmica da sociedade política no Brasil," *Revista Brasileira de Estudos Políticos (Belo Horizonte),* 1:23–38.

1956b. "O inconsciente sociológico: um estudo sôbre a crise política no Brasil, na década 1930–1940," *Cadernos do Nosso Tempo,* 5(January March): 225–236.

1957a. *Condições sociais do poder nacional.* Rio de Janeiro: Instituto Superior de Estudos Brasileiros, Ministério da Educação e Cultura. Pp. 37.

1957b. "Fundamentos sociológicos do poder nacional," *Revista do Clube Militar,* 140: 12–19.

1957c. *Ideologias e segurança nacional.* Rio de Janeiro: Instituto Superior de Estudos Brasileiros, Ministério da Educação e Cultura. Pp. 55.

1957d. *Introdução crítica: A sociologia brasileira.* Rio de Janeiro: Editorial Andes. Pp. 222.

1958a. "Os camões ideológicos da programação econômico," *O Semanário,* 135(November 13–20): 4.

1958b. "O contrôle ideológico da programação econômico," *O Semanário,* 136(November 20–26): 6.

1958c. "Estabilização versus desenvolvimento," *O Semanário,* 137(November 11–December 4): 6.

1958d. "Estrutura atual e perspectives da sociedade brasileira," *Revista Brasiliense (São Paulo)* 18: 48–59.

1958e. *A redução sociológica: introdução ao estudo da razão socioógica.* Rio de Janeiro: Instituto Superior de Estudos Brasileiros, Ministério da Educação e Cultura. Pp. 169.

1959a. "A crisie brasileira: tipologia do nacionalismo," *O Semanário,* 152(March 26–April 4): 3.

1959b. "O nacionalism é um meio," *O Semanário,* 146(February 5–11): 4.

1959c. "O nacionailsmo e a revolução por cima," *O Semanário,* 171(August 8–14): 4.

1959d. "Nacionalismo e problemas brasileiros." *Revista Brasiliense (São Paulo),* 21(January/February): 35–50. Published under the pseudonym "XXX," which has been attributed to the author.

1960. *O problema nacional do Brasil.* Rio de Janeiro: Ediora Saga. Pp. 265.

1961. *A crise do poder: problemas do poder no Brasil.* Rio de Janeiro: Zahar Editores. Pp. 197.

1963. *Mito e verdade da revolução brasileira.* Rio de Janeiro: Zahar Editores. Pp. 218.

1966. *Administração e estratégia do desenvolvimento: elementos de uma sociologia especial da administração*. Rio de Janeiro: Fundação Getúlio Vargas. Pp. 453.

1968. "A Typology of Nationbalkism in Brazil: A Case of Political Breakdown." Los Angeles: School of Public Administration, University of Southern California. Pp. 104 (mimeographed).

1983. "A modernização em nova perspectiva: em busca do modelo da possibilidade," *Revista de Administracão Pública*, 17(1/January–February): 5–31.

1984[1981]. *The New Science of Organizations: A Reconceptualization of the Wealth of Nations*. Toronto: University of Toronto Press. Pp. 210.

Rangel, Inácio. 1957. *Dualidade básica da economia brasileira*. Rio de Janeiro: Instituto Superior de Estudos Brasileiros, Ministério da Educação e Cultura. Pp. 113.

1960. *Recursos ociosos na economia nacional*. Rio de Janeiro: Instituto Superior de Estudos Brasileiros, Ministério da Educação e Cultura. Pp. 62. Expanded and revised ed. published by ISEB in 1963. Pp. 136.

1963a. *A inflação brasileira*. Rio de Janeiro: Instituto Superior de Estudos Brasileiros, Ministério da Educação e Cultura. Pp. 138.

1963b. *Reforma contra reforma*. Rio de Janeiro: Tempo Brasileiro. Pp. 90.

1975. *Introdução ao estudo do desenvolvimento econômico brasileiro*. Salvador: Livraria Progreso.

1978a. "Dualidades e 'escravismo colonial," *Encontros com a Civilização Brasileira*, 3(September 1978): 79–92.

1978b. *Poder e política: crónica e política: crônica do autoritarismo brasileiro*. Rio de Janeiro: Foense-Universitária. Pp. 211.

1980a. "A quarta dualidade," *Encontros com a Civilização Brssileira*, 25(July): 11–21.

1980b. "Revisitando a 'questão nacional,'" *Encontros com a Civilização Brasileira*, 27(9/September): 47–58.

1981. "A história da dualidade brasileira," *Revista de Economia Política*, 1(October–December): 5–34.

1983. "Terceiro Painel: Guerreiro Ramos e o desenvolvimento brasileiro," *Revista de Administração Pública (Rio de Janeiro)*, 17(2/April–June): 63–92.

1995. "Interview (Given to Lúcia Lippi Oliveira and Alzira Alves de Abreu)," in Lúcia Lippi Oliveira, *A sociologia do Guerreiro*. Rio de Janeiro: Editora da UFR.

Reale, Miguel (ed.). 1984. *Figuras da inteligência brasileira*. Rio de Janeiro: Tempo Brasileiro and Fortaleza: Editora Universidade Federal de Ceará.

Ricupero, Bernardo. 2011. "Florestan Fernandes and Interpretations of Brazil," *Latin American Perspectives*, 38(3/May): 112–123.

Reis Filho, Daniel Aarão. 1990. *A revolução faltou ao encontro: Os comunistas no Brasil*, 2nd ed. São Paulo: Editora Brasiliense. Pp. 200.

Reis Filho, Daniel Aarão et al. 1991. *História do marxismo no Brasil: Vol. I: O impacto das revoluções*. Rio de Janeiro: Editora Paz e Terra. Pp. 208.

Ribeiro, Darcy. 1968. *La Universidad latinoamericana*. Montevideo: Colecciôn Historia y Cultura, Universidad de la República.

1980. *Os brasileiros: Teoria do Brasil*. Petrópolis: Editora Vozes. Pp. 177.

Ridenti, Marcelo. 1993. *O fantasma da revolução Brasileira*. São Paulo: Editora da Universidade Estadual Paulista. Pp. 284.

Rieznik, Pablo. 1995. "O intelectuais diante a crise," *Lutas Sociais*, 1. http://www.pucsp.br/neils/downloads/v1_artigo_pablo.pdf.

Rios, José Arthur. 1966. "Atualidade do Tenentismo," *Cadernos Brasileiros*, 33(November–December): 9–18.

Rocha, Ronald de Oliveira. 1980. "O 'capitalismo mercantil' de André Gunder Frank e Caio Prado Júnior," *Teoria Política*, 3: 60–91.

Rodrigues, José Honório. 1963. *Aspirações nacionais. Interpretação polítca*. São Paulo: Editora Fulgor. Pp. 162.

1965. *Conciliação e reforma no Brasil: um desafio histórico-político*. Rio de Janeiro: Editora Civilização Brasileira. Pp. 246.

1984. "O que é o Brasil; o que é a história do Brasil," *Folha de São Paulo* (October 16).

Rodrigues Netto, Leôncio Martins. 1966. *Conflito industrial e sindicalismo no Brasil*. São Paulo: Difusão Européia do Livro.

1970. *Industrialização e atitudes operárias*. São Paulo: Editora Brasiliense. Pp. 217.

1990a. *CUT: os militantes e a ideologia*. Rio de Janeiro: Paz e Terra. Pp. 143.

1990b. *Partidos e sindicatos: escritios de sociologia política*. São Paulo: Editora Atica. Pp. 115.

Rodríguez, Octávio. 1981. *Teoria do subdesenvolvimento da CEPAL*. Rio de Janeiro: Editora Forense-Universitaria. Pp. 345.

Rorabaugh, W. J. 1989. *Berkeley at War. The 1960s*. New York: Oxford University Press.

Rosa, Luiz Pinguelli. 1980. "Sumário dos pontos levantados e de algumas idéias surgidas no seminário," *Encontros com a Civilização Brasileira*, 24(June): 91–101.

Rosa, Virginio Santa. 1933. *O sentido do tenentismo*. Rio de Janeiro: Schmidt-Editor, Civilização Brasileira. Pp. 189.

Rossi, Bishop D. Agnello. 1960. "A igreja e o nacionalismo," *Síntese Política Econônica Social (SPES)*, 2(1/July–September): 29–30.

Sader, Éder, and Maria Célia Paoli. 1986. "Sobre 'classes populares' no pensamento sociológico brasileiro," in Ruth Cardoso (ed.), *A aventura antropológica*. São Paulo: Editora Paze Terra. Pp. 39–67.

Sader, Emir. 1988. *Quando novos personagens entrarem em cena: experiências, falas e lutas dos trabalhadores da Grande São Paulo (1970–80)*. Rio de Janeiro: Paz e Terra. Pp. 329.

1990. *A transição no Brasil: da ditadura a democracia?* São Paulo: Atual Editora. Pp. 92.

1995. "A primeira geração: ser comunista no Brasil," in his *O anjo torto: esquerda (e direita) no Brasil*. São Paulo: Editora Brasiliense. Pp. 67–101, 195.

2003. *A vingança da história*. São Paulo: Boitempo Editorial. Pp. 199.

Sader, Emir (ed.). 1986. *E agora, PT? Carácter e identidade*. São Paulo: Editora Brasiliense. Pp. 189.

Sader, Emir, and Ken Silverstein 1991. *Without Fear of Being Happy: Lula, the Workers Party and Brazil*. London: Verso.

Sader, Emir, and Theotônio dos Santos (coordinators) with Carlos Eduardo Martins and Adrián Sotelo Valencia (eds.). 2009. *A América Latina e os desafios da globalização: ensaios dedicados a Ruy Mauro Marini.* Rio de Janeiro: Editora da PUC and São Paulo: Editorial Boitempo Editorial. Reviewed by Ronald H. Chilcote. 2009. "The Life and Thought of Ruy Mauro Marini," *Latin American Perspectives,* 36 (6/ November): 131–133. In Portuguese translation as "Celebrando a vida e o pensamento de Ruy Mauro Marini," *Lutas Sociais (São Paulo),* 21–22(2010): 192–195.

Saes, Dêcio. 1984. "Do Marx de 1843–1844 ao Marx das obras históricas: duas concepcões distintas de estado," *Teoria Política,* 5/6: 82–94.

———. 1985. *A formação do estado burguês no Brasil: 1888–1889I.* Rio de Janeiro: Coleção Estudos Brasileiros (86), Editora Paz e Terra. Pp. 364.

———. 1987. *Democracia.* São Paulo: Editora Atica. Pp. 93.

———. 1994. *Estado e democracia: ensaios teóricos.* Campinas: Coleção Trajetória (1), IFCH/UNICAMP. Pp. 195.

———. 1995. "Marxismo e história," *Crítica Marxista,* 1: 39–59.

Saffioti, Heleieth. 1978. *Women in Class Society.* Trans. Michael Vale. New York. Monthly Review Press.

Salgado, Plínio. 1933. *O que é o integralismo.* Rio de Janeiro: Schmidt-Editor, Civilização Brasileiro.

Said, Edward W. 1996. *Representations of the Intellectual.* New York: Vintage. Pp. 121.

Sampaio, Plínio Arruda. 2005. "The Direction of the Government. What Has Changed after Lula?," *Brasil de Fato,* 97(January 5). www.brasildefato.com.br

Santos, José Rufino. 2005. "Nova História: Conteúdo histórico do último ISEB," in Caio Navarro Toledo (ed.), *Intelectuais e política no Brasil.* Rio de Janeiro: Revan. Pp. 43–57.

Santos, Sales Augusto dos. 2011. "The Metamorphosis of Black Movement Activists into Black Organic Intellectuals," *Latin American Perspectives,* 38(3/May): 124–135.

Santos, Theotônio dos. 1967. *El nuevo charácter de la dependencia.* Santiago: Cuadernos de Estudios Socioeconómicos.

———. 1970. "The Structure of Dependence," *American Economic Review,* 60(May): 231–236.

———. 1971. *La crisis norteamericana y América Latina.* Santiago: Ediciones Prensa Latinoamericana. Pp. 159.

———. 1973. *Socialismo e fascismo – el nuevo carácter de dependencia e el dilemma latinoamericano.* Buenos Aires: Periferia.

———. 1983. *Revolução científico-técnica e capitalismo contemporâneo.* Petrópolis: Editora Vozes. Pp. 169.

———. 1986a. *O caminho brasileiro para o socialismo.* Petrópolis: Editora Vozes. Pp. l70.

———. 1986b. *Forças produtivas e relações de produção: ensaio introductório.* Petrópolis: Editora Vozes. Pp. 89.

———. 1987. *Revolução científica técnica e acumulação do capital.* Petrópolis: Editora Vozes. Pp. 286.

———. 1991. *Democracia e socialismo no capitalismo dependente.* Petrópolis: Editora Vozes. Pp. 288.

1994. "A teoria da dependência: um balanço histórico e teórico." Rio de Janeiro, typescript. Pp. 29.

1996a. "Os fundamentos teóricos do governo Fernando Henrique Cardoso (nova etapa da polémica: sobre a teoria da dependência)," Rio de Janeiro, typescript. Pp. 18. (Published in *Ciências e Letras*, Porto Alegre, 1996.)

1996b. "Memória." Rio de Janeiro, typescript. Pp. 133.

Santos, Wanderley Guilherme dos. 1962a. "Desenvolvimentismo: ideologia dominante," *Tempo Brasileiro*, 1, 2(December): 155–192.

1962b. *Quem dará o golpe no Brasil?* Rio de Janeiro: Civilização Brasileira.

1963a. *Introdução ao estudo das contradições sociais no Brasil.* Rio de Janeiro: Instituto Superior de Estudos Brasileiros. Ministério da Educação e Cultura. Pp. 123.

1963b. "Quando a crítica é que dá golpe," *Tempo Brasileiro (Rio de Janeiro)*, 4, 16(March): 375–386.

1963c. *Reforma contra reforma.* Rio de Janeiro: Tempo Brasileiro. Pp. 90.

1966. "Uma revisão da crise brasileira," *Cadernos Brasileiros*, 1, 55(November–December): 51–58.

1977. "Liberalism in Brazil: Ideology and Praxis," in Morris S. Blackman and Ronald G. Hellman (eds.), *Terms of Conflict: Ideology in Latin American Politics.* Philadelphia: Institute for Study of Human Issues. Pp. 1–38.

1978a. "Paradigma e história: a ordem burguesa na imaginação social brasilieira," in his *Ordem burguesa e liberalismo político.* São Paulo: Livraria Duas Cidades. Pp. 17–63.

1978b. *Poder e política: crónica e política: crônica do autoritarismo brasileiro.* Rio de Janeiro: Forense-Universitária. Pp. 211.

1986. *Sessenta e quatro: antomia da crise.* São Paulo: Verice. Pp. 195.

1988. "Política do caos," *Presença: Revista de Política e Cultura*, 12(July): 15–23.

Saunders, Frances Stoner. 1999. *The Cultural Cold War. The CIA and the World of Arts and Letters.* New York: New Press. Pp. 509.

Schwartzman, Simon. 1979. *A formação da comunidade científica no Brasil.* São Paulo: Companhia Editora Nacional-FINEP.

Schwartzmann, Simon, Helena Maria Bousquet Bomeny, and Vanda Maria Ribeiro Costa. 2000. *Tempos de Capanema.* São Paulo: Paz e Terra/ Editora FGV.

Schwarz, Roberto. 1967. "Nota sobre vanguarda e conformismo," *Teoria e Prática*, 2: 127–132.

1978. *O pai de família e outros estudos.* Rio de Janeiro: Editora Paz e Terra. Pp. 147.

1990. *Um mestre na periferia do capitalismo.* São Paulo: Livraria Duas Cidades. Pp. 227.

1992. *Misplaced Ideas: Essays on Brazilian Culture.* London: Verso. Pp. 204.

2001a. "City of God," *New Left Review*, Second Series, 12(November–December): 102–112.

2001b. *Machado: A Master on the Periphery of Capitalism.* Durham, NC: Duke University Press.

Serra, David, 1957. "Que é nacionalismo?," *O Semanário*, 89(December 10–26): 4.

Serra, José. 1980. "A UNE e o golpe de 1964," in *História da UNE*, Vol. 1. Butantã, São Paulo: Coleção História Presente (94), Livramente. Pp. 23–30, 127.

Serra, José, and Fernando Henrique Cardoso. 1978. "As desventuras da dialética da dependência," *Estudos CEBRAP*, 23: 33–80.

Shills, Edward. 1972. *The Intellectuals and the Powers and other Essays*. Chicago: University of Chicago Press. Pp. 481.

Silva, Eliete de Queiroz Gurjão. 1985. "Estado, intervencão, e capital monopolista na agricultura brasileira," *Ensaio*, 14: 203–215.

Silva, Geraldo Bastos. 1957. *Educação e desenvolvimento nacional*. Rio de Janeiro: Instituto Superior de Estudos Brasileiros, Ministério da Educação e Cultura. Pp. 53.

Silva, Golbery Couto e. 1955. *Planejamento estratégico*. Rio de Janeiro: Biblioteca do Exército Editora. Pp. 296.

1957. *Aspectos geopolíticos do Brasil*. Rio de Janeiro: Biblioteca do Exército Editora. Pp. 81.

1967. *Geopolítica do Brasil*. Rio de Janeiro: José Olympio.

Silveira, Cid. 1966. "Teoria marxista da revolução brasileira," *Revista Civilização Brasileira*, 8(July): 127–146.

Silveira, Ênio. 1978. "Por quê e para quê," *Encontros com a Civilização Brasileira*, 1(July): 7–8.

Simonsen, Roberto. 1937. *História econômica do Brasil, 1550–1820*. São Paulo: Companhia Editora Nacional.

1973[1939]. *Evolução industrial do Brasil*. São Paulo: Companhia Editora Nacional.

Singer, Paul. 1968. *Desenvolvimnto e crise*. São Paulo: DIFEL.

1980. *Guia da inflação para o povo*. Petrópolis: Editora Vozes. Pp. 77.

1981. *Dominação e desigualdade: estructura de classe e repartição da renda no Brasil*. Rio de Janeiro: Coleção Estudos Brasileiros (49), Editora Paz e Terra.

1982. *O que é socialismo, hoje*. Petrópolis: Editora Vozes. Pp. 72.

1996. *Um governo de esquerda para todos. Luiza Erundina na prefeitura de São Paulo (1989–1992)*. São Paulo: Editora Brasiliense. Pp. 262.

Singer, Paul, Francisco Weffort, José Ibrahim, and José Arthur Giannotti. 1986. "Opinões sobre o socialismo," *Socialismo e Democracia* 3, 9(January–March): 35–64.

Soares, Fabrício. 1959. "Conceito atual de nacionalismo," *Revista Brasiliense*, 23(May–June): 76–94.

Sodré, Alcindo. 1933. *O gênese da desorden*. Rio de Janeiro: Schmidt-Editor, Civilização Brasileiro.

Sodré, Nelson Werneck. 1941a. "Fronteira," *Cultura Política*, 1(2/April): 24–30; see also 1942, 2(18/August): 93–102.

1941b. *Oeste: ensaio sobre a grande propriedade pastoril*. São Paulo: Livraria José Olympio Editora. Pp. 206.

1941c. "O problema da unidade nacional," *Cultura Política*, 1(6/August): 116–120.

1941d. "Um sentido político," *Cultura Política*, 1(4/June): 152–159.

1942. *Orientações do pensamento brasileiro*. Rio de Janeiro: Casa Editora Vecchi. Pp. 190.

1943. "Sentimento da nacionalidade na literatura brasileira," *Cultura Política* No. 3, 27(May): 115–130.

1944. *Formação da sociedade brasileira.* São Paulo: Livraria José Olympio Editora. Pp. 338.

1957a. *As classes sociais no Brasil.* Rio de Janeiro: Instituto Superior de Estudos Brasileiros, Ministério da Educação e Cultura. Pp. 51.

1957b. "Estudo histórico-sociológico da cultura brasileira," *Digesto Econômico,* 135(May–June): 159–183.

1957c. *O Tratado de Methuen.* Rio de Janeiro: Instituto Superior de Estudos Brasileiros, Ministério da Educação e Cultura. Pp. 50.

1958. *Introdução à revolução brasileira.* Rio de Janeiro: Coleção Documentos Brasileiros (98), José Olympio. (3rd ed). Rio de Janeiro: Civilização Brasileira, 1967. Pp. 259.)

1959. *Raízes históricas do nacionalism brasileiro.* Rio de Janeiro: Instituto Superior de Estudos Brasileiros, Ministério da Educação e Cultura. Pp. 40.

1961a. *A ideologia do colonialismo.* Rio de Janeiro: Instituto Superior de Estudos Brasileiros, Ministério da Educação e Cultura. Pp. 270. (2nd ed., Rio de Janeiro: Editora Civilização Brasileira, 1965. Pp. 253.)

1961b. "Literatura e política," *Semanário,* 267 (September 14–21), 8.

1962. *Formação histórica de nacionalismo brasileiro.* Rio de Janeiro: Instituto Superior de Estudos Brasileiros, Ministério da Educação e Cultura.

1963a. "A burguesia brasileira e a República," *Revista de Estudos Sociais (Rio de Janeiro),* 5(17/June): 19–45.

1963b. *Introdução a revolução brasileira.* Rio de Janeiro: Editora Civilização Brasileira. Pp. 226.

1964a. *Formação histórica do Brasil.* São Paulo: Editora Brasiliense. Pp. 417.

1964b. *História da burguesia brasileira.* Rio de Janeiro: Editora Civilização Brasileira. Pp. 418.

1965a. *História militar do Brasil.* Rio de Janeiro: Editora Civilização Brasileira. Pp. 439.

1965b. *As razões da independência.* Rio de Janeiro: Editora Civilização Brasileira. Pp. 274.

1966. *A história da imprensa no Brasil.* Rio de Janeiro: Editora Civilização Brasileira. Pp. 583.

1968. "Nationalism and Development." Paper Presented at the University of California Project "Brazil-Portuguese Africa," January 24, 1968. Riverside and Los Angeles: African Studies Center, Los Angeles, Latin American Research Program, Riverside, Latin American Center, Los Angeles.

1970. *Síntese de história da cultura brasileira.* Rio de Janeiro: Civilização Brasileira. Pp. 131.

1975. *Os ricos não fazem greve – porque?* Lisbon: Colecção Universidade do Povo (4), Diabril Editora. Pp. 111.

1976/1977/1978. "História do ISEB-1.Formação," *Temas de Ciências Humanas* (1) 1977 "História do ISEB-2. Crise" (2) 119–144; 1978 "História de ISEB-3 Fechamento" (3), 69–91.

1977. "História do ISEB-2. Crise," *Temas de Ciências Humanas,* 2: 119–144.

1978a. "História de ISEB-3 Fechamento," *Temas de Ciências Humanas,* 3: 69–91.

1978b. *A verdade sobre o ISEB*. Rio de Janeiro: Avenir Editora. Pp. 69.

1980. *A coluna Prestes*. Rio de Janeiro: Editora Civilização Brasileira. Pp. 119.

1980–1981. "História do PCB," *Temas de Ciências Humanas*, 8(1980); 9(1980): 181–218; 10(1981): 169–208.

1984a. *Contribuição a história do PCB*. São Paulo: Global Editora. Pp. 119.

1984b. *Vida e morte da ditacura: vinte anos de autoritarismo no Brasil*. Petrópolis: Editora Vozes. Pp. 133.

1986. *História da história nova*. Petrópolis: Vozes.

1988. *Nelson Werneck Sodré (depoimento, 1987)*. Rio de Janeiro: CPDOC/FGV/ Servico de Comunicação Social/Petrobras (Projeto Memória da Petrobras).

1990. *A luta pela cultura*. Rio de Janeiro: Bertrand Brasil.

1992. *A ofensiva reacionária*. Rio de Janeiro: Bertrand Brasil.

Sorj, Bernardo. 2001. *A construção intelectual do Brasil contemporâneo*. São Paulo: Jorge Zahar Editor.

Sorj, Bernardo, and Sêrgio Fausto. 2011. "The Sociologist and the Politician: An Interview with Fernando Henrique Cardoso," *Latin American Perspectives*, 3(3/May): 160–193.

Sousa, Herbert José de. 1962 "Radicalizaao da teoria social," *Revista Brasiliense*, 41(May–June): 161–171.

Souza, Antônio Cândido de Mello (aka Cândido, Antônio). 1959. *Formação da literatura brasileira (momentos decisivos)*. 2 vols. São Paulo: Martins.

1963. *O método crítico de Sílvio Romero*, 2nd ed. São Paulo: EDUSP.

1964. *Os parceiros do Rio Bonito*. São Paulo: José Olympio.

1965. *Literatura e sociedade*. São Paulo: Companhia Editora Nacional.

1968. "Literature and the Rise of Brazilian National Self-Identity," *Luso Brazilian Review*, 5 (1/June): 27–44.

1969. "Literatura e consciência nacional." Suplemento Literário de Minas Gerais (Belo Horizonte), IV, 158(3rd year special ed.), September 6.

1981. "Os brasileiros e a literatura latino-americana," *Novos Estudos CEBRAP*, 1(1/December): 58–68.

1995. *On Literature and Society*. Trans. Howard S. Becker. Princeton, NJ: Princeton University Press. Pp. 198.

1996. "Marxismo e militância," *Praga: Revista de Estudos Marxistas*, 1(September): 5–24.

Squeff, Enio, and José Miguel Wisnik. 1982. *Música*. São Paulo: O Nacional e O popular na Cultura Brasileira, Editora Brasiliense. Pp. 190.

Stedile, João Pedro. 2007. "The Neoliberal Agrarian Model in Brazil," *Monthly Review*, 58(February). http://www.monthlyreview.org/0207stedile.htm.

Tavares, Assis. 1966–1967. "Caio Prado e a teoria da revolução brasileira," *Revista Civilização Brasileira*, 11–12(December 1966–March 1967): 48–80.

Tavares, Claudio. 1960. "Caio Prado e a questão agrária no Brasil," *Revista Brasiliense*, 32(November–December); 143–154; response from Caio Prado. Pp. 155–157.

Tavares, Maria da Conceição. 1972. *Da substituição de importações ao capitalismo financeiro: ensaios sobre economia brasileira*. Rio de Janeiro: Zahar Editores (11th ed., 1983). Pp. 263.

Telles, Edward E. 2004. *Race in Another America: The Significance of Skin Color in Brazil*. Princeton, NJ: Princeton University Press.

Telles, Jover. 1962. *O movimento syndical no Brasil*. Rio de Janeiro: Editorial Vitória. Pp. 301.

Teixeira, Anísio. 1957. *Educação não é privilégio*. Rio de Janeiro: Livraria José Olympio Editora. Pp. 146.

Teixeira, Erios Martins. 1957. "Nossa revolução," *Novos Rumos*, 1(September): 23–29.

Teotônio Júnior. 1958. "Review of Guerreiro Ramos," *A redução sociológica*. *Revista Brasiliense*, 19(September–October): 189–195.

Teres, Harvey. 1996. *Renewing the Left: Politics, Imagination, and the New York Intellectuals*. New York: Oxford University Press. Pp. 326.

Terres, Harvey. 1996. *Renewing the Left: Politics, Imagination, and the New York Intellectuals*. New York: Oxford University Press.

Toledo, Caio Navarro de. 1978. *ISEB: Fabrica de Ideolgias*, 2nd ed. São Paulo: Ática Editora. Pp. 195.

1986. "Teoria e ideologia na perspectiva do ISEB," in Reginaldo Morães, Ricardo Antunes, and Vera B. Ferrante (eds.), *Inteligência brasileira*. São Paulo: Brasiliense. Pp. 224–256.

1995a. "A modernidade democrática da esquerda: adeus a revolução? "*Crítica Marxista*, 1: 27–38.

1995b. Prefácio à nova edição, in his *ISEB: fábrica de ideologies*. Campinas: UNICAMP. Pp. 9–15.

1998. "Intelectuais do ISEB, esquerda e marxismo," in João Quartim de Moraes (ed.), *História do marxismo no Brasil. Teorias. Interpretações*. Vol. 3. Campinas: UNICAMP. Pp. 245–274.

Toledo, Caio Navarro de (ed.). 1997. *1964. Visões críticas do golpe. Democracia e reforma no populismo*. Campinas: Editora da UNICAMP. Pp. 168.

Toledo, Caio Navarro de (ed.). 2005. *Intelectuais e política no Brasil: a experiência do ISEB*. Rio de Janeiro: Editora Revan. Pp. 262.

Topik, Steven. 1978. "Middle-class Brazilian Nationalism, 1889–1930: From Radicalism to Reaction," *Social Science Quarterly*, 59(June): 93–104.

Torres, Alberto. 1933. *O problema nacional brasileiro; introdução à um programa de organização nacional*, 2nd ed. São Paulo: Biblioteca Pedagógica Brasileira, Série V Brasiliana (16), Companhia Editora Nacional. Pp. 277.

Unger, Roberto Mangabeira. 1990. *A alternative transformada: como democratizar o Brasil*. Rio de Jdneiro: Editora Guanabara Koogan. Pp. 399. See also Unger's three-volume work, *Politics: A Work in Constructive Theory*, 1987, Cambridge: Cambridge University Press.

Vale, Antônio Marques do. 2001. "Papel de formação do intelectual e o planejamento da educação nos "históricos" do ISEB." PhD Dissertation. Universidade Estadual Paulista (UNESP), Marília.

Vianna, Maria Lúcia T. Werneck. 1984. "Ser ou não ser nacionalista?," *Presença. Revista da Política e Cultura*, 3(May): 53–65.

Vianna, Luiz Werneck. 1983. "Problemas de política e organização dos intelectuais," *Presença. Revista da Política e Cultura*, 1(November): 137–151.

1984. "O popular e operário na história recente do PCB," *Presença. Revista da Política e Cultura*, 2(February): 55–63.

Vianna. Luís Werneck et al. 1984. Series of Unpublished Papers on Intellectuals. Rio de Janeiro: Instituto Universitário de Pesquisas do Rio de Janeiro (IUPERJ). Presented August–November 1984.

1994. "Cientistas sociais e vida pública: o estudante de graduação em ciências sociais," *Dados*, 27(3): 35–52.

Vieira Pinto, Álvaro Borges. 1958. *Ideologia e desenvolvimento nacional*. Rio de Janeiro: ISEB. Pp. 52.

1958b. Series of Lectures, April 9, 16, 30; May 5, 7, 12, 14. Curso Regular de Filosofia, Instituto Superior de Estudos Brasileiros, Ministério de Educação e Cultura. Each lecture 8 or 9 pages (mimeographed).

1959. "Textos selecionados para o ensino." Rio de Janeiro: ISEB (mimeographed).

1960[1956]. *Ideologia e desenvolvimento nacional*. Rio de Janeiro: Instituto Superior de Estudos Brasileiros, Ministério da Educação e Cultura. Pp. 52.

1960. *Consciência e realidade nacional*. 2 vols. Rio de Janeiro: Instituto Superior de Estudos Brasileiros, Ministério da Educação e Cultura. Pp. 442, 633.

1962?. *A questão da universidade*. Rio de Janeiro: Editora Universitária. Pp. 163.

1963. "Indicações metodológicas para a definição de subdesenvolvimento," *Revista Brasileira de Ciências Sociais (Belo Horizonte)*, III, 2(July): 252–279.

1975. *Os ricos não fazem greve – porque?* Lisbon: Colecção Universidade do Povo (4), Diabril Editora. Pp. 111.

Wald, Alan M. 1987. *The New York Intellectuals: The Rise and Decline of the Anti-Stalinist Left from the 1930s to the 1980s*. Chapel Hill: University of North Carolina Press. Pp. 440.

1994. *Writing from the Left: New Essays on Radical Culture and Politics*. London: Verso. Pp. 243.

2002. *Exiles from a Future Time: The Forging of the Mid-Twentieth Century Literary Left*. Chapel Hill: University of North Carolina Press. Pp. 412.

Weffort, Francisco. 1966. "Estado e massas no Brasil," *Revista Civilização Brasileira*, 7(May): 137–158.

1971. "Notas sobre a 'teoria da dependência:' teoria de classe ou ideologia national?," in Fernando Henrique Cardoso et al. (eds.), *Sôbre teoria e método em sociologia*. São Paulo: Edições CEBRAP. Pp. 3–24.

1972. "Participação e conflito industrial: Contagem e Osaco." São Paulo: Cadernos CEBRAP.

1975. "Sindicatos e política." São Paulo: Livre-Docência, Universidade Federal de São Paulo.

1978. *Populismo na política brasileira*. Rio de Janeiro: Paz e Terra. Pp. 181.

1980. *O populismo na política brasileira*, 2nd ed. Rio de Janeiro: Estudos Brasileiros (25), Paz e Terra. Pp. 181.

1984. *Por que democracia?* São Paulo: Editora Brasiliense. Pp. 133.

Wright, Angus, and Wendy Wolford. 2003. *To Inherit the Earth: The Landless Movement and the Struggle for a New Brazil*. Oakland, CA: Food First Books. Pp. 365.

Wright, Erik Olin. 1978. *Class, Crisis and the State*. London: Verso.

XXX (pseudonym). 1959. "Nacionalismo e problemas brasileiros," *Revista Brasiliense*, 21(January–February 1959): 35–50. Author is Alberto Guerreiro Ramos.

Zarifhetto, Jorge. 1957. "Análise do nacionalismo," *O Semánario*, 83(November 7–14): 2.

Zilio, Carlos, and João Luiz Lafetá. 1983. *Artes plásticas*. São Paulo: Editora Brasiliense.

Index